Gentile Tales

The Narrative Assault on Late Medieval Jews

Miri Rubin

Yale University Press
New Haven and London

Set in 10.5 on 12 pt New Baskerville by Best-set Typesetter Ltd., Hong Kong
Printed in Hong Kong through World Print Ltd

Library of Congress Cataloging-in-Publication Data
Rubin, Miri, 1956–
    Gentile tales: the narrative assault on late medieval Jews/Miri Rubin.
    Includes bibliographical references and index.
    ISBN 0–300–07612–6 (cloth: alk. paper)
    1. Host desecration accusation.   2. Judaism—Controversial literature—
History and criticism.   3. Host desecration accusation in Literature.
4. Antisemitism in literature.   5. Antisemitism in art.   6. Literature,
Medieval—History and criticism.   I. Title.
BM585.4.R83   1999   98–49996
305.892'404—dc21   CIP

A catalogue record for this book is available from the British Library.

10 9 8 7 6 5 4 3 2 1

Gentile Tales

In memory of Bob Scribner
(1941–1998)

Contents

Illustrations

MAPS

FIGURES

Acknowledgements

It is the greatest of pleasures to thank friends for their help and support in archives, homes, libraries, lecture halls and hotels in several countries, languages and climes. Their help was particularly appreciated when offered during periods of research which took me away from home and while writing this book on events which could, and sometimes did, induce in me feelings of great sadness. My trips to Austrian and German towns and villages, the sites of too many acts of violence, would have been inconceivable without the companionship of Peter and Inge Johanek of Münster, whose own lives have been touched by violence, but whose faith in friendship and understanding has never failed. It is the possibility of such friendships that has given this work more meaning than other historical enterprises.

Shulamith Shahar, friend and role model, was the first to read the book in its entirety, and to offer encouragement and criticism. Willis Johnson read a later version with the enthusiasm, generosity and sternness which betokens true friendship. What they read was the product of my work with the help of many friends, treasured cohorts of generous experts. Some old friends were rediscovered as inspired and erudite authorities in fields I had never studied so closely, above all Ora Limor and Israel Yuval. Simcha Goldin and Stefan Reif answered numerous questions on Jewish liturgy and occasionally even buckled down to the joint deciphering of texts.

Those engaged in several adjacent and parallel projects, including Denise Despres, Sarah Lipton and Robert Stacey, offered the intimate encouragement of close conspirators and shared with me their work in progress. My work would have been the poorer had I not learnt from the efforts of a group of young German historians, devoted to the reclamation of Jewish history as part of German history, a task they approach with responsibility and commitment: Christoph Cluse, Gerd Mentghen, W. Treue. Their seniors have also shared findings and conclusions most generously: Friedrich Lotter who has written so authoritatively about the violence which followed host desecration accusations in Germany, Volker Honemann who has disentangled the facts and images of Sternberg (1492), Friedrich Battenberg who shared archival material with me. Austrian historians such as Klaus Lohrmann and Gerhard Yaritz responded warmly to my interests and queries. Suzannah

Burgharz responded to a telephone call out of the blue and shared some transcribed material from the Zurich archives with me, and Valentine Groebner still keeps his erudite eyes open for mentions of hosts, Jews and Christians.

The spatial range of this study – from Paris to Poznań – and the regional aspect of the events examined meant that I was using materials encoded in dialects and microworlds. Faced with a barrage of linguistic peculiarities, I benefited continuously from the lexicographic erudition of Roy Wisbey, as we worked in parallel in the Cambridge University Library, and enjoyed some intensive 'brainstorming' sessions with Hajo Schiewer of Berlin during his stays in Oxford. Sarah Kay kindly offered her boundless expertise in checking my translations from Old French texts, as did Peter Linehan with medieval Castilian, and Alfred Thomas in translating a crucial medieval Czech phrase. In interpreting images I shared moments with Peggy Smith and learned from as yet unpublished work by Stephen Greenblatt and Catherine Gallagher.

Even single meetings could create a memorable link and an enduring debt: with Hana Zaremska I discussed the Silesian cases over lunch in Budapest, and the intricacies of the Church of St Gudule as well as current Belgian politics were elucidated by Peter de Ridder in a café in Brussels. Peter Spufford explained the size of medieval coins at a party in Cambridge.

Unexpected group responses to the work in progress helped me design the book and apply greater rigour to it. I experienced such encounters at the universities of Bristol, Columbia, Duke, London, Oxford, St Andrews and Warwick. I benefited greatly from the critical exposure which the Davis Center Seminar at Princeton offers to its guests and am most grateful to Natalie Davis for devising, chairing and illuminating that session. A memorable event was the delivery of a paper to the Center for Medieval Studies at the University of Connecticut at Storrs, which I visited for a while in the summers of 1996 and 1998 at the invitation of its directors David Benson and Tom Jambeck.

Most of this work was conducted in the nurturing environment of the Cambridge University Library (and special thanks to Tony Rawlings of the Map Room), but librarians and archivists far and wide – in Paris, Münster and Vienna – offered welcome and assistance. A particular delight was my meeting in Klosterneuburg with Wolfgang Huber, himself a historian, keeper of the treasures stored in that abbey. He both guided me through the library and museum and expedited the sending of reproductions to me. The staff of the Haus-, Hof- und Staatsarchiv in Vienna helped turn my short visit into an extremely productive one; similarly helpful were the staff at the Archives Nationales in Brussels and the Österreichisches Nationalbibliothek in Vienna. Work at the Bibliotheca Apostolica Vaticana was a particular pleasure, as it has become in recent years, under the leadership of Father Leonard Boyle, a particularly congenial research library. Institutions lent important support for my travels and for the technical assistance required: the Discretionary Fund of the Regius Professor in History at Oxford, the Foundation for Jewish Culture in New York, and several small but crucial research grants from Pembroke College, Oxford.

My friends Sarah Beckwith, David Feldman, Sarah Kay, Gabor Klaniczay, Jon Parry, Paul Strohm and David Wallace offered their personal examples, while David Miller, friend and agent, and my colleagues Debbie Banham and Carl Watkins helped turn a typescript skilfully and intelligently into a book. Gareth Stedman Jones read and commented and encouraged as only a brilliant historian can.

My son Joseph was born in the midst of work on this book. The hopes I have for his future and for children like him are nourished by the certainty that even though deadly tales have their committed makers and unthinking followers, they can also be unmade with humane scepticism and with courage. These hopes have been gently nourished by the writing of a book.

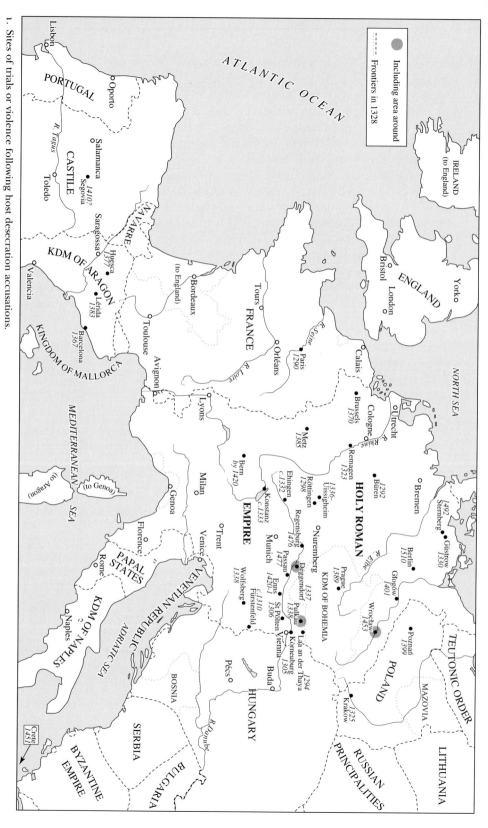

1. Sites of trials or violence following host desecration accusations.

Map labels:

ATLANTIC OCEAN

Lisbon
PORTUGAL
○ Oporto
R. Tagus
CASTILE
Salamanca ●
Segovia ● *1410?*
Toledo ○

NAVARRE
Saragossa ○ Huesca *1377*
KDM OF ARAGON
Lérida *1383* ●
Barcelona *1367* ●
Valencia ●

KINGDOM OF MALLORCA

MEDITERRANEAN SEA
(to Aragon)
(to Genoa)

(to England)
○ Bordeaux
Toulouse ○
Avignon ○
Lyons ○

Tours ○
FRANCE
Orléans ○
Paris *1290* ●
R. Seine
R. Loire

Calais ○
Brussels *1370* ●
Cologne ○
○ Utrecht
R. Rhine

Metz *1365* ●
Remagen *1323* ●

Bern *by 1420* ●
Milan ○
EMPIRE
Konstanz *c.1333* ●
Ehingen *c.1332* ●
Röttingen *1298* ●
Üssigheim *1336* ●
Regensburg *1476* ●
Nuremberg ○

HOLY ROMAN

1292 Büren ●
○ Bremen
1492 Sternberg ●
Güstrow *1330* ●
Berlin *1510* ●
Głogów *1401* ●
Wrocław *1453*
Poznań *1399* ●

TEUTONIC ORDER
MAZOVIA
LITHUANIA
POLAND
Kraków *1325* ●
RUSSIAN PRINCIPALITIES

Prague *1389* ○
KDM OF BOHEMIA
R. Elbe

Munich ○
Deggendorf *1337*
Passau *1477*
Wolfsberg *1338* ●
Enns *1420-1*
Fürstenfeld *c.1310*
St Pölten *1306*
Pulkau *1338*
Vienna ○
Korneuburg *1305*
Laa an der Thaya *1294*

Trent ○
Venice ○
VENETIAN REPUBLIC
Florence ○
PAPAL STATES
Rome ○
KDM OF NAPLES
Naples ○

ADRIATIC SEA
BOSNIA
SERBIA
BULGARIA
BYZANTINE EMPIRE

Pécs ○
Buda ○
HUNGARY
R. Danube

IRELAND (to England)
ENGLAND
Yorko
Bristol ○
London ○
NORTH SEA

Crete *1451*

Legend:
● Including area around
---- Frontiers in 1328

1

Introduction

This book attempts to understand a powerful narrative about Jews that developed in late medieval Europe, the host desecration accusation. The enormity of the offence which it imputed to Jews was defined by the holiness of their victim: the host – the consecrated eucharistic wafer – was believed to be Christ himself, in the generous form within which he offered himself daily and ubiquitously at the altar, consecrated by priests during the mass. The host was the most precious symbol of Christian community and identity, while the Jews carried difference in their bodies, in their rejection of Christian truths, in their palpable mundane otherness.[1] The very practices through which medieval Christian culture was experienced in the centuries after 1100 held the eucharist to be central and precious and led to a growing sense of discomfort about the Jew's proximity to it within Christian spaces. Inasmuch as the eucharist came to symbolise much that was possibly shared among Christians in their communities and estates, those who could never aspire to eucharistic wholesomeness became more clearly distinguished as different, as not belonging. It is hard to tell how deeply and how evenly these attitudes penetrated medieval regions and social spheres, but they are evident in pastoral writings and in visual representation, and were captured in the growing desire for separation between Christians and Jews.

All too often narratives of abuse, particularly those about Christians and Jews, are taken as eternal, unchanging.[2] Yet as historians we cry out for the solace of change, for the hope embedded in it, the variety of human experience and difference it encompasses. The narrative studied in this book was *new*, born around the end of the thirteenth century and re-enacted tens of times in the two centuries that followed. Cast in tragic mood, the host desecration narrative opened with a Jew's intention to procure the consecrated host, worked its way through a series of cruel Jewish attacks on the host, climaxed in the manifestations of eucharistic power through the show of blood or flesh, and ended with punishment of the Jew and recovery into cultic triumph of the, now miraculous, host. The narrative emerged dense with internal reference and logic, rich in its *dramatis personae*, resonant in its appeal to an ideal order of justice and piety which emerged again and again victorious over Jewish unfaith, filth and cruelty. The accusation of host desecration was

1

both *history* and *story* and thus encompassed authority and universality while allowing space for individual participation and the working of fantasy.

All myths ground meaning in the past, but also claim that the past is part of the present in tangible and demanding ways. The myth of Jewish deicide took its form from strong notions about the *present* disposition of Jews, and about appropriate action towards them which followed in the present. All these notions – about Jewish unfaith and Christian vigilance in countering it – were shaped in narratives which offered entries and roles for participation.[3] Inasmuch as host desecration accusations and their enactment both told a story and became stories to be told, it is interesting to consider their narrative form as a particularly persuasive, necessary and effective mode. Narrative has a mimetic function: narrative prefigures and refigures action.[4] Narratives which give sense to violence are encoded within local frames of reference. When an outsider – a medieval observer or a later historian – misunderstands or judges the actions of those who belong, that very criticism can be turned into proof of the difference which the tale endorsed and the violence sought to annihilate. It is difficult to find here a common ground for conversation or ethical discussion. The experience of violence and playing out the narrative creates a distinct identity which marks apart those who lived it, enacted it – and those who did not.

Some might take the study of narratives as a step away from an authentic historical reality, from pain and suffering and the responsibility which violent action imparts. One truth which emerges from confronting the host desecration accusation as narrative is that even the most pervasive representations – visual or textual – can only be understood fully when observed embedded within the contexts that accredited them and gave them meaning. Yet it is impossible to deal with historically specific events without addressing the textual quality of almost all remaining traces. Textuality and the narrative dimension of texts are not qualities appreciated *only* at the cost of losing the claim of the texts to truthfulness and authenticity. Textuality provides the conditions within which meaning and self-knowing are possible, and is thus intimately related to processes by which people have represented their violence as justifiable and necessary.[5] It is through narrative – historical, didactic, parodic – that we come to encounter the host desecration accusation, its effects and the memories it bequeathed to later generations.

Narrative has been the subject of many recent theoretical discussions and applied studies.[6] Let us think of narrative as a mode of organising events, unified by a plot, which follows movement from problem to resolution, from violation of order to restoration. Whole cultural systems are carried in myths, and myth is carried in rituals and through narratives. People act through narratives, and they remember through narrative. Willed acts are probably both conceived narratively and also understood and used as such. Experience is most often made historically available through representations in narrative form. It is thus inherently historical, just as history itself is so frequently narrative in character.[7] Hayden White's famous dictum that 'all narration is moralisation' is helpful when it is brought to bear on narratives told within bloody disorder and violent action. It allows us to ask: How did the narrative of Jewish host desecration encompass a world? Where was its moral and ideal centre? How did it make its appeal, and what was the price paid by those who rejected it?[8]

Once the narrative mode of action, self-understanding and memory is appreciated, the writers of history are forced to consider the terms in which we explore powerful and deadly narratives, narratives which were rich and immediate in consequence, authoritative and commonsensical in their familiar logic, and yet utterly futile in their claim to reveal Jewish intention and action. It is hard to write about events which were so redolent of meaning and exciting to participants, so vindicated by most commentators and observers, from a position that is distanced. It creates a tedious type of prose littered with disclaimers such as 'it was alleged' or 'the Jews were unjustly accused'. Most remaining traces represent the position of Christian authorities – chroniclers, preachers, town officials – who were almost always writing in defence or celebration of the events. It has been through reading and writing quite against the grain of surviving texts that those glimpses of doubt and contestation, guilt and embarrassment felt by medieval persons when apprehending the host desecration accusation in any of its forms have been produced. The book is thus entitled *Gentile Tales*, and – although an interjection in midstream stops to reflect on Jewish attitudes – it informs and perhaps illuminates the workings of the host desecration accusation within a broad medieval frame of religious and political sensibilities.

Powerful as it was, the host desecration accusation, which bound Christians, Jews and the eucharist in a narrative of abuse and indignation, was not so powerful as to leave no space for evasion, doubt and rejection by those to whom it made its appeal. If a sacramental language contained prevailing meanings of the holy for late medieval people, then the diversity, disagreement and strife within medieval communities and regions also produced a plurality of attitudes to that very language and its related narratives. If several late medieval representations described and explained the place of Jews in Christian society, the variety of treatment experienced by Jews and the varied ways in which narratives involving them unfolded must be explained through close attention to the use and interpretation these narratives underwent in the political cultures that saw them unfold. We return here to the need to think of narrative as historically *situated*, as drawing its meanings and weight, its relative urgency from performance, enactment and deployment. By looking at action through narrative – formal, yet always flexible in practice – we may be allowed moments of 'dialogic' insight into the past. Through the study of narrative plenitude we become aware of 'alternative possibilities in formulation and valuation' which people in the past may have taken, and which we may in turn consider.[9] Narrative can reveal to us the work of persuasion and the condition of its own transmission.[10] Following its trail may help us to observe medieval people reasoning for and against violence, embracing or rejecting opportunities for exclusion, expulsion and excision of neighbours-now-culprits which were offered by the central narratives of their religious universe.

This book will thus aim to situate one of the most compelling anti-Jewish tales within the contexts of its production and telling. Like so many chameleons, the narratives are coloured by the shadings of their telling, by the conditions of their reception and the exchange implicit in their transmission.[11] The tale's reception is characterised by an ease and eagerness in those who claimed it, which is akin to a process of transference by which a story heard, a narrative offered by others, can emerge and be used as utterly relevant and intimately fitting to the highly specific subjectivity of I or we, here and now.[12]

The question of responsibility and blame is closely related to any use and interpretation of materials such as those offered by the host desecration accusations. Before we can imagine who moved others to abusive action we must have some idea of how alternatives and choices of action are generally represented and communicated. If responsibility is to be sought for mass violence, we ought to think hard about whether crowds are incited, led on, or live a spontaneously collective life. The problem of agency and the problem of historical distance are closely linked. Do we approach the men and women of the past as moral entities quite different from ourselves, as interesting subjects for inquiry by virtue of that *difference*, or do we expect them, within the bounds of historical variation, to be able to discern good and evil in ways recognisable to us? After all, even today people and communities differ as to the contours of violence to be tolerated – in their homes, schools and streets, by their states and armies.

Does the fact that late medieval culture was suffused with ideas and representations of Jewish otherness, and fears of the danger which Jews posed to the physical and spiritual well-being of Christians, provide a sufficient explanation for patterns of violence, and the willingness of people to participate in collective acts against Jews? The enactment of the host desecration narrative was a possibility offered to medieval people well tutored in a eucharistic lore which repeatedly and imaginatively invoked the danger posed by Jews. While chronicling the rumours, the actions of crowds, the trials, tortures and executions that followed host desecration accusations, I shall seek to measure and assess the limitations of those representations and identify those who chose *not* to follow the route to violence offered by the tale. The cases which lend themselves to such scrutiny are few. But we will discern among the cases moments of choice *not* to believe, *not* to be lulled into the rhythms of eucharistic indignation which afforded the licence to kill.

Discerning such moments is not to discover 'Jew-lovers', but rather it is to encounter discursive moments which challenged the rule of the host desecration narrative, and which emphasised some other mode of making sense and seeking action. In order to discover such voices one has to believe that choice is possible at all, and thus see in violence not the inevitable, spontaneous and culturally 'expected' reaction, but a choice which favoured *some* rather than *other* manners of self-presentation, self-fashioning.

This is a book about the making of dangerous representations and the processes which empower their users or inhibit their application. It is situated within a historical field in which Christians (and sometimes very new Christians, converts from Judaism) were freer to act and initiate, and Jews were to a large extent recipients of their actions. Yet it is hard not to ask what Jews *did* think about the eucharist and the violence it incited, when they had occasion or need to formulate positions about it. The interjection into the story of the *Gentile Tales* is offered in midstream to satisfy that curiosity and bring into the discussion some Hebrew sources which shared the space and the times of the host desecration accusations.

To concentrate on the birth of a single anti-Jewish narrative is also to set up a context in which some larger questions can be asked. This points us towards an investigation of the power of narratives, and of the choices of those past actors who accepted and acted upon them. Such investigation will also reveal the complexity of Jewish existence at the heart of the mysteries of Christian cultures, at the heart of European towns and villages. It will suggest some of the terrifying mechanisms which move or facilitate that awful transformation of neighbour into persecutor, of community into murderous crowd, of tolerated other to the object of all phobic energy and destructive desire.

The distinction which lends meaning to the title *Gentile Tales* is also one which we may wish to dissolve by the end of this book. The host desecration tale was told by Christians, to Christians, to make Christians act and redefine that which made them Christian. That they could do so most easily and rewardingly through thinking *about* Jews, and acting *upon* Jewish bodies, books, dwellings, is proof of the intimacy which prevailed between the two groups.[13] As put by Toni Morrison in an essay on the centrality of racial sensibilities in American narratives, it has led to 'an astonishing revelation of longing, of terror, of perplexity, of shame'.[14] This book will begin with an exploration of early medieval narratives, in chapter 2, and trace the emergence of new types of tales about Jews in the thirteenth century. These coalesced into a narrative of host desecration, which was told and enacted by 1290 in Paris, and became known and established in various regions of Europe, as shown in chapter 3. Chapter 4 offers an analysis of the tale, of the protagonists, actions and situations which both express its variety and underpin its structural uniformity. The contexts which provided the immediate background for a number of cases of accusation and violence will be the subject of chapter 5 – these are cases for which sufficient materials have survived to allow a more detailed, closer analysis; here the conditions and interventions which could encourage, quell or undermine an accusation will be considered. The containment of memories of accusations and avenging violence is the challenge faced by chapter 6, as we consider the echoes of narrative and the forms – visual, dramatic, literary – within which attempts to preserve them were made. The book will conclude with reflections on changes in the force of the host desecration narrative over the centuries, leading to its virtual disappearance in the early sixteenth century.

The challenges posed by this book have been legion: those faced by any historian of the Middle Ages but many more. There was the constant struggle in the face of the consoling allure of pat generalisations about Christianity, about human nature, about Germans. There was the compelling feeling of personal involvement when touching headstones or reading texts in Hebrew, when thinking of all the different ways in which memory and fear coalesce into contemporary historical consciousness. There was the cruel beauty of places which change little, where a chapel still stands proud since its erection in the late Middle Ages on the site of a synagogue destroyed following a host desecration accusation, testimony to the dramatic buffeting of a Jewish community in a place which presents itself as so little touched by time. But there has also been the beauty of history and the few glowing examples of humane doubt and courage by medieval people which make us appreciate more recent examples of resistance. There clearly is poetry after Auschwitz, and history too – we cannot do without them.

2

From Jewish Boy to Bleeding Host

Early medieval tales reflected the official Christian position on the historic role of Jews. Having rejected Christ, Jews were condemned to a life as ever-present reminders of the inception of Christianity, and of the error and evil of their ways. Their state of servitude and general abjection in the world was useful testimony to the truth of the Gospel tale. Contemporary Jews were always present, in flesh or in image, bearing witness.[1] Jews who converted to Christianity similarly fulfilled this role and presaged the fate of all Jews at the approach of Judgement Day. With their eschatological role and their rhetorical stance as witness to Christianity's truth and triumph, Jews formed a familiar presence in the theological discussion, homiletic reflection and didactic tales of early medieval culture. Such tales usually had a 'happy ending': that of conversion following the realisation of Christian truth, and the incorporation of such converts into a Christian world.

One of the cultural frames within which stories about the conversion of Jews were elaborated was the powerful world of the Marian tale. In this chapter I have chosen to trace the transformation of attitudes through story types. This will allow a closer look at the ways in which suggestive knowledge about Jews was represented and contained. Within this context, Jews were to acquire a poignant identity, as this benign discourse, which crystallised in the twelfth century into a formidable repertoire, embraced the Jew as the opponent of the Virgin's grace, but also as a needy recipient of her mercy.[2] The Marian world was made of early medieval tales and related images, strung together like pearls into a dazzling ornament by a few monastic writers in the twelfth century. These writers created a body of powerful tales, which were to become ubiquitous. Old stories, like that of Theophilus or of the Jewish Boy, became, through their incorporation into the Marian repertoire, the stuff of popular homiletics and of widespread visualisation of the supernatural. Once the collection of Marian tales was defined, in the Latin collection of Anselm of Bury St Edmunds in mid twelfth-century England, it was transmitted, translated and disseminated all over Europe, shedding and acquiring local colour with an ease reminiscent of the flexible genre of *exempla*. The stories told in this vein were miracles of resolution, of forgiveness, about the victory of persuasive mercy, of reception at a maternal bosom which only the perverse would reject or deny.

In the early medieval collections of religious tales from which the compilers of Marian collections drew most of their material, Jews were familiar protagonists. Their part in such stories was as doubters and offenders (often inadvertently) against Christian truths. The tale might begin with attendance at a Christian ritual or with a viewing of a sacred image, in jest or doubt, and end with persuasion under the influence of manifest wonders, and conversion to Christianity.[3] A Jew in the guise of a magician featured in the most famous and recurrent Marian tale, the story of Theophilus.[4] The protagonist was the secular deputy (*vidâme*) to the Bishop of Cilicia – he had entered into a pact with the devil, at the instigation of a Jewish *magus*, after having lost his worldly position and goods.[5] In this story the devil's power is rendered quite palpable in tempting Theophilus into a Faustian pact, but the Virgin is shown to be even more effective. The Jew begins as the partner of the devil, as clearly depicted in a variety of visual representations, ranging from a lancet window in the cathedral at Le Mans, where he wears a pointed hat and stands right behind Theophilus and the devil, to a relief from Notre Dame in Paris, and in a string of illuminations which accompany this tale in Marian Books of Hours from later centuries.[6]

In an attempt to appreciate the qualities of early medieval tales about Jews, and to trace the changes in such tales throughout the medieval centuries, we will concentrate here on a single tale from the Marian repertoire. This is the story of the Jewish Boy, a tale of witness and conversion, but also one of punishment and violence. Of Greek origin and written down by Evagrius Scholasticus of Antioch (*c.*536–600) in his *Historia ecclesiastica*, the story spread westwards and attracted the attention of Gregory of Tours (d. 595), winning a place in his *De gloria martyrum*.[7] This early Latin version had as its protagonist a Jewish glazier of Constantinople, whose son went to school with Christian boys. Once the son accompanied his school-mates to a local basilica and partook there 'of the Lord's body and blood'. The child then returned home, and told his father what he had done. The Jewish father declared that he would avenge this offence to the law of Moses, and threw his son into an oven. The boy's mother rushed to his rescue, but seeing the heat of the fire she despaired and began wailing and shouting so that the city filled with her cries. When Christians inquired and were told of her calamity they approached the fire, only to see it subside, and find the Jewish boy in it, unscathed, with the following explanation of his felicitous state: 'The woman who was sitting on the throne in that church where I received the bread from the table, and who was cradling a young boy in her lap, covered me with her cloak, so that the fire did not devour me.' The Jewish boy then converted with his mother, and his example led many other Jews to do so, while his father was thrown into the oven.[8]

This is a perfect tale of the Virgin's mercy, in saving an innocent child, and opening the eyes of misguided Jews.[9] As the twelfth-century collection of Marian tales coalesced, the tale gained a place in this most important vehicle of religious lore. The story is significant as a typical example of the *witness* tale, where a Jew effects the conversion of others through the personal experience of miracle and illumination to Christian truth.[10] It acquired such emphasis at the hands of Paschasius Radbert (d. 859) in the ninth century. In the *Liber de corpore et sanguine domini* (831 × 3) the story of the Jewish Boy was detached from its Marian context and made to serve, together with three other miracles, as support for the monk of Corbie's polemic in favour of a physical interpretation of the eucharist. Here the Jewish boy not only attended the mass but was privileged with a eucharistic vision of Christ at the moment of reception of the host:

> Who, when he approached, what I take to be divine providence revealing itself in him, saw a woman on the altar, of fine shape and seated on a throne, holding a little boy on her knees, who stretched out his hand with the holy communion to the priest so that he might distribute it to the people faithfully approaching.[11]

Here the Virgin and Child come alive and participate in the priestly office of communion.

The story thus came variously to be placed within a more defined field of eucharistic proof, in which the Jewish boy bore simple witness and the Jewish father revealed himself as the eucharist's enemy. Some versions described more clearly than others the details of the eucharistic moment. In the twelfth-century *Liber de miraculis* attributed to Botho of Prüfening the boy answered his father's question about his whereabouts and tardiness: 'the priest gave us a whole lot of white bread, and we ate it all up.' After being pulled out of the fire he reported that the woman who had offered particles to eat from the altar had helped him in the fire.[12]

Gregory of Tours' version dominated the sporadic telling of the story of the Jewish Boy in the early Middle Ages, and until its incorporation into the Marian corpus in the 1120s. Thus it is mentioned by Siegbert of Gembloux in his Christian chronicle (*c.*1030–112), placed in the year 552:

> At this time in the Orient a Jewish boy was led to church with his Christian peers, to receive in the Holy Mother of Christ's church the body and blood of Christ, for which he was then thrown into a burning fire by his father, and when he was pulled from it unhurt by Christians, he claimed that the woman, who was depicted in the church holding a child, had fanned him in the flames of the fire with her cloak.[13]

In the twelfth century, Honorius of Autun drew out the eucharistic threads more explicitly in his version in the *Historia ecclesiastica*: the Jewish boy saw the Virgin and Child on the wall as he approached communion, and just when the priest distributed the hosts to the people, the Jewish boy saw another child, like the one on the wall, being divided among the communicants. When his turn came he received 'raw flesh from the priest' and took it home.[14] As in Gregory's version the boy identifies the woman who saved him in the fire with the one seen by him earlier in church during communion. The Virgin is thus strongly invoked both as traditional saviour and as mother and bearer of the eucharistic Christ.

It is this tradition which reached England to be codified by Anselm, monk of Bury St Edmunds, by 1125 in a collection of some forty Marian tales, and then elaborated and extended by William of Malmesbury (*c.*1090–1143), one of the most important contributors to the Marian genre in this formative stage.[15] Some years earlier Herbert de Losinga, Bishop of Norwich (d. 1119), incorporated the tale of the Jewish Boy into a Christmas sermon, a tale of Christians and Jews in a Greek city.[16] Interestingly, and unusually, here the Jewish mother was the parent who responded angrily to her son's experience. When she heard that he had received communion ('had accepted a sacred portion from the Christian altar')[17] she was moved by 'feminine fury' ('femineo furore commota'), summoned the father and incited him to take action. The father in 'madness and cruelty' threw his son into the flames, then blocked up the oven with stones and cement. As in other versions of the tale the mother was then moved to pity and ran to Christians with her terrible tale, and they came to the rescue, discovering the child unscathed in the oven. The boy told everyone that the lady who sits on the altar of the Christians, and the little one whom she holds in her bosom, stood and stretched their hands out to him in protection. Bishop Herbert's telling of the tale at Christmas emphasises the child, abandoned and hurt by parents, and thus highlights the miraculous protection given by God's mother, she who gave birth on Christmas Day, as merciful saviour to the Jewish boy.[18]

William of Malmesbury's version of the tale forms part of his collection of fifty-three Marian miracles, adapted from the work of Dominic of Evesham, and written no later than 1141.[19] William emphasises the eucharistic meanings of the story in ways reminiscent of Paschasius Radbert's version: the child-Christ is seen on the altar and perceived as the eucharistic offering. The Virgin is described by the boy she saved as: 'That beautiful woman, he said, whom I saw sitting on a throne, and *whose son was divided among the people*, was with me in the burning oven.'[20] William ends with the comment that the Jewish boy had been shown that which most people are expected to imagine, the eucharistic truth.[21]

Nigel of Longchamp (*c.*1130–*c.*1200), monk of Canterbury, an accomplished man of letters and satirist, adapted William's story with its Pisan location in his verse poem on the miracles of the Virgin. Nigel emphasises the eucharistic moment within the miracle (the boy had received the 'panis angelicus' from a priest, and the Virgin was described as the mother of the child who had been distributed and given as food), and grants the Jewish mother a prominent role side by side with the Virgin.[22] The fire into which he had been thrown embodies the Virgin's own qualities: 'she made the flame of the oven as tepid as a breeze of dew', invoking powerful images of the Virgin's delicacy and purity.[23] Similar imagery is used in John of Garland's *Stella maris* c.1240, a collection of Marian tales used in the course of Arts instruction, and which was widely used in monastic houses. The short poem (24 lines) describes the Virgin as a cloud of dew, a cell of the honeycomb, with an emphasis far removed from the eucharistic one which prevailed in some earlier versions.[24]

Marian tales were being refined, embellished and collected by English monastic writers, and by mid-century the three prominent and over-lapping collections of Anselm, Dominic of Evesham and William of Malmesbury were arranged by Master Alberic, Canon of Saint Paul's, to create a *corpus* ready for translation into French by the Anglo-Norman poet Adgar c.1165–72.[25] The Jewish Boy in the French guise of 'le petit juitel' was now poised for further transmission in Anglo-Norman England, just as he was to make a wider appearance in the French language.

This story is as much a tale of child abuse as it is of the power of the Virgin; the father's cruelty, the danger which seemingly befell the boy, the terror of his helpless mother, equally the father's victim. A family drama is thus created, with particularly potent dynamics, which fed upon existing tensions within the patriarchal family: the paternal vio-lence feared by mother and son alike, which is resolved in the punish-ment of the father, as many versions of the tale had the Jewish father thrown into the oven after his son's miraculous salvation.

While in the twelfth century the tale circulated in the exclusive circles of monastic devotions, with its translation into the vernacular – Castilian, Netherlandish, English and French – in the thirteenth cen-tury, its reach was greatly extended. It was incorporated into the forma-tive collection of miracle tales, the *Legenda aurea* c.1260, but here the emphasis had shifted: the Jewish Boy's tale was provided for the feast of the Virgin's Assumption.[26] The child was protected by the Virgin, the father was burned to a cinder, but no conversion followed, no happy end, just eternal punishment of the Jew 'who was continuously burnt and utterly consumed'.[27] Vernacular collections such as the *South English Legendary* of 1266 × 88 contained some of the *Legenda aurea*'s material and included the tale of the Jewish Boy under the rubric of St Theophilus, which contained Marian tales.[28] The story line has the child wisely associating the saving Virgin with his earlier eucharistic vision:

Certes quaþ he þe faire womman. þat ich at churche isey
þat stod anhei up bi þe crois. & þo ich was ihouseled also
Me þogte he[o] stod upe þe weued. & tollede me þerto
And to me suþþe hider he com. & hure kerchef nom
And helede me þat nu fur. ne hete ney me com.[29]

[Verily, he said: the beautiful woman whom I saw at church / who
stood on high by the cross / when I received communion / I thought
she stood up on the altar and drew me there / and she came to me
again and took her kerchief / and protected me in the fire, so that the
heat did not reach me.]

In addition to its appearance in devotional collections, the tale of
the Jewish Boy also entered the preaching ambit in *exempla* collections,
many of which were composed by monastic writers, and relied heavily
upon Marian lore. The *Solsequium* is such a Latin guidebook composed
in 1284, not by a friar, but by a Franconian secular priest, Hugo
von Trimberg (*c*.1235–*c*.1313), rector in charge of the scholars of S.
Gangolf's monastery on the outskirts of Bamberg. This work contains
166 legends and *exempla* for the use of secular clergy in the preparation
of sermons, and Hugo included the story of the Jewish Boy in the book's
second section, one containing thirty-six Marian tales.[30] It was similarly
used as an *exemplum* in the highly influential fourteenth-century collection of tales, the *Scala coeli* compiled by the Dominican Johannes Gobius
Jr (*fl.* 1323). This alphabetically ordered collection was self-consciously
'modern'; it preferred *auctoritates* and informants of the thirteenth
century to patristic lore. Yet under the letter C and the subject 'Corpus
Christi' the Jewish Boy's tale is told following a story of the miraculous
transformation of the host into a young boy.[31] So from the exclusively
devotional to the context of instruction, here still in the Latin, the tale
was moving on, with the potential for even wider dissemination in
pastoral and preaching situations. *Exempla*, the performative tokens of
medieval culture, the persuasive enactments of cultural tropes, carried
the story of eucharistic enlightenment and conversion to many new
users.[32]

Translation and interpretation could bring with it a noticeable
change in the tale's register and mood, a fact which must be borne in
mind in the face of the uniformity often suggested by genre. By far the
most influential translation was that of Gautier de Coinci (*c*.1177–1236)
the monastic compiler and translator of Marian lore whose *Les Miracles
de Nostre Dame*, written in verse between 1223 and 1227, lent to the story
of the Jewish Boy a quite different emphasis and mood.[33] The tale is full
of detail: it is set in Bourges, and the Jewish Boy is said to have been the
son of a malicious Jewish glazier ('gïu verrier mesdisant', line 2) while
he himself was intelligent and beautiful ('mielz entend ait et mout plus

bel / De toz les autres giuetiaus', lines 6–7; 'plaisans et biaus', line 8).
The boy is described as tender, soft of flesh and much loved by Christian
boys. This tender person was to receive the blows of his Jewish father.
When the boy attended communion it was a veiled figure holding an
infant that offered him the host:

> Qu'en liu del prestre vient l'ymage;
> Deseur l'autel prise a l'oblee
> Que li prestres avoit sacree
> Si doucement l'en commenie
> Que toz le cuers l'en resaste.³⁴

[In place of the priest the image / came onto the altar and held the
host / which the priest had consecrated / and gave him communion
so sweetly / that his heart was fully sated.]

Upon his return home the boy's resplendent face raised his father's
suspicion, and led to cruel punishment. The father grabbed the child by
the hair and dragged him to the oven and then went to gather more
wood to stoke the fire. The mother was desperate, she wailed and tore
her hair out, crying out for help 'Hareu! Hareu!' (line 68). People came
and saved the Jewish boy while his father, the 'dog', was thrown into the
fire. The child told of his saving in the knowing religious idiom of an
adult:

> 'Par foit, fait il, la belle ymage,
> Qui hui matin me sousrioit
> Quant ele me commenioit
> Avec moi vint en la fornaise
> Luez m'endormi, si fui aaise.'³⁵

[By faith, he said, the lovely image / which this morning smiled /
when she gave me communion / came with me into the furnace /
immediately I fell asleep so was I at ease.]

Mother and son received baptism together with many other Jewish
witnesses of the miracle. But this is not the end, as there were those who
saw the miracle and chose *not* to believe. Gautier's passion for Mary is
fully matched by his horror of the Jews and, in other places in his
collection, of the devil.³⁶ It is with a terrible alliterative ending, playing
with the syllable 'dur' that the story concludes, dwelling upon the hard-
heartedness of the Jews:

> Vers us sui durs si durement
> Que, s'iere rois, pour toute Roie
> Un a durer n'en endurroie.³⁷

1. The Jewish Boy. Gautier de Coinci, early fourteenth century, Paris, fol. 35rb.

[I am so very hard towards them / that if I were king of the whole Kingdom / I would not tolerate even *one* of them.]

Gautier's version became very popular, with the survival of tens of manuscripts, many of them illuminated (figure 1).[38] Gautier was loyal to his twelfth-century source, probably a German manuscript of Marian tales, but he goes further in interpreting and embellishing, turning the innocuous, even forgiving, twelfth-century heritage of Marian tale, and of Jewish witness within it, into a much harsher, adversarial set of tales, insistent on Marian mercy but forcefully aware of those who failed to merit it. In Gautier's telling the Jewish boy is a Christian in the making, redolent with Marian qualities of softness and pliancy; but other Jews were less than potential witnesses. Their very witnessing power is brought into question, and the verse tale achieves a bitter and evil ending, incorporated into its harsh concluding *moralitas* clause.

Other worries inform the tales, beyond the desire to be incorporated into a loving and saving Marian nest, and destabilise the Marian mood discerned in early medieval tales. In this quintessential mid thirteenth-

century language of devotion, aggression and danger still loom even after
the tale's last verses have been read or declaimed. Although the verse tales
of Gautier de Coinci became extremely popular and were known to lay
audiences, he was writing within and for a monastic world, a distinct
world where fantasies of otherness and danger abounded. Thus, more
than most writers Gautier expressed hatred and disgust for Jews:

> Mout les hä et je si fas
> Et Diex les het et je les has
> Et toz li mons les doit här
> Car leurs erreurs ne vielt chär.[39]

[It (the Holy Spirit) hates them a lot and I do too. / And God hates
them and I hate them / and the whole world must hate them /
because they do not wish to desist from their errors.]

So the Marian tale was moving out of monastic contexts through
translation and insertion into devotional *exempla* material in a variety of
ways. Another important vernacular rendition is the *Cantigas de Santa
Maria* of Alphonso X, King of Castile (1252–84). The tale of the Jewish
Boy is situated here fourth among 427 Marian tales (thirty of which
contained Jewish figures), and is rendered as a poem of eleven stanzas,
each ending with the burden:

> A Madre do que livrou
> dos leões Daniel,
> essa do fogo guardou
> un menyõ d'Irrael.[40]

[The mother of He who delivered / Daniel from the lions, / she saved
a boy of Israel / from the fire.]

In another verse the father is said to have been a glazier, and the parents
were named Samuel and Rachel. Here the traditional mood of the tale
is restored, with a happy ending as mother and son convert and father
is put to death:

> Por este miragr' atal
> log' a judea criya,
> e o menyõ sen al
> o batismo recebia;
> e o padre, que o mal
> fezera per sa folia,
> deron-ll' enton morte qual
> quis dar a seu fill'Abel
> *A Madre do que livrou* . . .[41]

[Because of this miracle / the Jewess believed / and the son was baptised / without delay, / whereas the father, / who in his fury / had done the evil deed, / was put to death in the same manner / which he had tried to inflict on Abel his son.][42]

The story retains its Marian inflection, emphasising the mother's role and the Jew's reception into Christianity. Yet in the court of Alfonso X other sentiments were also nurtured, at least in connection with the heightened sensibilities of Holy Week. In the compilation of laws associated with him, the *Siete Partidas*, the section on Jews reports their habit of kidnapping Christian children in re-enactment of the Crucifixion.[43]

The Riojan poet Gonzalo de Berceo (*c.*1196–*c.*1264) based his version of the tale on the Latin tradition which located the events in Bourges.[44] His boy, 'el Judiezno', was much liked by all, and he was moved by the image of the Virgin and Child. The eucharistic context is very thin, and the miracle and conversion are simply and dramatically related. The son innocently recounts his morning's experience to his father, and the father responds harshly and cruelly, not only throwing the boy into the fire, but also lighting it expressly for that purpose. In turn, the Jew's end was bitter: his hands were tied and he was thrown into the oven, reduced to ashes and charcoal ('cenisa e carbones'). Sixteen lines of praise to the Virgin end the poem, whose source was the early set of miracles from the monastery of Chiusa.[45]

The world which embraced the tales of Gautier de Coinci and the *Cantigas* also produced a variety of images to accompany them: in glass, in stone and on painted parchment leaves.[46] In a Marian context, in the chapel of the Blessed Virgin in the *chevet* of Le Mans Cathedral, around 1241 the abbot of the monastery of Eron (dedicted to the Virgin) commissioned the making of images of the Jewish Boy, the story appearing in the north choir triforium in three scenes: a group of boys receiving communion, the father in a pointed hat throwing his son into the oven, and the mother holding her hands to her chest and looking dejected, while the Virgin protects the boy in the oven.[47] A similar rendition in glass appears in Lincoln Cathedral: eight scenes of the life and miracles of the Virgin survive, two of which retell the story of the Jewish Boy (figure 2).[48] The two scenes are in the north choir aisle: the Jewish father, wearing a red pointed hat, throwing his son into the oven, and the Virgin crowned with a halo and dressed in purple and white, saving the child from the fire. Similarly lofty surroundings embrace the image carved as a ceiling boss in the North Alley of the cloister of Norwich Cathedral.[49] Although it forms the centre of a cross-shaped cluster of nine bosses, and was thus hardly visible for clear inspection, this depiction is nonetheless evidence of knowledge of the tale, with its

2. The Jewish Boy. Lincoln Cathedral, mid thirteenth century, window S1.

central emphasis on the taking of the eucharist by a Jewish boy indistin-
guishable from his friends, and side scenes depicting the father's punishment and the saving of the boy.

From *exempla* collections and illustrated miracle-books the images
could also be transposed on to walls, for a close and effective encounter
with viewers. Late medieval collections such as the *Alphabetum
narrationum*, and its fifteenth-century English translation *The Alphabet of
Tales* offered *exempla* grouped by theme. Under the rubric dealing with
the eucharist, the tale appears with the caption 'The eucharist, received
by an unbeliever, saves him from fire' ('Eukaristia sumpta ab infideli a

combustione eum protexit'), rendering quite a novel emphasis in the story. As a eucharistic tale it nonetheless retains the Virgin's agency as the woman who had wrapped her son 'in a clothe' and who then covered the Jewish boy 'with hur mantyll'.[50] A similar context was given to the tale in the fourteenth century in the Chapel of the Corporal of Orvieto Cathedral of *c*.1330. Here an encyclopedic cycle of eucharistic tales covered the walls surrounding the tabernacle, which contained the bloodstained eucharistic napkin (corporal) of the Miracle of Bolsena.[51] The tale of the Jewish Boy appears here in a eucharistic setting, quite divorced from its Marian origin, appropriated into a strongly didactic, and still miraculous, eucharistic frame.[52] In the chapel at Eton, the themes for the fresco series of 1479 × 8 and 1487 × 8 were chosen from Marian miracles. The story of the Jewish Boy appears on the south side, and is told through scenes of communion, throwing into the oven, and saving by the Virgin. A similar thematic arrangement was made soon after in the related stained-glass images of the Lady Chapel at Winchester Cathedral in 1498 × 1524.[53]

During the fourteenth century the narrative was incorporated into the hand-held prayer-books of the rich. The emergence of a book of prayers for the laity, the Book of Hours, rendered as a sequence of psalms combined with devotions to the Virgin, provided a space for visual representations of Marian lore. These are often placed on the *bas-de-page* of leaves of Latin psalms, to be touched by a holder's fingers as she leafed through her Hours. The dramatic tale of a child's suffering and salvation is starkly depicted in these, with emphasis upon the Jewish father's act, the mother's pain, and the Virgin's secure saving lap, all held close to the praying person's own body at moments of silence and introspection.[54] A good example is the Carew-Poyntz Book of Hours

3. The Jewish Boy (a) (*below*) receiving communion; (b) (*right*) being thrown into the fire. Carew-Poyntz Book of Hours (*c*.1350–60), fols 188ᵛ, 189ʳ.

of *c.*1350–60, probably produced for the wife of Sir John Carew, Lord Deputy of Ireland (d. 1363). Here the tale is told in a pair of *bas-de-page* scenes, a quarter of a page high, at Psalm 142, 1 'Domine exaudi oracionem meam': the communion of the children over a prominent housling cloth on fol. 188ᵛ, and a tug-of-war between Virgin and Jewish father near the hot oven, on fol. 189ʳ (figures 3a–b).[55] It follows a number of folios on which a host desecration tale was depicted.

The illuminator of the Carew-Poyntz Hours not only devoted space at the bottom of its psalm pages to such scenes, but also juxtaposed new eucharistic knowledge with the traditional liturgical imagery of the mass. Thus on fol. 56ᵛ, which opens the section of elevation prayers, the initial has a background of punched gold and a fine scene of the elevation. The *bas-de-page*, however, contains an unexpected scene: under a broad arch stand four Jews, two on each side of a hexagonal table, and the two nearest to the table pierce a crucifix with their daggers as bloods flows (figure 4). This is a choice similar to one made later, in the early fifteenth century, by the illuminator of the Lovel Lectionary, who chose to depict a dignified procession as an initial for the Corpus Christi section, but who then added at the *bas-de-page* an angry and bloody scene of two Jews piercing the host on a table covered with a white, bloodstained, cloth (figure 5).[56]

The Bohun Hours of the Virgin of *c.*1370 depicted the tale of the Jewish Boy in two scenes: the communion of a row of children, and the father throwing his son into the oven, in which the boy is shown being protected by the Virgin.[57] Another manuscript made for Mary de Bohun (d. 1394), first wife of Henry IV, has the tale at the Prime of the Virgin (Psalm 69: 2), 'Deus in adiutorium meum intende', in three scenes:

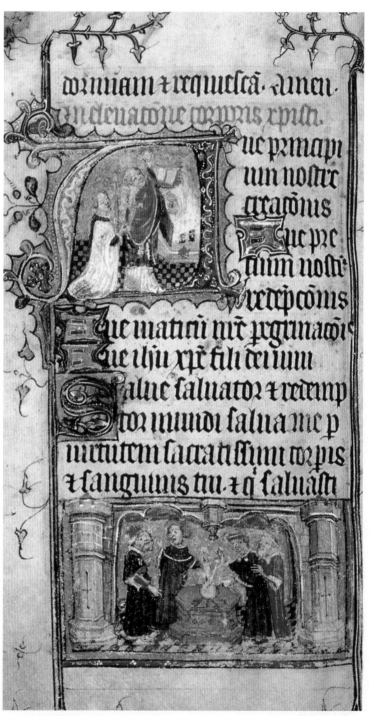

4. The elevation of the host (*above*) and host desecration (*below*) on the page opening the canon of the mass, *Te igitur*, Carew-Poyntz Book of Hours (*c.*1350–60), fol. 56^v.

5. Desecration of the host by two men. Lovel Lectionary (*c.*1400), fol. 13ʳ.

6. The Jewish Boy. Thirteenth-century psalter, Thott MS 547, fol. 14ᵛ.

communion, the throwing into the oven (with recoiling mother), and protection by the Virgin (figure 6).[58]

Similar visual treatment was provided in the large leaves of that intriguing devotional miscellany, the Vernon Manuscript of *c.*1390.[59] This copiously illuminated vernacular book, which may have been made for reading within a large household community, provided a dramatic setting for the tale, one which emphasises the family drama, to the exclusion of the Virgin herself.[60] Other European manuscripts similarly depicted the drama in manuscript illumination. A Parisian workshop produced in 1325 × 30 a collection of Marian tales which had the boy dressed in blue, the Virgin's special colour.[61] A book of the Marian miracles of Gautier de Coinci, made in the principality of Liège in the mid-thirteenth century, shows the boy being rescued by Jesus and Mary in the oven. A later collection, made in Brabant for the Charterhouse at Zelhem *c.*1328, includes an illustration to the tale of the Jewish Boy: the scene chosen was the throwing of the boy into the oven.[62] The tale was also included in the collection of Marian miracles composed by Jean Miélot, made for Duke Philip the Good *c.*1456, and illustrated by two scenes: communion, and burning and saving from the fire.[63]

Through such readings and sightings of lore about Jews, children and the eucharist, the Marian collection was gaining values which were new, related to violence and often overtly eucharistic. Gone, in the late medieval world, was the unambiguously testimonial quality of the Jew through the innocent allure of the Jewish boy and the power of a single Jew to lead to the conversion of many more. By the fourteenth century and within the Marian repertoire, the story of the Jewish Boy was introduced into a multiplicity of contexts – literary, devotional, visual – and could acquire a variety of tones, eliciting differing moods. An early fourteenth-century French version from England, which borrows from Gautier de Coinci, elaborated the liturgical setting of the boy's communion magnificently:

> Al muster vint cum altres firent,
> les enfanz deu le covirent.
> Les pareis esteient curtinees,
> les ymages bele deorees,
> verines beles, le alter bel;
> mult se delita le Gyutel.[64]

> [To the minster he came with others / the children surrounded him / the walls were curtained off / the images were nicely gilt / the glass was lovely / the altar beautiful / all this much delighted the Little Jew.]

The boy was also privileged with a vision and received communion from the Virgin:

Avis lui fu ke le ymage bele
de la gloriouse mere e pucele
s'entremetteit a cele feste
d'acuminer la gent, cum fist le prestre.[65]

[It appeared to him that the lovely image / of the glorious mother
and virgin / had intervened at the celebration / to give communion
to the people, as the priest did.]

He was able to recount his vision when he was saved from the fire. The
Lady who had 'given the people to eat' ('duner a manger a la gent')
earlier that day,[66] became his saviour, while his father was thrown into
the oven:

la mere se fist mein tenant
baptizer oveske l'enfant
e tuz les Gyus sanz targer
pur poi se firent baptizer.[67]

[The mother immediately had herself / baptised with the child / and
almost all the Jews without delay / also had themselves baptised.]

Here a strong Marian emphasis is merged with a heightened eucharistic and liturgical sensibility. The child is no longer a metonym for
the mercy of the Virgin but a prophet of eucharistic truth, elicitor of
eucharistic revelation. What was told in this edifying tale could then be
observed in reality. The Dominican *Annals of Colmar* under the year
1290 reported the case of a youngster from a village near Colmar, who
saw a lovely boy in the host elevated by the priest, and asked his parents
to give it to him all day long.[68] The tale of the Boy's eucharistic vision,
transmitted in a Marian context, came to acquire qualities with evident
pastoral value and power to disseminate eucharistic probity. It was to
travel even further within the *Legenda aurea* and in collections of *exempla*,
increasingly strong in its resolution.[69]

The sensibility that concerns us here revolves around a child and the
altar – the underlying image of both parts of the Jewish Boy tale – and
can be seen on a growing number of altars all over Europe, with the
development of the altarpiece of Virgin and Child from the thirteenth
century.[70] This is the devotional image which most frequently accompanied sacramental action, and which contributed to the linking of Christ
Child and consecrated host. Among the miracles recounted in the *vita*
of Peter Martyr (1205–52) is the case of a rumour that spread in the
region of Milan that the Virgin and Child had appeared on the altar of
a heretical church. When he was summoned to the church, Peter
unmasked the vision as no more than a figment of diabolical delusion.[71]

In visual images of this story, artists rose to the challenge of representing the Virgin and Child as devils, and in one Venetian polyptych panel of *c.*1450–60 Peter Martyr confronts the altarpiece with the *real* thing, the host in a monstrance.[72] The juxtaposition of child and altar was also a disturbing one, which conjured images of infanticide, and to the learned perhaps also the images of Circumcision and the Sacrifice of Isaac.[73]

Images of a child in the consecrated host appeared frequently in visions, and are thus often told in *exempla* and other tales. Such appearances could move hearers to pity, but their true nature was far from easy to discern. Thomas Aquinas (d. 1274) attempted to clarify the meaning of 'the child in the host' in the *Summa theologiae*. The question posed is 'Does the body of Christ really remain in this sacrament when there is a miraculous appearance of a child or flesh?'[74] The answer is 'No': 'the sacramental species sometimes still remain in their entirety, sometimes only the more important ones.' The form of Christ's body which appears as a child is thus a miraculous one, during which the bread and wine remain consecrated.[75] Aquinas earlier distinguished between 'subjective' visions which are visited upon individuals for the strengthening of their faith, but which are perceived only by them, and 'objective' ones, where many witnesses observe the child simultaneously. In any case, the appearance of the child does not detract from the sacramental nature of the vision, rather it is to be understood devotionally. Indeed, as we have seen, the appearance of the child in the host fits in well with the mood of eucharistic sensibility, acquiring the meaning of Christ's suffering body in the consecrated host. In the later medieval centuries it allowed the Jewish Boy to be the carrier of eucharistic insight reinforced by his own victimised tenderness.

The story of the Jewish Boy allowed the conflation of violence and compassion, powerful and contradictory sentiments which cannot but stir unease. The centrality of the figure of a child, and its convergence with Christ in the host, recurs repeatedly and invokes pathos. People were moved by the vision of the child in the host and by the complementary image of a child observing it, both chastising presences which evoked suppressed questions and doubt. Around these children – the Jewish boy, the child on the altar – strong fears of abuse and loss could be crystallised. Indeed, in the tales of the abuse of hosts, it is often the wounded Christ Child who comes forth to proclaim the suffering eucharistic presence. Christ and child, Christ as child, introduced victimhood and with it, of necessity, crime and danger. It may have resonated with sensibilities related to Jewish martyrdom, and the martyrdom of children.[76]

The sense of danger posed by Jews – linked so frequently to the utter vulnerability of children to any adult malefactors – was represented in a northern tale about Jews, children and ovens. In the French version of the Gospel of Christ's childhood, *L'Evangile de Enfaunce de Jesu Christ*, which appears in the later thirteenth century, the story of Christ's infancy was made up of apocryphal material in Latin, based on the Greek (pseudo-)gospel of Mark,[77] and formed into a version of His early life, containing interesting and otherwise absent details of Christ's infancy.[78] Among the thirty tales is a story of the Children in the Oven. In Jericho, Jewish parents intervened to prevent their children from playing with the boy Jesus by hiding them away in an oven. When Christ came to look for his playmates and asked what was in the oven, he was told that these were 'pigs', to which he answered 'Let them be pigs' ('Pors soient, puiz que cy sont miz') and the children turned into pigs and ran away from their parents.[79] The English illustrated Holkham Bible of *c.*1327 attaches a miniature to this tale, and one which resembles closely the scenes of the Jewish Boy: Jewish children put by parents into a dark and forbidding oven.[80]

The oven is rich in connotations: it often represented the womb, the place where children were 'cooked', a secret place. It could be familiar, domestic, warm and vibrant,[81] as well as a destructive place where children were destroyed.[82] This duality also lent itself to a specifically late medieval connotation, one which made of the oven or hearth a token of eucharistic meaning.[83] In this meaning the dual aspect of the oven's work is realised: Christ's body was made as bread or as paschal meat in an oven, but it was also destroyed as a sacrifice. Ovens were thus both food-giving and life-denying, dark and dangerous places for children, while remaining useful spaces for adults.[84]

The association of child, danger and Jews is invoked further in a eucharistic context in a vernacular sermon of the Dominican preacher Berthold of Regensburg (*c.*1210–72). In a rhetorical exchange he engages with those who question the peculiar forms of the eucharist: Is it a big body residing within a small wafer? Why does God not allow us to see Him? Berthold answers these questions with brutal realism: 'Who would want to eat raw flesh or drink red blood? Who would want to bite off a little child, its head or its hand, or its foot?'[85] In the same decades the *Tabula exemplorum*, a French handbook of preaching material, made in passing a sinister connection between the devil-Jews and child-killing. In his exposition on *Dyabolus* the author notes that the devil, like a wolf, is defined by his actions, and his are nothing but malign. The *exemplum* then tells of a wolf who pretended to be dead in order to devour a bird.[86] The *moralitas* which follows concludes that the devil acts like a wolf, as do Jews 'who in the place of Christ crucify waxen images, and sometimes boys' ('qui loco Christi crucifigunt ymaginem ceream et quandoque pueros'). The slight hesitation introduced by 'sometimes' ('quandoque') underscores the enormous leap in gravity between the

abuse of wax images and the killing of a living child.[87] A sinister world
which associates Jews with the slaying of the innocent is reinforced here
by the prevalent fear of wolves.[88]

Thus the Jew as the foe of children appears in several related contexts.
Not only is this a world in which popular belief in Jews' need for
Christian blood had become established, but one which was able to
associate all types of Jewish difference with danger to innocence, to
children. A powerful representation of three kinds of usury appears in a
roundel of a *Bible moralisée* of *c*.1220–30. There is a man carrying a chest
on his back, another holding a scale for coins which is being tipped by
a devil's head, and a third taking a baby away from a woman/mother. Is
the child the woman's only possession, pawned here to a Jew?[89]
Although usury is not named as a specifically Jewish vice here, the right-
hand column of the page is devoted to enemies of the faith, and the
lowest roundel on that side directly juxtaposes the mass (a scene of
elevation) with the adjacent group of grotesque Jews holding a lamb,
their own type of filthy and redundant sacrifice.

The Jews also suffered from association with the universal sin of greed,
and the greedy were seen as the particular enemies of children. Was not
a cruel man who oppressed the poor and their children a devourer of
children? John Gobius recounted a tale in his *Scala coeli* about a prelate
who abstained from eating meat but who was famed for his rapine
and unjust exactions. A widow, surrounded by her children, once
approached him: 'Sir, you do not eat dead and cooked meats but rather
live ones, those which you force out of us. So devour now my two sons
and eat them.'[90] The prelate immediately repented and made restitution
for his ill-won gains.

In the hands of some writers and image makers the dangerous juxtaposition of child/vulnerability/Christ and Jew/abuse/father is emphasised in the traditional Marian tale, while others continue to underline
in the tale the drive towards resolution through mercy. The emphasis of
a tale is inflected by the context of telling and use. Travelling within the
Marian frame of cultural reference, image and performance, the story
emphasised the possibilities and limitation of inclusion. In Books of
Hours or other devotional settings, the violence of the tale was encased
within schemes of certainty and mercy. Violence was circumscribed,
unfaith turned into faith, cruelty into the vehicle for miraculous and
salvatory happenings. Yet, when set in another frame, that of eucharistic
lore and the miraculous, the story of the Jewish Boy gained undertones
of danger and bespoke a promise of violence.[91]

A family romance seems to have emerged from the tale: the Jewish
Boy acquires a new parentage, an engulfing mother acting as a conduit
to a new father, Christ.[92] The family drama embedded within the tale of
the Jewish Boy could lend itself to new emphases, away from the Marian
matrix of inclusion. The German versions of the early thirteenth

century, rendered as free-standing poems known as 'Das Jüdel', were redolent of adversity and polemic.[93] There are lengthy exchanges between the boy and his father (Why was the boy late to his meal? What was the boy's vision of the Virgin really?). It has turned into a polemical tract rather than a Marian tale. The end sought is punishment, rather than witness or conversion.

The Marian context is one which explores the promise and the danger of mother-love. The oven into which the Jewish boy was pushed by his father beckoned as a womb, and stands metonymically linked to the Virgin, who inhabited it as the boy's saviour. In the Marian tale eucharistic associations are implicit, juxtaposed with Mary's image of nurture and inclusion the pollution and danger represented by the Jew. In the tale the Virgin as mother is further reinforced by actions of the earthly Jewish mother, whose maternal quality outstrips her quality as Jew. The oven-hearth is related to the punishment of the Jew but also gestures towards Christ's own death and rebirth as bread. The tale of the Jewish Boy thus allows a number of fantasies to be expressed: return to the mother, rejection of the father, enclosure within the saving grace of Christ through his mother. The Jew could have no part in these.

Throughout the thirteenth century, the juxtaposition of Jew and children became more heavily weighted with episodic rumours of ritual murder. Preachers such as Giordano da Rivalto (da Pisa) retold stories of Jewish abuse of children as one of the many ways in which they attack Christians. In a sermon of 9 November 1304 he reported that Jews circumcised poor Christian boys ('fanciulli de'poveri, essi li circuncidono'), then told the host desecration tale from Paris, the tale of the Jewish Boy in a version which included the appearance of a child in the host, followed by a case of ritual murder in Apulia which resulted in the expulsion of the Jews from the Kingdom of Sicily.[94]

As the juxtaposition of Jew and eucharist became more laden with meaning throughout the thirteenth century, narratives increasingly came to include the host as the object of Jewish abuse, as bearing the tenderness of a child within it. Ritual murder accusations took hold in the Empire in the mid-thirteenth century and host desecration rumours in the century's very last years. These narratives inhabited quite separate geographical spheres, but, as we have seen, they possessed the potential for convergence which was to become most evident in the second half of the fifteenth century. Even a thirteenth-century case, such as that of Werner of Oberwesel (d. 1287), was rewritten with eucharistic flourishes during the canonisation process of 1426 × 9. Two witnesses, Johann Selig and Johann Fudersack, interpreted the alleged killing of the boy by the Jews as a substitute for the abuse of the host.[95] Several cases later in the century would see one of the narratives incorporating, in the course of its unfolding, the other.[96]

It is increasingly within the world of religious instruction and ecclesiastical regulation that the possibilities of the encounter between Jew and
the host were being rethought and tested. The world of the eucharist
was that of promise, but also of punishment. Its truths were taught as
much by rules of belief and practice – the belief in transubstantiation,
the communion in a state of purity – as by exemplary instruction on
infringement and its dire consequences.[97] This process of forging a
Christian identity depended on the articulation of perceptible differ-
ences, and it occurs in this period through the use of a variety of types
– heretic, Jew, woman, incontinent priest – and with the deadliest of
consequences to the Jew.[98]

The elements embedded in the figure of the Jewish father, who in the
Jewish Boy tale was always sent to his death in the fire he had stoked for
the destruction of his son, come to predominate in some new or
reworked narratives. While the story of the Jewish Boy was to be told and
retold throughout the later Middle Ages, as were other traditional tales
of Jewish witness, a new type of narrative frame was emerging with
particular force, a new story *à la mode*: one which saw Jews as an ever-
present danger to the faith, and which all but excluded the chance of
conversion and incorporation. Its rhetoric was accusatory and vindic-
tive, describing heinous Jewish crimes and the just retribution these
deserved. No longer the potential convert in life, the Jew's mission of
witness was worked through his death, through the erasure of the doubt
and danger he represented.[99] This new frame included the tale of ritual
murder, but also a less well-known and even deadlier narrative, the
accusation of host desecration. This narrative was produced through the
intersection of two discursive frames: that which reflected on Jews and
attempted to separate them from Christians, and that which defined
Christian identity around the sacramental promise and practice of the
eucharist.

A strange and dangerous relationship between Jew and eucharist was
gradually tested in narratives of the thirteenth century, revolving around
eucharistic dignity and the dangers posed to it by Jews, in their intention
to test it, at the very least, or abuse it, at the very worst. Jews were
increasingly seen as being true to their nature in the enactment of
contempt for Christianity and evil intent towards its God in His eucharistic manifestation. Encounters between Jews and host thus came to be
imagined and located in the streets and houses of medieval towns and
villages, producing a new and powerful narrative which came to affect
hundreds of communities and many thousands of Jews and Christians.

The new design of the eucharist, becoming increasingly widespread
from the late twelfth century, provided a new location for encounters
with God and for experience of the sacred. This powerful and necessary
eucharist came to require careful containment and surveillance, just as
new rituals around it – visitation of the sick (*viaticum*), processions –

exposed it to the open air, to the unpredictable surroundings of people's homes, streets and roads. Just as the eucharist's power was emphasised and increasingly realised, the myriad dangers and mishaps which could befall the host became clear. This led to attempts at regulation and legislation of the environment and safety of the host.[100] The exposition of the host was becoming more frequent, and it was often public in nature: elevation at the mass, reservation of the host for the sick, processions to the dying which passed through the streets of town or village, festive expository processions, and from the fourteenth century regular processional exposition on Corpus Christi and its octave.[101]

All these were occasions which might detract from the host's safety and dignity, so bulwarks of practical protective measures were provided with the aim of securing the host from harm and indignity. The Fourth Lateran Council of 1215, which legislated for the doctrine of transubstantiation as an article of faith,[102] also laid down measures to limit the spheres of Jewish contact with Christians, through work, residence and sexual relations. Jewish presence in the streets during Holy Week was prohibited, so that they would have no occasion to deride Christ and Christian grief at His Crucifixion.[103]

Lateran IV did not lay down a strict connection between Jews and the exposition of the host, but the principle of separation between Jews and representations of Christ was to become clear as the century evolved, the century which saw the growth of preoccupation with the safety of the host.[104] Synodal action inspired by the papacy was particularly felt in Central European provinces, where statutes habitually required Jews to stay indoors during part of Holy Week. Cardinal-Legate Guido of San Lorenzo in Lucina brought the papal programme to northern Europe, incorporating striking clauses referring to Jews in his statutes for the Austrian church.[105] The synod of Vienna (10–12 May 1267) devoted five clauses to matters related to Jews such as employment of Christians by Jews, sexual intercourse between the peoples, limitation on the construction of synagogues. In the clause 'On their festivities' ('De conviviis eorundem') Jewish presence near the host in mentioned:

> And if it happens that the sacrament of the altar be carried in front of the houses of the Jews, those Jews, having heard the heralding sound [of a bell], should be made by us or by the church's bishops to enter into their houses and close their windows and doors; lest they presume to dispute the Catholic faith with simple folk.[106]

There is little evidence that these canons were widely disseminated. They were probably the expression of local ecclesiastical unease at the granting of extensive privileges to Jews by the Dukes of Bohemia-Austria and Poland-Silesia.[107] But they fit in with the interest that the newly established inquisitorial process in the region displayed towards Jews. If indeed the Passau Anonymous, the author of the mid thirteenth-century handbook for inquisitorial examination of heresy, was a native of northern Austria, then he may have been expressing some of the ideas prevalent in the region about the need to curtail and limit the activities of Jews, to mark them as enemies, to make them the subjects of scrutiny and separation.[108]

It is on the pages of the canon of the mass that a stark distinction between the historical fates of *ecclesia* and *synagoga* came to be placed. This representation of the opposition between Christianity and Judaism became a popular choice for the decoration of Romanesque and then Gothic church portals, of fonts, of stained glass and of the initial of the canon of the mass, the initial T of *Te igitur*.[109] The initial of the canon in the Cholet Missal of after 1261 even dispenses with the crucifix, as the letter T provides the central separating line between the two figures: one crowned, holding a cross triumphant in one hand and a tabernacle with a draped chalice in her left hand, the other turning her blindfolded head, holding a broken staff and letting slip from her hand the tablets of law. *Ecclesia* is calm, *synagoga* is all confusion and loss.[110] Similar is the representation in the Amesbury Psalter, where the figures flank a crucifixion, *synagoga* holding a broken staff, her oil spilt, unable to face Christ or the reader.[111]

The anxiety about the Jewish presence could be dealt with in other ways, through the efforts of secular rulers. A whole set of legislative acts could be initiated as political necessity and religious awareness dictated. Communities could also pursue the principles of separation laid down by ecclesiastical legislation. The commune of Avignon decreed in 1243 that Jews and Jewesses over the age of nine should hide away from viewing the host, or else pay a fine:

> And we ordain for God's honour and reverence that when Christ's body will be carried to the sick, no Jew or Jewess older than nine years old should stay in the Jewish street in Its presence, had rather go away and hide, and whoever acts against this should be fined 5 *sous*.[112]

The papal justices of Avignon presented a number of cases of Jews who dared to stay out of doors during Holy Week. Bellicadra, wife of Salves Jaqura the Jew, was denounced by Jacomardus lo Camus in 1364 for having walked through the town (*per villam ivit*) on Ash Wednesday in contravention of the statutes. She was fined 10 *sous*.[113] In 1374 the Jewess Bonanada (*alias* Rasiassa) was denounced by a servant for having obstinately walked in the butchers' street (*carreria parvi macelli'*), while Christ's body was being carried through the town, and failed to hide ('non se abscondit'), or show it reverence. She was fined 5 *sous*.[114]

Jurisdiction over infringements of eucharistic codes by Jews could become the business of authorities secular and ecclesiastical. The town-book of Meissen in Saxony (fifteen miles north-west of Dresden), the *Meissener Rechtsbuch* of 1357 × 87, included a set of regulations about Jews' work and life, among them a clause on behaviour during the passage of the host. A Jew should remain indoors when Christ's body was being carried, and if he was in the street, he should enter a house or go into another street.[115] In Avignon not to do so was seen as an offence against public order, dealt with by the secular papal judges; it could also be deemed spiritual business for episcopal treatment. A mandate of 1275 from the Bishop of Worcester, Godfrey Giffard, to the deans of Westbury and Bristol ordered them to refrain from contact with the Jews of Bristol who had insulted and blasphemed the body of Christ and the chaplain while he carried it to a gravely sick woman of the parish of St Peter, and passed through the Jewish quarter (*placea Judaism' Bristoli*) en route.[116] The letter ordered the deans to have the deed proclaimed in all the parish churches of Bristol on three Sundays.[117] Avignon Jews who failed to kneel before the host, spoke Hebrew in its presence, or made gestures which could be taken as mockery found themselves brought before the papal justices in the fourteenth century.[118] In 1281 while on a visit to Vienna, King Rudolph sat in judgement in the case of a Jew 'who, it is said, wounded a priest walking with Christ's body with a lump of mud or a stone'.[119] The moment of exposure at the taking of the host to the sick was singled out by King Peter IV of Aragon in 1340, in a series of legislative attempts at the correction of morals, as an occasion from which Jews and Muslims should be banished, lest they indulge in wild laughter and derision ('cachinationes et derisiones') to the distraction of the faithful.[120]

Such ecclesiastical and secular attention to the possibility of encounters between Jews and the host was paralleled in the testing of new narrative lines which linked the two. Elaborate stories of mani-pulation and testing of the host were inserted into collections of older miracle-tales. In these, Jews exhibit great ingenuity in procuring the host – through the help of Christian friends or converted Jews, by bribing the weak-willed, or simply by pretending to be Christians. A whole field for competition and persuasion opened up around the eucharist. As the eucharist emerged more potent in itself, through the claims of transubstantiation, the relative proximity allowed to Jews in observing it and commenting on it grew problematic and menacing. Between the wish to make the Jews act as guarantors and witnesses of Christian faith and the fear of the danger they posed to Christ's public body, interesting interpretations and stories could develop.

It was in this mood that Innocent III wrote his letter to the Bishop of Sens in 1213, concerning the Jewish convert N. The Pope was recom-mending to the Bishop's support and patronage the young man N. who had witnessed the following events:

a certain Christian woman was living in the home of this man's father, and, by Jewish seductions, she was estranged from the Catholic Faith, so that she constantly asserted . . . that bread taken from any ordinary table is as efficacious as the host of Christ . . . she pressed on to church . . . on the feast of the Resurrection . . . and she received the host, and hid it in her mouth. Then, giving it into the hands of the father of the above-mentioned N. . . . she burst forth in these words: 'Behold my Savior, as the Christians say.' Just as he wanted to put this into a certain empty box . . . he was called to his door, and fearing lest someone by chance come into the house, he unwittingly and on account of his haste, placed it into another box in which were seven Parisian *livres* . . . When hurrying back from the door he returned to the closet and did not find it . . . in the empty box in which he believed he had placed the said host, he looked into the other in which he kept the money, and he saw it full – not with coins – but with wafers. Astonished and trembling . . . the people standing about perceived the greatness of the divine miracle, and decided to become converted to Christianity.[121]

Within the setting of a household engaged in monetary dealings, the eucharist was vindicated through miraculous self-protection against Jewish manipulation. Here the Jew had not even committed the intended misdeed, but rather displayed pathetic curiosity and unspoken intention. This tale about a Jew and the eucharist is still oriented towards resolution (conversion, penance); abuse is only implied, danger suggested rather than enacted. The tale invokes the 'Midas principle' of punishment for avarice through the generation of a superabundance of gold without the ability to control it. The Jewish father's crime is ultimately transferred from an incipient crime against the eucharist (he hid the host till later . . .) to one concerned with greed. His worldly logic led him to think that through his riches he could gain all – control over Christians (maid), and through them, their God (host). His inability to distinguish his coins from the host is yet another manifestation of Jewish blindness, to intrinsic truth, to true value, invoking vertiginous fascination with gold and riches.[122]

The accusation of host desecration was being born among narratives which countered the doubts of the misguided, the feeble, the heretical, with myriad examples of eucharistic vindication. As we trace the emergence of the host desecration accusation, it is important to remember the many tales which described abuse by other 'dangerous groups'. In his *Gemma ecclesiastica* Gerald of Wales (1146–1223) recounted several cases of doubt and ridicule by heretics, new and old: the Patarins of Ferrara side by side with the early medieval tale of the doubting woman at the Mass of St Gregory, a spontaneous miracle of transformation into flesh and blood in Chartres and Reims, a testing by heretics in Flanders, and the edifying miracle of the eucharist and the bees.[123] In Gerald's chapter 'Of examples which affirm the faith' tales follow a line of associations; old and new stories mixed and merged in an edifice of danger and relief to the eucharist.[124]

Such an old-fashioned narrative of 'recognition' could now link eucharist and Jew, as it did in a widespread tale which inserted Jewish avarice and magical action into the plot. A Jew conjured up the devil in order to strike a deal with him, and the devil appeared to him crowned and robed. Suddenly, and inexplicably, the devil knelt down and removed his crown; he later rose and knelt again. When the Jew asked for an explanation, the devil admitted that when the parish priest passed by carrying the host to a sick person, he was obliged to kneel and venerate the host with a bare head; and when the priest returned with the empty pyx, he merely knelt in respect.[125] Hearing this, the Jew was led to conversion, moved by the eucharistic truth, which even the devil was forced to acknowledge, in this tale so embedded within familiar eucharistic practices (*viaticum*, kneeling), and the even more familiar belief in the devil.[126]

Jewish access to the host was most frequently enabled by networks of friendship and employment. Female servants in Jewish households recur as lowly mediators of the sacrament. Anxiety about their presence there led to recurrent legislation against the practice, which began in earnest under Pope Innocent III (1198–1216).[127] The imagined horror of the presence of Christ's remains in the body of a Jew inspired further anxiety in both groups. In July 1205 Innocent III requested of the Archbishop of Sens and the Bishop of Paris that they prevail upon the King of France, the Duke of Burgundy and the Countess of Troyes to prevent the employment of Christian wet-nurses by Jews in his domain. The Pope claimed that after Easter communion Jews required their Christian wet-nurses to express their milk into a latrine for three days, rather than feed it to their infants.[128] The canonist Henry of Segusio, Cardinal Hostiensis (1200–70), also reported in his *Summa aurea* that some Jews had wet-nurses express the milk into a latrine in the days following communion, thus committing Christ's body to the filth.[129] It is hard to discern the degree to which such cases are reports of practice, widespread perceptions of Jewish practice, or the figment of a heated casuistic scholarly mind;[130] Jewish law allowed the employment of non-Jewish wet-nurses so long as they were supervised, particularly lest they bring into the house 'unclean foods'.[131]

An abiding conundrum faced scholars in the challenges posed by the enhancement of the reality and presence of Christ's body in the host. The promise which the directness of bodily assimilation of the host held was matched by the danger that such closeness harboured. This led to quite novel reflections on the fortunes of the host within the human body. The first Dominican master in Oxford, Roland of Cremona (d. 1259), commented on the reception of the host, in its nature as food for the soul rather than for the body ('non nutrit corpus humanum sed animam'). Following William of Auxerre's *Summa aurea*, Roland develops the notion of food which could be nourishing to some and nauseating to others. The host would thus be unsavoury when taken by a Jew or a heretic. Just as the amounts of manna which had been greedily accumulated by some when granted in the desert could not be savoured, so the other God-given, perfect food – the host – would nauseate those who took it to be no more than a morsel of bread: heretics, Jews and other unbelievers.[132] The ever offered, wholly given eucharist was dangerously located at the mercy of weak persons – women, poor lower clergy – and thus potentially in the hands of its deadliest enemies, the Jews.

Contact with Jews, to the detriment of the safety of the host, could also come about in the course of business affairs, especially those of a shady character. Or at least such events could be imagined. A most interesting picture arises from a roll recording cases bought before the English Justices Itinerant on their Norwich rounds of 1285. The jurors required the arrest of Abraham of Warwick, Petithake, Isaac the Chaplain of the Jews of Norwich, and many other Jews and Christians, for having broken into the churches of Newton and Swainsthorpe (four miles from Norwich): 'at night, [they] stole chalices, vestments, books, and other ecclesiastical ornaments, and vilely broke a pyx in which Christ's body (*corpus Christi*) had been placed, and crushed the Lord's body beneath their feet.'[133] Here the dry language of legal process controls the description, and the details of the abuse of the host are strung together with other offences. This is not the language of homiletics, and if popular outcry against the offence was raised, it would not have been recorded in the Justices' rolls.

Similarly 'mundane' if more robust in its consequences is a case recorded in a collection of legal precedents, the *Schöffenbuch* of the Bohemian town of Brno (Brünn), which reflects the decisions of town officials up to the early fourteenth century. This is a case of two students who stole four consecrated hosts in a gilt pyx from the village church of Modricz (Modrice) and offered them to the Jews of Brno. Horrified, the Jews reported the thieves to the authorities. The case posed the townsmen with a legal dilemma: whether the attempt to sell the hosts to Jews turned the offence, theft, into the graver crime of heresy, an offence which fell within ecclesiastical jurisdiction. The townsmen decided

in a definitive sentence that in this case the desire to sell should be judged as graver than the act of theft. Thus the said malefactors should be handed over as heretics to the fire for the sake of the faith rather than, as thieves, suffer the punishment of torture by the gibbet.[134]

The Jews seem not to have been considered as the focus of legal consideration here. A later but similar case is contained in the formula of sentencing recorded in the sentence-book of the Alsatian town of Schlettstadt in a theft case of 1409. One Henselin Glaser undertook under oath that after his release from prison he would never again repeat the offence of bringing the host to a Jew's house.[135]

Tales of eucharistic recognition by Jews which reached peaceful resolution through conversion were still told throughout the thirteenth century, but as the century advanced even these increasingly emphasised Jewish ill intent and machinations in descriptions which were ever more detailed and sophisticated. A story included by Herman of Bologna in the *Viaticum narrationum* of *c.*1280–90 told of a Jew of Cologne, well acquainted with Christians and their ways, who received communion as a Christian and kept the host in his mouth. As he stepped out into the churchyard he heard heavenly voices, speaking German, and when he took the host out of his mouth he observed it turn into an attractive little child on the palm of his hand.[136] The Jew's fear of discovery and his attempts to avoid it are described in a comic manner. He first tried to eat the little thing, only to find it so hardened that he could not chew it. Then again he heard the mocking voice: 'For it is not meet to take the children's bread, and to cast it unto the dogs' (Mark 7: 27). He then tried to rid himself of the host/child and leave the churchyard, but whenever he tried to step out he found the devil at his side forcing him back in. The repeated interventions of the heavenly voice convinced him that he was witnessing a true miracle, not diabolical delusions, so he asked a passer-by to summon the bishop to whom he confessed his misdeed and from whom he begged forgiveness. The host/child, refulgent in miraculous luminosity, was unearthed from the place of its hiding/burial and was carried into heaven by angels, while on earth many Jews converted. Versions of this tale circulated throughout the later Middle Ages. The chronicle of the Lübeck Dominican Hermann Korner, compiled in the 1420s, included a Low German version which enhanced the earlier tale with greater emphasis on demonic manipulation through speech, while still retaining the 'happy ending' of conversion.[137]

The tenor of such stories, even those which end in conversion, became more dangerous and violent as the century progressed, just as what the host represented became weightier, more precious. A story in the *Tabula exemplorum* (compiled in northern France in the late thirteenth century) tells of a priest in Rome who received communion at Easter. On his return from church some Jews known to him stopped him and asked, 'Where is now that body of Jesus Christ, which you claim to have received today?', to which the priest answered, 'It is in my soul.' The Jews retorted, 'And where is your soul?', to which the priest answered: 'I believe it to be in my heart.' They then killed him and extracted his heart, and just as they cut it open, a lovely little boy appeared to them in it. Seeing him the Jews went quite mad, and shouted so amazingly that nearby citizens came forth and saw the miracle. The little boy told the assembled crowd that he was Jesus Christ, reciting the words 'He that eateth my flesh and drinketh my blood' (John 6: 56). He then re-entered the priest's body, which was resurrected whole, and it was he who lived on to tell the tale.[138]

The danger posed by Jews in the presence of the host became 'common knowledge', and even medieval writers admitted that this might lead Christians to misattribute ill intent to Jews. Among the tales which the Dominican preacher John of Sterngassen, prior of the Strassburg convent from 1316 (*fl.* 1310–36), used in his sermons to Dominican sisters of St Nicholas *abundis*, a Jew engaged in reflection on God in the host was taken to be a potential abuser. The Jew was said to have approached an image of Christ saying: 'Creator and saviour, judge and guardian, you who are God and man, pour your mercy upon me a poor sinner.'[139] Once he saw a priest carrying the host on the road. He knelt with the Christians, but spoke different words from the others: 'if you are God and Man, so pour mercy on me a poor sinner.'[140] A Christian who suspected the Jew of mocking Christ threw a stone at his head. But the priest witnessed the Jew's soul raised to heaven by angels. The Jew had obviously shown faith, and for this he was rewarded. In a rather quaint and old-fashioned manner, John here uses the Jew as a witness, rather than as an abuser, and inverts the act of abuse, as the perverse act of a single misguided Christian.

Tales which linked Jews and the host were thus becoming more complex in their descriptions of the trails of danger and the paths of ill intent. A fourteenth-century thematic collection of *exempla*, that of the English Dominican John Bromyard (d. 1409), included under the rubric 'Eucharistia' the following complex tale about the instability of conversion and the ease with which Jews might invade Christian spaces. Following an expulsion, a Jewess moved to another region where she was unknown, and pretended to be a Christian. When she lay on her death-bed and was visited by a priest, she confessed to him that she had never been baptised. The priest tried to persuade her to convert but failed, until he remembered that in the early church ('primitiva ecclesia') people were often healed following baptism, as Constantine's case amply illustrated. On hearing this, the Jewess decided to be baptised, and she was healed. On a subsequent visit to her he learned from the woman of her regret. Whereas in the past she had always received a vision of a pretty little boy in the priest's hand at church, this vision disappeared once she had been baptised. The priest patiently explained that faith is not proven by seeing but by belief. Before she was converted the vision was sent to persuade her; as a Christian she no longer needed such proof.[141]

In this tale neither danger nor punishment affects the mood; patience is manifested in the gentle beckoning of the Jewess to Christian truth. The affirming visions are inserted in passing, as a common occurrence, just as natural as eucharistic truth. The crucial element which allows this tale to take a benign turn is the fact that the Jewish person is a woman: less knowing, and in consequence less culpable.[142] As we will see, the tale of violent host desecration and its aftermath always employed a Jewish man as protagonist, and he was *never* forgiven or treated with forbearance.

The embellishment and shifts of emphasis in narratives that linked Jew and eucharist are part of a long and complex process, of which we can only glimpse fleeting moments. A particularly interesting one is provided by an *exemplum* which is said to have been preached by the Parisian Franciscan scholar James of Provins in a parish church in Paris in 1272 or 1273.[143] This *exemplum* appears under the rubric 'Eukaristia' in the collection of some 300 sermons attributed to Raoul of Châteauroux, one of the first scholars of the Sorbonne College. It brings Jews and eucharist even closer in a dangerous and abusive narrative embrace. Here a group of Jews procured the host from an old woman (*vetula*)[144] and proceeded to test it in three ways: by water, fire and metal. The host remained intact, and then began to bleed. Astonished, the Jews decided to consult a famous rabbi from a neighbouring town, and sent an emissary with the host and a letter to inquire: should they convert following the miraculous manifestation? Even before the letter reached its destination the host was discovered and in consequence the Jews were punished. This is less than a full host desecration accusation: the story retains the possibility of witness, it is less than whole-hearted in imputing evil intent to the Jews. It shows the fissures of an unstable narrative; but one which, at least in the parish of St-Jean-en-Grève in Paris, was to achieve cohesion and persuasive power some seventeen years later.

By the 1280s a version told in south Lorraine was captured in a series of painted glass medallions in the church of St Dié. A building and decoration campaign which lasted from the late 1270s to around 1290 employed an extremely able stained-glass master, who alongside scenes related to the patron saint recounted two tales involving Jews: a tale of a Jewish sorcerer who excised a Christian girl's womb, and a tale of intended host desecration. The latter tale is depicted in two scenes; in one a Christian holding a sack full of hosts is approached by a Jew (figure 7), and in the other the citizens of St Dié approach the Duke to punish the Jew.[145] The source of the host desecration tale survives only in a seventeenth-century version traced by Meredith Lillich, according to which a Jew procured the hosts from a Christian, but was caught by a suspicious local priest, as he was about to take them home.[146] The Christian was made to provide the church with 1,000 hosts every Easter,

7. The Jew buying the hosts. Medaillon in the parish church of St Dié, Lorraine, *c.*1285.

while the Jew was evicted from the Duchy. This version assumes the Jew's intention and ease of access to the host, but denies him the execution of his act and thus allows him to be spared the full punishment, death, the end of most later host desecration cases. While we know that the artist worked between 1285 and 1289, we cannot ascertain the age of the story. For our purpose it is important to situate the story as current in the later thirteenth century, and in an intermediary form, very close to the full host desecration tale, in which abuses of the host are fully realised and later avenged by severe punishment of the Jew or Jews. The narrative was spreading in Lorraine, put into images by an artist from Alsace, who invented a visual pattern in the absence of well-established precedents.

The danger implicit in the association between Jew and host was growing, in tales which increasingly emphasised Jewish evil intention and the apt response of severe punishment when eucharistic miracles led to the Jewish abuser's discovery. This trend would ultimately produce the eucharistic tale of abuse, the host desecration accusation against Jews, which offered no place for forgiveness, ending in revenge and destruction.[147] This happened at the convergence of Jews with a central strand within the culture, that which placed the eucharist at the heart of a system which made the supernatural efficacious.[148] Here also, the Jew was made into a doubting, testing figure, an enemy, to be excised and removed from the Christian body. Several such painful excisions followed the working of the emergent narrative, in the wake of the accusation of host desecration.

3

Patterns of Accusation

THE 'FIRST' TELLING OF THE TALE IN A WELL-GOVERNED CAPITAL: PARIS, 1290

While most of the legislative and administrative acts, as well as the narratives, which linked Jew and eucharist are to be found in the southern and eastern reaches of the Holy Roman Empire, the first fully documented case of a complete host desecration accusation, from discovery to punishment, occurred in Paris in 1290. This case is usually singled out as the first manifestation of a new kind of fantasy about Jewish abuse. Yet, as we have seen, the narrative's elements, the juxtaposition of Jew and eucharist and the suggestion of bad intention on the part of the former towards the latter, had already evolved by the late thirteenth century. The first complete telling of the accusation story is known to us from Paris, but it could have occurred in any number of German towns, and indeed soon did.[1] We need not insist on a linear development by which the Paris tale begat all other versions, but rather think of the parallel development of the narrative in a variety of regions, some of them gaining buoyancy from the fame of the Paris case, and some probably not. The Paris case became particularly well known since it took place in Europe's greatest city, the seat of a monarchy for which an official historiography had already developed, a renowned city, home to Europe's foremost university, with hundreds of travellers and foreign visitors in its streets. A case which occurred in Paris in the reign of the formidable monarch Philip IV was bound to be reported and retold, especially within the cultural ambit of the *langue d'oïl*, both in French and in Latin. The Latin trajectory disseminated the tale through monastic chronicles and scholastic discussion. It spread even further since Paris was also the centre for a great number of Europe's professional communicators, the friars.[2] News of the Paris case was to provide the inspiration for historical *exempla*, plays, painting and liturgy. Its representation was often used by communities which had not known such violence as the quintessential manifestation of a host desecration.

The Paris host desecration accusation is known to us from a number of Latin and French versions, none of which can be dated before 1299. There is a particularly striking Latin homiletic version 'Of the miracle of the host' ('De miraculo hostiae') in sermon form; a Latin version in the chronicle of St Denis with a number of shorter derivatives; a French version in the *Grandes chroniques*; and what may be a report of the ecclesiastical court ruling, preserved in a monastic chronicle of Ghent.[3] There are also copies of deeds relating to land transfers which preceded the erection of a commemorative chapel and some leaves from liturgical books from the parish which experienced the miracle.[4]

This is the core of the tale: during Holy Week 1290 a Jew tempted a poor Christian woman in the parish of Saint-Jean-en-Grève – either a maid in his household upon whom he prevailed, or a debtor who had pawned a valuable item of clothing as security for a loan, to whom he promised the return of the pawn and the cancellation of her debt if she were to bring him the host received at Easter communion. The woman (maid or debtor) was tempted and proceeded to take communion at Easter and hand the host over to the Jew. Once it was in his possession the Jew 'tested' the host through a series of injuries, saying 'I shall know whether the insane things which Christians prattle about this are true.'[5] He put it on a table or a chest, took out a feather-knife (perhaps a pen-knife?) (*cultellum pennarium*) and struck at the host, but it remained intact and simply began to bleed. He then picked up a hammer and nails and pierced it through, but again the host remained whole and bleeding. He threw it into a fire, hoisted it on a lance and, attempting final destruction, threw it into a cauldron of boiling water. The water turned red ('aqua sanguinea facta'), and the host was transformed into a crucifix which hovered above the cauldron. The Jew's instruments are those of Christ's tormentors, the instruments of the Passion (hammer, nails, lance), and judicial pain (lance, fire). The host's response was a truly eucharistic one, manifesting its real character: indestructible, changeable, full of mystery. Its power was revealed even to the Jewish family as his wife and children came to appreciate the miracle, while the Jew remained blind to it. The reactions to the powerful revelation were thus conditioned by the inherent characteristics of the members of the Jewish family: father – cunning, violent, obstinate; mother and children – misguided but pliant, impressionable, open to conversion.

It is a strange task to try and tease out of the reports of a host desecration something akin to the familial and social relations which prevailed between Jews and Christians in a community such as the parish of St-Jean-en-Grève (see map 2). We can, however, find a sense of foreboding in the accounts of the tale, as some chroniclers noted that 1290 was a year in which Easter and Passover coincided, Holy Week (*la semaine peneuse*), being the annual occasion for reception of communion by the laity. A discerning understanding of female nature and familiarity with Christian practice were attributed to the Jewish culprit: he tempted the Christian woman by promising to return her garments in time for Easter communion, an occasion on which she wished to appear well groomed among her neighbours ('ut inter vicinas cultior appareat')

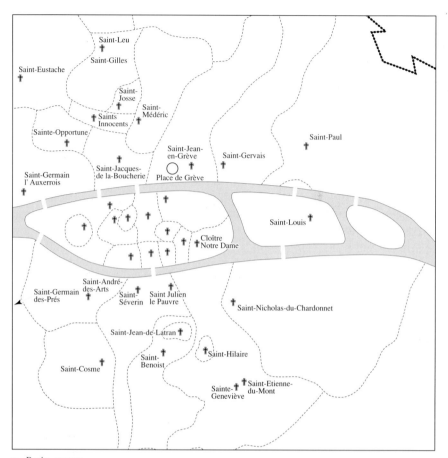

2. Paris, *c.*1290.

(figure 8). Motivation is also explored in the differing accounts. The Christian woman acted out of vanity and greed, the Jew out of the perverse desire to challenge Christian eucharistic truth by testing the captured host. The Jewish family is also described in detail: it disintegrated as it witnessed the desecration and the ensuing miracle. In perfect symmetry to the figure of the greedy woman (*avara mulier*) there was another, pious, Christian woman, who discovered the abuse. According to one version she was informed by the Jewish boy that she need not seek her God in the church since He was being tormented by *his* father at that very moment. Intrepid in her devotion the woman hastened to the scene of the crime (according to another version, she entered the Jewish house in search of an ember to kindle her fire, a touching display of neighbourly relations at the climax of the tale). What she encountered terrified her, and her discovery frightened the Jew. He tried to entice her into collaboration, offering her 20 *sous* in return for her silence and

8. The Case of Paris: a Christian woman exchanges the host for a garment. Late fourteenth-century illustrated manuscript of Giovanni Villani's *Cronica*, fol. 110ʳ.

for help in getting rid of the indestructible host. But the woman stood fast and declared that she would rather burn (hinting at the end of any host-abuser, and that which awaited the Jew) than be party to the abuse, and she initiated collective action for the host's recovery and the Jew's punishment.[6]

The reaction to the miracle in their midst was handled with great efficiency by the parishioners of St-Jean-en-Grève.[7] Following eucharistic logic, the woman who discovered the abused (now miraculous) host called for the parish priest. The host, after all, was only to be handled by priests, carried in their hands alone, never by a lay person or by a cleric of lower orders. The priest himself summoned the Bishop, or his representatives, as the offence fell under ecclesiastical jurisdiction. The Bishop of Paris, Simon Mattifart de Bucy (1290–1304), sent his sergeants to lead the culprits in chains, and took advice as to the appropriate action in the case, the counsel of 'expers en theologie et decrets'.[8] The Jew was found guilty (presumably of sacrilege) and was released to the secular authority for burning. A tragi-comic anecdote is told in the Latin version: that the Jew asked to hold his 'book' when in the fire and thus to be saved.[9] The book and the Jew were burnt to ashes, while his wife and children converted and, according to the French chronicle of St Denis, the daughter became a member of the nunnery of Filles-Dieu.[10] His fate mirrors that of the father in the tale of the Jewish Boy: a family saved and converted at the price of its father's destruction.

A whole set of familial, social, liturgical and judicial relations was woven into the telling of this powerful tale. In its domesticity, familiarity and localised setting (it is no fable, no ancient tale retold) it demanded legitimation and credibility from hearers. Such authority defined, for good and for evil, its actors: host and Jew. A realistic style was habitually deployed in the telling of the Paris case: its accounts are full of names, times, circumstances, even as it dealt with the horrific and the miraculous, abuse and its punishment. A man who converted following this case and who gave evidence about it in Paris claimed that the Jew had called others to observe the host, to deride it with the words 'Are not the Christians foolish, to believe in this host?' and then fall upon it as a group with knives and pointed instruments.[11]

The narrative of abuse reached closure and resolution as the accused Jew was burnt, his family converted, a host was elevated to miraculous and cultic heights, a bad Christian woman was punished, a good one praised and a community vindicated, a new and untested bishop acted wisely, and a city dwelt in harmony. But the story left a powerful legacy which transcended the parish of St-Jean-en-Grève; it introduced into the repertoire of tales a Christian communal drama, and more immediately, it sharpened sensibilities towards Jews in the environs of Paris and under the gaze of the French crown.

For Parisians the host desecration became enshrined in local traditions and liturgical practices, as cults developed around the miraculous host and the knife (*canif*) which had pierced it and had become holy by association with it. Soon after the event, the Jew's house, confiscated following his arrest, was sold for the creation of a chapel there. By July 1295 Pope Boniface VIII had sent a mandate to the Bishop of Paris directing him to allow Raynier Flaming, one of the richest bourgeois of Paris, to build a chapel on the site of the alleged crime.[12] In 1291 Jehan de Marle, the Provost of Paris, approved the sale of the house adjacent to the emergent *capella miraculorum*, to the priest Gui Morel, and after his death in 1308 it passed to the Charity of Notre Dame.[13] The brethren of this order became the Brethren of the Charity of the Blessed Virgin, charged with the guardianship of the chapel, which came to be known as the chapel 'des Billettes', a name which refers to the badge in the shape of a lozenge (*billette*) which the brethren wore on their habits.[14]

Besides the newly constructed chapel which housed the *canif*, the miraculous host of Paris rested in the parish church of St-Jean-en-Grève. There a special liturgy evolved, now contained in a booklet copied and authorised by a notary in the sixteenth century.[15] An inventory of the parish fabric and plate taken in 1602 recorded ornaments which celebrated the special relic:

a great reliquary of gilt silver with images of Jesus Christ and the Magdalene and a tree in the middle, and a little pillar on which a little golden sun, decorated with 25 pearls and two big hanging oriental pearls, a diamond encased in gold and an oriental emerald also encased in gold; on this sun is the Holy Host mutilated by the Jews.[16]

The relic's importance as a focus for processional celebrations is evident in the presence of processional crosses and canopies mentioned in the inventory.[17] The cult in the parish church flourished to such an extent that the building required extension in 1326, and the small parish church gained a place on the liturgical routes of the French capital.

The narrative enacted in Paris in 1290 contained the salient elements of the emergent host desecration narrative which would be enacted many times over in future decades.[18] These are:

An encounter between a Jew and a Christian willing to hand over a consecrated host in return for money or favours. The accomplice is most frequently a woman, often a debtor and sometimes a maid employed by Jews.

The abuse – at home, in a synagogue, in a secret room – includes piercing, cutting, cooking, boiling, all of which initially bring forth bleeding, and then some secondary form of miraculous transformation of the host into a child or into a crucifix. Occasionally this miraculous change so terrifies the Jew(s) that attempts are made to dispose of the host (by burial, by throwing it into water or into a place of filth).

Once hidden, the host begins to produce signs which reveal its location (lights, voices) and lead to discovery. The agents of discovery are frequently women, who summon a priest. In some cases a self-appointed layman may lead an urban crowd on a spree of unofficial violent revenge; some of the perpetrators are killed, others convert and still others may be banished.

A cult develops around the host now contained in precious vessels and housed within a purpose-built chapel on the site of the Jew's house, or of the synagogue, frequently razed to the ground by fire. News of miracles attracts pilgrims.

It is intriguing yet ultimately impossible to fathom the many ways in which tales such as the host desecration of Paris were disseminated and became established within the horizons of regional cultures. Even when it is possible to trace a single line of dissemination, this often intersects with other possibilities for its transmission. Yet it is evident that the host desecration narrative was known in the Low Countries, in south-west Germany and in northern Italy by the very late thirteenth and early fourteenth centuries.

The news from Paris very soon existed in Latin and in French, and travelled to adjacent regions thanks to the efforts of the monks of Saint-

Denis, the court chroniclers. The Florentine businessman, public official and chronicler Giovanni Villani (1280–1348) wrote his *Cronica* in the 1330s and 1340s, and included an account, 'D'uno grande miracolo ch'avenne in Parigi del Corpo di Cristo' under the year 1290.[19] He may have learnt of it during his stay in Bruges in 1302–7 as the representative of the Perruzi.[20] Or he may have heard it from preachers such as Giordano da Pisa, who integrated the tale into a powerful anti-Jewish position in their sermons to Florentines.[21]

As the expulsion of the Jews from France occurred in 1306, there are traditions which linked the two events. The chronicler Jean Hocsem of Liège, writing around 1402, related the two in general terms: 'A.D. 1306 All the Jews living in France, were seized by royal command, on the feast of Mary Magdalene for the nasty crime which they committed on the sacrament of the altar and for which they were accused before the king.'[22] Yet nowhere in formal pronouncements is the expulsion explicitly linked to the host desecration accusation. What is more likely is that Philip IV noted and considered the possible meaning of the case, just as he supported its cult, and kept a watchful eye for signs of Jewish abuse. In 1299 he instructed his justiciars that inquisitorial powers should apply not only to instances of Christian error and blasphemy, but also to Jewish blasphemy in the form of heretical influence on Christians, effected through clever manipulation and abuse of the sacrament.[23] Conversely, in an answer to an occasional theological (quodlibetal) question written some time after the expulsion in 1306, the Cistercian Jacques of Thérines expressed the view that, though Jews may pose danger to the faith, they were also the begetters of miracles, such as the one which had occurred in the parish of St-Jean-en-Grève.[24]

In his encyclopedic book of arguments against the enemies of the church, the *Fortalitium fidei* of 1458 × 61, the Franciscan Alfonso da Spina discussed in a section on Jews the circumstances of the many expulsions imposed on them. When discussing the expulsion of the Jews from France in 1306 Alfonso claims to have heard from a pair of Cluniac monks visiting Medina del Campo that the case of Paris had prompted the expulsion.[25] In his version the Jew was a money-lender, and the story of his abuse of the host was reputedly famous in France and elsewhere and depicted widely in images in churches.[26] An earlier theologian and promoter of church reform, Jean Gerson (1363–1429), held the living of the parish of St-Jean-en-Grève, and mentioned the case of Paris in his *Collectorium super magnificat* when referring to Nicholas of Lyra's claim that Jews perpetrated idolatries, as a proof. He claimed that the miracle of Paris led to the confounding of the Jew and the conversion of other Jews.[27] The reform movement, which was supported by some bishops and theologians and which called for purification of the Christian bodies politic in wide areas of Europe, was carried forward by preachers and skilful writers such as Alfonso, who often provided justification, recommendation and rationale for drastic actions against Jews. One hundred and fifty years after the event, the Paris story thus became useful again.

The Paris story is a good starting point for our exploration of the working of the fantasy of abuse and the accusation against Jews, but it is atypical in its relatively 'benign' result. The Jew and his family, as well as the Christian accomplice, were chained and brought to trial, the main culprits were tried and burnt by the royal sergeant of the Châtelet, while the innocent bystanders, the Jewish family, converted. One version of the tale claims that there was some doubt as to the culpability of the Christian woman,[28] a theme pursued by Paolo Uccello in one of the scenes on the *predella* (executed in 1465 × 8) which represented the Paris case. The last of six scenes has devils and angels arguing over her soul.[29] The Jew's house was confiscated and dedicated to the erection of a chapel, but there is no other sign of violence, regional persecution or further destruction. The aftermath of the Paris accusation is unusual compared to the majority of cases which followed in the decades after 1290. It happened in a much governed, well-policed city, Philip IV's Paris, where judicial process was followed: arrest, examination, deliberation by judicial and theological experts, execution. As we will see, in most other cases of a host desecration accusation, community action preceded that of officials and magistrates. The chronicle accounts capture here the sense of neighbourhood outrage, but also of bureaucratic efficacy. The latter element would be missing in most cases which were to occur in imperial lands.

The English crown evicted its Jews in the very year in which 'Dieu fut bouilli' in Paris. The Capetian crown retained its Jews under a regime of high taxation and close supervision between 1290 and 1306, and then again in the years 1326–95, the Jews' last sojourn in the French domain in the medieval centuries.[30] Large parts of Italy saw no Jewish settlement in this period; the Jews of Sicily were expelled in 1292. Most Jewish settlement concentrated in the Iberian kingdoms, in the south of France and in imperial lands, especially in the Rhineland, Franconia, Alsace, Swabia, Bavaria, Austria and, increasingly throughout the fourteenth and fifteenth centuries, in Bohemia and Silesia. It was in the areas of dense Jewish population that the host desecration tale was to experience deadly longevity. It was in such settings that the host desecration accusation became a narrative of violence, of destruction and of annihilation of Jewish communities. By the fifteenth century it was frequently the last tale to be told of Jews, as host desecration accusations were used to justify mass regional expulsions.[31]

The host's vulnerability came to signify a more general susceptibility of Christian life to Jewish harm. It was paralleled by another powerful narrative which was particularly current in the Rhineland: the ritual murder accusation. In this, older, narrative the child rather than the host is the vulnerable victim, the subject of Jewish desires and ill intent. Within the emergent cosmology that developed around sacramental orthodoxy and parochial participation, a particular link was forged between the host's inherent value and vulnerability and the ubiquitous rejection and difference which Jews represented. The cases we will examine occurred in bursts in regions of the Holy Roman Empire – Franconia, Bavaria, Austria, southern Bohemia and, later, Silesia – and remained endemic in them for centuries. Their rhythm and trajectories raise historical questions about legitimation (who could begin the narration?), authentication (who could pronounce the truth of a rumour of desecration?) and evidence on the technologies of punishment (trial or mob execution), and touch upon the very structures of authority and social and political organisation within the Empire. The narrative was so powerful, so definite in its virtue, that those who could claim it acquired with it leadership and a licence for violence. This is nowhere more evident than in the events which led to the months-long regional wave of violence which has come to be known as the Rintfleisch movement (*Rintfleischbewegung*).

REGIONAL MASSACRES: RINTFLEISCH 1298, ARMLEDER 1336–8

While the news of the case of Paris was spreading in northern France and the Low Countries, parallel accusations were brewing in the German-speaking lands, culminating by the late 1290s in regional accusations and massacres. The earliest documented reference to a host desecration accusation in the Empire comes from Büren in Westphalia, where in 1292 the Bishop of Paderborn, under whose protection the Jews lived, and the town were locked in conflict.[32] A document which settled their dispute refers to a recent massacre of the Bishop's Jews. In 1299 a chapel dedicated to the sacrament was founded to commemorate 'various negligences which have occurred in the diocese, both by Christians and by Jews who maltreated the eucharist'.[33] These events augured the introduction of the recently founded and as yet little celebrated feast of Corpus Christi to the diocese, an act of eucharistic affirmation. Put together, these snippets of evidence suggest that the massacre of Jews may have been related to eucharistic abuse which was then fittingly commemorated by the construction of a chapel dedicated to Corpus Christi. In 1294 the little town of Laa-an-der-Thaya in north-east Austria accused its Jews of host desecration and a 'small' massacre followed.[34] But by far the most unequivocal readiness to act violently through the narrative of host desecration was displayed in Franconia. Probably the least stable region of the Empire, with no overarching territorial lord to mediate between Emperor and localities, apart from

3. The Franconian region.

the authority of three prince-bishops and a multitude of petty lords whose castles chequered its many river valleys. Franconia was rich in pockets of imperial land and *Reichstädte*, and was the most densely urbanised region of the Empire. Yet power there was fragmented. Its knightly landholders were many, and closely integrated into exchange and trade in its towns: the marketing of grain, cattle and wine were its main commercial activities, in which Jews played a crucial part.[35]

The sources informing us of the bloody events which swept Franconia in 1298 are mainly urban and monastic chronicles (see map 3).[36] These usually provide only short accounts of the burning of a number of Jews in a given locality because of eucharistic abuse. The chronicle of Regensburg reports that the rumour of a Jewish offence, the crushing of Christ's body in a mortar and the flowing of blood, led to revenge against the Jews of Würzburg, Nuremberg and Rothenburg and the whole of Franconia.[37] A more sophisticated view is that of Gotfried of

Ensmingen, a notary in the court of the Archbishop of Strasbourg, who describes a persecution of Jews which lasted from 25 July to 21 September, at the hands of a Franconian noble who was called Rintfleisch. Gotfried assessed the number of victims at 10,000 Jews of Würzburg, Nuremberg and other villages and castles, and explained that the persecution followed an offence to the host so great that 'God permitted such persecution'.[38] He also opined that had it not been for King Albert of Habsburg's intervention on his return from Aachen, the persecution would have continued and annihilated the Jews of the whole kingdom.

The more detailed accounts tell of the beginning of events on Sunday, a fortnight after Easter, 20 April 1298, as twenty-one Jews were killed in Röttingen, in the mid-Tauber valley, in revenge for a host desecration.[39] The chronicle of the Archbishop of Trier describes the events as a vengeful uprising of Swabian nobles against Jews who had cut the throat of a knight's son, a sin so heinous that it could not be hidden.[40] They were like rabid wolves falling upon a sheepfold, led by a nobleman – 'Reyntfleis' – sparing no Jew as they marched adorned with banners and warlike insignia, killing thousands.[41] The identity of this leader remains a mystery; most likely a knight, he acquired the appellation 'Rintfleisch' which has led some to claim that he was a butcher.[42] Avenging cohorts also arose in outbursts which occurred primarily in the valley of the Tauber, first in Röttingen and its environs (from 20 April), then in the mid- and upper Tauber (23–30 June), reaching Rothenburg and its area (18–22 July), Würzburg and the lower Tauber valley (23–24 July), the Jagst and mid-Necker valleys (25–29 July) and on to Nuremberg (27 July–1 August).[43] It reached other regions and into Swabia, Hesse and Thuringia.[44] The massacre progressed despite the *Landesfriede* announced by King Albert in late 1298, a call for peace under imperial sanction.

Jewish sources, on the other hand, are few and mournful; they are poetic laments for the dead and necrological lists of victims for the purpose of commemoration. The Nuremberg lists number 146 affected communities; that of Charleville knew of seventy-eight.[45] The twenty-stanza lament 'I cry for the day's tribulation' (*Evke li-kshe yom*) highlights the particular plight of the communities of Röttingen and Rothenburg, where the killing began, and of the great cities of Würzburg and Nuremberg. It states as the reason for the violence:

> They conspired with their plots and added treachery
> to that bloody bread, so vile and disgusting.
> To say of the finest of the holy and exalted people
> 'You've stolen our God' that dweller of darkness.
> *May my viol become a mourning song and my flute the voice of tears.*

And you crushed it fine and treacherously
Even the driest grain in a mortar, unto the flow of his blood therein.
And you divided and split him and hung him on a frame,
and sent him to all your confounded and dispersed camps.
May my viol become a mourning song and my flute the voice of tears.[46]

The lament attempts to reproduce the accusation: Christians claimed that Jews had abused their God – crushing him, hanging him, and ultimately sharing him in pieces with their brethren. This was the logic attributed to the perpetrators of the ethnic cleansing of Franconia.

The same justification was to be deployed by a most interesting writer on the Rintfleisch massacres. A collection of *exempla*-like tales was written down around 1303 by the Dominican Rudolph, prior of Schlettstadt in Alsace. The tales survive in a single copy, a manuscript copied in 1562 which includes other Dominican material.[47] Of the fifty-six tales which have been named *Historiae memorabiles* after the compiler's description, twenty involve Jews and others are tales of witches, demons and prodigies. The stories involving Jews relate occurrences which are set in the heat of the Rintfleisch movement and its aftermath. Rudolph strives to give the recent bloody events an explanatory frame and moral purpose, and to draw out lessons for an imagined audience.

Rudolph's anecdotes about 1298 are not told chronologically; they are moralising rather than historical. One explanation for the events is offered in a tale about the local lord, Kraft I of Hohenlohe (1256–1310), whose castle was perched on the River Tauber at Weickersheim, at the heart of the region where the massacres took place. Kraft was deeply indebted to the Jews, and as his embarrassment mounted the Jews feared the worst at his hands.[48] They petitioned the territorial lord, the Prince-Bishop of Würzburg, to intercede with Kraft, not in order to make him pay (which he evidently could not do), but rather to hold him fast to a promise not to hurt the Jews in his lordship. Having gained their wish, Rudolph goes on to say, the Jews became audacious and contemplated further abuse. They tempted a bell-ringer (or sacrist) to let them into Weickersheim church and spent the night there on the eve of Maundy Thursday. They joyfully entered the church that night and flung hosts on the altar and abused them with knives, only to witness the hosts bleed the purest blood, which gushed and stained the Jews' hands. The hosts further sounded Christ's words on the cross: 'God, my God, this is my God, my God, why have you foresaken me?' ('Hely, hely lamma sabatchani? hoc est deus meus, deus meus, ut quid deelequisti me?').[49] The cry summoned poor Christians to the church, who were shocked by the sight of the bleeding hosts, and the parish priest, who informed Kraft. The knight announced that he would stick to his oath but informed the Bishop of the developments, and the Bishop gave his consent that justice be done, saying 'You know the penalty for killing a man, how much more so for killing Our Lord Jesus Christ son of the Virgin Mary . . .'[50] Thus advised, Kraft of Hohenlohe proceeded to burn all the Jews he could find. For Rudolph, it is not Kraft who is the hero, but his followers, the simple pious folk who kept him to his task, and away from the 'love' of Jews which characterised so many rulers.[51] Kraft's lordship also came to host a burgeoning regional pilgrimage centre, that at Iphofen.[52]

Abbot Peter of Zittau (d. 1339), chronicler of Königsaal monastery in Prague, reported the events from a distance. According to him, Rintfleisch was a butcher, a base, poor and hot-tempered man ('vir deneger et pauper mente acer'), who led a popular crowd, a rabble ('surrexit conturba plebeia . . . convolabat mox ad istum iudaeorum tortorem innumerabile vulgus plebeium'), which considered in its killing neither sex nor age.[53] Popular opinion had it that the reason for the disaster ('plaga') had been the event in Röttingen, when Jews cruci-fied Christ in a consecrated host which they had bought from a maid. This Bohemian chronicler also claimed that some doubted the motives for killing the Jews, judging these to be the wish to rob Jews of their money, rather than piety.[54] Yet Peter concluded that whatever the reason, he was sure that God was pleased with the slaughter, and ends with a poem celebrating 'King' Rintfleisch's revenge:

> Jewish people! this King Rintfleisch has dealt you a sad destruction, for he has suddenly rejected you, and all but destroyed you, since God has recently spurned you and has set him up as your torturer, so that in this way you may be drawn to His love, and His grace work upon you.
>
> Mourn, Jew! because you will always be pressed by a double burden, you will suffer both here and there.[55]

A number of political themes inform different versions of the Rintfleisch events: the complicity of those in power with Jews, the protec-tion granted them by the mighty, and the need for simple folk to take just revenge by wresting violence into their own hands. The events broke out during a period of singular political instability, which was only to be resolved by the Battle of Göllheim of 2 July 1298 and the subsequent return of King Albert of Habsburg to his throne. From Aachen he moved through the Rhineland and finally reached Rothenburg in Sep-tember. There he meted out some punishment by imposing fines and banishment decrees against some, although few, of those who had injured his Jews. In Nuremberg seventeen burgesses were banished for inciting a crowd, and a woman of Bern was banished for arson.[56]

Returning to Rudolph's tales of the Rintfleisch massacres, they appear to be offering, and echoing, the pervasive logic of violence. He explained the justice of the violent events of 1298 by imputing to his actors pious reasoning and complex judgement. In Rudolph's narrative a grand cosmic drama was unfolding in which communities and individuals played their parts by following signs and reading clues. The power of simple folk to interpret such signs is valued highly and accorded great trust in his narrative. In the case of Möckmuhl on the River Jagst (near Heilbronn), another town in the Hohenlohe dominions, on a riverine peninsula, a wet and nasty habitation fit only for paupers and prostitutes, certain burning lights appeared and terrified all who saw them.[57] The town fathers (*maiores opidi*) decided to look into the matter, but rumours of a Jewish crime were already in circulation, since they lived not far from the place ('Nam erat magna suspicio Judeos, qui non longe de hoc loco habitabant, aliquid crimen perpetrasse, quod deus manifestare velet'). On the following day an examination took place, and a loosely covered opening in the ground was discovered, in which hosts had been hidden by the Jews. The hosts were carefully recovered and taken to the church with reverence. In the same town, a peasant lying down to sleep was woken by voices which prompted him to examine the house of a Jew, Wivelin. Having heard the voices a second time he informed his priest. The priest thought the peasant was drunk and did not believe him, but was ultimately moved to examine his claims, and found five perforated hosts hanging from a string. Seventy-six Jews were shut up in a house and when Rintfleisch came to town, they were all burnt.[58] The chronicle of St Peter's, Erfurt, described in similar tone the finding of tell-tale hosts buried in the remains of Jewish houses, after the killing.[59]

What have we here? In the closing words of *Fiction in the Archives* Natalie Davis has suggested that narration can serve to facilitate self-forgiveness.[60] A few years after the events, Rudolph was recounting and moralising stories about horrifically violent deeds. He brought to his tales the generic form of *exemplum*, as well as what purported to be common sense and local knowledge (like the claim that prostitutes and paupers lived at the edge of town). He is not without irony (presenting Kraft of Hohenlohe as the meek servant of the Bishop of Würzburg), but always enthusiastic when describing the ability of simple folk to discern truths, and the inexorable working of divine justice. He often confuses sequences of dates: fixing the discovery of hosts in Möckmuhl during Holy Week, when the Jewish account situated the accusation later in the summer.[61] But he is authentic in sounding the sort of narrative strands which would have motivated action and sustained self-justification within a community engaged in the parallel actions of exaction of revenge and narration of abuse.

Rudolph is never more powerful in his commitment to such moralisation than in his treatment of the regional logic of the Rintfleisch massacres. The events of Röttingen in April 1298 – the movement of hundreds of men, the destruction of 146 communities and the killing of over 3,000 Jews, in the lands of 21 lordships – could be justified only through the working of a narrative which decreed the spread of blame and of revenge. In providing this line, Rudolph uses some widespread truths about the eucharist, as well as beliefs about Jewish culpability. He invented the regional conspiracy, using an idea already familiar from previous elaborations of the ritual murder accusation in the Rhineland, on the basis of a eucharistic dynamic. According to Rudolph, the army which moved from town to town, village to village, burning Jewish houses and Jewish bodies, was on a trail of vindication and recovery, in search of *all* the hosts, *all* those parts of Christ's body which had been allegedly disseminated by and among Jews. Thus as the crowds moved they stumbled upon evidence, in nooks and crannies in smoking houses. The crowd worked as an instinctive avenger, divinely guided but always vindicated by unambiguous eucharistic proof.[62] Such an account made perfect sense in eucharistic terms; after all, at every consecration of the host, Christ's very body, the historical body which suffered on the cross, was realised, unlimited in quantity or location. Even a single host could be infinitely broken down, and each of its crumbs would be fully Christ, flesh and blood – wholly worthy of worship and recovery, veneration and revenge.

Rudolph was not alone; the Thuringian chronicler Sifried of Balhuisen (d. 1308) wrote in his *Compendium historiarum* of the purchase of a host by Jews from the church warden of Röttingen, and its distribution to Jews in other cities and towns. Discovery was occasioned by the presence of women who were keeping a vigil in the church (over Christ's sepulchre, before Easter), and who suddenly saw two lights above the guilty Jew's house. The Jew and the warden were caught and the latter confessed to the crime. Recovery was difficult, since the host had been distributed and variously abused, but miracles brought about through the particles led to the discovery of the pieces of the host and to the killing of the Jews of many places.[63] Rumours of the supernatural abounded in accounts of the events. Under the caption 'Of a miracle' Sifried also described the attempt of Jews to defend themselves by congregating in a castle. When a young woman cried out to the Christians to pull her out and baptise her she was dragged away by the Jews and thrown from the height of the tower. Angels miraculously saved her falling body from harm and she later converted.[64]

Some towns attempted to resist and came to be known as 'Jew-loving':[65] Regensburg and Augsburg were distinctive in having succeeded in withstanding the Rintfleisch force once, perhaps because they were peripheral to the region of greatest tumult and density of disruption. The town fathers of Regensburg clearly preferred the honour of a well-governed town to the fleeting satisfactions of murderous pleasure.[66] But in Würzburg it was the townsmen who led the killing. The Jews were protected by their episcopal lord but were exposed and led out to Rintfleisch's followers by citizens.[67]

Rudolph's account addressed the first regional pogroms, which produced memories etched into townscape, local memory, liturgy and civic life. Just a generation later, in the 1330s, the area covered by Rintfleisch and his followers experienced a similar wave of violence. This is the *Armlederbewegung* – a movement of killing named after its leader, King Armleder (*Rex Armleder*), anchored in Franconian soil but destined to spread far beyond that region's confines.[68] Chroniclers were less willing to describe the cause of the Armleder movement as a host desecration than their predecessors had been in 1298 in the case of the Rintfleisch movement.[69] They sought and found other motivations for its leader, Arnold of Uissigheim, and his followers. The Franciscan chronicler of the Basel region, John of Winterthur (1302–48), described it as an act of revenge by Arnold for the killing of his brother by Jews.[70] Under the pretext of piety he incited a crowd to cruelties against Jews. John of Viktring (d. 1345 × 7), writing in a Carinthian monastery, emphasised the desire to rob and the resentment bred by usury.[71] The force and pleasure of existing tales about Jewish abuse were attached to accounts of the Armleder violence. An English manuscript containing *exempla* recorded the tale of the Jew who shamed the host by walking around with it in his shoe. On Corpus Christi day during the procession, he taunted a Christian by asking what was being carried so solemnly. When the answer came, that it was God in the form of bread, the Jew claimed that God was with him, in his shoe. Having heard this the 'German knights' combined to avenge the offence to God and his body, with a special licence granted by Pope Boniface.[72]

The upsurge of violence was so overwhelming that the events have sometimes been seen as a veritable uprising.[73] A letter written by one Nicholas, from the court of the Archbishop of Trier to Master Rudolph Losse, the Archbishop's procurator in Avignon, recounts the violence as that of peasants ('rustici') of Franconia, around Bischofsheim, who had elected a king called Armleder and proceeded on foot to kill all the Jews in the towns and cities of Kitzingen, Oxenfurt, Owe, Mergentheim and four other towns he could not name.[74] John of Winterthur's chronicle emphasises not only the social breadth of the movement but also its leadership by a notorious knight, whom the crowd made into its king. A knight, Arnold, was banished from his lordship in 1332 by his lord, Count Rudolph IV of Wertheim, for a period of ten years for an offence committed with his father and brothers against the comital privileges.[75] With his following, King Armleder went on the rampage, slaughtering Jews in towns and cities: Kitzingen, Oxenfurt, Mergentheim, Bischofsheim. After Armleder was beheaded in Kitzingen on 14 November, the leader of the Alsatian branch, a hosteller named John Zimberlin, took over. John of Winterthur was unclear as to his motive: 'I do not know for sure what motive moved him, he rose against the Jews closely followed by a great multitude and hit them with a great disaster, claiming to have received divine inspiration and heavenly oracles as commands.'[76] Zimberlin ceased his actions only in 1339, when his lord, Lord Rudolf of Andlau, was bound over to ensure that in the next ten years John would refrain from warfare.[77]

The movement which began in the diocese of Würzburg spilt over into Alsace, Austria, Styria and Swabia. Sometimes imperial authorities were able to intervene and stop the violent tide: in Franconia it was stopped with the arrest and execution of Arnold by imperial decree in November 1336; in Alsace it was stopped by Louis of Bavaria in 1338. In Bavaria the movement continued, enflamed by the case of the Danubian town of Deggendorf on 30 September 1337.[78] Here revenge for an alleged host desecration was led by the ducal official in the town, and helped by ducal forces. In the following year the ducal town of Straubing near Deggendorf was burnt, as were Cham, Dingolfing, Eggenfelden, Kelheim, Landshut and Vilsbiburg.[79] The Bavarian pattern is related to the lenience with which the Duke, Henry IV of Landshut-Bavaria (Lower Bavaria), treated the leaders of the Deggendorf violence; his own man led a group of knights and townsmen who gathered at Schaching church, some 700 metres from the town centre and outside its walls, to take an oath of revenge against the Jews.[80] A charter of October 1338 pardoned the leaders of the killing, Hartwig of Deggenberg and Konrad Freiberger, and released the townsmen from debts to the killed and dispersed Jews.[81] The movement finally came to an end in 1338 with an armistice arranged by the Archbishop of Strasbourg.[82] The year 1338 also saw some imperial efforts to exert influence on towns: on 16 May Louis wrote to the council and burgesses of Gerlach (in Limbourg) requesting them to receive back Jews who had fled and to restore their goods.[83]

The movement's name *Armleder* suggested the fact that its origins were not in knightly violence but in the initiatives of townsmen and lesser men, whose armour was the simple thick leather armbands of a town militia, rather than the metal mail of a knight. John of Winterthur gave a list of crafts and named the singular instruments which their masters brought to the assault: hatchets, rakes, swords, hammers, threshing sledges, knives, axes, battle-axes, hunting spears, bows, missiles and lances.[84] The chronicle of the Bavarian dukes painted a similar picture in autumn 1338, reporting rumours that

> Jews cut up the catholic host each in their synagogue and amongst other mockeries, pierced it with sharp thorns until it bled. Therefore, around the feast of St Michael in all the towns of Bavaria and Austria except for Regensburg and Vienna they were miserably and cruelly killed by poor folk.[85]

The chronicler concludes that God's will must have been with the army, as all the efforts of the princes and their officials to stop them failed. Even Duke Henry of Lower Bavaria, who stood up to the 'poor', was all but trampled under their feet, and ended by admitting 'Now I know truly that this . . . is vindicated by God, who wishes no one to resist.'[86]

Contemporaries emphasised the unruly and contagious nature of the violence. Henry of Diessenhofen (1300–1376), Doctor of canon law and Canon of Konstanz Cathedral, reported events which took place in January 1336 in Konstanz and Basel, where almost all the Jews were killed, and similar acts in Austria and Styria. In the dioceses of Würzburg and Mainz, similarly, almost all the Jews were killed over the following three years. He could find no reason for the violence 'except that in Austria Christ's body had been molested by Jews, as I heard from someone who came from there'.[87] Although imperial justice here was relatively swift and Arnold was arrested, tried and beheaded, commitment to him and his actions coninued to flourish. Arnold's tomb in his native village of Uissigheim became the centre of a cult, as if he had died a martyr. The Carinthian abbot John of Viktring recounted that many miracles occurred at Arnold's tomb (figure 9).[88]

It is hard to assess how the rumour of host desecration was kept alive or how necessary this was for the continued nurturing of the violence. But in 1337 and 1338 a recurrence of accusation and violence occurred in the sphere of the Armleder movement, with two spectacular cases, at Deggendorf in 1337 and Pulkau in 1338. Awareness of this hovering accusation led to Jews remitting their debts in several towns and villages.[89]

A TOWN AND ITS PRECIOUS MIRACLES: KORNEUBURG, 1305

Further east in the Empire, in Austria, the host desecration accusation was implanted relatively early and with recurrent resonance. The violence it inspired in this duchy was never as wide-ranging as in Franconia, but rather occurred in towns and in the villages and townlets of their immediate hinterland. The accusation at Korneuburg in 1305 reflects ways in which the narrative might be circumscribed by doubts about its authenticity, and problems with procedures of proof. The examination of the authenticity of the eucharistic material involved in the case was headed by one Ambrose, of the Cistercian monastery of Heiligenkreuz. His investigation led him to pose the question 'Whether Jews should be killed in such a case?'.[90] On the streets of Korneuburg the answer was a resounding 'yes', and yet we will encounter here some recurrent elements which suggest that, while powerful and dominating, the eucharistic tale of abuse could also encounter resistance and questioning. Such opposition was rarely expressed in terms of justice to Jews, but rather as scepticism regarding some of the narrative's salient parts:

9. The tomb of Arnold of
Uissigheim in the parish
church of Uissigheim,
Franconia. Mid-fourteenth
century.

popular claims of miraculous action, Jewish access to the host, and ill intent towards it.

The commission led by Ambrose of Heiligenkreuz was appointed by Wernhard of Prambach, Bishop of Passau (1285–1313), to examine the miracles worked by an allegedly abused and miraculous host, found in a Jewish house earlier in the year 1305. Ambrose presided over a panel made up of Master Albert, Canon of Regensburg and Doctor of canon law, Gotfried, Dean of Krems, and Master Conrad of Steinheim. Their brief is laid out in the notarial account of the investigation:[91] it was to establish the truth of the claims that candles lit up spontaneously, that sight was restored to blind people, that lame persons regained the ability to walk and that the possessed were liberated, by virtue of the miraculous, desecrated host. Twenty-one witnesses – six clerics and fifteen laypersons (of whom one was a woman) – were examined by means of a series of identical questions, and their answers, recorded by the commission's notary, have survived.

The scenes at the abbatial residence of Lillienfeld near Vienna, where the investigation took place, were noisy and tumultuous, as the citizens of Korneuburg rushed to bear witness to Jewish abuse and the miracles they had seen. Those who could not be heard waited outside in a throng. There were so many potential witnesses that after a while some were sent away. The cool reception of these eager informants by the chief examiner Ambrose earned him the wrath of the citizenry, and accusations of sympathy for the Jews, which impeded the business of investigation. In an apologetic tract written after the investigation and before 1312 Ambrose described his predicament: 'The wrath of the said citizens having being aroused against me, as if I had sided with the Jews and impeded the progress of the trial.'[92] He wrote a working report which reveals the many questions that were on his mind: How were miracles to be proven? In whose authority did such a decision reside? And finally: should Jews be killed in such cases? It was such doubt that earned Ambrose the wrath of the citizenry of Korneuburg.

Every word in the opening statements of Ambrose's report expresses his frustration in dealing with the Korneuburg case. This feeling must have mounted as witnesses filed in for investigation, and the results of the case were confronted: the charred bodies of ten Jews, the cures and enthusiasm around the bloody host reserved in the spontaneously created miracle-chapel. Ambrose's distrust persisted and Korneuburg's status as an impeccable site of a desecration and miracle was never quite established, at least not officially. That popular belief held it in esteem is clear from the continuation of the cult well into the fifteenth century. The cloth in which the host had been wrapped became the object of adoration, and was placed in a gilt portable altarpiece of *c.*1470 (figures 10a–b).[93] The central panel held the (now missing) bloodied cloth, while the wings showed two scenes each, miraculous scenes with

10. The altarpiece of Korneuburg, *c.*1470 (a) (*above*) open and showing scenes of miracles of the host and the place of the blood-stained cloth; (b) (*right*) closed with the image of a monstrance containing a host.

explanatory captions in the vernacular. When folded, the wings combined to create the image of an elaborate gilt monstrance containing a pristine rounded host.

The witnesses were called to testify in order of importance: first priests and then townsmen, each group arranged by status. The town's priest (*plebanus*) was Frederick, who opened with a detailed testimony about the host found in the Jews' house (*in domo iudeorum*). He answered the following questions, which made up the form of inquiry:

whether he believed that the host had been consecrated;

whether the blood on it was produced by human or divine operation;

whether the blood was liquid or dry, and whether its nature or quantity changed over time (3 questions);

whether the host he saw held in the Jew's hands was white or bloodied;

whether the human or other blood had been put there by some person;

whether it was a Christian or a Jew who brought the host to the Jews' house in the first place;

whether such a person had been asked or hired, or was an enemy;

whether he (the witness) had seen the host trampled under foot;

whether the blood had emanated from the host as a result of such trampling;

whether the blood had stained the hands of the Jew who held it;

who was present at the finding of the host;

when was it found;

where was it found;

at what time of the day was it found;

was it whole or partial in shape;

why did he believe that it was Christ's body if he had not seen it consecrated;

how long had the Jews had the host;

whether there had been a rumour about the host *before* it was found;

whether he could not have carried away the host (held by the Jews) from the Jews' house;

whether the person who confessed to having given it to the Jews had been sent to Rome for judgement;

whether it is that very same host which is now venerated by the people;

whether he gave witness because of his hate of Jews or favour towards Christians;

whether he believed Christ's real blood, or some other miraculous blood, to be in the host;

whether he had agreed with others on the contents of his testimony.

The inquiry then went on to ask specific questions about the miracles allegedly performed by the miraculous host.[94]

To these questions witnesses occasionally answered 'I do not know' or 'I did not see but heard'. Frederick the priest answered only two questions more than others: about a person who confessed to a fellow priest to having given the host to the Jews. Frederick, like all the others, asserted that he firmly believed that blood appeared in the host by divine intervention; that it was first fresh and liquid, and then turned dry; that only a part of the host was found (most said it was a third of a host, to Frederick it seemed like a quarter in size); that the host which received veneration was the one found in the Jews' house. He had no views on whether it had been fraudulently bloodied in answer to the question 'Did he believe or had he heard that some man had put human or other blood onto that host?' ('Credat vel audierit aliquem hominem apposuisse eidem oblate humanum vel alium sanguinem'); nor had he seen it in the hands of a Jew, or trampled underfoot by a Jew.[95] He was certain that it had been found in the presence of Walter the Shoemaker's wife, a servant called Sidlin, and the citizen Conrad Hochstrasse, with many others whose names he did not know, on St Lambert's day (17 September) around the hour of the mass, on the stone threshold of the Jew Zercl's house ('in domo Zaerclini ludei super limen in lapide'). The priest Frederick was careful in his statements; he refrained from elaborating on details he could not have known, but was confident that the miracle of spontaneous candle-lighting was indeed caused by the blood of the host, and that it occurred around vespers on Sunday following the finding of the host, at the showing of the cloth which had held the bloody relic. He responded in detail to questions about the cure of a blind person, who had been sightless for some twenty years, but whom he had, admittedly, not known before the cure was effected by the cloth. As to liberation from demonic possession and the cure of the lame he had only heard rumours. Frederick was followed by Henry, a priest, Jacob, a cleric, Rudiger, Provost of Klosterneuburg, the priest Conrad, Vicar of Lebendorf, and by Wernhard Shawbach, Canon of Klosterneuburg, who knew very little.

With the seventh witness began a stream of layfolk eager to tell their tales, beginning with a string of prominent townsmen. The leading citizens dramatically recounted the events. They had been alerted during the town council's deliberations, which involved most prominent local men, among them Conrad, *alias* 'of Hochstrasse'. With Conrad's account the consensual tale of the townsmen unfolded, as details previously absent in the evidence of the priests came to light. The townsmen had heard the alleged confession of the Jewish schoolmaster, as he was being dragged to the fire. According to Conrad, the Jew claimed to have been an innocent victim; Conrad suggested that the Jew was innocent ('quod ipse scholasticus innocenter cremaretur') while Zercl, his master, was the culprit. Three years ago that Christmas Zercl had procured the host from a servant, and the Jews wished to get rid of it but could not. So Zercl hired a (Christian) servant (named, significantly, *Ribaldus*), for two pounds of silver, and charged him with the task of getting rid of the host. But when Ribaldus realised what he was meant to destroy he exclaimed that he would not destroy his creator even for 1,000 pounds and ran away in fear of the Jew's revenge. It was as Zercl ran after him shouting 'Catch this servant' that the Jewish schoolmaster followed, host in hand, shouting 'Take your God, whom a servant has thrown into our house, and who should be burnt for the deed, rather than we.' But no one approached to help him (or save the Christian God). Zercl made his way home where he stamped on the host in frustration, and all was revealed as the Christians entered the Jews' house, and saw the schoolmaster, the informant of the tale, holding the bleeding host in his hands.[96]

Were the Jews of Korneuburg framed, and was the assault on them being turned into a host desecration accusation by a prominent burgess of Korneuburg? The witnesses who followed Conrad supported the story in various ways, and confidently stated that the schoolmaster stood on the threshold of the Jews' house with a host in his hand. The core of the accusation was put thus into the mouth of a Jew as he was led to the stake. *He* was able to know what happened in the privacy of the Jewish house, as no Christian could. Witness number ten, Henry, otherwise known as Shem, recounted the full version, but added a powerful walk-on role for himself. As Zercl ran in the streets among a crowd of Christians, he turned to Henry himself: 'O Sir Henry, this nasty man threw your God at my house and then withdrew.' And as he went to the Jewish house to check, Henry found on the threshold Christ's body 'bubbling blood-drops, like an egg sweats when it is cooked' (an image used also by witness fifteen, Prehlin, citizen of Korneuburg). This version does not include a description of the Jewish schoolmaster's accusation of Zercl, but it may have preserved the phrases shouted by a desperate Jew at a neighbour as he discovered the accusation unfolding at his doorstep.

The townsmen's testimonies take a further twist with the version offered by an apprentice baker, the young Sidlin, elsewhere referred to as *famulus.* On the Friday in question, as he was baking alone in his father's house, he heard a mysterious voice which directed him to the Jew Zercl's house, and which materialised into a force which dragged him there, pulling him by the arm, when he hesitated to move. When he arrived he saw Christ's body lying on the ground, and he guarded it lest some new offender come upon it, and while he waited he saw it sweat beautiful blood, bubbling into drops. He picked it up between index finger and thumb, and placed it on the stone threshold. His index finger remained bloodied by a small mark, as if he had been pricked by a needle. He had no idea whether a Christian or a Jew had planted the host in the Jew's house and contributed no information to the investigation of the miracles.

Sidlin's version is an interesting one. The thirteenth witness, Pertha, wife of Conrad Reuz, attested to having seen him hold Christ's body, although she had no knowledge of the circumstances of its arrival at the Jews' house. Sidlin described himself as baking (the host was after all a piece of baked dough!) alone, his action could be described as running to the Jews' house, planting something there on the threshold and being seen while doing so. His place in the tale diminished as townsmen developed a version which placed themselves and their personal experience in the centre: rushing out of the council chambers in the middle of a meeting, entering the Jews' house, being entreated by the schoolmaster and spurning his supplications, dragging him to the stake, hearing a confession which implicated Zercl too, and ultimately witnessing the gushing of blood and the working of miracles. It was that blood and those miracles which were being investigated, and the townsmen presented a narrative which covered unambiguously any question which Ambrose of Heiligenkreuz might put to them. What they could not do without destroying their own version was to claim knowledge of what happened prior to the Jewish abuse, an involvement which might have implicated them in neglect or failure to act to prevent Jewish possession of the host and the abuse implied. In the face of such certitude, the stranger, the theologian, was suggesting through his questions that all the fuss may have been over an unconsecrated host!

Ambrose had extricated himself from the dangerous task of adjudication by writing to the Bishop of Passau that so grave a matter required a papal commission of inquiry, just as canonisation processes did. Yet seven years later he was still haunted by his experience at Korneuburg. The victims of Korneuburg were long dead, the shrine's status was doubtful.[97] In 1312 he composed a tract 'Of the acts of the Jews under Duke Rudolph', and in it told of the case, in Styria, of a pyx containing the host found in a bag left behind by a Jew after napping under a tree during his travels.[98] This was said to have led to a massacre of the Jew and many others. This is probably the case at Fürstenfeld, in which another source describes the found host as a bleeding one.[99] Ambrose continued to monitor and reflect on the possibility and veracity of the miracles of host desecration.[100]

Korneuburg had its shrine, but doubts surrounded it, especially in official circles, and these were to influence the reception and impact of another host desecration accusation in the region, that of Pulkau in 1338.

LOCAL UPHEAVALS, A TOWN AND ITS HINTERLAND: PULKAU, 1338

The question 'Should Jews be killed for such a matter' which Ambrose raised in his tract was not only a scholastic conundrum, but a practical dilemma. Thirty years after the case of Korneuburg, duke, bishop, pope and townspeople were again confronted with an accusation which was quick in claiming victims but also in producing doubts and rumours about its veracity. This was the host desecration accusation enacted in 1338 in the little town of Pulkau in Lower Austria (twenty-five miles north of Vienna) not far from the Bohemian border, which cost the lives of 150 Jews. The duke and bishop acted quickly to investigate its circumstances. The 1330s were hard times in the region of Pulkau, as it saw constant incursion by the Bohemian forces of King John, during which towns like Pulkau were abandoned by their Duke Otto, and left unprotected while he established his power in the Duchy of Styria, recently annexed to Austria. Duke Otto did not defend, but he *did* tax, annually and heavily, to support his campaigns in 1332 and 1336. He was not popular; and even less so when he sowed doubt around the alleged miracle that had taken place in 1338 in Pulkau, and which led to regional violence against the Jews in the small towns of this borderland: Retz, Znoyma, Horn, Eggenburg, Neuburg and even Zwettl to the west.[101] The account of the events claimed variously that a host had been found on a Jew's threshold, and that Jews had tried to rid themselves of an abused host by throwing it into a dung-heap, over which a miraculous light appeared – or in the well of the rabbi's house, now the site of the chapel.[102] The violent repercussions travelled well into Bohemian territory and interest in Pulkau was excited near and far.

The accusation and massacre in Pulkau and its vicinity were reported by a variety of Austrian and Bohemian chroniclers. Some, like the annalist of the neighbouring Cistercian monastery of Zwettl, noted that in the year 1338 the Jewish Passover and Christian Easter coincided.[103] Others specified that on St George's day a bleeding host bought from a sexton was found in a dung-heap which produced lights and led to its discovery.[104] Zwettl monastery's calendar also recorded that the host had

been found in the house of a Jew, and was recovered with great ceremony and processions.[105] The Annals of Neustadt on the Mürz vaguely
refer to persecutions 'in many regions', but add that persecutions did
not occur in those Austrian towns where the duke and other lords could
offer protection, like Vienna and Neustadt.[106] Abbot John Neplacho of
Troppau monastery in Bohemia reported that the persecutions broke
out in 1338 in Bohemia, Moravia and Austria, and that the host was
found in Pulkau, for which many Jews, their wives and their children in
cribs were killed.[107] The Carinthian Abbot John of Viktring emphasised
the robbery and the extensive suffering caused: the Jews were despoiled
of their treasures, goods and letters; they were drowned, burnt,
beheaded, eviscerated and punished miserably. In some places princes
protected them as far as they could. But, claimed the Abbot, Christ's
case was vindicated spectacularly in Pulkau in Austria and in Wolfsberg
in Carinthia.[108]

These are short reports biased by regional perspectives, but they build
up to a picture of widespread violence in the north-eastern borderlands
of Austria. Habsburg policy throughout the thirteenth century had
attracted Jews and encouraged them to settle and involve themselves in
finance and trade within the commercial sphere which linked Bohemia
and Austria, and which contained tens of tiny towns along the road from
Vienna to Prague.

Pulkau itself became a pilgrimage site once miracles had been performed by its host. Yet within months, Otto, Duke of Austria, appealed to
Pope Benedict XII (1334–42) for an investigation of the persistent
doubts about the circumstances in which the host had been found: not *in*
the Jewish house, but *outside*, it 'was found by a layman in the street under
some chaff in front of a certain Jew's house, that is outside its threshold'.[109] The papal response of 29 August 1338 reproduced the arguments of the ducal letter and went on to mandate the Bishop of Passau,
Albert of Saxony (whose predecessor Wernhard had instituted the
Korneuburg examination by Ambrose of Heiligenkreuz), to set up an
inquiry around the events in Pulkau and to punish the perpetrators: be it
those who desecrated the host or those who falsely accused the Jews.[110]
There is further evidence of sceptical rumours about the case being
raised by chronicles from a variety of regions. Abbot Peter of Zittau
reported that the Bishop of Passau had taken precautionary measures
around the 'found host' ('hostia inventa'): he placed another, consecrated, host right behind it, so that whenever people turned their eyes in
devotion to the 'miraculous' host, they would always see the one that
was undoubtedly consecrated, and thus be saved from the danger of
idolatry which might result from praying to an unconsecrated and falsely
venerated 'miraculous' host.[111] The Bishop of Passau was not sufficiently
convinced by the circumstance of discovery and by the rumours to deem
the host found by the Jewish house unambiguously miraculous.

A position which discredited the Pulkau accusation altogether appears in the chronicle of the Franciscan John of Winterthur.[112] After recounting the Armleder events and the uprising of 1336–8 in great detail, he goes on to report the persecution of the Jews in Pulkau. According to him a needy priest of Pulkau had sprinkled a host with blood, hid it by the Jews' house, and then falsely accused them.[113] John lamented the fact that the culprit, who became rich on the offerings to his church, had not been properly punished by his bishop, and escaped through bribery. Such rumours of fraud, and precautionary measures to control or stifle the cult of the miraculous host, were pursued by bishop and duke, and remarked by knowledgeable observers.

It is interesting to note the contexts within which a local event such as the Pulkau accusation could be inserted. Chroniclers often sought a larger universal plane when describing some local occurrence. Thus Abbot Peter of Zittau, writing from Prague, reported the events of Pulkau in a meaningful setting. The chapter 'De miraculo quod circa corpus Christi acciderat' begins with a miraculous survival of the pyx, host and cloth during the fire in St Andrew's church in Prague that year. In the same year in the hill-town of Pnyewicz, a merchant discovered a host pierced through in three places and bleeding; he saved it and took it to the church where it began to work miracles. In Kaurim in Bohemia in the same year a host whipped by Jews was found and this led to massacres in Bohemia with the miraculous discovery that Jews did not bleed when mutilated. The culmination of this passage is the miracle of Pulkau, where a host was found tormented, and given special care by juxtaposing a consecrated host with the new one.[114]

The investigator chosen in the case of Pulkau was Frederick, Canon of Bamberg Cathedral, Doctor of canon and Roman law. The report he submitted to the Bishop of Passau has survived in a manuscript devoted to questions of miraculous proof concerning the eucharist.[115] Frederick of Bamberg was as unambiguous in his views as Ambrose had been hesitant. His report to the Bishop of Passau was nothing less than a fully-fledged eucharistic tract. Adopting a well-established rhetorical device, he set it out in the form of a dialogue between master (*Doctor*) and disciple (*Discipulus*) in which ten questions posed by the former were answered with full theological and canon law backing by the latter. Only in point eight does the discussion turn to the recent events at Pulkau.[116] To the disciple's question 'What is the sin and what is the due punishment of Jews who are drawn to the sacrament?' Frederick's answer came in the form of a description of the case of Pulkau, and the elaboration of the principle that the greater the glory of the subject the greater the offence; and an offence against the sacrament was clearly the greatest, deserving the most severe punishment.[117] The recurrent theme of 'Jew-loving' rulers motivated by financial need rather than piety and religion is powerfully deployed by Frederick.[118]

The Pulkau narrative, as cast by the Franciscan chronicler John of Winterthur, reflects a possible action brought about by tension between Jews and local clergy. The parish church of Pulkau belonged primarily to the 'Scottish' Monastery of Vienna (*Schottenkloster*; monasteries of Irish foundation were often so called). This meant that two-thirds of its income was appropriated to the monastery. Such annual incomes could be allocated to creditors in repayment of a loan. Twenty years before the accusation, Pulkau church had been appropriated to the Viennese monastery, and a portion of its income 'farmed' to a Jewish creditor. This is a background against which narratives of hate might be suggested, and forensically established almost at will. The local priest was after all the most readily available authoritative arbiter of truth in most of the host desecration accusations encountered so far. An entry added at the bottom of a folio in a fifteenth-century collection of sermons from the Cistercian monastery of Göttweig reports the case: the accused Jew is named Marquard (Merchlein?), and the host is said to have been found on the threshold of his house ('iuxta valvas domus').[119] Might Marquard have been the creditor who was paid annually from the parish's meagre income? The narrative of Pulkau admits no such collusion. Its clergy led the recovery of the miraculous hosts, and the processional celebration of their presence, even as the fires burnt for 150 Jews of Pulkau and for many more of the region on the days following.

In Pulkau, Count John of Hardegg, *Purg*-Count of Maidburg, financed the construction of the Holy Blood chapel in 1339, consecrated in 1396 (although only the apse was ever built).[120] Did the glory of Pulkau wane with the rumours of its fraudulent origins? Was episcopal censure brought to bear on further large-scale construction? In 1520, Abbot Benedict II of the Scottish Monastery of Vienna offered a magnificent winged altarpiece. The centre-piece depicted carved scenes of the Crucifixion, while the wing panels, most probably painted by a master of the Danube School, Master Nicholas Breu, represented the host desecration: three Jews around a circular table, and their attempt at hiding the miraculous host.[121]

Within fifty years of the first known occurrence of the accusation of host desecration against Jews, its shadows were cast permanently, if intermittently, over three areas of Europe. Franconia saw two major outbreaks of regional violence, maintained over months, led by a self-appointed knight, executed by an itinerant crowd of townsmen (artisans, journeymen) and rustics. Towns which had resisted on the first occasion, in 1298, succumbed to the violence in 1336 or 1337. Bavaria developed its own series of local accusations in the 1330s and fell in with the general upsurge of Armleder violence emanating from Franconia.[122] Austria, and particularly its northern parts bordering Bohemia, experienced a series of cases which led to less protracted but nonetheless regional repercussions, following accusations whose resulting miracles also led to the emergence of important pilgrimage and cult sites.

The narrative of host desecration was also told in these decades about Jews in communities outside these areas: in *c.*1323 there was a case in northern Germany at Remaghen, and accusations were made in Silesia in 1323 and 1325, and no doubt there were other cases which we will never come to know. In the later Middle Ages the tale becomes increasingly elaborate, and travels into new areas: Catalonia, Brabant, Silesia. Events followed the establishment of the narrative within the local religious culture, through the dissemination of tales, or more directly as a result of the promptings of insistent and charismatic preaching. We should bear in mind the multitude of accounts, continuing up to that time, which related the truth of the new accusation against Jews. Writers such as Rudolph of Schlettstadt transmitted not only the accusation but the news of its realisation in a given place, in *real* time, not 'story' time. Each case reflects the nuances of local colour, power relations, memory and cultural variation, and yet there is a deep structure to the tale and its telling. Within the host desecration accusation, the effects of the sacramental materials, violence and justice all come together in specific structures of relations. These lend meaning to our discussion of them as a single narrative in cases ranging far and wide. They involve fundamental understandings of human agency, gender roles and inclinations, communal duty and the nature of social action.

4

Persons and Places

The host desecration tale recounted an outrage committed by Jews upon the eucharist, but put this act within a familiar, even mundane setting. Its protagonists were 'ordinary' Jews, made to seem like those neighbours, who went about their business in ways somewhat different from Christians, but ways which were also familiar. The access they gained to the eucharist and the occasion this created for desecration often arose from the possibilities offered by work and travel, bolstered by advantages created by Jews' family networks and communal solidarities. Similarly, the Christian purveyors of rumours and detectors of host desecrations were ordinary Christians who called upon their neighbours and their parish priests to act. The logic of action within the tale was embedded in the unexceptional, in routines of local knowledge and common sense.

Yet the banal setting of the tales merely served to reinforce the truth-value of the claims they made. The clichés of context contributed to the conjuring of a mood of likelihood, familiarity, uncontestability, which the tales came to enjoy in the minds of many. The mundane scenery and background against which desecration was said to have occurred was carried over as a guarantee for the more outrageous events these settings were made to contain. The town streets, urban neighbourhoods, parish churches, communal wells, labouring people, matrons and children at work or at rest brought forth a sense of utter relevance, as if to say that the events unfolding probably did happen, since they could happen anywhere, everywhere. The genre was realistic, inasmuch as its narrative was presented as 'a plausible construction which refers to known patterns of human character, behaviour and event'.[1] Behind the common lives of ordinary people lurked the unusual, the dangerous, the menacing.

How were the setting and the plot made to bear such fruitful banality and engender so powerful a narrative, one which we have already seen in action and in use? Before looking at the characters, locations and plots, the paths of action which the tales reported to listeners and suggested to actors, let us reflect on the nature of familiar and conventional representation. The mundane is, after all, itself a set of conventional representations – the woman at her loom, the man at his plough, the merchant at his counter. Such stereotypes were undoubtedly as conventional then as the representation of, say, American suburbia is in television and popular drama today. The interplay is between sets of conventional representations of 'normality', which audiences can relate to and identify with, hope for and fantasise about. They can be temporal (like the setting of most host desecration accusations at Eastertide) or topographical (Jewish houses as built of stone). Teasing out these representations will tell us about some of the conventions of social expectation which empowered the fiction. In this sense the cliché makes 'commonplace the untrodden territory of a new story, amplifying audience identification'.[2] It will also suggest the ways in which new representations can emerge – as the host desecration narrative did – from juxtapositions and reconfigurations of conventional signs. Here is the cast and here are the locations of many of the host desecration accusations enacted in late medieval Europe.

THE PERPETRATOR: THE (MALE) JEW

Men and men alone were the culpable parties in the host desecration accusation. Singly, and later in groups, the quintessential abuser was a man, with women only very occasionally cited as accomplices. This preference mirrors the general tendency to mean *male* Jew when medieval persons referred to a Jew; the male carried the distinctive sign of Jewishness – circumcision. This is easily understood: the Jew, lacking in faith and perversely wedded to a distorted type of reason, had to be a man in order to act as a fully moral person, as capable of (evil) choice and guilt. The Jewish man was the circumcised Jew, the Talmud-Jew, the carrier of the intrinsic qualities and external signs of Jewish difference.[3] Female Jews were, like other women, seen as pliant and impressionable, lacking in reasoning and moral faculties. They were thus more frequently cast as subjects of attempts at conversion and the beneficiaries of instinctive insights into the Christian truth which their fathers, brothers or husbands were barred from sharing.

Whereas the narrative began as one involving an individual (Röttingen) or a man and his family (Paris), by the fifteenth century it was frequently told of groups of Jews and was often associated explicitly with a festival or a gathering. Alternatively, a single Jew might be seen as the activator of a whole group of Jews, even a series of regional groups, to whom particles of the eucharist were sent for serial desecration. This was the case in Wrocław in 1453, in Passau in 1477 and in Sternberg in 1492.

The abuse perpetrated by the Jews upon the host is variously described as either testing or shaming: the almost playful testing of the veracity of the much-publicised presence of Christ in the host, or the knowing and purposive abuse of that which was or might be the

Christian God. In either case the Jewish plot was shown to unfold in stages: first the Jews faced the challenge of procuring the host; then they had to keep it until an opportune occasion arose for abuse, and it was often reserved, appropriately, in a silken purse, box or pyx; the abuse then followed, with the use of metal instruments such as needles, lances, knives, axes; when this initial attack did not succeed in destroying the host, but rather brought forth blood, the host was thrown into a cauldron of boiling water, or a frying pan (as in Konstanz and in Uccello's *predella* scene). Frustration with the indestructible (and thus miraculous) host led the Jews to greater acts of desperation and ingenuity: hosts were buried in the ground, thrown into streams or swamps, sent away to another town. Sometimes while ridding themselves of the host the Jews were made to add insult to injury by throwing it into a dung-heap, or a stable (as in Laa-an-der-Thaya in 1294). In cases of testing, the host is sometimes treated differently: as in the case of a Jewish woman who placed it in an oven to see whether the host would behave like ordinary bread.

Rich Jewish men were particularly dangerous potential abusers, as all the qualities of Jewish power were inflated in them: their control of money, and thus of destinies of Jews and Christians alike.[4] The protagonist of the host desecration of Brussels was such a rich man, Jonathan of Enghien. Professional moneylenders and keepers of pawned goods were often cast as initiators of abuse: from the Jew of Paris, who was situated by Uccello in an ample pawnshop, to the rich man Meir, upon whom the accusation at Wrocław hinged.

Eastertide was considered to be the favoured time for Jewish eucharistic abuse, close as it is to the Jewish Passover. In the case of Pulkau we are told that in 1338 Passover and Easter coincided.[5] Easter Week was also the season most likely to produce anti-Jewish riots or revelry, and much effort was invested by rulers in removing Jews from the streets on such days. Even a very laconic report of a host desecration accusation and its violence did not omit the emphasis on the date, as in Glogóu (Silesia) in 1401: 'The Jews were burnt outside the town of Glogóu after Easter.'[6] The effects of heightened religious awareness, heated preaching and intensive ritual activity, as well as the continuous evocation of Passion imagery, with its related themes of Jewish guilt, suffice to explain the danger of this season. A further explanation was offered *c.*1400 by the great rabbi of Prague, Yomtov Lippmann of Mühlhausen. In his *Book of Contention* for Jewish disputants, the *Book of Contention*, he argued that Christians mistook Jewish Passover rituals for sinister manipulations of host-like materials (figure 11).[7]

The quintessential Jewish person was a man, a person in a position of economic power and patriarchal authority, and bound to other men by ties of sociability and shared ill intent. Over the decades of the retelling of the host desecration accusation, the single male protagonist turned into a group of perpetrators. He no longer acted alone, but planned his deeds with other men, or drew them into the action once he had begun an act of abuse. Jewish men were thus poised for action, as men were in medieval understanding, as opposed to women who were easily led and influenced. But the male Jew was not simply like other men. In medical, theological and homiletic discourses he was represented as the harbourer of strange desires, a sufferer from physical afflictions such as menstruation, dropsy and a sickly pallor.[8] It was this ambivalent figure, strangely feminine in body although male in the plenitude of his responsibility for the crime, that sought an accomplice in the planning of host desecration. Jewish men needed help in procuring the Christian God; their helpers were most frequently Christian women.[9]

WOMEN

While women were rarely accused of perpetrating violent acts in abuse of the host they were nonetheless important participants in the events, as it was almost invariably through women that the Jews came to acquire the sacrament. Poor debtors or Christian maids in Jewish households, the female 'familiar' of the Jew was dependent on Jewish favour; occasionally they were said to have been simply greedy, easily tempted by Jewish money. An early account of the accusation at Paris described the procurer of the host as a maid in Jewish service, but other versions set the scene in a moneylender's shop, a tradition depicted in an illustration to a fourteenth-century manuscript of Villani's *Cronica* (see figure 8, p. 43) and in Uccello's *predella* scene.[10] Slippage between these types of female agency is evident in the accounts of the desecration at Poznań in 1399: the chronicle of Jan Długosz (1415–80, notary and secretary to the Bishop of Krakow) claimed that a poor woman stole the host from the Dominican church and sold it to the Jews, while an *exemplum* which was circulating by the late fifteenth century spoke of her as a servant who received the host at communion and sold it to the Jews.[11] Servanthood emerges as particularly detrimental to a woman's faith (as it was to her chastity). Since she was likely to partake of the food, conversation and company of her Jewish employers, joint activities which late medieval legislation repeatedly attempted to uproot, her character and morality were constantly endangered.[12] Such was the case of the Christian servant of an old Jewish teacher and scholar, Moses of Rothenburg (Franconia), who worked for him for over fourteen years and during that time 'she did not go to services, failed to confess, nor did she receive the sacrament during that period, and her soul became badly blinded'.[13] When her employer was moved to interest in Christianity, he asked her to go to church, confess, receive communion and bring the host to him for examination. Even this 'lapsed' Christian identity could be activated at

11. An example of Passover ritual. Castilian Haggadah, late fourteenth century, fol. 87^r.

will and be made to penetrate the most sacred Christian spaces. Such a perversion of Christian practice is described by John of Winterthur in an account of a host desecration accusation at Koblenz *c.*1332, where 'a woman, Christian only in name' removed a host from St Paul's church and sold it to the Jews so that they could mock it. But when she witnessed the abuse it was she who ran in the streets shouting for help: 'Christ's body is being horribly tortured by the Jews.'[14] In an *Urfehde,* a peace bond, signed by three Jews settled in Neustadt (Hesse), the signatories admitted that they had been offered the eucharist for sale by a certain woman, Notzin.[15] The men were allowed to go free after signing the bond, but the woman's fate is not known to us.

Women and Jews met in regions of magic and manipulation within the religious culture. In the account of the desecration at Remagen (Rhine Palatinate) *c.*1323 by the monk-chronicler of Egmont, William the Procurator, the woman was linked to the Jews through demonic kinship: just as they were sons of the devil, she was his daughter, and thus sister to the Jews. She sold Christ's body to them in return for her pawned clothes and five marks of silver.[16] Similarly greedy was the rich widow of Metz who, in 1385, when corn prices were low and times were hard, consulted a Jew, who promised to help her if she would bring him the 'sacred body of our Lord and sacrament'. She feigned illness and received communion on her 'death-bed', but saved the host and handed it over to the Jew, who placed it in a box with a toad, which he hid in a cupboard. Her servants rushed to her chamber when they heard cries from her closet, and found in it a box with Christ's body bleeding from the toad's bite marks. The discovery led to the capture and burning of both Jew and widow.[17]

An occasion for female detection of female crime was told by the mystic Margaretha Ebner (*c.*1291–1351) in one of her 'showings' (*Offenbarungen*). In the summer of 1346 a terrible thing happened: a woman from the village of Medingen, led astray by the devil, stole from the pyx of the abbey church of St Mary at Steten two *un*consecrated hosts. She removed these to the nearby town of Lauingen (Swabia), and meant to sell them to a Jew or borrow money against them. The Jew would have nothing to do with her and called the authorities, who arrested and executed the woman by burning, her unborn child being cut out of her body and baptised.[18] Margaretha exclaims that she could not rid herself of the thought of this case all summer long, of the horror of what had befallen Christ her God.

Through weakness of mind and moral judgement, women acted variously as deceivers of Christians and accomplices of Jews. But as we have seen, individual women, and often groups of women, could also act as arbiters of eucharistic probity, judges of eucharistic truth and leaders of neighbourhood action in recovery and revenge of the abused host. Women were quintessential detectors of abuse, skilful and alert spotters of unusual events amongst neighbours, some of whom were Jews. After initial recognition or identification, they then handed matters over to men – clerical or lay – who were authorised to wield sacerdotal power and violence.

Female agency is particularly complex in the case from the Swabian town of Ehingen near Nördlingen *c.*1332, where female guilt seems even to have displaced that of the Jews. A woman is said to have taken the host from her church and hidden it in some 'disgusting' place. Once the parish priest discovered the disappearance the Jews were suspected and a mob fell upon them, killing eighteen Jews. But *other* women, worthy Christian women, had seen her carrying the eucharistic purse and trying to sell its content to the Jews, and they had her caught, whereupon she confessed and was executed.[19] The chronicler comments here drily that although the Jews had committed no crime, they were killed.[20]

In tales in which a Christian man delivered the host to the Jews, attention was frequently directed towards his wife as the one who persuaded him to act. In Enns in 1421 it had been a church custodian's wife who provided the host which prompted the accusation of abuse; this accusation ultimately sanctioned the expulsion of the Austrian Jewry in that year.[21] According to one of the versions of the events leading up to the host desecration trial of Wrocław in 1453, a group of Jews was said to have approached Peter, the custodian of the church of St Matthew, for the purchase of some hosts. The man initially refused, but when they insisted, he went home and discussed the offer with his wife. He agreed 'having had a short consultation with his wife'; his wife evidently did not object, and by implication even encouraged him to collaborate with the Jews.[22] Ten hosts were thus handed over for testing by the Jews of Wrocław and the neighbouring Silesian towns.[23]

Jewish women rarely appear as abusers of the host, and were often punished only by implication and by association with the guilt of their menfolk. When agency is imputed to them this takes the form of more innocent or simple-minded transgressions. Rudolph of Schlettstadt tells of a young Jewish woman who confessed to the Würzburg council that she had put a host into one of her shoes in order to see whether indeed it was God.[24] Alternatively, a woman may be found guilty for crimes 'inherited' from her husband. Thus in Sternberg in 1492, the wife of the Jew Eleasar, who had abused the host and provided some to other Jews, was left with the task of getting rid of the bleeding wafers after her husband had absconded on the morrow of the alleged desecration. One version of the tale had the desecration take place on 20 July, and her attempts to return the hosts to the priest who had provided them on 21 August. Another version describes the efforts of the woman in the interim: she tried to throw the hosts in a stream, only to find that she had become glued to a stone on the bank whenever she tried to throw them away. When interrogated and under pressure she revealed not only her absent husband's name, but described his act as the realisation of a long-standing desire to procure hosts, a project which he had intermittently promoted over a number of years.[25]

Women in the host desecration narrative were thus the weak and easily tempted accomplices of Jewish plans, but they could also be high-minded and pious and quick to identify abuse. Women in poverty were particularly vulnerable to seduction, but the pious matron was ever vigilant for the eucharist's sake. Women introduced the home and the hearth into these tales, and offered modes of participation for other actors who deepen the pathos of the tales, actors such as children.

CHILDREN

Children appear regularly and in diverse positions in host desecration narratives.[26] In some cases the abused host was said to have taken the shape of a child, or to have emitted child-like sounds, as in the case of the Jew of Cologne in whose hand the misappropriated host sounded like a child of 'around three years'.[27] In the heat of the accusation an abused host, boiled in fat, was said to have turned first into a child and then into a young man.[28] When the Jews of Remaghen pierced and punctured the host and finally invoked the devil over it, the 'venerable substance' produced noises which could be heard by Christians. Since the voice resembled that of a little boy, they thought that a child was being held in the house, and broke down the door to save him, discovering traces of the desecration.[29] After abusing three hosts in a cellar in their quarter and observing the miracles worked by them, the Jews of Poznań in 1399 tried to get rid of the troublesome hosts and threw them into a swamp. A shepherd boy discovered them in the shape of three hovering butterflies which he reported to the parish priest, to the detriment of the thirteen Jews who were then tortured and slowly roasted to death.[30]

Child-like innocence paralleled the child-like persona of Christ, the innocence of Christ, and raised the level of compassion and drama in the narrative: the host itself could turn into a child, and the painter of the Pulkau altarpiece around 1520 chose to recreate this very image.[31] Children were agents of discovery, and symbolic victims as abused hosts turned into child-like figures. In the Franconian town of Röttingen, the home base of the Rintfleisch regional massacres, it was the sound of childish cries from the house of childless elderly Jews which prompted action by the worthy women of the neighbourhood and led to the discovery of abuse.[32] Whatever the dynamics of neighbourhood rumour and accusation (of the types the Korneuburg protocols reveal), the narrative privileged the particularly innocent witness of children, and the instinctive discerning piety of women. A short and puzzling interjection in Rudolph of Schlettstadt's collection of tales appears untitled and retells the power of the testimony of a child who was also a convert. When asked what her mother did with the sacrament, a little Jewish girl ('Judea puella parvula') who had been baptised answered:

> My mother seized a small piece of wood and dug in the ground and found the host there, and with her hand put it on a tunic and pierced it repeatedly with a needle. She also pierced it repeatedly with a sharp knife. She then put it in her mouth and dirtied it with spittle. And cursing she heaped maledictions on it. She then dug the ground and buried it again, placing a stone on the spot and she sat on it as if to press it down.[33]

Children could be used as unassailable witnesses about the happenings within private spaces, in the intimacy of homes. Once their tale could be elicited or staged, it would have been difficult to mount a defence against it.

PRIESTS, SEXTONS AND ANTI-CLERICAL SENTIMENT

In most narratives of host desecration, a woman procured the host for the Jews and another woman or women detected the abuse, and then turned to a parish priest to assist in its recovery and in according it the treatment appropriate to a now miraculous host. The clergy were the saviours in this drama, the only liturgically privileged actors who could put into motion a whole ritual process of appropriate gestures for translation, containment and display now so richly merited by the miraculous matter.[34] These actions usually culminated in the triumphant placing of the miraculous host on the altar of the parish church, to the sound of chants and prayers.[35]

Yet the clergy could play another role in the tales, one more sinister though ensuing equally from their privileged status. In numerous cases they were represented as transgressors rather than saviours. Even more than an erring poor Christian woman, the priest had easy access to the eucharist. Thus it is priests, or clergy in lower orders who could gain access to the pyx, who were sometimes cast as the Jew's accomplice. When cast in this manner, the clergy appear symbolically equivalent to Jews, occasionally merging with the rich anti-clerical discourse of the time: they are portrayed as exploitative, greedy, unproductive, sexually incontinent and predatory. When a priest acted in a manner true to this character or caricature, he posed as much danger to Christians as did the Jew. There are also some instances of laws drawing parallels between Jews and priests. The *Sachsenspiegel* law-code treats them together in the clause on the carrying of arms.[36] And when popular wrath was unleashed in scenes of urban violence, it was often Jews as well as priests who were its victims.[37] A poor or greedy priest might plant a bloodied host and forge an accusation, as John of Winterthur believed to have been the case at Pulkau.[38] A scholar, a hireling of a church in the diocese of Aqui, was the collaborator who sold a consecrated host to the Jews there not long before 1365, at the instigation of the devil ('instigante diabolo').[39] In 1305 in Lower Austria the investigator of the host desecration and miracles at Korneuburg, Ambrose of Heiligenkreuz, reported that he had heard from the Bishop of Passau that the Jews had not been solely to blame, a version supported by the priest Frederick, one of the witnesses to the inquiry, who had heard that a Christian man had confessed to selling the host to the Jews.[40] In his tract, written some years after the events, Ambrose even went so far as to claim that the real culprit was that priest, rather than the Jews who had been executed.[41]

A priest who lived in concubinage might also become a victim of multiple pressures. The most powerful convergence of the theme of 'woman as source of evil' and 'priest as beholden to Jew through penury or lasciviousness' is evident in the famous case of Sternberg (Mecklenburg) of 1492. Here the priest Peter Dane, who had broken up a relationship with his concubine following the corrective chastisement of his bishop, pawned her cooking pot to the Jew Eleasar. The spurned concubine demanded the return of the pot and under the pressure of her drunken taunts, and unable to redeem the pot, Peter was forced to comply with the Jew's request that he bring a consecrated host in return for it.[42] In those early days of print, the popular shrine which developed in Sternberg was quickly supplied with broadsheets and pamphlets in the vernacular telling the tale. Their tone often resembled themes in the anti-clerical rhetoric of early Reformation pamphlets, drawing from the same rich seam of abusive figures.

The most elaborate narrative involving members of the clergy is that presented in 'De persecutione iudaeorum vratislavensium a.1453'. The writer begins by invoking God's mercy in the production of miracles for the correction of obstinate Christians and to instil terror in perverse Jews.[43] In Wrocław on Wednesday in the octave of Corpus Christi 1453 (6 June) the Jews held counsel and decided to try and discover 'whether that round figure of unleavened bread and snow-white in colour is Jesus Christ', by procuring a host and testing it. They approached a town-herald known to them and expressed their need for a host, offering him 100 florins for his trouble. The herald promised to try and, having received a florin on deposit, he set off to the town of Olsawa, where he met a shepherd known to him. He greeted him profusely, and after a while expressed his need for a host, promising him a florin in turn, and another after the deed was done. The shepherd claimed to know a priest in another village who failed to keep the hosts locked up, and promised to go and procure one. The shepherd went to the village while the herald waited. He found a shabby married cleric ('clecham coniugatum lacerdum') who looked no different from a rustic, and greeted him warmly, professing his friendship and pleasure, asking after the cleric's health and that of his wife and children. He then asked for the host, expressing a great need for it. The cleric agreed to help but only after they had spent some time refreshing themselves at a tavern. They then went on to the church where they found the rector snoring away on his mattress in the middle of the day. The cleric approached the place where the host was reserved, took one that had been consecrated, and handed it over to the shepherd, who wrapped it in a cloth and went on his way, and thus the host ultimately reached the Jews.

We have here a cutting representation of the clergy, priest and cleric, perverse in having become not keepers of the host, but its negligent merchants. The term *clecha* used throughout for the cleric who handed over the host is an abusive term for a married priest in the Polish Latin of the later Middle Ages.[44] The association with marriage (licit for clerics in lower orders but always a subject of some ambivalence in the church's attitude), with drink, with dishevelled and tattered appearance, all went against the code of clerical propriety. Furthermore, it is also the rector, he who was the guardian of the eucharist, who is upbraided. Snoring in the middle of the day, keeping his hosts unlocked in defiance of centuries of church legislation and custom, he was as much of an accomplice to the betrayal of Christ as were the laymen and cleric involved. The text is satirical in nature, with elements of generic estate-satire in this, its first section (the description of the Jews' end is quite different in tone). A resonant representation of the clergy and priesthood is here allied with the tale of host desecration: two types of abuse and a fiendish camaraderie.

THIEVES AND THEFT-PLOTS

Ecclesiastical legislation from the thirteenth century onwards emphasised the exclusive right of priests to handle the host and thus reduced occasions for other folk to gain access to consecrated hosts. The challenge seen as facing those Jews who wished to abuse the host was thus that of gaining access to it. The host was nonetheless made widely available to layfolk at communion, and this offered opportunities for tempting recipients to keep a part of their communion wafer, a possibility exploited by the makers of host desecration narratives.[45] Another group, that of custodians and sextons, could also be approached to help steal consecrated hosts, which were regularly kept in churches for the communion of the sick.[46]

From the fifteenth century, theft narratives similarly served to fill the narrative gap between the host in the safety of a church chancel and in the hands of Jews in the privacy of their homes or synagogues. In reality, robberies from churches supplied the trigger for a set of investigations based on suspicion. The search for stolen vessels might raise the question of stolen hosts, as consecrated hosts were reserved in vessels for up to a week for use in emergency for the benefit of the sick and dying. The hosts contained in a pyx represented an irksome complication to the thief's plan of action: in Magdeburg in 1315 a thief stole a pyx from the sacristy of the monastery of St Paul, and fearful of simply placing the hosts on the altar, buried them in the churchyard between two stones in the mud. He then took the pyx, the object of his robbery, for sale to the Jews. Here the supernatural intersects with the trivially criminal: as a water-carrier ('bornekopenfurer') was returning from the Elbe on horseback and reached the spot of the burial, all stood still and then knelt. His servant dismounted, looked around and found the host, while a miller joined them and extracted the sacrament from the mud. Meanwhile the thief Conrad was arrested, and a chapel was built on the spot.[47] That theft in and of itself could raise suspicions which might lead to a dire end is suggested in the laconic entry of the Salzburg chronicle for the year 1404: 'the Jews of Salzburg were burnt because of the eucharist stolen in the mills.'[48]

Thieves and thefts might be involved in the narrative of host desecration in a number of ways: it might be claimed that a Jew approached a Christian and tempted him or her to steal the host, as was the case in the version of the Wrocław case of 1453, in which a Jew approached a town herald.[49] Alternatively, a thief might offer a Jew some hosts for sale, often the by-product of thefts of precious vessels from churches.[50] A justices' roll from thirteenth-century Norfolk describes the unexpected dilemmas posed when a run-of-the-mill church robbery provided loot of consecrated wafers.[51] A thief might also hope for the displacement of some of his guilt during questioning for suspected theft by involving Jews as initiators or instigators of the theft. Such seems to have been the logic reflected in the version of the Wrocław case of 1453 which told of a series of men implicated in the theft of hosts – town herald, shepherd, cleric – and which pointed to Jews as the instigators of this chain of events.[52] In Passau in 1478 it was the thief Christoph Eisengreissamer who informed the authorities of the theft of hosts which he had been asked to procure for a group of local Jews and their co-religionists in other towns. One of the striking woodcuts in the broadsheet which publicised the Passau case shows the scene of a monstrance on an altar, and a later scene demonstrates that Christoph's end was as gruesome as that of the Jews he had denounced (c.1490) (figure 12).[53]

12. The Case of Passau from theft to punishment in twelve scenes. Passau broadsheet (*c.*1490).

Similar elements of theft, abuse and dispersal are embedded in the records of a theft of hosts from the Nonnenkloster at Leipzig in 1489. Here the town's account-book reveals, through the records of occasional expenses reimbursed in that year and the next, the activities of its officials in pursuit of the theft perpetrated by a convert ('getawfte jude'), aptly named Paul. The transport and upkeep of the suspected thief in jail, the efforts of councillor Hieronimus Cleinsdorf on repeated journeys to Zeytz and Pegaw in July in pursuit of the Jew who had bought the host, and the transport of the suspect to Leipzig for trial are listed as so many incidents of expenditure in a busy town's accounts.[54] As late as December 1489 a town councillor and a scribe travelled to Sleutz in pursuit of the Jewish purchaser and in the roll for the following year expenses for travel and the arrest of Jews (note the plural) were still being entered.

Accusations of host desecration through theft tended to reflect patterns of judicial control. Thus a cluster of three accusations in the kingdom of Catalonia-Aragon in the second half of the fourteenth century all began with the confession of a thief, which activated the exalted, and willing, judicial attentions of the Infant John. In Barcelona in 1367 it was a Christian thief with an accomplice, who was later hunted down in France, who began the series of accusations. In Huesca in 1377, similarly, a Christian thief accused the Jews, but then retracted his accusation in the presence of his confessor before execution.[55]

Poverty could motivate the thief, especially the poverty of a misguided woman. As already mentioned, the visionary Margaretha Ebner described a case which occurred near her nunnery in 1346. A pregnant woman from the village of Medingen stole two hosts from a monastery-church in the hope of selling or pawning them to a Jew. But the Jew did not wish to buy the hosts, informed on her and had her arrested and executed. Ebner tells this story since it moved her greatly and invoked in her strong feelings of pity and sadness for the woman and for her God, feelings which overwhelmed her all summer long. A report on the case of Wrocław in 1453 had a poor 'Polish' peasant ('ein pawr von Polan von der Älss', 'der Polakch') as the protagonist who stole the host, but he had been tempted by a Jew who offered in return for the host the return of an old coat ('ainn alten rokch'), as well as a coat for his wife.[56]

A fascinating case in which a woman was involved in a theft-narrative is of interest here, even though it is not related to the sale of hosts to Jews. In 1447 Anna Vögtlin was arrested at Triengen (Sursee, eighteen miles north-west of Lucerne) on suspicion of the theft and mishandling of some hosts which had been discovered among nettles by a young girl. Anna's confession recounted a tale of poverty and misery, which had led to temptation when a man from her native region taught her a form of words which would give her the power to affect others. He had, in fact, taught her to make a pact with the devil, and gave her a guide and familiar by the name of *Lux*, who was to 'rule, guide and govern you'.[57] She was incited by him to steal the host from the parish church of Bischoffingen, and shared it with him. Ten weeks later she repeated the act and they used the hosts in black magic in order to destroy her enemies' crops. A third theft occurred, but this time she was unable to leave the churchyard, so she buried the host among the nettles and went on her way. On the road to Triengen she was apprehended by two parishioners of Ettiswil, one of the robbed parishes, who led her to trial and execution by fire. The account details that the woman, who confessed all her crimes, also repented and thus died devoutly in contrition in the fire.[58]

CONVERTS

Since the host desecration narrative had to stage an encounter between Jew(s) and the host within a Jewish space, the liminal figure of the Christian thief was often invoked to realise the transfer of the host. Alternatively a convert was made to do this work. Converts appear in the host desecration narrative as morally ambiguous figures: as procurers of the host for Jews, as informers who denounce Jews as desecrators, as adept translators who penned vernacular confessions voiced under torture. The host desecration narrative was also a begetter of converts: moved by the evidence of the miraculous transformation of the desecrated host, or fearing for their lives in the aftermath of discovery, Jews were frequently said to have chosen conversion in the wake of the host desecration drama. Sometimes children were spared in order to be baptised and raised in 'good Christian homes'.[59]

Women, like children, were more likely than men to become good converts as they were seen as pliant, easily influenced, and lacking in the adamant and obstinate preoccupation with Jewish law.[60] In the tale of the Jewish Boy we have already noted that while the father was invariably punished, the mother and child converted. A similar distancing was represented in a version of the Paris story: the Jewish child ran into the streets of the parish of St-Jean-en-Grève shouting: 'Your God is being tortured by my father.'[61]

One of the memorable tales recounted by Rudolph of Schlettstadt concerned a Jewish woman who gave the following account in the fever of the Rintfleisch persecutions. Her father had asked her to light a fire for him, and he proceeded to heat a pot of fat over it. He then threw something into the pot, addressing it thus:

> If you are Jesus Christ of Mary the Virgin, as the Christians say, real son of God and Man, who is carried by the Christians daily in streets and squares and minister to them daily, and if you will judge on the day of judgement the dead and the living, show me your power, so that I may believe in you and preach of your power. If you do so I shall relinquish my Jewish faith and observe the Christian one loyally and extol you as God Almighty for evermore.[62]

After a short while the host turned into a lovely boy, the Jew proclaimed his faith and the child jumped out of the pot and stood up as a young man. He offered a third sign by disappearing and bathing the room in light. The Jew was terrified and moved. He and his daughter converted, as he had promised they would.

Rudolph stops the sequence of blood and mayhem created in the wake of the movements of Rintfleisch's crowd to tell this story with a happy ending, the 'old-fashioned' story of witness and proof. Yet it acquires its edge from its context, as a story which begins very much like the others, but turns into an *exemplum* rather than a report on a killing. The narrative's power to educate is here strongly demonstrated, as the Jew's address to the host is all but a paraphrase of the Lord's Prayer, and the Jew adopts the triple pattern of Christ's temptations as the pattern for his own questioning of the host/God. A variety of eucharistic figures is displayed here: the host, the child, the man. This is a parenthesis within the larger drama of desecration, blood and destruction which swept Franconia and which came to be told so cunningly by Rudolph in this collection.

In Rudolph's tales, converts were the carriers of knowledge of the secret actions of Jews. A female convert fled from Würzburg to Colmar to escape the pressure of her Jewish friends. She told her new landlady of Jewish wickedness, and of the monthly haemorrhage and dysentry which afflicted Jewish men, and which was only cured by the use of the blood of a Christian, baptised in Christ's name.[63] She also told of the procuring of hosts from a priest or a sacrist, their abuse, and the issue of blood which was followed by the appearance of a child.[64] Another female convert told of her own mother's habit of hiding a host and occasionally taking it out of the ground to torture it. Throughout these tales the pervading sense is one of incomplete conversions, a process never quite put to rest, and thus of the danger which followed from the integration of converts into Christian secrets, spaces and rituals.

Converts also appeared as denouncers of Jews, as enthusiastic adherents to their new religion, committed to their new solidarities. One convert was moved to inform on a Jew as a way of resisting the claims Jews were still making on her. In the case of Brussels of 1370, the female convert Katherine was approached by a Jewish widow with the request that she return some stolen hosts to their proper place. Katherine, in turn, approached Michael, the vice-rector of St Gudule, confessed, and the theft was thus discovered.[65]

Converts could offer inspiration and open new avenues of inquiry in the course of a trial. John of Capistrano who led the inquisitorial trial at Wrocław in 1453 was approached by a poor Jewish convert, the wife of a local artisan, with information about a host desecration and ritual murder in which her father had been involved. So detailed was her knowledge that the investigators followed her to her native town of Lamberg (Löwenberg), and in the cellar of the rabbi Cayphas the bones of a child were found.[66] Even more complex is the evidence contained in the small register of an Aragonese inquisitor of *c.*1377 (probably the Dominican Nicholas Eymerich, *c.*1320–99) which lists denunciations made to him. Most informers told of magical practices or statements made against the sacraments, and some cases were brought against Jews. In one, the convert Jacob Bisnes, a tailor of Monso (Lérida diocese), accused Lupus Abnatan of desecrating hosts. This was alleged to have

13. Cupboard and pyxes as depicted in a Jewish Haggadah. Catalan Haggadah, late fourteenth century, fol. 13ʳ.

occurred on an occasion when Jacob and other Jews had been invited to Lupus's house and were shown two gilt-silver chalices with their patens, in which rested two hosts (Were they consecrated? Were these not chalices but pyxes?) (figure 13). Lupus told those assembled that these had been sold to him by a chaplain, and that he had had them for a while and could do as he wished with them, but that he preferred money to hosts (meaning that he might sell them?). He then threw the hosts with contempt on to a table, so that they fell to the ground, showing how little he valued them. Jacob swiftly added that he and others had reprehended Lupus for his actions. The convert named all those who had been present and added that Lupus had sworn them all to secrecy.[67] We have no further knowledge of the inquisitor's actions in pursuing the denunciation.

What can one, responsibly and usefully, make of such a record? It combines so many of the stock elements of the accusation narrative: Jewish men gathering in secret, the availability of hosts through Christians and Jewish money-lending practice, the ease of abuse once hosts were obtained.[68] The denunciation reflects the anxiety prevalent among Christians about the vulnerable host as wholesome divinity, about the very claims made in its name. It also reflects the convert's desire to be trusted and to be immersed in the new community. That Jews, roused by festivity and fellowship, may have played about, even played a practical joke on their neighbours and their beliefs is all too believable. That hosts were left in pawned vessels is less likely but surely possible. What truth-value does such a denunciation carry except as a masterful narration and as a mark of the radical alienation which conversion can bring about, and the price the chronic insecurity it bred could exact?[69]

Converts were not only actors in the unfolding of accusations, but the product of their cruel outcome. Reports of the punishment of Jews after accusations often detail the numbers of converts. Death as Christians meant for some converts a neat and swift beheading rather than the agonising torture and execution by fire, the death saved for heretics.[70] The broadsheet which eloquently told the story of Passau of 1477–8 shows the different forms of execution for the accused: beheading for the converted, burning after torture for the others (see, again, figure 12, p. 82). It is gruesome indeed to imagine the events which led to the full confessions of those accused in this case, all named in the court records in their old (Jewish) and new (Christian) names: Mandl, now Sebastian, Kalman, now Stephen, Valk, now Hans. Banishment was often the lot of those Jews not directly involved, but who were tainted by association with the accusations of other Jews.[71]

Even where Jews and their quarters were destroyed, converts remained as lingering traces after the violence. In 1464 the Dominican inquisitor for the diocese of Wrocław, Gregory Heyntze, recorded the reacceptance into the bosom of the faith of a convert who had returned to Judaism and abused his new religion. The letter was a safe-conduct which confirmed that the carrier had been properly confessed after in a fit of madness he had rejected his new faith and had shouted in public that he wished to die in the faith to which he had been born.[72] The inquisitor who issued the document was now convinced that the Jew truly wished to adhere to the Christian faith. Was this man, unnamed in the letter, a forced convert of 1453, eleven years earlier, who managed to escape death?

There was something in the palpable physical continuity of the converted person, something about the radical physical difference which

Jews represented, that stood in the way of an easy integration of the convert into Christian society. This was particularly acute in the case of male converts; attached to men was an extensive array of Jewish characteristics, in body and in soul. It is thus that converts were able to fill the role of betrayers of the eucharist and to execute crucial actions within the narrative of eucharistic abuse – in their newly licensed proximity to the host, and their persistent refusal to embrace it wholly.[73]

THE CROWD AND ITS VIOLENCE

Conversion was induced in these cases through the operation of the menace of mass violence or judicial torture. The Christian crowd, moved by religious zeal, is represented most frequently as a swift and just actor in the tales of host desecration. It countered Jewish violence with its own brand of action: burnings, slayings, hangings, drownings. The scope for such action was closely dependent on local political and institutional arrangements: as we have seen, violence was minimal in Paris and very extensive in Pulkau. The crowd is represented by most reporters as avenging the abuse and mockery of Christ. It was motivated not only by the desire to vent its wrath, but sometimes also by the fear that failure to do so would in turn incur divine revenge. The rhetorical stance of Jesco, the leader of the crowd of Prague in the spring of 1389, which so affected his hearers, was to warn that God's wrath would fall upon them.[74] The crowd was thus presented as intuitive, pious, and sometimes out of control. So enthusiastic was it in St Polten (Lower Austria, thirty miles west of Vienna) in 1306 that some of its own number were trampled to death in the heat of its violence.[75]

The crowd did not stop long to think: it acted on a simple set of signs and prompts, almost like an animal lacking reason. Thus it could get things very wrong, even in terms of its own objectives. When the hue and cry was raised at the discovery by the parish priest of the disappearance of hosts from the parish church of Ehingen in *c.*1323, a furious crowd responded to the priest's tearful entreaties ('he turned to the townspeople with tears and horrible cries')[76] and killed eighteen Jews. Only later was it revealed that a Christian woman had stolen the hosts for use in magic. When a crowd appointed its leaders or accepted one who offered himself, an even more elaborate pattern might emerge, leading to enduring and wide-ranging violence, as was the case in the Rintfleisch and Armleder movements.

Where rulers were deemed as failing to act against Jews for reasons of greed and convenience, the crowd was presented by recorders of the events as being moved by pure and selfless zeal. Around 1333 the citizens of Konstanz rose as a crowd to avenge the injury and degradation caused by the Jews, leading the Jews away and 'slaughtering them like cows'.[77] Twelve Jews were burnt, nine were pressed to death and the rest were spared through the protection of *potentiores*. The Cistercian monk who compiled the annals of the neighbouring Zwettl abbey described the events of Pulkau in 1338 as the actions of a crowd moved by divine zeal. Its actions resulted in the killing and burning of Jews and their reduction to dust.[78] The crowd in Prague is described by a number of chroniclers as having been moved and inspired to action by its preachers in the heated setting of Easter week.[79]

When Jews were caught and taken to be the guilty party in a host desecration they were most commonly thrown into a fire, not at the ordered stake of secular punishment, but fires lit by townspeople or groups of people who assembled for the task of revenge. The Jews were thus destroyed in the final annihilation of fire, the punishment reserved for heretics, which contained an element of totality, but also of purging. Some descriptions of killing in fires say no more than 'Iudei cremati sunt'.[80] The well-documented case of Korneuburg has the fire lit by townsmen, and the terrified Jew running in the streets claiming his innocence.[81] Punishment following inquisitorial trial saw corporal punishment in many more elaborate forms. Torture occurred in the context of the trial, but torture could also be part of the punishment.[82]

A particularly detailed report is given by the 'De persecutione iudaeorum vratislavensium' on the case of Wrocław, 1453.[83] The tribunal assembled in the city centre under John of Capistrano, special legate with inquisitorial powers, and in the presence of the bishop and four town officials known as consuls. After interrogation and the eliciting of confessions, public punishment was arranged. The Jews were tied back on to a board and four torturers ('tortores') tore the flesh off their bones with iron pincers and put the pieces to burn in pans heated by coals. This continued until the whiteness of bones was revealed.[84] The Jews were then hung at the crossroads 'as was the custom', to instil terror in the hearts of Jews and Christians alike. John then had a pyre built and by its side set up a baptismal font flanked by priests. The choice presented to those city Jews, those who had not been found guilty of the alleged desecration: fire or baptism. Fearing the fire ('terrore ignis perterriti') twenty adolescents chose baptism; the rest, young and old, were burnt.

ORDER RESTORED: SYNAGOGUE INTO CHAPEL

Following the discovery of the *corpus delicti*, its containment and loving care were the next challenge faced by the community. The miraculous, bleeding host had to be contained in fine cloth, within a precious vessel, inside a cupboard or a *Sakramenthaus* located in a church or a specially built chapel. This stage of recovery and keeping of the miraculous host is evocatively, even mysteriously, depicted by Paolo Uccello in his *predella* scene, where a procession including a cleric dressed in a triple tiara passes through the night and into the protective space of an apse (see figure 16c, pp. 146–7). Many of the communities which saved and savoured their miraculous, abused host also witnessed the erection of a chapel dedicated to its cult. Such chapels were almost invariably on or near the site of the alleged abuse.

No full-blown host desecration accusation which resulted in vindication and violence was complete without the creation of an enduring sign to mark the events. The narrative of abuse and revenge thus most frequently ended with the growth of a cult following the working of miracles. Narrative closure was achieved as destruction of the Jews found its counterpart in the establishment of commemorative edifices and practices in the vacated space. The yawning gap in town centres following massacres and expulsions was filled not arbitrarily but knowingly with memorials of the events and vindicating symbols, which sanctioned violence by making it into a begetter of grace.[85] Ruins were not allowed to stand as traces of a still open past, but were assumed into new, polished structures. Jewish spaces, which had been seen as marginal, in or near unhealthy or unattractive parts of the town, were to become refulgent sites of great attraction.[86] As it was succinctly put in a description of the town of Lauda in the diocese of Würzburg, following the Rintfleisch massacres in the throes of which a Jew was accused of procuring a host from a Christian woman for money, the transition was complete and neat: 'The truly impious crime was revealed by a shining light . . . and the Jewish houses having been demolished, the current chapel was founded'; all this was recorded in a bull of the year 1300.[87]

Absence and loss were thus turned into presence and power and affirmation, from the very earliest case known to us, that of Paris, with the triumphant set of commemorative locations which the narrative spawned, parish church as well as *capella miraculorum*. In 1299 Bishop Otto of Paderborn provided an indulgence to encourage the construction of a chapel in Büren (Westphalia) following a host desecration accusation.[88] In 1337 a chaplaincy was endowed by a knight who may have been prompted by the recent Armleder accusations and violence: Albero Kloit supported a commemorative chapel under the supervision of a Cistercian abbess, Elisabeth of Hothausen, in whose hands the right of presentation to it was to be placed.[89] The laconic description of the case at Laa-an-der-Thaya in northern Austria in 1294 reports the construction of a chapel there, dedicated to the Corpus Christi, a dedication shared with others, such as the chapel at Schweidnitz (Silesia), built after the accusation in neighbouring Wrocław.[90]

Another common dedication for chapels built to commemorate host desecrations is that to the Holy Blood, the substance which always issued from the desecrated host and which was often absorbed into napkins and altar-cloths, thus creating additional relics from a single miraculous host. One of the earliest Holy Blood chapels must be that at Iphofen, a Franconian town ravaged by Rintfleisch, as described by Rudolph of Schlettstadt: 'And they considered faithfully how a church might be built there.'[91] The Holy Blood shrine at Pulkau drew people from near and far. The annalist of the neighbouring monastery of Zwettl emphasised its widespread attraction: 'it was visited and devoutly venerated not only by poor folk, but by all people of the surrounding lands.'[92]

Construction of these commemorative buildings depended on the fervour associated with the event and place. In Pulkau the host of 1338 came to be contained in a chapel consecrated in 1397; that of Deggendorf (1337) was consecrated in 1360.[93] Impressive in its swiftness is the response to the Poznań case of 1399. By 9 July 1401 Pope Boniface IX had granted an indulgence to the local Carmelites who guarded the chapel in answer to public demand: 'because of the miracles a great multitude of people was flowing to it.'[94] Commemoration was achieved through the building of a chapel dedicated to Corpus Christi, as described in a grant made to it by King Ladislaus II in 1406:

> a church with a monastery of the said order in praise of almighty God and in honour of the sacrosanct body of Our Lord Jesus Christ in the suburb of our city of Poznań, in the place where it is known that the same body of the Lord was once miraculously found.[95]

As in the case of Poznań a new miraculous host could prompt not only the building of a chapel but the creation of a new religious community. Following a claim that a Jew had buried a host in a latrine, and his discovery by the Bishop of Coimbra, a pious founder and his family endowed a hermitage and a church dedicated to Corpus Domini near the cathedral.[96]

After a host desecration accusation, the world was in better order; a mark of its 'improvement' was the safe-keeping and control of miraculous remains, and the creation of a new space devoted to veneration and commemoration. All these were signs of a community's pious engagement with crisis, its success in meeting the challenge to its resources and spiritual stamina. Host desecration narratives dwell with poignancy on the emergence of sacred spaces and applaud the replacement of ruins with celebratory edifices which provide the narrative with its resolution.[97]

In attempting to understand the narrative, we have found that it abounded in clichés which hinted at particles of knowledge about difference – of gender, of religion, of authority. Why so many? It is exactly the use of clichés, rather than the appeal to specificity and uniqueness in the tales, that made them so familiar and affecting. The unreliable wife, the prying neighbour, the ruthless but just knight, the shameful convert – all are stereotypical characters deployed in other narratives and other discursive frames. The familiarity lent by the deployment of clichés creates a 'common' frame, one validated by people's experience. It also invokes an 'intertextual' frame, one which derives from its interaction with other textual traditions.[98] In our tale *both* modes are used.

It is the very frequency and repetition of clichés that enhance their effect. A narrative which only occasionally invokes stereotypical characters may seem odd or old-fashioned, yet one which abounds in them or is made of *nothing else* is a powerful construct which draws the listener-reader in, as a participant in a game, a spotter of interrelated clichés which enjoy something akin to a 'relationship'. Umberto Eco described these relationships: 'because we sense dimly that the clichés are talking among themselves, celebrating a reunion . . . the extreme banality allows us to catch a glimpse of the sublime.'[99]

Once established and known, once cases were reported and recorded, the accusation of the host desecration received affirmation from the enactment of the narrative. Each telling added repetitions of the salient components, which emerged reassuringly familiar from contexts of practice and fields of knowledge. And yet the people who witnessed sequences of artifacts and actions which could fit into the narrative of the host desecration accusation were faced with the need to decide: Is this feasible? Is this real?[100] Is the suggested to be rejected or acted upon? That decision, that leap, happened in differing moods and circumstances; inasmuch as these were strongly affected by interest and predisposition, we might conclude that they were the products of a politics – a field of power and persuasion. We shall look at some such cases in chapter 5, but not before we pause to listen to some new voices in the assessment of the host desecration accusation.

Interjection: What did Jews Think of the Eucharist? According to Jews and According to Christians

What indeed did Jews think of the eucharist, the Christian sacrament around which a whole world of meaning and practice revolved? Evidence of the celebration of the sacrament was ubiquitous in late medieval communities, and growing in frequency and elaboration: the sound of bells calling to mass and at the elevation, the rush into churches to witness the elevation, processions to the sick with the host at which believers knelt and recited prayers, and from the early fourteenth century sumptuous eucharistic processions on Corpus Christi and its octave.[1] There was a virtual silence in Jewish writings on matters related to the eucharist before the mid-thirteenth century. Polemical energy was usually directed to the issues of Virgin birth, the Incarnation and the Trinity.[2] While these topics were debated with vigour, and the despised views and figures were systematically derided by Jewish writers, the eucharist received little attention. This is not wholly surprising; after all, even for Christians, transubstantiation became a requirement of faith only at the Fourth Lateran Council of 1215, and its liturgical and catechetical enhancement was realised through the efforts of bishops throughout the long thirteenth century.

It is only with the growth of the sacrament's prominence and with the precision of new Christian formulations on the nature of the eucharist that Jewish attention was drawn to it.[3] Two polemical writings of the thirteenth century which are closely interrelated addressed the conception of bread and wine as containing Christ's body. The *Book of Joseph the Zealot (Sefer Yosef ha-mekaneh)* was written soon after 1240 by the Parisian Rabbi Joseph Official, a scion of a great rabbinical family associated with the Archbishop of Sens, whose teacher Rabbi Yehiel of Paris defended the Jewish faith in the famous Paris Disputation of 1240.[4] Later in the century, somewhere in Germany, the *Old Book of Contention (Nizzahon Vetus)* was composed, a collection of quite outspoken and explicit polemical claims against Christianity.[5] This book follows the order of the books of the Pentateuch (Torah), and contends with Christian interpretations of passages from them.

In the *Book of Joseph the Zealot*, the eucharist is mentioned on only two occasions.[6] At the section on the Prophets the following case is made about the eucharist:

93

Makers of evil say: 'Why do you not believe in the sacrament?' And more 'Why do you not believe that the bread we eat is the salvation of our souls?' We answer them: 'As Hosea has prophesied: "They shall not pour libations of wine to the Lord; and they shall not please him with sacrifices" [Hosea 9: 4], because this sacrament is made with wine. And see also what follows: "Their bread shall be like mourners' bread; all who eat of it shall be defiled", and "polluted food" [Malachi 1: 7].' And another . . .[7] evil that they say is that the bread called 'pain' is for the salvation of their souls, since '[their bread] shall not come to the house of the Lord' [Hosea 9: 4], all this worship is a nonsense.[8]

Another version is:

> Damned are those who say of their sacrament that the blood poured is that of the hanged one, and the polluted bread which is called *oyta* is the flesh of the hanged himself, may their name be erased, since these are terrifying things . . . all that they do is a nonsense.[9]

These formulations provided a new type of argument: it was cast in biblical language, but addressed novel criticisms to Christian rituals. Earlier in the book Rabbi Joseph refers to the eucharist in passing when discussing the story of Melchizedek as a prefiguration of Christian clergy and tithe-giving. He opens with a question which had been presented to him by a priest, a 'tonsured one': ' "And Melchizedek king of Salem brought out bread and wine" (Genesis 14: 18), why did he bring out more than one thing? Because this is how the sacrament is made, of bread and wine, he said.'[10]

The author of *The Old Book of Contention* addresses the eucharist in a section of objections to the Gospels and Christianity which follows the book's rebuttal of Christian biblical exegesis book by book:

> It is written in their books in the account of Mark: 'When they were sitting on the eve of Passover, Jesus took the bread, broke it, recited a blessing, and gave it to his students, saying, Take this bread, for it is my body. In addition, he took the cup, recited a blessing, and gave it to all of them, and they all drank it. And he said unto them, This is my blood of the new testament' [Mark 14: 22–4]. In what sense was it his body that they ate and drank? Did he cut a piece off his body which he gave to them, or did his body first become bread and wine and he gave them pieces of it? Moreover, where did that body which they ate and drank descend? Did it go on its way separately or was it mixed up in the stomach with all the other food?[11]

So in the context of biblical polemical confrontation, the eucharist appears seldom and in a limited manner. It is only a whole century later that a new type of engagement with eucharistic claims will become evident. Perhaps in response to the growing visibility and centrality of the eucharist in Christian public rituals, or to the ability of host desecration accusations to wreak disaster, these later references to the eucharist appear in two contexts: rebuttals of accusations and attempts to find their misguided roots, and philosophical discussion of the theology of the eucharist. The awareness of 'new types' of accusations is reflected in the business of community leaders in Aragon in 1354. The confederation of the Kingdom's Jewish communities, which assembled to formulate clauses for a petition to the Pope and the King, commented that 'transgression in bread' by a single man could result in collective punishment, as a recent case in Seville had amply shown.[12]

In the early years of the fifteenth century (c.1401–2) Rabbi Yomtov Lippmann of Mühlhausen (1387–1423) referred to the eucharist in a context not much different from that of the *Old Book of Contention*.[13] His *Book of Contention (Sefer ha-nizzahon)* was probably produced following the Prague disputation of 1399, which saw him argue with the convert Peter (once Pesach) and which ended with the execution of eighty Jews.[14] The *Book of Contention* was structured according to the order of the books of the Bible, and divided into seven sections. His intervention on the eucharist appears in the book of Genesis. In the chapter which deals with the text 'For on the day that thou eatest thereof thou shalt surely die' (Genesis 2: 17), following the prohibition against eating from the Tree of Life, he develops a discourse on eating within which he claims,

> Furthermore they believe that he stands always in heaven in a bodily manner, and crucified for no purpose, and his qualities are null and void, and that he descends every day once in all the thousands of thousands of breads and in each of them he is whole. And how very unacceptable this is both to reason and to nature![15]

Rabbi Yomtov informs his readers of the Christian accusation voiced by his opponent Peter against the Jews in relation to the eucharist:

> he added falsehoods malignly and said that the dough which you knead and some of which you burn is done in derision of their god, and also that on Passover eve, which is the time of the Passion, you burn the bread. These are falsehoods with which he wished to alter all that is known since even from your cradles an offering is made to the priest from the dough that is used for the making of the *hallah*, a sacred contribution which must not be eaten (since it may have been kneaded by an impure woman) . . . and, therefore, we must burn it.[16]

Rabbi Yomtov here associates Christian accusations with a misinterpreta-
tion of two Jewish practices, that of setting aside a portion of all dough
to symbolise the tithe once offered to Temple priests, and that of
burning the remains of leavened bread in preparation for Passover.
Preparation for Passover also involved the cleansing of vessels in cauldrons of water at a rolling boil.[17] It is striking to note the similarity
between visual representation of cauldrons of abuse in the course of
host desecration and that of cauldrons for communal Jewish use in
preparation for Passover (see figure 11, p. 73).[18] The *Book of Contention*
both reflects the trauma of a recent host desecration massacre (1389)
and a deadly disputation (1399), and furnishes ready arguments for
future rebuttal and self-justification.[19]

The later fourteenth century, especially in Spain, saw the arrival of a
crop of polemical writings produced after the massacres and mass conversions of 1391.[20] Profiat Duran's (*c.*1345–*c.*1414) *The Reproach of the
Gentiles (Sefer kelimat ha-goyim)*, addresses the philosophical argument
about transubstantiation. Duran begins with the claim that wheaten
bread can shed its bread-like appearance and receive Christ's corporality
while retaining the accidents (the Aristotelian term denoting external
attributes) of bread alone. He further discusses the belief that Christ
moves from altar to altar while also remaining in heaven. Duran bases his
work on Peter Lombard's seminal but outmoded discussion, even using
his examples (such as the likening of the host to a mirror: both retain
their qualities even when broken into the smallest of pieces).[21] He is also
familiar with the tradition of casuistic insistence on 'what happens if a
mouse eats the host', rendered by him 'what if a polluted pig or mouse
eats and drinks Christ's body'.[22] The objections subtly refer to Christian
difficulties with these claims, and invoke the indignity which the claims
about substance without accidents inflict on the Christian God. Duran
attacks not only the theology of the sacrament's operation but its very
scriptural basis. The story of the Last Supper as told in Matthew 26: 18–
28 is not to be taken literally; indeed, claims Duran, Jesus never intended
it to be taken so when pronouncing 'This is my Body'. Rather, Jesus was
a parable teller (*mamshil meshalim*) and the passage is meant to induce
Christians to remember him, rather than to eat him.[23] In a striking and
ironic reversal Duran calls Christians to understand the gospel *spiritually*,
as Jesus meant them to, rather than to build a whole city on his words, a
city with few true men (Eccles. 9:14).[24]

The contemporary writer and community leader Hasdai Crescas
(*c.*1340–1412) argued more directly against Christian theology in his
Refutation of the Christians' Principles (Sefer bittul iqqarei ha-nozrim). Here in
ten chapters the articles of Christan faith are subject to a philosophical
demolition.[25] He reminds the reader that the rejection of the Trinity in
itself destroys arguments about the niceties of sacramental presence, for
'if the Trinity does not exist, and the Son does not exist, then he would

not be incarnated, nor appear on the altar'.[26] On the argument for transubstantiation, he presents a double attack: if Christ is not in the bread before consecration, and cannot be created there, he must have arrived there from a distance. Christ's 'travel' to the host after the consecration must last some time, and given the vast distance between heaven (where God dwells) and earth, this must be a long journey in time (and space). Furthermore, Christ's frequent descent would create many holes in the firmament as he passed, unless, of course, it is claimed that he is 'glorificado' – glorified – and thus has no real presence which might damage the celestial layers, but this then becomes unreasonable. For Crescas, eucharistic theology causes so many offences to reason that it simply cannot be sustained. He even makes a rather alarming reference to the perceived involvement of God and excrement, which Christians discussed, and for the good reason that the host is eaten and thus must turn into bodily refuse.[27]

Similarly vigorous is Profiat Duran's polemical epistle *Be Not like thy Fathers (Al tehi ka-avotecha)* (1396), written in response to the conversion of David Bonet Bongoron, the son of a prominent family of physicians from Perpignan, in which Duran disputes each of the articles of the Christian faith in parodic fashion. He questions a troubling aspect of the eucharistic edifice, the claim of clerical efficacy, that any priest can work the transformation at the altar:

> And this [transubstantiation] is said to happen after this choice utterance has come from the mouth of a priest – not a high priest, but any priest, great or small, wise man or fool, good or bad, god-fearing or sinner. For this special power inheres in this utterance, which was handed down from the mouth of the Messiah after he ate and drank with his prophets and wise men, his disciples and apostles.[28]

When discussing the impossibility of divergence between accident and the substance to which it belongs, Duran argues:

> But do not believe in the metaphysical principle that affirmation and negation cannot exist at the same time, further that transformation of an accident into essence is impossible . . . that the being of an accident depends on the object which carries it. For the body of the Messiah who sits on the throne in heaven does not move while that on the altar moves in every direction. The wafer is, before the utterance of the priest, nothing else than bread, but by this utterance the essence of the bread becomes an accidental quality and disappears entirely, and the previous accidental qualities become independent and enter the stomach of the priest who eats the wafer.[29]

In Spain the arguments about the relative cleanliness of the eucharistic sacrifice had developed as an issue for discussion, which was taken up in *The Touchstone* (*Even Bohan*) by the physician and polemicist Shemtov ibn-Shaprut (*c.*1340–*c.*1410),[30] and raised in the Tortosa Disputation (1413/14) as a point which clearly proved Christian superiority.[31] The tone of the Iberian arguments grew in acrimony as the fifteenth century unfolded and as anxiety about the penetration of Jewish converts into the Christian body grew fiercer. Such sophisticated philosophical discussion was not taken up by most Ashkenasi rabbis. Yet there were a few mediators of Iberian thought; among them R. Yomtov Lippmann, whom we have met, and Avigdor Kara, whom we will meet presently.[32]

   By the early fifteenth century, the terms of such Iberian debates were known to scholars such as Rabbi Yomtov, but he rejected them in favour of simple imagery, which was more accessible for popular use.[33] Nonetheless, by the later fifteenth century the acrimonious philosophical debate was having some impact on northern discussions. A collection of texts assembled *c.*1466 for the Jewish community of Sandomierz (150 km north-east of Krakow) contains an argument about the eucharist.[34] This Polish-Jewish text develops the types of argument we have already encountered in Iberian Jewish tracts from the later fourteenth century. It abounds in the philosophical terminology of Aristotelian categories and reaches the discussion of the eucharist through an engagement with the Trinity, by way of reflection on the ability of a single body to contain another (or two others):

> they also say that the substance is in two utterly different places – above in heaven and here below in the lowest of places in a little cake – so that if the cake is subdivided into the tiniest most insignificant parts, that large substance is thought to be in heaven in its plenitude and amplitude and in all its parts. And this is said to happen not in one cake but in a hundred thousand cakes daily, when priests merely pronounce that is his body and that is his blood, so that immediately the cakes change, and the substance of each returns to that imagined body in heaven wholly and according to its size.[35]

Whereas Jewish discussions of the eucharist ranged from exegetical opposition to visceral rejection of libellous accusations, Christian attitudes to Jewish beliefs varied too. As we will see, the accusation narrative might shift between the imputation to Jews of 'testing God' and ascription of evil intention in causing injury to Christ. But here too a plethora of contradictions and ambiguities arises, as it did in general discussions of Jewish intention in the theology of the twelfth and thirteenth centuries: to what extent could Jews sin in rejecting that in which they did not believe? Did not the ascription of evil intent to desecrate God also require some degree of Jewish faith in the eucharist? Theologians developed positions which often provided pegs for casuistic exertion, using Jews as extreme cases for the testing of hypotheses. In a discussion of 'Jews, Muslims and their servants' in the *Summa aurea* of the canonist Henry of Segusio, Cardinal Hostiensis (d. 1271), consideration for toleration is then followed by reasons for restriction.[36] Among these he recounts a nefarious practice:

> Because there are some, who having Christian wet-nurses, do not allow them to breast-feed their sons, after having received Christ's body, unless they had over the previous three days expressed their milk into the latrine: since they understand that Christ's body had been incorporated into the wet-nurse's body and would descend to evacuation. But it is wrong to believe so.[37]

Hostiensis raises here a problem which vexed Christian theologians, as to the exact nature of what was experienced by the host in digestion and disposal from the body.[38] Jews were simultaneously seen as believers in Christ's presence in the host and inflicters of harm upon that presence, to the detriment of Christians.[39] This is a contradictory view which will inform many later tales about Jews and the eucharist: in inflicting pain on the host, the Jews are taken to believe that it is indeed a worthy recipient of injury. From the Jewish perspective, as we have seen, there is total rejection of the possibility of divine presence in the eucharist, and the host is treated more as a perplexing joke.

Occasions of polemical discussion with Jews were often used as the setting for strong rebuttals of 'error' and a restatement of orthodox positions by didactic writers. Thus, in St Bonaventure's *Collations on the Ten Commandments* (1221–74), the Jewish understanding of the second commandment provided an occasion for the affirmation of sacramental presence. The Jew is made to raise three objections to the way in which Christians fulfil the commandment's three parts: belief in one God alone, the prohibition against graven images, and against the use of any other likeness than God.[40] In dealing wth the third part:

> Of the third point of opposition, which they abhor most of all, that is of Christ's body, this was the most secret, but is now made open to all. Once upon a time some said, God is there only in sign; but it is to be understood that at the pronouncement of the words of the priest and at the intention of the speaker, the substance of bread is immediately converted into the real body of Christ, which is united in soul with the Divinity, and this is just so. But the Jew says: how can this be? I say, that He who can separate substance from accidents, can cause that the substance which is under alien accidents should not appear to our senses. Thus I say that we venerate the true body of Christ and God three in one; and in that the power of God, his force, wisdom and goodness are manifested.[41]

Bonaventure's answer to the third objection is a heated defence of the eucharist.

An anonymous thirteenth-century tract against Jews from Uncastillo (Navarre) collegiate church, known as *Qui captum*, adopts a similar dialogic stance. Addressing a Jew, the author argues:

> and you mock and reproach us for making a sacrifice of bread and wine and for saying that it is Christ's body, while you claim that it is impossible that the substance of Christ's flesh and blood be present there, and I prove to you in your law that it can be transformed into the substance of flesh and blood and I shall prove to you in your law that the substance of fire turned into the substance of water, and then returned to the substance of fire, and I say to you that when the children of Israel were led from Babylon to Jerusalem the priest Nehemiah came to a well full of ashes and fire . . . and found there fresh water.
>
> O, miserable Hebrew, just as the substance of water turned into the substance of fire so it is possible to convert the substance of bread and wine into that of Jesus Christ's flesh and blood.[42]

In the following century the great polemicist and biblical exegete Nicholas of Lyra (*c*.1270–*c*.1349) rebutted Jewish biblical exegesis with a multitude of Christian readings which authenticated eucharistic claims. In his tract against a Jew's attack on the Gospel of Matthew, written by 1334, he countered the Jews' claim:

> Christians eat Christ's body, which is horrible. It should be said that this would have been true had it been received in its actual species, but to receive it under the species of bread is not horrible, but rather sweet and venerable. It is not Christ himself or his body that is broken, that is injured by the thorns or lacerated in such an eating, as the Jews imagine it to be; only the species of bread is broken and impaired.[43]

Profiat Duran was to raise similar objections a few years later, as had the Cathars decades earlier in southern France and as did the English Lollards decades later.[44]

A painful context of eucharistic rejection around the abhorrence of eating Christ's body is recorded in the French royal chronicle under the year 1307. A Parisian convert from Judaism by the name of Perotus was brought before the inquisition by the Bishop of Paris for returning to his original faith. At the instigation of 'one of his brothers, Moses' (may this not just mean another Jew?) he was dipped in hot water and circumcised, and he claimed that his conversion had been a pack of lies expressed out of hatred for his brother, who refused to pay back a debt. The Bishop of Paris decided to adhere to Perotus's previous confession of faith and to impose a prison sentence on him as on a Christian. When in prison he claimed that he was not Christian, but a Jew by the name of Samoe, and that Christians eat their God; he also asked that when he died, he be buried as a Jew.[45]

Most of the texts we have just encountered emanate from scholarly attempts at refutation, which are ambivalent in their motivation and multivalent in their rhetorical impact. In them Christians ascribe to Jews views which are misguided and abhorrent, and yet ones which we know to have been current in Christian discussion and often in popular objection. Jewish views, on the other hand, range from indignant rejection of accusations made about them in connection with the eucharist to a philosophical rebuttal which exposes the intellectual weakness of eucharistic claims. The two sets of discussions sometimes refer openly to each other, as in the case of Nicholas of Lyra and Profiat Duran. Traces of ideas emanating from less formalised endeavours and from the context of daily encounters are fewer and harder to interpret.

How did Jews react to the evolving accusation of host desecration? As we have seen the lament on the Rintfleisch massacres 'I cry for the day's tribulation' ('Evke li-kshe yom') describes the Christian accusation as a plot:

In the bloody, foul disgusting bread
They contrived their plot, adding treachery to it.
Saying to the chosen of the holy and exalted people
'You have stolen [our] god (who walks in darkness).

And you crushed him fine, and betrayed him,
in a mortar, so as to gather his blood.
And you cut him and divided and hung him on a hanger,
and sent pieces to your despised and confused camps.'[46]

Rabbi Joshua son of Rabbi Menachem composed a poem of forty-three quatrains to form his lament on the Rintfleisch massacres, the 'Lord, loyal king' ('El melech ne'eman'). The final line of each stanza contains the word 'fire' (*esh*), and interacts with many other images of burning and immolation: the Sacrifice of Isaac (lines 19–20), the baking of foods for holy offerings (lines 11–16), and above all, their painful parallel in the burning of Jews. Stanza 10 describes the Christian conspiracy which caused the eruption of violence:

They pinned on me a lie in their treachery, as they
Break up this foreign God to undermine their customs
As if in my heart I had aspired to destroy the bloody bread.
It is polluted and would be burnt by fire.
It is never to be found explicitly, neither in scripture nor in any
    sensible mind.[47]

An earlier lament, after a massacre in Erfurt in 1221, may also have made a passing and very early reference to Christian eucharistic views, although not in relation to a host desecration accusation. The author, Rabbi Shlomo son of Abraham, opens the poem with reference to persecution at the hand of Christians. He relates the Christian sense of superiority to their violence against Jews. Christian potency is related to Christian faith, which is here mocked:

> Speaking falsehoods you ate the man;
> They ate me, flesh and blood;
> Yet they alone inherited the earth.
>   If it so please the king let him order their destruction.[48]

The fifteenth century saw the elaboration of popular disputation in some vernacular texts. These include the urban poems of Hans Folz of Nuremberg in the 1490s, and the report on the host desecration accusation of Wrocław, rich in reported speech by Jews and their Christian accomplices. In Folz's verse staging of a discussion between *Christ und Jude* the Jew opens with the age-old objection about the size of Christ's body which was repeatedly expressed by doubting Christians:

> So said the Jew: 'Tell me one more thing.
> If Jesus is indeed also a man,
> How is it that his body is divided so much
> In the form of bread and unblemished,
> As is the case many times a day?
> No man could be so much divided.'[49]

To this apparent familiarity with Christian ideas displayed by the Jew, the Christian retorts with the mockery of a seemingly equally unreasonable claim made by Jews: that the prophets Enoch and Elijah attend every Jewish circumcision ceremony. How could they be everywhere, summoned at each ritual?[50] This is an argument familiar from the late fourteenth century: Rabbi Yomtov Lippmann mentioned it in his *Book of Contention*. Placed here in the mouths of lay discussants, Jew and Christian, and in the vernacular, are fragments of exchanges which might have taken place in the shared spheres of neighbourhood and business. In a record of an inquiry which took place in Zurich in 1420, a witness describes a discussion of religious difference in town streets. A Jewish woman was asked by a few assembled Christians: 'Do you not have a mass?'[51]

Scholars or neighbours, in late medieval towns Jews and Christians were more aware of claims about their difference than ever before. Ivan Marcus has suggested that ceremonies, such as the initiation of

Jewish boys to the study of Torah, may have incorporated elements of Christian ritual, in form and imagery, but also that these were eventually discarded from the fear that any emulation might be interpreted as satirical mockery.[52] The host desecration accusation heightened the stakes and the tensions around eucharistic moments in the culture. The narrative offered a role to every Christian, man or woman, child or adult, layperson or priest. It was particularly empowering to those who could make it *work* in elaborating claims to virtue and authority in the contested streets of late medieval towns.

5

Making the Narrative Work

A new tale was being told about Jews in late medieval Europe. In some places it inspired actions by those who saw the narrative enacted in the world around them; for others it simply became part of local knowledge and accepted lore. Not all believed in it, nor were all willing to perform it. The narrative's strength was derived from its deep embeddedness in central issues of Christian self-understanding. It was reinforced by lore about sacraments, and ideas about Jews, nuggets of knowledge which contributed to a 'repertory of tales for future use'.[1] Yet despite this rootedness, there were those who questioned the narrative, resisted it. It is difficult to gauge the degree of resistance and doubt involved, as chronicles celebrated only the cases in which the narrative swept all before it, and ended in spectacular and noteworthy violence. To assess the true value of narratives, their power to motivate and structure action, it is also necessary to appreciate the contingent nature of every telling, the dependence of the narrative on the actions of agents, carriers, bearers, makers, realisers of its powers.

The tale's force derived from the rich world of eucharistic knowledge and myth which was being imparted at the very heart of the religious culture, and was bolstered by an ongoing interaction between eucharistic claims and the realities or appearances which most people apprehended in and around it. It also derived from the strange vulnerability of Jews: even when legally protected (and their status was very clearly defined in those very imperial lands in which most accusations took place), their lives were always liable to be thrust into the heart of the anti-Jewish discourse which turned them from neighbours, friends and business partners into polluting, bestial and life-denying creatures whose very existence depended on a cost or a loss to non-Jews. The host desecration tale was a narrative produced within this frame and the unfolding of a host desecration accusation was the creation of a *mise-en-scène* for the enactment of gestures and the making of utterances learnt and legitimated within it. Versed in these parts, women, priests, children, dukes and Christian knights all had compelling roles to play.

The intimate affinities between the host desecration tale and representations of everyday life within powerful discourses of the day could add coherence and interest to enterprises related to it. The tale was claimed by later writers for periods before its inception and currency.

Thus Abbot Aymeric of Peyrac (1377–1406), chronicler of Moissac Abbey, told of a case which had occurred under Abbot Durand of Bredon (1048–72), and which involved the purchase of a host by a Jewess from a Christian woman at Easter ('corpus Domini cum in die sancto Pasche a quadam judea emitur de una maleffici christiana').[2] The culprits were discovered and punished together with most of the Jews of Moissac, while some Jews chose to convert. This is a full telling of the host desecration accusation of the late Middle Ages in all but the casting of a female Jewish protagonist, but it is said to have occurred under a Count Alphonse, and no Count of Provence was so named before 1189.[3] This perfect host desecration tale is suspicious. Aymeric of Peyrac may have embroidered upon the expulsion of Jews in 1271 with elements of the desecration tale, situating the amalgamated account in the eleventh century, in the hope of providing the monastery's sacred host with an attractive myth about its provenance, suited to the fourteenth century.

The possible range of doubt and official resistance to the narrative can be imagined and plausibly reconstructed through attitudes which some priests and bishops brought to bear in playing down enthusiasm for the accusations. As we have seen, a monk-scholar, some bishops, an emperor and a duke transmitted the criticism, while local priests, townsmen and others, such as a cathedral canon, supported it. Evidence of resistance to the tale is very elusive and context bound, but let us examine some clues. We have already encountered the reaction of a city like Regensburg, a heavily governed imperial jewel, with a flourishing Jewish community and a strong grip on law and order, which was able to withstand the crowds at its gates in 1298. Its citizens desired to keep their town's order and peace, and to leave vengeance to God. Yet, while Regensburg, known as 'Jew-loving', could resist the violence of a crowd again and again,[4] for the sake of its own peace and property,[5] Würzburg, the seat of the Prince-Bishop, was unable to withstand the crowd, and Regensburg itself later relented in the face of accusations against Jews, ending in the expulsion of 1518.[6] A high degree of political awareness and control, through a system of guilds which reached craftsmen as well as their apprentices and journeymen, functioned fairly well in Regensburg. But most Franconian and Bavarian towns were different, like Röttingen or Wertheim on the Tauber, lively centres of trade with many active Jews. Bishops and emperors, protectors of Jews through the system of *Landesfriede* and attendant fines, were far away from the tension and provocation which close contacts between Jews and Christians could create. Little Röttingen, the corn-trading centre of the Tauber valley, thus became the rallying point for regional massacres twice over. Some accusations could end in death for a few, conversion or banishment for others. The spectacular and archetypal Paris case thus resulted in the burning of the Jew sometimes called Jonathan, and in the conversion of his wife and children and others. Among the 'others' may have been one Jew, newly named John, whose report formed the basis of the version of the Paris tale recounted by the monastic chronicler of Ghent, John of Thilrode.[7]

While the power of the host desecration narrative to move to action and to lend shape to unfolding events has been emphasised in our attention to its details and structure, this power was nonetheless far from being constant or certain. If the process by which the narrative animated action is related to its ability to seem apt and fitting, then contrasting narratives could counter, diminish or unsettle each other. That is to say that the narrative possessed the power *in potential*, which could be activated and animated, but which might also be made to seem inappropriate, unfitting or ill-judged. There is an inescapable problem in trying to evaluate the type of narrative encounters and clashes which might silence or disable the telling of a host desecration tale; chronicles, after all, recount the violence which occurred, not that which was averted, the killing rather than the saving. Only occasionally and obliquely are we able to glimpse the testimony of a host desecration accusation and action which did not quite achieve full dramatisation, which were halted in their tracks. An extraordinary document of 1469, an *Urfehde* (peace bond) copied out in German, in both Latin letters and Hebrew ones, attested that David, Saul and Abraham, Jewish subjects of Count William of Wertheim, who resided in Neustadt (Hesse), were bound over for having been offered the holy sacrament for sale by a woman, Notzin (figure 14). This peaceful resolution conceals the full extent of the events: Did they not buy it and inform on Notzin? Did they pay a high fine? Here the Jews suspected of being offered the host were not killed, but bound over. The dangerous proximity of Christian woman, host and Jew did not result here in the telling of a host desecration tale, as it had done elsewhere; the case ended without bloodshed, although we do not know the end met by Notzin.[8]

Such cases show that not all suspicion of intention to desecrate the host (of which in most cases the purchase of the host seemed to be a sufficient indication) ended in mass violence or even in official judicial treatment in torture and execution. An entry in the court book of the Alsatian town of Schlettstadt for the year 1409 notes that a rumour of the theft of a host and even the presence of such a host in a Jewish house could be traced back to a Christian culprit without inculpating the Jews. In this case the legal record imputed bad intent to the Christian thief 'who roguishly carried a host into the house of Jews', and failed to impute ill intent to the Jews.[9] In about 1460, Moses, a venerable teacher from the town of Rothenburg, converted to Christianity with twenty-four of his disciples and their families. What had begun as an attempt to test the host ended in conversion under the impression of its ensuing miracles. A letter by the vicar, Philip, who had baptised the group, issued on

14. *Urfehde* (peace bond), *c.*1490. Wertheim, Hesse.

behalf of one of the converted disciples, Peter (and his wife and two daughters), recommended the now Christian family to the charity of believers who might meet them on their wanderings. The parish priest of Rothenburg deemed it better to help the culprits convert than punish and destroy them. This letter claims that after having been proven wrong in doubting Christian truth, and after the miracles of bleeding had been reversed, the Jews approached the local priest and told their tale ('Illo facto ipsorum tres abeuntes ibant ad sacerdotem sibique singula gesta revelabant'). It is hard to determine the causes which would have led to the conversion of an extended group of families and their rabbi. But if there had been a rumour which linked the Jews to the handling of a host, clearly their sponsor preferred to launch them on a Christian life rather than have them punished. Peter and his family travelled far in seeking that new beginning; the letter has survived as a copy in the town book of Osnabrück! A 'happy ending' indeed.[10]

In the case of other accusations, we encounter even more comprehensive dismissals of the rumour. In 1301 the Jews of Barcelona were accused of having murdered a little boy: the attempt to frame them was foiled and the conspiracy exposed.[11] In 1329 an accusation of child murder was made in the Duchy of Savoy against a Jew, Acelinus of Tresserve, and a Christian, Jacques of Aiguebelle. They were said to have kidnapped several Christian boys and made a Passover dish (*aharace*) from their blood and flesh.[12] The Christian cooperated with the authorities and the Jew confessed under torture. But a Jewish defence was mounted, based on the papal bulls of Innocent IV and Gregory X denying the Jewish ritual use of Christian blood. The confessions were also shown to be invalid, both on theological and judicial grounds. A letter from the Chancery of the Duke of Savoy, Edward the Liberal (1284–1329), summarises the case and deems it to be a misguided attempt at inculpation, to be thrown out of court.[13]

The accusation of host desecration licensed violence against Jews and the promotion of sites of piety through a narrative dense in references to common experience, religious teaching and political and administrative conventions. This was also a narrative which offered ample space for imagining transgressive behaviour and the airing of doubt and discomfort. It was the very intimacy and proximity of Jewish social life and liturgical practice to those of Christians that made the narrative so potent, rendered it so easy to use. It offered a blueprint for action, in the naming of abuse, discovery of miracles, recovery of the host and punishment of the Jews. But as powerful and compelling as it was, as false and necessary to the self-vindication of the eucharist, this was a narrative which required actuation. It did not *make* action, but structured energies embedded within political and religious structures, in the negotiations of social and political life. A charismatic preacher, the heat of crusade, the dynastic struggles between father and son, the infectious power of regional unrule – these are the contexts within which the narrative of host desecration by Jews unfolded to a deadly conclusion. But we will also witness occasions when the story did not take hold, in regions where identity was realised through means other than collective violent action – through law, as in Venice where councils controlled the streets and preachers failed to convince or impress with their claims about the necessity of violent revenge. In such regions Jews remained, for a while at least, just strange neighbours, not the target of homicidal piety.

The doubts expressed by Ambrose of Heiligenkreuz, together with the following examples of host desecration and other accusations which failed to unfold fully, suggest that the narrative's success depended greatly on context and on the forces which supported it and attempted to promote its persuasive effects. The host desecration tale was an accusation in the making which, despite its compelling truth-value, required a degree of active support with polemical energy for its unfolding. This is demonstrated not only by the failure of accusations, but even more so in the workings of some spectacular collective narrations. The narration could also remain unresolved and contested, bitterly and without closure, as the following cluster of Aragonese/Catalan cases shows.

CATALONIA-ARAGON: DYNASTIC TENSIONS AND HOST DESECRATION ACCUSATIONS

A string of host desecration accusations was brought against Jews in quick succession in some towns of the Crown of Aragon in the space of some sixteen years in the second half of the fourteenth century. These were not related by parish priests, nor instigated by angry knights, and the violence was perpetrated by no unruly mob. These were accusations initiated on the basis of flimsy evidence by the Infant, the crown prince John, in two cases (Barcelona 1367, Huesca 1377), and by a count, the King's nephew, in another (Lérida 1383), in their capacity as provincial governors. In the first two cases a family drama unfolded in parallel with the cruel accusations, a drama which tested the King's policy towards the Crown's Jews against the zeal of a restive heir keen to follow Dominican advisers and independent policies.[14] Relations between King Peter III (the Ceremonious) of Catalonia-Aragon and his son John (the Infant) had deteriorated particularly after the death of John's mother, Eleanor of Sicily, in 1375 and the King's subsequent remarriage.[15] The Infant's attempt to assert autonomy in areas under his rule was tested in the host desecration accusations brought by him against his father's Jews (map 4).

The sources from which these events can be reconstructed are treasury notes related to the property seized from the Jews accused, as well as a rich set of epistolary exchanges between father and son, father and nephew, from royal court to provincial town. These accusations

4. Catalonia–Aragon in the fourteenth century.

display several of the components of those already encountered in other parts of Europe, bad Christians and collective Jewish intent, but interestingly an accusation of active abuse, in the form of piercing, laceration, boiling or baking, is never fully articulated. It is also possible that the case of 1367 was not the first to be brought against Aragonese Jews. Among the list of abuses which the Jewish confederation of Aragon, created in 1354, determined to pursue by petition to pope and king was the habit of collective punishment for individual crimes such as 'transgression in bread done by one and the wrath fell on all' recently experienced in Seville.[16] The existence of the host desecration accusation was thus known, but it found its first activator in Catalonia and Aragon in the Infant John.[17]

The case of Barcelona unfolded following the confession of a thief, P(ere) Fuster of Morella, before the Infant and his council. Fuster and an accomplice had stolen a silver pyx (*custodia*) with seven hosts in a pristine linen cloth from the church of St Mary of Muntblanc (a town some fifty miles west of Barcelona, on the road to Lérida) and sold five of them to a Jew.[18] The confession formed the basis for the institution of a tribunal which included the Infant's advisers, jurists (Berenger d'Abella, Jacme des Monell, Berenger de Relal, P(edro) ça Costa, Micer des Pug) and citizens of Barcelona (Romeu de Busquets and Fracesch de Castalri). Under interrogation the thief divulged that he had sold the pyx for 12 florins, and the five hosts for 60 shillings. As he could not name the Jewish purchaser, the thief was brought to St James's square from which he could observe many Jews passing and identify the culprit. In this medieval version of an identity parade Fuster did recognise the Jew in question, one Provençal de Piera, who was brought to the royal palace in the town. Having achieved all this the Infant wrote to inform his father of the trial, adding that he had taken care to warn the Christian not to incriminate 'even a Jew' falsely ('no le volgues dampnar, car si bens seren juheus sin seria dampnat, si acusava negu, qui colpa noy hagues').

The trial then moved on to the interrogation of the recently arrested Jew, Provençal, who spoke after having been tortured 'a bit' ('apres que feu un poch turmentat'). He confessed to having sold the hosts and pyx to another Jew, Struch Biona, at the price of 70 shillings for the hosts (10 shillings profit) and 13 florins for the pyx (1 florin in profit). The Infant then ordered the interrogation of Struch Biona, who first denied and then confessed after torture to having given the hosts to a Jew, Salamo Sescalta, the community secretary. Salamo was seized and questioned with a variety of tortures ('fiu molt e en diverses maneres turmentar lo dit Juheu'), but he denied the accusation and died of his torments. This turn of events prompted Struch to claim that his accusation against Salamo had been a lie. However, on the basis of Provençal's first confession, Provençal and Struch were both sentenced to death, together with another accomplice, Mosse Badroch Gallart, to whom they were said to have sold some of the hosts. So two Jews and the Christian Fuster were submitted to 'justicia corporal', and were tortured and burnt, whereas Mosse was only burnt. Among the Jews originally arrested had been the community leader and scholar Hasdai Crescas, who had also written a refutation of Christian theology.[19]

The Infant intended to leave no loose ends in this affair, so he sent a messenger to find and arrest Fuster's accomplice, Guillem Terraça, who was then known to be serving on a galley in France. When he was found his confession agreed in all details with that of Fuster ('es acorda en totes coses ab lo dit del dit P. Fuster'),[20] except in the age of the Jew to whom the host had been sold: whereas Provençal had a white beard, Terraça claimed the Jew to have been about forty years old and with a black beard. Terraça died in prison, but his body was also burnt. The profits generated for the Infant's coffers by this trial were noted in June

1367 in the treasury rolls recording the payments by relatives of the accused towards the 'ransoming' of the property of their unfortunate kinfolk, required of Bonadona, Struch's wife, and Ascaro, Mosse Gallart's wife, both widows-to-be, during their husbands' incarceration.[21]

The only flaw in this masterpiece of criminal investigation was that the hosts in question were never recovered. The object which justified in its holiness the whole effort, indeed the very category of blasphemy and sacrilege under which the offences were tried, could not be accorded the suitable treatment and care it would have deserved. When the Infant left Barcelona he committed the task of searching for the hosts to two jurists. Another open question was that of further complicity. If three Jews were involved in a sequence of purchases, why not more? It is perhaps this thought which ultimately prompted a royal mandate on 30 November 1367 to seize all Jews for up to three days and see whether they would divulge further information. Men and women, young and old, were duly arrested but to no avail; they were released 'because they were not found guilty', and royal protection over them was renewed.[22]

A decade later in Huesca the tension between father and son became even more evident, and is captured in an extended correspondence between the two. The Jewish community of Huesca was already in decline when the host theft accusation was brought against it. Suffering from heavy taxation in Aragon, many Jews had migrated to the neighbouring territories of Castile. The Infant John arrived in Huesca as Duke of Girona and Governor-General in November 1377.[23] The accusation again followed a confession by a Christian thief, Ramon Rafart. This ruffian claimed to have sold hosts to a Jew, Haim Andalet, who confessed under torture to having sold them to a couple, Jaffuda and Manases Abmabez. Haim Andalet swiftly left town with his family and a mandate of 1 December directed the Infant's officials to seek and arrest them.[24] On the same day an order was issued for the arrest of a woman of ill fame, to whom Rafart the thief had made a gift of two of the three rings with which the Jew had paid him for the hosts.[25] Some confusion arises from the testimony as to the woman's identity: was she Constança or, as a letter of 6 December named her, Johanela?[26]

Concurrently, other initiatives were taken aimed at promoting the Christian faith among Jews in the heat of the accusation. A letter of 3 December was addressed to all royal officials and granted the Infant's support to the convert Arnau d'Estadella, an expert in Old and New Testament and organiser of disputations. He directed the bureaucrats to facilitate Arnau's work in every way and force Jews to congregate wherever his teaching was to be provided, with the help of local Dominican priors and Franciscan lectors.[27]

A series of letters now appears in which the son informed his father of his actions and justified them. On 7 December, before leaving for his winter stay in Saragossa, the Infant wrote with a request for permission to continue his trial, asking his father not to intervene, and to allow it to reach its conclusion.[28] He wrote again upon arrival in Saragossa despite having already approved the Jews' sentence before leaving Huesca. He reported to his father the killing by quartering of the Christian thief Ramon Rafart, and the burning of the Jewish couple, the Jewish man's genitals having been severed and hung up. The trial had clearly moved quickly, producing three capital punishments in three weeks. Under terrible torture the victims had confessed that they had sold the hosts to Salomo de Quatorze, Mosse Ambinax and Abraha Abolbaça, who went on to desecrate them. The first accused managed to flee from Huesca, but the remaining two were brought to Saragossa, where on 11 December the Infant presided over the trial, with the Archbishop of Saragossa, the Bishop of Taraçona, the Justiciar of Aragon, jurists and nobles. In his letter to his father the King, the Infant clearly stated that on this occasion the defendants were allowed to mount a defence. Preoccupied by the news from Huesca, the King also sent word to the Infant reminding him of Barcelona, a case which he claims to have been ill founded ('trobam que no era vera'), and recommended that the Jews of Huesca be assembled and asked to answer the accusations so that the culpable be punished and the innocent be freed.[29] He also decided to send his own observer, the Procurator-Fiscal of Aragon, Bernat Planes.[30] But events were moving fast and before the arrival of the letter on 15 December, the friends and relatives of Salomo de Quatorze were being arrested: his father, his son and five other Jews of Huesca.

At his father's royal request the Infant was now required to assemble the documentary evidence and send it for central scrutiny; the tension between father and son was mounting. The Infant wrote to the notary H. Guillem of Alcolea with a request for the documentation on 21 December 1377. Whereas the outrageous case of Barcelona had been a new but suggestive possibility, which was ultimately left unproven, the Huesca accusation was a wilful repetition. Indeed, on 8 January 1378 the King directed that all accusations in the Huesca case be dropped since they had been made out of 'hatred and ill will'.[31]

Clearly, every criticism of the case was a potential rebuff to an erring son. The royal council was fully engaged in examining the Infant's actions in Huesca. Rafart was found to have confessed under duress, as were the Jewish couple who named the three currently accused. The only truth in the matter was that a pyx (and hosts) worth some 5–6 florins had been stolen.[32] The King suspended all proceedings until the Vicar-General arrived in Barcelona, and he enlisted the services of the great Aragonese nobleman Dom Lope de Guerrea in his attempt to restrain the Infant.[33] The King was clearly afraid that such victimisation would result in Jewish migration. His frustration was colourfully expressed in the letter of 26 January 1378: 'We, who have striven to

preserve them in our lands and kingdoms in times of war and tribulation, can and should indeed do so in times of peace and well-being.'[34]

Another advantage for the defence arose when the King received a
letter from the Jews of Huesca claiming that some trial documents had
been suppressed, namely, a declaration by Rafart to his confessor in
which the chief witness exculpated the Jews. The petitioners suggested
that the original be shown to the King, who had asked to examine all the
relevant documentation.[35] Yet on 4 February a mandate for the arrest of
Haim Andalet (Royo) as an accomplice in stealing the hosts with Rafart
was issued. Jewish efforts to stop the trial continued into February 1378,
putting the whole premise of the trial into doubt with the claim that the
Jewish couple had no knowledge of the events, had never touched any
hosts and did not know what they were.[36]

The trial was reaching an impasse, with punishments already executed
and some of the accused and their relatives still imprisoned; with clear
royal/parental wrath and much embarrassment in the Infant's circles.
The King could not fully alienate or disempower his son, so he allowed
the investigation to proceed and required that the accused be allowed a
proper defence ('justes y llegitimes defenses'). The King also attached
two of his own men to the court in a supervisory role, Lope de Guerrea
and Miguel de Capella.[37] It was a difficult time for such a distraction at
court, as a campaign to Sardinia and Sicily was being prepared and the
King's most reliable officials were needed close at hand. Indeed Miguel
de Capella, the Auditor of the King's Court, was called back on 3 May.[38]
Soon afterwards the Infant fell ill, his wife died and the King freed the
Jews under his protection.

The Huesca case demonstrates a more determined commitment on
the part of the Infant to pursue his policy and a more suspicious royal-
paternal attitude, as well as a more contorted set of accusations and
recriminations. Whereas royal policy focused on the peaceful existence
of the Jews, the King was not always able to enforce protection. Even the
very weak case of Barcelona had claimed three victims; in Huesca
months of suffering and three victims, a Christian and two Jews, were the
toll, as well as numerous displaced people obliged to leave their homes
and families.

The third case of a host desecration accusation involved not the
Infant but his cousin, the Count of Urgel, in his position of provincial
governor (similar to that of the Infant). In Lérida in the spring of 1383
the Jewish community was much more able to act quickly in its own
defence. Following the theft of a monstrance from the church of
Castelló de Farfanya, two Jews, Sentou Levi and Moses Xicatella, were
accused of having purchased it. A royal missive of 26 September to the
Count of Urgel directed him to drop all charges since the accusation
had been motivated by 'false treatments and measures by people of ill
will'. He requested that these be found and punished for bringing false

accusations.[39] On this occasion the Jews of Lérida put forward the claim that the accusation was unreasonable: 'according to their precept and beliefs the said Sentou is not guilty of the deed, for various reasons, according to which, such acts cannot and should not reasonably occur to a Jew.'[40] We encounter here the entry of a Jewish voice into the trial narrative, a rare occurrence, as most Jewish voices recorded in trial reports come from confessions extracted under torture. This entry ruptures the *chronotopos* which the accusation narrative attempts to evoke, the particular blending of time and space, which displaces the Jew as a passive figure, lacking in agency, following his arrest and in anticipation of his annihilation.[41] The Jewish protest against the very assumptions on which the accusation was based ruptured the process of separation which placed the Jews outside the text's production; here, astonishingly, the Jews' voice is allowed in by the logic of judicial documentation. Wiser after two recent host desecration accusations, the Jews were able to gain authority by applying directly to the King and questioning the hitherto unquestioned.

The host desecration accusations of Catalonia-Aragon display some peculiar features. They arise from the initiatives and nurturing of the very greatest men, and they concentrate on trade in stolen hosts procured from criminal Christians. They do not dwell on the details of abuse nor develop into mass violence. They are highly controlled show trials, and were considered to be such by the King and his officials. They caused deaths but seem to have little other resonance. They drew their power to convince only from the artificial setting of the Infant or the comital court and thus lost their power when the initiators lost interest or were forced to withdraw. The fifteenth century would see a number of cases which were to end quite differently, like that at Segovia in 1411–12.[42]

VENETIAN DOUBT: CRETE 1451–2

As we have seen, an accusation that was aborted could nonetheless cause a great deal of pain and suffering. An interesting case occurred in Venetian Crete in 1451–2. It began with an accusation of host desecration, of which we have no details, but which was brought against the Jewish community by a (Greek) priest's wife, Ursa.[43] Venetian law applied to the Jews of Crete and to religious crimes, so the case was brought before the investigating judge Antonio Gradenigo, who began proceedings in the Republic's highest court, the Avogaria di Comun. An order then arrived from Venice on 26 January 1452 for the Duke of Crete, Brando Balbi, ordering the arrest of nine of the Jewish community's notables. After thirty-five days of imprisonment they were shipped to Venice, in chains, for trial. Forty-nine days later seven of the men arrived in Venice alive for the incarceration and torture which accompanied the investigation. On 15 July a judge and the representative of the Avogaria recommended that the Grand Council condemn the Jews, but the eloquence of Antonio Diedo, Nicolò di Bernardi and Claudio Bollani swayed the Council. The vote which followed produced a different verdict: 220 votes favoured the Jews, 130 condemned them and 80 abstained ('non sinceri'). On 9 August the Jews were freed to make their way back to the island.[44]

Unhappy with the result, the investigator Gradenigo accused some council members of corruption: that they had received bribes in return for a favourable vote, so another trial followed. The Jews were reaccused and on 26 May 1454 the Grand Council deliberated the case and voted: of 310 members 143 condemned the Jews, 95 favoured them and 72 abstained. This small showing did not suffice, so another vote was taken on 7 June 1454 and the 506 members present voted: 261 in favour of the Jews, 120 against them and 125 'non sinceri' who were added to the majority that favoured acquittal.[45]

HERESY, CRUSADE AND THE LOGIC OF EXPULSION: AUSTRIA, 1421

In Austria in 1421 the host desecration met – with dire consequences – the passion of crusade and the fear of the challenge of heresy. As German armies marched eastwards to Bohemia to engage in battle with Hussite forces in the crusade led by Emperor Sigismund and strongly supported by Albert IV, Duke of Austria, his son-in-law,[46] rumours of Jewish collusion with Hussites began to circulate. The traditional crusading logic was activated: why travel so far to fight the heretic when the Jews among and around us perpetrate abuses and blasphemies against our Lord?[47] Already in June 1419 the theologians of the University of Vienna had discussed the danger posed by a coalition of heretics and Jews. Political insubordination and religious heterodoxy were merged into a powerful threat:

> In the same meeting, there was talk about a plot of Jews, Hussites and Waldensians; about the multitude of Jews, about their luxurious life and their despicable books, which they keep as an insult to the Creator, and in blasphemy of Christ and all the saints, and to the greatest injury of all Christians.[48]

The lively trade between Vienna and Prague, in which Jews played an active role, was seen as a cover for the sale of arms to the Hussites.[49]

The fight against the political and religious challenge of Hussitism, recurrent failures to unseat the league created by the Bohemian nobility, and the reforming attitudes of several high ecclesiastical figures, which included criticisms of Christian as well as Jewish life, all came together in a ground swell of frustration and disapproval which could find echoes in university halls as well as among the German armies. The royal court and the university were closely linked in the person of Leonhard Gaming, the Austrian Duke's Dominican confessor and a university theologian. The Duke had attempted to quell this rise of accusations and violence in Vienna a month earlier, when his officials directed the university to refrain from insulting Jews.[50] In the midst of the preparations for a new crusade, called by Pope Martin V on 1 March 1420, a host desecration accusation began to circulate from the city of Enns, which by the next spring had led to the expulsion of Jews from the whole of Austria.

Vienna University was a centre of intellectual discussion and reforming ideas, which often included fierce diatribes against Jewish usury. The work of Henry of Langenstein (1325–97), which included tracts against usury, was translated there into German in the early fifteenth century by Ulrich von Pottenstein, under the patronage of Ulrich von Wallsee. Henry's career had begun in Mainz diocese, he studied in Paris, became canon of Liège, and in 1383 was invited to the University of Paris. He was a Doctor of Theology and wrote works of biblical criticism, tracts on astronomy and tracts proposing reconciliation during the Schism.[51] In his reforming tracts he also addressed the question of usury and repeatedly blamed rulers, rather than Jews, for the harmful and exploitative practice of Jewish usury.[52] The Duke was seen as chronically crippled by debt: Had he not pawned his household silver to the Jews in 1415? Had he not renewed the Jews' privileges in 1417?[53] This connection is not meant to suggest the direct involvement of ecclesiastical figures and scholars in the accusation at Enns, but rather to delineate the sorts of arguments informing intellectual discussion in Austria in this period, as a provincial host desecration accusation led to major changes in the status of Jews in the capital and elsewhere in the Duchy.

It is hard to describe precisely the role played by the accusation, nor can we ever hope to fully document its emergence, circulation and implantation.[54] It is noteworthy that the monastic annalists who describe the expulsion of the Jews refrain from mentioning the host desecration accusation as its cause.[55] Only Thomas Ebendorfer (1388–1464), the author of the *Chronica Austriae*, refers to it at length. He describes the rumour as reaching the Duke after his return from the failed siege of Prague Castle, while the Jewish *Wiener Geserah*, written in German-Yiddish in the mid-sixteenth century, later describes it as happening *before* the Duke's departure for Bohemia.[56] Like the records of the Duke's judgements, which survive in several copies, Thomas recounts an event in Enns as germane to the ensuing arrests, killings and expulsion of Jews. A Jew, Israel, bought a host which had been stolen by a sexton's wife in Enns. Israel and his wife proceeded to distribute parts of the host to Jews throughout the Duchy: 'they bought many particles of the host and sent them to their relatives to be mocked and treated with sacrilege.'[57] When the Christian woman was arrested and the abuse came to light, there were mass arrests of Jews as well as mass conversions. Thomas reports that some Jews killed themselves in prison, including Israel's wife and a Jew of Tulln. Finally, in March 1421 the remaining Jews were burnt on a pyre erected in a meadow, the Erdberg, on the bank of the Danube just outside the city walls of Vienna.

Royal accounts relate that the Jews had been arrested on 23 or 24 May 1420 and executed on 12 March 1421. The delay in execution may be explained by some details contained in the *Wiener Geserah*: whereas the poor Jews were put on a rudderless ship and sent to their death on the Danube, the rich Jews were pressed to reveal the hiding places of treasures.[58] It may be that the richer Jews were kept in the Viennese prison for negotiations over a possible settlement. Although the host desecration rumour was a wild, provincial one, there is a sense of administrative control: the documentation is exact, the richer Jews in their prisons were kept alive and safe for months. The Viennese synagogue was destroyed but its stones were used for the fabric of university buildings.[59]

A region excited by the preparations for and the aftermath of war, a duke forced to make extreme expenditure in pursuit of his dynastic commitments and religious politics, a rumour of Jewish collusion with Hussites, all these fed the Enns accusation. An interesting parallel, if unconnected, preoccupation of Jews with the Hussites is worth notice. In Jewish circles, the rumours of a new, reformed church, the enemy of the Roman church, offered hope of a new phase in relations between Jews and Christians. A Jewish chronicle written by R. Zalman of St Goer of Mainz, an emissary of the Ashkenasi spiritual leader, the Maharil, tells of certain intellectual and political alliances between Jews and Hussites, and particularly of a benign 'Hussite' king, the good King Wenzel. The chronicle continues by recounting the contacts with R. Avigdor Kara, the scholar of Prague, whose hymn to the unity of God was sung by Jews and Hussites alike.[60] On the Jewish side, there may have existed a yearning for any change in the Christian polity, which could only produce greater tolerance. Yet the Hussite sects displayed little interest in Jews. Some Hussite calls for reform focused on a resounding critique of usury, such as that of Jakubek Stříbro;[61] while a few Hussite fundamentalist sects observed some Mosaic dietary laws. But there is no evidence of *rapprochement*, much as this would have been desired by some Jews.[62] Even knowledge of such sects is somewhat dubious, as they are usually described in the polemical accusations of mainstream Hussites, such as the condemnations of John Pribram.[63]

The flourishing Jewish commercial traffic between Prague and Vienna must have aggravated the anxieties of Catholics who were fighting the Hussites and had been fed on horrific tales of Hussite atrocities, nourished by the facts of Hussite military supremacy and the repeated crushing of German challenges by them. As we have seen in the records of Vienna University for 1419, there was a preoccupation with a variety of groups which might have offered help to the Hussites. The year in which the accusation of host desecration emerged was one in which Sigismund and his allies were defeated by the combined forces of the Hussite coalition ranging from Bohemian nobility to Hussite Prague and the Taborite forces. This defeat, the Battle of Vyšehrad, took place in November 1420 and may have fuelled the rumours already in circulation, since moves against Jews had begun earlier in the year, in the heat of preparation rather than in the anger of the crusade's defeat.[64] The Jews who had been held for months were soon dealt with summarily, at the end of the winter of 1421: denuded of property, in the depth of despair after a long period in prison, mindful of some conversions and other deaths and suicides, the remaining arrested Jews – men, women and children – were executed.[65] Thomas Ebendorfer triumphantly declared that Jews were never to settle in Austria again. In reality, the Dukes of Silesia and Carinthia were allowed to retain their Jews, and probably received some of the fleeing refugees.

The Austrian case is one in which we hear strangely little of the details of the host desecration accusation, but we can appreciate much of the context which evoked it, the multiple associations which lent it credibility and the momentous repercussions it had. What is striking is that most chronicles did not consider it to be a serious argument in a historical account of the events, leaving it out altogether and favouring the political explanation for the expulsion. Business transactions aplenty followed the expulsion as Jewish houses were sold, and fabric was reallocated from synagogue to university. The chronicler Peter of Pulkau could exclaim: 'Behold the wonder! The synagogue of the Old Law is miraculously transformed into the school of virtue of the New Law.'[66] The host desecration narrative was useful as an ordering and legitimating element in this dense political and religious field. Its elusive presence demonstrates its partial utility; for some it was a story worth retelling, re-enacting, as part of an unfolding drama of crusade, religious revival and the political need to mask defeat. Similarly, the tale became a prelude to expulsion in Wrocław in 1453.

PREACHING AND INCITEMENT: WROCŁAW, 1453

Wrocław was built on the Oder in 1241 as a defensive outpost against the Mongols, and became a flourishing episcopal see, the sort of town which saw the development of strong and prosperous guilds, and which soon attracted Jewish settlement. Situated in Silesia, it was by the fifteenth century a royal city within the Kingdom of Bohemia, after the separation of Silesia from Poland and its attachment to Bohemia under the terms of the Agreement of Trenč in of 1335.[67] In the year of the jubilee, 1450, Pope Nicholas V (1447–55) sent four legates with indulgences and plans for reform to France, Bologna, the Empire and, a special envoy, to the east of the Empire. These eastern regions, now attacked by Turks, were also seen as rife with heresy, so the greatest preacher of the day, the Observant Franciscan John of Capistrano, was given the task of reforming and correcting them.[68] He was to generate reform and preach against error, with the authority to teach and to set up inquisitorial tribunals when necessary: 'The pious father John of Capistrano, of the Observant Order of St Francis, famed for his life of holiness, was sent against the Bohemian heretics armed with the great authority of the apostolic see.'[69]

King Ladislaus of Bohemia welcomed John and permitted him to preach, teach and write against heresy, especially against the 'heresiarch Jan Rokycana' (c.1395–1471, archbishop of the Hussite Utraquist church), and to found numerous Observant convents.[70] John moved confidently and effectively through Bavaria in 1452 and on through Austria to Bohemia. It was during the Silesian part of his Bohemian sojourn that the host desecration accusation and show trial began to unfold. He spent some eight months (13 February to 31 August 1453) in the city of Wrocław and transformed it; the lives of Silesian Jews were never to be the same again.

Armed with inquisitorial powers and basking in the papal blessing, John spent the years 1451–4 promoting reform as well as a new attitude to Jews: in his wake not only were the privileges of Jewish communities revoked but massacres sometimes followed, such as the one in Erfurt in 1451.[71] His preaching had a powerful effect on enormous audiences who received it through simultaneous vernacular translations. Capistrano's progress through Bavaria saw the revocation of the legal basis for Jewish life there, a situation which was quickly deteriorating into a series of expulsions. His preaching heightened religious enthusiasm and the reception of reform; the Austrian Observant house in Egenburg was founded immediately after his sojourn in the town in 1451. In Silesia he attempted to do the same, and further east he petitioned King Casimir of Poland, ultimately inspiring the King's expulsion order in the wake of his defeat at the hands of the Teutonic Order in 1455.[72] The events of Wrocław in the summer and autumn of 1453 were enacted against the background of John's preaching campaign, the incipient wave of expulsions further west, and the pattern of accusation and violence which could follow even in an area like Silesia, which had never before experienced it. Rumour, accusation, infectious culpability – the accusation of host desecration could quickly turn from local storm to regional, countrywide tidal wave.

Our main sources for the examination of the case of Wrocław are the legal documents of the trial, contained in the chronicle account 'De expulsione iudaeorum' and the city archives; the trial proceedings as compiled by one of the royal ambassadors sent to oversee the process, Oswald Reicholf; and a narrative account of great detail and colour which may have been used as a sermon, 'De persecutione iudaeorum vratislavensium a.1453'.[73] The legal records kept by the Bohemian chancery are varied and include confessions, appointments of judges, and inventories of the property of Jews seized after their arrest.[74]

The story begins with a thief's confession, like many others we have already encountered.[75] A peasant from Langenweise confessed to having stolen a pyx with ten or twelve consecrated hosts from his village church, which he attempted to sell to Jews. During the trial he explained that he had sold the hosts to Meyer, a Jew of Wrocław. Following the confession, the town council rounded up its Jews on 2 May – men, children and women – seized their moveables and sealed their houses. Some who attempted to escape were caught after four days' flight, and the town treasurer's accounts record payments to the 'poor' Christians who had joined the chase. A juror, Johann Soner, representing the town, together with a notary, Johann von Kiezingk, and in the presence of witnesses, composed over three days (5–7 May) a painstaking inventory of the Jewish goods, of which the lists for a few houses remain. After these swift preliminary actions the town turned to its sovereign, the King of Bohemia, for further instructions. A royal letter of 22 May expressed shock and appointed two plenipotentiary emissaries as investigators, Sigmund Polembrunner and Oswald Reicholf.

The gathering which began the investigation in early June enjoyed full secular and ecclesiastical competence, in the persons of the royal emissaries and John of Capistrano, theologian, jurist and inquisitor, assisted by the mayor (*Burgermeister*) and bailiffs. The town judge (*Hauptmann*) submitted the Jews to investigation under torture, and soon produced results. The Jews confessed all: they had bought the hosts from a Christian and brought them to the synagogue where they pierced them and struck them with birches, only to witness the miracle of blood issuing from the sacred substance. The forceful, as well as questionable, testimony of a converted woman, now a townswoman of Wrocław and married to an artisan, was then brought forth; she described with hair-raising detail events that had taken place when she was only six years old. As a child in Lamberg (Silesia) she knew that her father had bought the sacrament, and had seen many Jews assemble around a fire and throw hosts into it, hosts which remained intact. This was repeated again and again until finally an old Jewish woman fell to her knees in prayer to the host. Enraged, the assembled Jews killed her with clubs and hid her body in a corner of the house. The convert went on to relate that the Jews had kidnapped a boy of three, fattened him with fine food and finally sacrificed him for his blood. She named the location of his body, where John of Capistrano ordered its exhumation.[76] The royal emissary Oswald Reicholf, citizen of Vienna, reported to his city's council on his embassy. He detailed the boy's treatment in Jewish hands: he was gagged and pierced and, bleeding, was hidden away bound and wounded, and later taken out and his body washed with cloths dipped in wine. The wine and blood mixture was then squeezed into vessels which were sealed with wax and hidden away, with the boy, in a cellar.[77]

The convert's evidence is an artefact studded with literary and symbolic gems, a jewel of storytelling which brought together disparate tales and attitudes to Jews in a dizzying manner. The ritual murder and the host desecration accusation intersect here, as they would repeatedly later in the century, most famously in Trent in 1475.[78] The Jews standing around a cauldron of boiling water or a fire provided an image which could be seen during the preparations for Passover, the burning of remaining unleavened bread and the ritual cleansing of cooking and eating utensils (see figure 11, p. 73). Contemporary Jews, such as the polemical writer Rabbi Yomtov Lippmann of Mühlhausen, referred to the confusion of Passover rituals with desecration of Christian cult objects as one of the recurrent confusions which bedevilled Christian perceptions of Jewish life.[79] As we have seen, a convert's evidence was taken to be of paramount importance in securing convictions; it was evidence from within, an authentic commentary on Jewish practice.

An anonymous chronicle account of the case of Wrocław similarly combines narrative reporting and documentary evidence from the trial. This is the 'De expulsione iudaeorum' which places the beginning of the events during a procession which took place on Thursday after the feast of the Holy Cross (20 September 1453), as Christ's body was being carried in the streets. The pious fell to their knees in proper devotion, but the Jews, 'lying low in their small houses and synagogues', derided the Christians for believing that something made by them was their God. A few days later when assembled for collective celebration of the Sabbath, they summoned to them the custodian of St Matthew's church, which was close by, and asked him for the host. The custodian was reluctant, but when offered the (portentous) sum of 30 pennies of silver, and goaded by his wife, he sealed the deal with the Jews. This *alter Judas* handed over to a Jew called Meir ten consecrated hosts. The Jewish community leader raised the hosts for all to see, introducing them as the 'Gods of the Christians' ('Dii Christianorum'), and proceeded to examine their power. The Jews placed two hosts on a table, blasphemed and sang lewd songs, beat them with birches and pierced them with other utensils. Blood soon issued from the hosts, and this terrified the

Jews, some of whom were blinded at the sight. Some watchmen passing by looked through the window and saw what was being done: they hastened to call the clergy and the people. The table with the bleeding hosts was rescued and carried to the church. King Ladislaus was informed and ordered the Bishop of Wrocław, Peter Novack, to detain all the Jews in two houses.

The chronicle now moves into legal documentary mode with the words of the public notary, who recorded the confessions on Friday, 22 June 1453, in the palace before the hall of the consul near the pretorial tower of Wrocław. He attested that the (perfidious) Jew Jacob son of Solomon wrote his own confession in 'hebraico idiomate' on a paper codicil, which was translated by Dominus John, a physician, and Francis of Głogów (who are later described as converts). Jacob described his actions:

> I Jacob spoke with Boge the Christian about bringing me the Christians' Gods, for which I wanted to pay him, by the counsel and wish of the Jewish elders ('de consilio et voluntate seniorum Iudaeorum'). He left my home and went to Meir's and after a while Meir brought it to me in a box with his servant Kaulo. I brought it to Abraham of Oppel and then Abraham and ten Jews entered the synagogue carrying the box in which there were ten white spherical figures, as small as a *grosso lato*.[80] In the centre of the synagogue they placed a table and spread a silk cloth upon it, they laid two hosts on the table and, having cursed bishop Peter Novack, they hit them with birches and broke them so that they started to bleed. When this was seen they were terrified and many were blinded.

The two hosts ('figurae') were then disposed of by Moshe, Per, Israel and Kaulo in Olsawa:

> And four hosts ('figurae') were given to Jacob. Later I went to Schweidnitz and asked Israel whether he had the thing which represented Christ hanging and he said 'yes'. I wanted it to be sent to other cities, so that it be desecrated there, too.

Ten Jews were gathered in the synagogue to which the hosts were brought: Salomon the rabbi, Abraham, Tuneman, Isaac, Meir, Forchset, Zadoch, Salemlechem, Gimchen and the beadle.[81] As the Jews entered the synagogue with the pyx they sang the verse: 'He who offers to the Gods will be damned, except [those offering] to [one] God alone.'[82]

This testimony contains true and imagined aspects of Jewish communal life. The Jewish community is shown assembling under the rabbi in the synagogue, the ten men required for a *minyan*, a quorum for worship, scrupulously counted. The Jews are presented as being intent on injury, but shocked at the outcome – the manifestation of Christ's blood. They were awe-struck and struck blind, but this did not halt the abuse, as some of the hosts were salvaged for further circulation. The narrator forgot to subtract the two 'miraculous' hosts from the ten stolen, and claimed that nine or ten were circulated among the Jews of other cities for further abuse. This pattern of regional 'sharing' in the stolen hosts appears as early as the Franconian accusations of 1298 and provided the rationale for regional 'cleansings', the regional tours of host recovery and destructive revenge. The Jews are presented as adept stagers of ritual abuse: they set the hosts on a table which was dressed, like an altar, with a silk cloth. The 'confession' ends with the list of official witnesses.

The second confession, by Sweman the Jew, was similarly given in the king's court on Monday 9 July, this time in front of John of Capistrano, *inquisitor*, and Nicholas Lobin, canon and official of Wrocław and Vicar-General of the bishop. The notary public asserted that Sweman of Schweidnitz, without the pressure of torture, willingly offered his version. This was that Jacob son of Salomon, who was staying with Jacob Moses, a Jew, currently held in the castle for his involvement, gave Israel Kalio the Jew of Schweidnitz four hosts, each the size of a florin, which were held in a cloth. In the presence of Taler the Jew these were put on a copper paten and upon a table. The cloth was removed from the hosts as they viewed them but then they were carried in the cloth and on the paten to the synagogue where ten Jews, experts in Jewish law, had congregated. These were Sweman, Israel, Kaulo, Jacob, Moses, Faber, Joseph, Aaron, Effra and the synagogue bell-ringer. They put the hosts on the table, beat them with birches and then left the synagogue for Rabbi Isaac's house, who lay sick in bed. The sick rabbi used a knife and cut the hosts, until blood issued; terrified by the sight of the blood the rabbi cursed: 'May God give Rabbi Salomon a bad year.'[83] The hosts were then put in a cloth and given to Taler who took them away under the rabbi's instructions to the Jew Moses of Leignitz, who would in turn take them to his son Joel of Głogów, who 'would know what to do with them'. At the end of Sweman's confession it was noted that 150 Jews were burnt, and that the custodian of St Mark's, like an earlier Judas, killed himself. Forty-one were executed on 4 July and all children under the age of seven were baptised, while the remaining Jews were expelled.[84]

Although the trial in Wrocław did not deteriorate into mob violence, it followed the logic of regional extension, as local Jews were said to have shared the hosts with their brethren in surrounding towns and villages. On 17 June arrests and seizures of property began in Schweidnitz, Jauer, Striegau, Lamberg, Reichenbach and Leignitz (Eschenloer); nine days later the decree was extended to all towns and villages in Silesia. In Leignitz a fire broke out in the prison in early July and decided the fate of the Jews awaiting trial there. The Jews were gathered from their communities and brought to Wrocław for an *ad hoc* tribunal, bringing the total of Jews arrested to 318. The annals of Glogau reported the torture and punishment of Jews:

> *The Jews were torn apart with pincers.* Item, on Wednesday in the octave of the Visitation of Mary [4 July] two Jews were torn [*laniati;* some MSS *lacerati*] with burning pincers and then burnt. *Leignitz was burnt.* Item, as above on the night of that day much of the town of Leignitz was burnt and at the same time many Jews were killed by fire . . . *Jews were burnt in Wrocław.* On the day of St Hypolitus [13 August] seven Jews and Jewesses were burnt in Schweidnitz.[85]

Jewish silver was melted down and sold to a patrician of Wrocław, 1,800 guldens in value, of which 1,400 went to cover the trial's costs and the remainder was sent on to the king's coffers. The last chapter in the events at Wrocław occurred some years later when in 1455 King Ladislaus passed through it. Having already granted Brno (Brünn) and Olomouc (Olmütz) permission to expel their Jews, he promised on the day of his departure (30 January) never to allow Jews to settle. In 1457 he extended this to Schweidnitz and smaller Silesian towns.

   This record of torn flesh and burnt bodies is borne out by the claims made in the highly detailed narrative of the case 'De persecutione iudaeorum vratislaviensium a.1453' ('On the persecution of the Jews of Wrocław in 1453').[86] In this rich tale a Jew tempted a town herald, who approached a shepherd, who in turn contacted a clerk in an attempt to procure the host from a village church. Each stage towards the eucharist was lubricated by the payment of money. The Jews abused the host and were found out when a Christian maid who served them informed the city's pro-consul and thus led to their arrest. The wise councillors of Wrocław in turn sent emissaries to the Emperor and the King with a petition for advice on the appropriate process. The King instructed the town to employ John of Capistrano 'sent by God to our parts by omnipotent God's special grace'.[87] John presided over the trial in the town centre. He had four pans full of burning coals set up and had the Jews' bodies skinned and then bound back on to a table. Then four torturers tore out pieces of their flesh and burnt them in the pans and continued to do so until the bones could be seen. The consuls then ordered the Jews to be quartered and hung at the crossroads so as to deter other 'cursed' Christians and Jews.

   Apart from these fourteen, other Jews, who were not accused of being linked to the affair, were gathered together. Having requested the building of a rough wooden structure, which was set on fire, John placed four vested priests beside it and addressed the Jews: they could choose baptism or the fire. Twenty adolescents chose to convert and the remaining Jews were burnt. The text concludes with the consequent policies which were initiated in Silesia: that no town should have more than six Jews: 'because the increase in Jews causes great blasphemy and disgrace to Our Lord Jesus Christ, His mother the Virgin Mary and to the Catholic faith'.[88] An elaborate *Sakramenthaus*, the monstrance-like edifice for the keeping of the host, was constructed and set up in the church of St Elizabeth in Wrocław, the church from which hosts were said to have been stolen, some time in 1453.[89] Although there is no direct evidence to link the decision to build such a structure with the host desecration accusation and its aftermath, it is likely that so grand a shrine, not for a relic but for the eucharist, was inspired by the recent manifestation of eucharistic power. The pinnacled structure is of four 'storeys' standing upon a circle of eight columns. It was a partial copy and certainly an elaboration of the *Sakramenthaus* in the neighbouring Sandkirche, erected in 1437 by a Viennese artist (and now destroyed).[90]

Preachers such as John had already begun their activities in the first quarter of the century in Italy, where Jewish settlement was much sparser. The anti-Jewish preaching campaign was there related to a programme of moral renewal and reform which the newly constituted Observant Franciscan Order was promoting. As the disciple of Bernardino of Siena (1380–1444), John had already begun preaching in 1417, calling for inner conversion among the patrician urban groups, and proposing an alternative to the usurious indebtedness of their lesser neighbours.[91] The programme of *monti di pietà* was an imaginative platform for reform, if cruel to Jews and ultimately impracticable: the foundation of charitable banks which offered interest-free loans to the poor could remove the need to tolerate Jews within the communities of northern and central Italy. A flurry of activity in the 1410s and 1420s mobilised urban leaders under Observant Franciscan tutelage, energised by the frenetic anti-usury preaching which implicitly condoned most Christian lending as it condemned that by Jews. A reinvigoration of the Christian body was to be achieved by the excision of the Jewish presence, small as it was.[92] Later in the century the Observant Franciscans were to become enthusiastic facilitators of the Trent ritual murder trial and its resonances in Venice and Lombardy.[93] Town fathers were set a double task – financial and religious – which some met with enthusiasm.

A preacher's work could be highly suggestive, but its consequences depended on the authority he could deploy and on his audience's interest. Capistrano was a famous preacher of unparalleled charisma.[94] A local preacher might *try* to foment agitation against Jews, and fail. An intriguing instance of such an attempt is preserved in the records of the town of Zurich, in an investigation conducted by the town council in 1420.[95] The council was attempting to decide between two possibilities: 'We are here to judge, whether a Jew in our town had said, when the priest was passing in the street with our Lord's body, "What are you doing here with the whore's son?" or "What need have you for a whore's son?"[96] Nine witnesses were called and asked how they had heard of the Jew's misdeed. The source of the rumour was clearly a Dominican preacher at a specific sermon. Buerkli Schmitt claimed to have attended a sermon at the convent where a friar accused the congregation of being Jew-lovers since they had tolerated the Jew's mockery of Christ. But Buerkli also added that he was not sitting close enough to be able to report accurately.

Rudolph Trotter next told that the Dominican had accused them of loving Jews: once a Jew who was standing in the street during the passage of Christ's body taunted them with the words 'What have you to do with carrying the whore's son?' Rudolph added that the friar had also told them that recently a similar case had occurred in Bern, and led to the expulsion of the city's Jews. Eberhard Stadel explained that he could not recall well but that he had heard that a Jew had spoken during the passage of the sacrament about 'Our Lady's . . . and Our Lord's sack [of excrement]' ('do gat unser froewen . . . unsers herren sack hin'). But he was very unsure. Ulrich im Steinhaus sat so far from the pulpit that he could hear none of the friar's words. Jeckli Stark was much better informed: he had heard the accusation of Jew-loving, that a Jew had called Christ a whore's son, and that in Bern a Jew who had spoken of Our Lady as a 'sack of shit' was fined 300 gulden, and with the other Jews was expelled from the city. He wished them a Good Year and added that one should have no contact with Jews under pain of excommunication. Conrad of Ravensberg and Heinrich Gugleberg remembered only that there was some talk of a Jew speaking against the Virgin in Bern.

Two later witnesses were far more loquacious and knowledgeable: a priest and a layman. The priest, Herr Heinrich Stuerer, was full of interesting detail. He had heard the friar tell of Jews speaking during the passage of the host as reported by others. He also added that during the time of his service in the minster he once rode with the sacrament to Neumarkt,[97] where a person he took to be a young Jew was standing before the tower, in his way, and did not remove his cap as he should have done to a priest. Heinrich asked him whether he was indeed a Jew, and the youngster answered 'Yes'. He warned him to leave the street when a priest rode by with the eucharist. He then entered the town and passed in a narrow street and there too met a Jew who stood and failed to remove his cap. Angered by this Herr Heinrich shouted, cursed and struck the Jew, saying: 'You know full well that when you hear the bells you must leave the road.' And although he made a formal complaint against the Jew, a Jewess appeared at the clerk's house and begged for his release, promising that the young man would never repeat the offence. A colourful tale was thus added to the already colourful accusation made in connection with the sermon. The danger of Jews to the eucharist clearly lurked everywhere; their disrespect was ubiquitous and they frequently went unpunished. What indignation Herr Heinrich manages to whip up in a few phrases![98]

Heini Etter claimed similarly to know nothing of the case in question, but had something of interest to offer. A while ago he stood in front of Inkenberg's house with a friend as Heini Scherrer's mother, a Jew, passed by with a rubbing-mill in her hand. She stopped to chat with them, and then Heini asked her 'Do you have masses or anything similar?' to which she answered 'No, we do not have masses as you do, we only follow the ten commandments. But you are *torracht* [?] people and believe that Our God allows himself to be or to appear in the hand of a priest or a dirty monk.' Inasmuch as eucharistic issues might be discussed by neighbours in the street, one eucharistic tale involving a Jew could conjure an association with another. Moreover, the current investigation might have led Heini to rethink the Jewess's words and to perceive their potential meaning and relevance to an inquiry into Jewish disrespect towards the eucharist. The six last witnesses knew nothing at all and were ignorant of the whole affair.[99]

The Dominican preacher of Zurich failed to make a significant and lasting mark on his audience, or maybe the expectation that only half his hearers would retain what they heard is a realistic one. We have no knowledge of the action taken by the council, whether a Jew was punished or expelled. What is clear, though, is that rumours about Jewish abuse often came from pulpits, guided by preachers. The reported sermon opened with 'This is a town of Jew-lovers' (who but a Jew-lover would tolerate actions such as these?), as a prolegomenon to an accusation of disrespect for the eucharist.

The coincidence of campaigns of preaching and host desecration accusations cannot be without significance, even if the process of influence is one which can only be suggested rather than proven. The presence of an instigator, an element of excitement which lent the host desecration narrative a particular poignancy and relevance in a community, can sometimes be traced. The host desecration accusation in Segovia in 1412 followed the sojourn of the Dominican Vincent Ferrer (*c.*1350–1419) in the town in the winter of 1411/12 and his energetic campaign of preaching for Jewish conversion.[100] Ferrer's is an interesting example of the position of many energetic preachers: while he decried wanton violence, he recommended that pressure be applied by secular rulers and by the preacher's word: 'The apostles who conquered the world did not carry a lance or a knife, and therefore it is manifest that Christians should not kill Jews with a knife but with words.'[101] Collaboration between secular lords and preachers alone could produce the desired results: temporal lords should convert the infidel of their lands, but not with injurious force; they must enforce the attendance of Jews at preaching, for only by teaching will the truths of the faith be suitably publicised.[102]

REGIONAL INFECTION: THE NEIGHBOURING
DIOCESES OF PASSAU AND REGENSBURG IN THE 1470s

In the area of the *Donauraum* a series of host desecration accusations linked major cities and the Jewish communities within them, and produced quick responses in printed word and image. In 1465 the cautious town council of Nuremberg received a report accusing the Nuremberg Jews Mairlin, Lesar and Reich of the killing of a two-year-old boy – a case of ritual murder uncovered in Nordlingen – but decided not to act on it.[103] In this period, information was shared by cities, under the assumption that regional Jewish conspiracies to abduct Christian children and to abuse hosts were under way. In 1473, Nuremberg wrote to the Emperor with a request for permission to expel its Jews, on account of the harm they caused, but this was refused.[104] In May 1470 in Regensburg, an accusation involved a wavering potential Jewish convert to Christianity, Cantor Kalman, who had been swayed by viewing Christian worship. He moved into the suffragan bishop's household in Regensburg in preparation for conversion, but following an argument with the bishop's cook he returned to the Jewish fold. Kalman was investigated as a renegade Christian on 6 May by the ducal judge, and came up with the accusation of host desecration against Rabbis Israel, Byman and Yossl. The accusation resulted in no action, as the Duke intervened to protect the accused. Kalman himself was condemned to death and the community was fined 100 florins by the imperial overseer.[105]

In 1474 a converted Jew, Hans Veyol, in custody on suspicion of theft, confessed to having sold a seven-year-old child to Rabbi Israel of Brünn. The rabbi was arrested but released by imperial intervention, while the accuser was interrogated until he admitted that he had incriminated the rabbi in an attempt to save his own skin. He was condemned to death and executed on 14 May.[106] In the following year another convert, Rupert of Mosbach, also told his tale while in custody under suspicion of theft. He claimed to have stolen many hosts for the use of the communities of Krautheim, Bamberg and Regensburg. These accusations fitted in with the town council's desire to expel their Jews, a wish expressed in a series of petitions to Emperor Frederick III (1452–93). Easter was an occasion for the staging of a disputation between the Dominican Peter Schwartz (1431–84) and the Regensburg rabbis. Despite the rumours, the town council moved carefully and in September of that year renewed its protection for the Jews on a temporary basis. The accusations grew stronger when the Bishop of Regensburg returned from a trip to Rome in 1476; during his journey he passed through the town of Trent, bringing with him a copy of the Jews' confessions in the ritual murder trial of 1475, in which twenty Regensburg Jews had been named.[107] Jews in Regensburg were now arrested for a combination of ritual murder and host desecration. Six men on 29 March and eleven others on 9 April were seized and tortured, and in April 1477 workers in Rabbi Jossel's cellar found the bones of four children. In its appeal to the Emperor for the right to try the Jews the town council amassed dossiers from Endingen and Augsburg. The Jews appealed to the Pope and the Emperor while their leaders languished in prison.[108]

In 1478, Regensburg sent an emissary, Hans Friesshaimer, to investigate a possible connection between the Jews of Regensburg and those of Passau in the business of host desecration. In that year a servant from Passau, Christoph Eisengreishamer, had been arrested for theft. Under interrogation he confessed that a year earlier he had been sent to Prague by two Passau Jews, Ungar and Mendl (also known as the *Schulklopfer*). Upon his return he decided to offer hosts to the Jews. He broke into St Mary's church in the episcopal precinct and took eight hosts, which he sold for a single gulden. He also stole seven hosts for the Jew Sütteling of Regensburg. The Jews of Passau took the hosts to the synagogue, where these were stabbed, and began to bleed copiously, finally turning into a little boy. Jews, who became Christians in the course of the trial, attested that when the hosts were thrown into Veygel's oven for destruction, two angels flew out of the flames.[109]

All of this was recounted by the Jews in their confessions, and condemned them to death by fire; the four who had converted were beheaded before the execution of the others, on 10 March 1478 (see again figure 12, p. 82). The remaining Jews of Passau were expelled, and forty-six chose to convert. The synagogue was razed to the ground in 1479 and on its site the Chapel of the Holy Saviour was erected, completed in 1484. The remaining Jews were made to pay 1,000 florins in compensation: to the Emperor for his trouble in intervening and saving them, and to the town for its expenses in conducting their trial.[110]

In his poem on the event, written *c.*1490, Fritz Fellhainer claimed that in the course of the trial it was discovered that a trial at Schärding had found that Veygel had paid 12 shillings for a Christian child.[111] We note here the convergence of the host desecration tale and the ritual murder tale, which had already led to violence in neighbouring Regensburg in 1477. It was probably inspired by that *cause célèbre*, the trial of Simon of Trent, news of which was spreading rapidly and seizing the imagination of bishops and judges in southern German cities. Meanwhile in December 1490 to November 1491, a trial was taking place in Avila (Castile) which brought together ritual murder and eucharist. The case of the Little Boy of La Guardia – who could never be identified or connected with a child's disappearance – was a spectacular inquisitorial trial which created a mood that facilitated the last preparations for the expulsion of the Jews a few months after its end. But this was a different set of accusations from those we have encountered in more northern regions: the boy's heart and the consecrated host were materials which the Jews were meant to have used in magical manipulations aimed at rendering the inquisitorial efforts against them powerless. Although, in the course of the prime Jewish suspect's investigation, it was claimed that some disparaging comments were made by the perpetrators, ridiculing the host in matter and in meaning, this is not a host desecration accusation. Yet the La Guardia case demonstrates the proximity in symbolic meaning which child and eucharist could occupy.[112]

The host desecration accusation offered frames of meaning and action which were ubiquitous, and amenable to reproduction and elaboration. The events which followed from accusations could raise a town to regional prominence and produce a sense of 'community' through action, and then memory of past actions, which was captured in chapels, poems, shrines and images. In those areas where the narrative had become endemic – in the Habsburg lands, and particularly on the Austrian-Bohemian border, in the lovely little towns of Franconia, later in the towns of Catalonia-Aragon, and in parts of Bavaria – it was a real presence, of atrocities remembered, commemorated in local shrines (like the hallowed tomb of Arnold of Uissigheim) just as the events were marked in the liturgical laments of the Jewish communities which reconstituted themselves in a fragile manner, supported by imperial privilege and by the hesitant need to rebuild upon the ashes.[113]

As the fifteenth century unfolded, it was no longer single Jews, curious or malevolent, who were discovered following attacks on hosts with their kitchen knives, but conspiracies of Jews, often Jews from a number of regions, and sometimes this was coupled with the other horrendous accusation of child abuse, child murder. Here we witness a process of elaboration and extension familiar from other contexts: rumours coming to encompass a variety of symbolically related elements, in a similar process to that which psychoanalysis calls *overdetermination*.[114] The two arch-narratives about Jewish abuse underwent elaboration at different stages in the thirteenth century, but became increasingly intertwined, producing by the fifteenth century a dense tale of Jewish abuse at once of the human and the divine.[115] The narrative coexisted and collided with desires for the separation and excision of Jews from central European urban communities. But even when Jews were made to leave and when their quarters were burnt, their property redistributed and their streets renamed, the memory of violence in townscape, in pious offerings, in moving images, in laments heard in home and synagogue could facilitate their return and realise their presence.

6

Violence and the Trails of Memory

The commemorative tokens of the violence we have been exploring can be easily found in the celebratory edifices, magnificent altarpieces and joyful rituals which were established within communities that had accused Jews of host desecration and punished them for it. It is much more difficult to touch the memories of victims, survivors. Pain can be suppressed, it can be passed on to offspring ineffably through attitudes, silences, in the avoidance of certain spaces or in a fixation upon artefacts which come to represent the dead, the loss.[1] In the aftermath of the host desecration violence of 1298 some Franconian towns, such as Rothenburg, came to be known among Jews as 'blood cities'. In the words of the Hebrew lament for the victims, 'I cry for the day's tribulation' ('Evke li-kshe yom'):

> And for the city red with blood, whose name is evil
> Woe, woe, city of blood, I cry and moan
> . . . .
> A corner-stone for our grief was put down in Röttingen
> . . . .
> For gracious Würzburg, that gay city
> . . . .
> My heart faints for Nuremberg's victims.[2]

Much of Jewish memory is lost to us, and yet it must have been vibrant and acute, even if it was not enshrined in a historiographical tradition.[3] Occasionally a trace of it can be glimpsed, as through the memoirs of Rabbi Joseph ben Moshe, a disciple of the Rabbi Israel Isserlein (1390–1460) of Austria, who noted that his rabbi used to 'tell of the events of the *Geserah* [calamity] of Vienna, God avenge their blood, to his old disciples'.[4] It might surface indirectly in the aftermath of violence, as rabbis were called to deal with the legal dilemmas created by dispersal and the disruption of lives. In the wake of the Rintfleisch pogroms, a synod of Jewish leaders assembled in Worms under Rabbi Asher ben Yehiel, and its aims were stated thus:

> After the Almighty has caused a severe breach in the ranks of our people and members of holy communities were murdered, we con-

vened . . . to declare unanimously matters pertaining to estates [of deceased] and matters of personal status because these became innumerable.[5]

Dilemmas arising round the status of kin and property of converts, like those forced to receive baptism in the wake of the Austrian expulsion of 1421, who later wished to return to their faith, appear in rabbinical *responsa* well into the later fifteenth century.[6] While Jews did not build in stone or have many images painted on wood or parchment, they did create literary and historical genres for communal, liturgical commemoration: the necrologies listing victims household by household, compiled for the purpose of commemoration in the synagogue (*Memorbücher*), and poetic laments (*piyyutim*) and penitential chants (*selihot*), a genre sustained throughout the Middle Ages, for stylised recounting of events through the use of biblical verse. Such laments were recited on religious festivals together with the biblical laments for the destruction of the Temples and other past afflictions.[7]

By and large, the memories of the perpetrators seem more readily accessible. Yet it is no simple thing to discern the meanings captured in the chapels, altarpieces, verses and rituals into which memories were poured and through which they were represented. Every act of memory is also an act of forgetting; an effort of will is required for the cherishing of a segment of past events, singling it out for the loving treatment of memorial nurturing. Such choices leave other events unmarked, unloved. Furthermore, *every act of remembering is a making of a narrative full of meaning*, which gives sense to the events thus chosen to be relived and never allowed to die. As narrative always requires a listener, it is deeply dialogic, so making memories is a process conscious of its audience; it seeks to be persuasive, it is rhetorically aware. The whole business of conceiving and making an accusation, pursuing its details, collecting the evidence, identifying the culprit, retaining the traces is one which involves constant narrative production. If the memory of famous, miraculous, violent yet pious events was to be preserved, then other voices had to be forgotten. If remembering is telling a story, and remembering involves suppressing other memories, then its narrative must be full of gaps and traces of the suppressed, of the forgotten.

Communities which indulged in extraordinary violence, which burnt and destroyed without trial or official sanction, which named their leaders and then followed them, were also to be the users and spectators of the rituals of memory which, on the whole, were designed by priests, and paid for by public funds. Like the telling of the past between an analyst and a patient, the story of the past acquires increased coherence from the process of telling and sharing with another. Thus what might have been fragments of memory, taken from the different positions which people inhabited during the violent events, were worked and

reworked, interpreted, indeed analysed – through the mills of production which go into the making and appreciation of an altarpiece, a
poem, or a procession, or a chronicle recounting the memories of
violence. Latin or vernacular, small-scale or monumental, private or
widely disseminated, memory-bearing artefacts were products of an
attempt to make sense of and give sense to extraordinary events.
These could be significant texts – *exempla*, poems, sermons; meaningful arrangements of words and images – drama, broadsheet,
illuminated books; or visual representations in altarpieces, chapels,
and the effect of ritual display.[8]

In the face of widespread destruction, of burning flesh, of the cries of
children, of the looting and razing of houses and shops, does the
making of memory not involve the act of self-exculpation, the action of
justification, and in so doing is it not also an admission of guilt? Is the
triumphant building of chapels and tabernacles, in the erasure of Jews
from the subsequent celebrations of miraculous hosts, not akin to the
half-anxious/half-hopeful gaze of a child who has done wrong and who
eagerly seeks from her parent reassurance that she is still loved, that her
transgression has been forgiven, indulged?[9]

Of the physical remains of such commemorative artefacts, very little
has survived. The efforts of Reformation iconoclasm, wars, and in our
century the well-meaning efforts which followed the Second Vatican
Council, have meant that the carriers of memory and habitual images
which commemorated Jewish abuse, images which educated and made
available and quotidian the knowledge of such Jewish abuses, are now
difficult to reconstruct or reimagine.[10] It is both frustrating and moving
when visiting Pulkau's Holy Blood Chapel, to find the panels of the host
desecration *predella* demurely hidden from view, and to receive in response to polite inquiry about its whereabouts the indignant complaint
of a local guide, that the much loved and age-old cult image had been
removed by 'Vienna'.[11] The parish church of Uissigheim, the natal
village of Arnold, first leader of the Armleder massacres of 1336, kept
his tombstone for historical interest but had removed any signs of the
cult which had developed around him. Yet the village's main street is
named 'Ritter Arnold Strasse' . . .[12]

TEXTS

The dramatic events which surrounded a host desecration accusation
were undoubtedly the subject of rumour, discussion, boasts and cruel
jokes. We will never be able to capture the dense texture of these. We
are, however, able to encounter some of the ideas and textual representations which came to be related to the events, inasmuch as they were
packages of knowledge and interpretation. Numerous genres were
deployed in the making of such texts and in what follows we will meet

laments, *exempla*, prayers, chronicle entries, poems, plays. Sometimes accounts of the events circulated without literary clothing, within the stark forms of trial protocols. By the later fifteenth century, a time by which accusations often involved numerous Jews and grand trials, copies of such records were made for monastic libraries. We thus find copies of the confession of Christoph Eisengreissamer in the Passau case copied into a book of miscellaneous texts belonging to the Benedictine Abbey of Ebersberg (eighteen miles east of Munich) together with some medical recipes, a catechism and devotional writings by John of Neumarkt, Bishop of Olomouc.[13] In many other cases the events were amplified and elaborated through generic shapes aimed at enhancing their veracity, credibility and justification.

Clerical Parody and Jewish Lament: Prague, 1389

The host desecration of Prague in 1389 produced an interesting experiment in genre, as the story is told in the literary form of a *passio* entitled *Passio judaeorum secundum Johannes rusticus quadratus* ('The Passion of the Jews according to John the Stocky Peasant').[14] The *passio* is a narrative form in which political events were rendered in the style and language of the scriptural passages depicting Christ's Passion.[15] *Passiones* 'rearrange and distort biblical passages' in an attempt to invoke authority from scripture for the narrative on contemporary occurrences. The result is usually parodic through the working of the incongruous juxtaposition of the profane and contemporary with the historical-yet-eternal sacred tale.[16] In this *passio* Prague became Jerusalem and its Jews, Christ's tormentors (paraphrasing Matthew 26–8). Here the accusation unfolded from the complaint that during a procession of Holy Week 1389 (11–17 April) a Jew threw a little stone at the monstrance carried by the priest not far from the Jewish quarter.[17] This prompted the anger of the people of Prague, as they were led by one Johannes or Gesco Quadratus (John the Square). The parodic representation aims to surround the events with biblical images: the Jewish children in the streets during the procession carried branches and cursed the entry of Christ (in the eucharist) with 'Stone him, for he pretends to be God's son'; the town jail into which the Jews were thrown was a Roman *praetorium*; the Jews congregated in their synagogue 'priests and Pharisees'. True to the biblical tale, here was no story of accusation followed by discovery and punitive massacre, but the unfolding of several stages of betrayal, abuse, judicial process and final execution. On the contemporary plane, the preachers of Prague moved their audiences to take revenge by following a self-appointed 'prophet', Gesco. Yet in Prague no lots were cast; according to the text, *all* Christians fell upon *all* Jews, amputating their limbs one by one. And the books of the Jewish law were burnt under a crown of burning twigs (parallel to the crown of thorns), as a string of prophetic biblical phrases followed. On the morrow the town fathers met and decreed that property taken from the Jews in the heat of action should not be used, because it was the product of illicit usury. The council called for a central collection of all the goods in order to amass a sufficient amount of money for the payment of what was sure to follow: a hefty fine imposed by King Wenzel.[18] The town council also feared for the air quality in Prague following the massacre: worried lest the fumes arising from the charred Jewish body fats affect the health of its citizenry, the councillors hired some poor Christians to pile the bodies up and reduce them to ashes.[19]

Who was the intended audience of such a text? *Passiones* were usually written by clerks and for a Latin-reading clergy; the *Passio* of Prague may also have been read by the capital's extensive officialdom.[20] The figure of 'rusticus quadratus' is that of a stocky, thick-set, rough character, simple of mind, but also of an honesty lacking in more sophisticated folk.[21] In this instance his testimony is that of a person worlds apart from the capital's royal officials and protectors of Jews, those who were also politically pitched against the city's clergy. Prague's clergy was a formidable group which boasted a large proportion of university men and a lively disputatious intellectual culture. Those who would appreciate a clever turn of biblical phrase, an amusing inversion of representation in this parody, were not, on the whole, the killers. But they were the facilitators, as the text confesses, preachers who encouraged a crowd on the rampage. Clerks, preachers and priests were particularly implicated in the undercurrent of the tale: the anti-usurious frame within which the massacre is set fitted neatly into one of the main lines of acrimony and controversy within late fourteenth-century Prague, the struggle between the clerisy and officialdom, between the Archbishop of Prague and royal servants.[22] King Wenzel came to be known as a 'Jew-lover', and his servants 'protectors of Jews', and thus fully implicated in the usurious gain enjoyed by Jews. The Jews and their protectors are represented as harmful to a Christian polity, to the Christian body – political and physical – as the gory tale of the destruction of their bodies clearly shows.[23]

Another Latin narrative of the event of 1389 is to be found in a manuscript now in Krakow. This is the 'De caede Judaeorum pragensi' ('On the slaughter of the Jews in Prague'), which accords well with the tenor of the parody, even in simple prose.[24] Here the account emphasises the time of the year: it was at Easter and during the taking of the eucharist to a sick person that the Jews made their verbal and physical attack. Their violence broke the monstrance and led to the dispersal of hosts on the ground; they ridiculed the host and the priest, and drew his polemical retort: 'How can you be so ungrateful to a God who has poured goodness onto you, leaving you Moses's books?' The shameful event is described as a shock wave which passed through the Christian body of Prague as preachers retold the event on the morrow in their

Easter sermons, and moved the crowd to action. As they killed all but the very youngest Jews, as they despoiled their homes and unearthed hidden treasure, with the chant 'Almighty God' on their lips,[25] the Christian crowd continued to polemicise: let your acts be remembered and avenged, let your bodies be reduced to ashes. Only the arrival of the King, with his ministers and his financial retribution against the city, marred the celebration of virtue won through the extirpation of Jewish pollution.

Bohemia had known relatively few eruptions of anti-Jewish violence before the case of 1389. In the wave of massacres and expulsions which followed the fears of the Black Death in 1348–9, only the western town of Eger had risen against its Jews. A strong dynastic investment in the protection of Jews stood up well to pressures from ecclesiastical magnates. Emperor Charles IV's Prague had a flourishing Jewish community, one which was tied through commerce, learning and travel with other imperial communities, particularly those of Austria, and with Silesia. Yet in the 1380s one can sense a gathering atmosphere of menace, as the university stood up to King Wenzel, the son of its founder, with an aggressive polemic over usury. This was clearly an attempt to assert ecclesiastical autonomy and leadership within the body politic.[26] The *Judenpolitik* stood as a contentious issue between clergy and King, between clergy and King's men. The synodal statutes of October 1381 railed against usury:

> since the sin of usury is a horrible and detestable crime and it occurs frequently nowadays not only among common folk but also among men of high status, in all sorts of ways, both under the guise of profit and through counterfeit, which we report with sorrow, because of the things done by the same Jews and by other infidels to taunt us, and this creates great scandal in the hearts of the faithful of God's church.[27]

One of the bearers of these complaints in eloquent homiletics and devotional poetry was the Archbishop of Prague, John of Jenstein (*c.*1348–1400). In a Christmas sermon delivered in the 1380s he argued that the property Jews accumulated and the privileges they enjoyed favoured them over clergy; their influence in high places rendered them more powerful than magnates and churchmen.[28] The subject of usury immediately followed, and Jews were accused of pauperising prince and magnate alike, and then using their riches in the service of antichrist their Lord.[29] Another vehement critic of the Jews and their protector was the Augustinian abbot Ludolf of Sagan (d. 1422; abbot from 1394), who saw the King, in a period of grave lapses in justice, rejected by clergy and people, by nobles, townsmen and peasants, and accepted by Jews alone.[30] Thus the treatment of the Jews was seen as leading to their pride which resulted in offences against Christians and their Saviour, as expressed in Prague in 1389: 'since the Christian people could no longer pretend and bear, in just revenge of the blasphemy [committed] against it . . . on a day . . . on the feast of Easter, moved by zeal, it burnt those very Jews and their houses by fire.'[31]

The 'Passion of the Jews' emphasises the agency of clergy and preachers as creators of public opinion and motivators of the crowd. The alleged offence against the eucharist is said to have happened during a procession to the sick. It was then proclaimed and elaborated in the churches of Prague, and the vengeful crowd was presented as a pious one. 'On the slaughter of the Jews in Prague' similarly emphasises the work of preachers: whereas the Jewish offence of throwing stones at a priest passing with the host took place on Easter Saturday, causing the breakage of the monstrance, it was only on the morrow, when preachers 'tearfully' embellished the tale in their Easter sermons that 'the people, hearing of such a terrible act, raised their voices, saying: Jewish perversity, from the blasphemy of which such enormity has sprung up, must indeed be annihilated.'[32] Like the 'Passion of the Jews' this version is also steeped in biblical paraphrase; as the crowd fell on the Jews it is reported that people exclaimed: 'Vach, you who have blasphemed the body, by covering it with stones, of the one whose resurrection it is today! It is written: . . . before the cock crows, not one of you will remain alive.'[33]

The political context and the discourse are emphasised in these reports of the city's actions. Because of the King's absence, the crowd was drawn by the leadership of John (Gesco); the city elders supervised the collection of Jewish property, on expectation of a heavy fine. Moreover, the King placed armed men around the Jewish houses to reclaim them. As mentioned in the 'Passion of the Jews', the bodies of the Jews were dug up and burnt, removing evidence and cleansing the city of their presence. In the face of the loot offered by the Jewish houses, some claimed that this should not be touched as it was the product of usurious gain. The rhetoric of the report on Prague, within the context of clerical complaints which we have already noticed, allows the offence of host desecration to reverberate as only one instance of a greater evil, that which was preached regularly and insidiously, Jewish usury. Indeed a highly developed discourse on usury was treated very seriously at the University of Prague and that of Vienna. The host desecration accusation and its aftermath are suffused with the anti-usury reference which so often stood as an argument against Jews and their political patrons.

It is this anti-usury discourse which structured some of the memories of the massacre. This peculiar association with usury, which intersected with the accusation of host desecration, was carried over into another type of writing, that of the physician and homiletic writer John Lange of Wetzlar (1365–*c.*1427). A scholar of the University of Prague and Doctor of Medicine, who wrote texts on the management of epidemics, John also composed didactic and devotional works, the most famous of which is the *Dialogus super Magnificat* ('Dialogue on the Magnificat'), a work of 2,668 hexameters dedicated to the Archbishop of Worms.[34] A supporter of Archbishop John of Jenstein in his struggle against the King in Prague, John Lange turned the telling of the events of Prague 1389 into a polemic against King Wenzel and his servants, especially minister Sigmund Huber. The King is cast, as we have seen before, as a supporter of Jews, while the crowd take just revenge. The King protected his Jews for nefarious reasons:

> O kings, kings! Be shamed for such a crime! The usurious gain on the capital which is earned by the accursed people, in which you yourselves are proven to be accursed usurers.
>
> You have done this not on account of them, or because of their virtues, in which they are experts, nor for reason of justice, which attaches to them, rather on account of their vile silver and other gifts of gold. You know that they frequently enact nefarious acts against Christ's faithful, and you have consumed gifts but have worn down the justice of the law again and again.[35]

Lange is confident of the moral opposition which the case of Prague demonstrated – between protectors of Christ's body and protectors of Jews. He accuses the royal councillors of having 'sharpened' the King against the citizens of Prague, thus allowing for the all too real possibility that Christ's body be abused again.[36]

The host desecration accusation of Prague was thus inserted into a pervasive anti-usury discourse which converged with the stance of reform-minded ecclesiastics, against royal exactions, in the Bohemian capital. The satirical rendition of the horrible violence of 1389 was one of the trails of memory full of complicity with the violence of others.

The Jewish memories of 1389 can only be imagined, except for a single relic, which served to commemorate the events for generations. A heart-rending lament, 'All the afflictions which have befallen us' ('Et kol ha-tela'a'), was composed by Rabbi Avigdor Kara of Prague (d. 1439) (whose tombstone still survives in the Jewish cemetery of Prague), and was recited according to the liturgical Use of Prague during the afternoon prayers of the Day of Atonement.[37] The poem is made of twenty-five quatrains; it offers a narrative of the massacres as seen and experienced by Jews through a lament composed of biblical citations. A note of bitter irony is sounded as the poet dates the massacre, in the year 5149 since Creation, on the last day of the feast of 'sweet salvation', Passover.[38] The images of baking and burning involved in the Passover sacrifice and in the baking of the unleavened Passover bread, the *matsot*, are made to represent the immolation of the Jews, as burnt and slaughtered sacrifice. Then a number of stanzas describe the murderous crowd: armed with weapons of all kinds (bows, arrows, axes), chanting and jubilant.[39] The emphasis then moves to the experience of death, indeed the choice of suicide calculated to ward off death at the hands of the Christian crowd: fathers killed their children, children obeyed and offered themselves for sacrifice, the rabbi abandoned his congregation, choosing death at his own hands over the humiliation of torture and death at the hands of the Christian crowd. The poet pretends to be an observer from the side, and moves deftly between the first person singular ('my people', 'I cry') and the voice of the third person narrator, who refers to the victims and sufferers as 'they', and describes remorselessly their terrible deaths. The Jewish community's books, as well as their authors, readers and interpreters, were all destroyed in the fire.

The rhetoric of lament is raw and heart-rending. The crowd of murderers is seen as cohesive, purposive, confident, numerous and swift, with chants on its lips. To Kara they seem to be numerous ('entering from every opening') and cunning, they attempted to mask their crime, pretend that they were guiltless by burning the Jewish bodies with Christian ones. They spared neither the young nor the very old, neither children nor women, and even attempted to destroy the evidence of Jewish settlement and belonging, by breaking the headstones in the Jewish cemetery. The poem ends with a sense of tragic confusion, with an invocation of God's memory ('they are your number'), and with the hope of consolation.[40] The tone accords with the words of the *Memorbuch* entry, 'May God remember the killed and burnt of Prague . . . for having given their souls for the sanctification of God . . . our teacher the Rabbi Menachem son of Rabbi Asher for having been killed and burnt for the sanctification of God.'[41]

It has been claimed that Jews failed to produce a historiography in the Middle Ages, yet this lament is eloquent and was probably effective as a conduit for memories of trauma.[42] Disaster is, after all, not easily analysed, explained, justified, it defies historical containment. How much more powerful the loyal return to the consolation of the Bible, and the loving remembrance of victims. The Bible provided the solemn justification of purpose and identity for the both clerics of Prague and for Jewish survivors.

Tales that Exemplify

The host desecration accusation was a didactic narrative. When Christian actors participated in it they claimed to be enacting Christian truths as revealed in their own time and lives. Writers about such events and witnesses to them often expressed their views in what resembled catechetical phrases. Inasmuch as the host was ubiquitous and Jews familiar even where they did not dwell (England, France), stories about Jewish abuse and eucharistic response could be recounted anywhere in the Christian world. They could be inserted into the parcels of religious tales that were designed to facilitate a preacher's work and provide didactic embellishment.[43] Moreover, these particular tales fed the desire for *novelle*, stories with current authority and relevance.[44] Such were the tales of Rudolph of Schlettstadt, some of which have come to be known as *Historiae memorabiles*.[45] Although we know little of the aims and circulation of Rudolph of Schlettstadt's tales, their qualities in length and tone, in simple characterisation of good and evil, in the tendency to end with a *moralitas*, demonstrate the apt transformation of recent event to *exemplum*. Even though we have no knowledge of the recounting of these tales to Alsatian audiences, their production and matter demonstrate the type of work and energy which went into the retelling of events connected with host desecration accusations.

Dominican histories and *exempla* were efficiently distributed in the Middle Ages, and Rudolph's collection, written by 1303, might just have already informed the preaching of the great Florentine Dominican, Giordano of Rivalto (of Pisa) (*c.*1260–1311) in 1304.[46] Giordano was the foremost preacher of his day, and his sermons were noted and copied down by members of the audience. He was famed for his critique of certain banking practices, and reminded Florentines of the strictures on issues such as the just price and money-lending.[47] His attitude to Jews reflects the impact of the developments of the thirteenth century, emphasising not the Jews' role in universal history and their utility as witnesses of the Christian faith, but rather their agency in Christ's death and their abiding desire to harm, to 'recrucify' him:

> they also remake Christ's Passion not only in their hearts . . . but they remake it in their souls . . . The other manner in which they remake it is in the sacrament of His body, doing cruel things to it . . . Another manner in which they remake the Passion of Christ is in His image, and this in two ways: the one in the person of some man . . . and the other, in an image, such as the painted figures of Christ.[48]

Each of the modes of 'recrucifying Christ' is illustrated by examples: when describing the second mode, that which is worked upon Christ's sacrament, Giordano drew upon experiences which he claims to have witnessed:

> I was once in those regions when it happened that a Jew sent his maid to the Christian church; and he made her, either by the power of money or in some other evil device, bring to him Christ's body. When he had it, he and some Jews gathered in a house, recommenced enacting the Passion so nastily, and with such rage, that a miracle occurred, and they ground him in a mortar cruelly. It so happened that a little boy appeared, and he was Christ Himself.[49]

The Christian woman was horrified at the sight of the miracle and sent for representatives of the secular and episcopal authorities. Up to now the story told is largely that of Paris. But Giordano continues to tell:

> A layman arose by God's will, a spiritual person, possessing zeal for the faith, and together with another artisan he led the crowd and placed himself at its head shouting: death to the Jews – and he passed through the whole city and the whole province with an army of over twenty thousand people. And all the Jews were killed so that it was impossible to find one in the whole province; and it was a blessed thing that he could kill them.[50]

This part of the tale is clearly related to the Rintfleisch events of 1298: the regional aspect, the leadership of an 'inspired' layman, the destruction of communities. In the well-known Dominican manner, immediate agency by personal witness, or that of another friar, is used to the full in authenticating the tale.[51] Giordano had in fact travelled very little in his life; is his 'Io era' anything more than a rhetorical flourish? The tale fits in neatly with his earlier assertions about the danger posed by Jewish presence and intent to 'recrucify' Christ.[52] This was a very popular preacher, and yet his harsh teaching, though it remained part of 'local knowledge', never re-erupted into further violence.

Preachers such as Giordano and Rudolph of Schlettstadt were digesting and re-expressing recent events for pastoral oratory. From the mouth of a Giordano, who could swear to having attended some of the events, these became arousing and topical tales. Far more mundane, and much harder to assess for impact and influence, are the versions of the host desecration tale, and especially the arch-case of Paris, when inserted in alphabetical order into, say, a workbook of *exempla*. Such is the *Ci nous dit*, a book for instruction through moral tales compiled in 1313 × 30, which was a friar's work. The book contains a version of the story of Paris in its section on the 'miracle du saint sacrement'.[53] It reported the purchase of Christ's body by a Jew from a Christian woman; the boiling of the host in a cauldron and the effusion of blood which heralded the transformation into a crucifix which hovered over the cauldron. The *exemplum* went on to tell of the wife and child's conversion and the Jew's burning. An account of the miracles which took place around Christ's body, a relic still kept in the parish of St-Jean-en-Grève, brings the short tale to a close.

A similar if far more ambitious project of collection was undertaken by another friar, the English Dominican John Bromyard (d. *c.*1352), who produced a wide-ranging and influential encyclopedia of *exempla*, and included a version of the tale. In the section 'Eucharistia' of his alphabetically arranged compilation, Bromyard chose to include three *exempla* with Jewish protagonists, of which one was broadly based on the case of Paris: 'of another Jew, who remitted a woman's whole debt on the condition that she bring him Christ's body'.[54] The woman received communion, took the eucharist in her mouth, and later gave it to the Jew, who abused it in front of her, perforating it with a knife and bringing forth much blood ('so they say,' adds Bromyard). The woman informed a judge of the Jew's action and he summoned the priest, while the Jews were caught and burnt and the host was collected and presented for worship. This story sounds much like the tale of Paris, or indeed like a censored version of Giordano's tale, an English version of a host desecration tale, which diminishes the violence and re-expresses it as disorder.

Even more didactic in tone through its reworking was the *exemplum* of the events of Wrocław (1453), by an anonymous Carthusian of the Windesheim circle, composer of the *Speculum exemplorum*.[55] The host desecration trial against several Jews presided over by John of Capistrano was obviously worthy material for dissemination, but even so it had to be set in a more universal frame. *Exemplum* 17 in the tenth section of this compendium of preaching tales recounts 'How the Jews cut Christ's body in pieces and miraculous blood gushed out of that body'. The telling began: 'lest the confidence and faith of simple people's minds on the awesome [*terrificum*] sacrament of Christ's body be weakened . . . even these days stupendous and wondrous prodigies occur around the sacrament of the eucharist.'[56]

Miracles thus occur in order to strengthen the weak faith of the simple-minded, rendering Jewish agency subordinate to a larger divine plan. The tale begins not with the theft of the host by a peasant, as most chronicle and trial accounts do, but with the image of a eucharistic procession in the streets of Wrocław on one of the Ember Days after the feast of the Holy Cross (19–21 September). While Christian folk gathered to venerate the host, Jews mocked it and derided Christian stupidity in believing that something they had made with their own hands and which the fire had cooked was indeed the creator of heaven and earth. They resolved there and then to test the host and assembled in a house to discuss their plans. The author has several doubts voiced at this gathering: could it be that the host became God? could the bread become flesh and blood and yet remain in its original form? They tempted a custodian, who was seduced by the promise of thirty gold pieces ('XXX aureos dabimus tibi'), and who together with one of the Jews entered the church and removed a host. This was now carried back to the waiting Jews, who exclaimed: 'Let us now see what hides in it!' They cursed the host, which was placed on a table, spat on it and perforated it with knives and small lances. They recrucified Christ, who began to bleed profusely and this confused and shocked the Jews. The commotion drew the attention of Wrocław's night-watchmen, who woke the citizens with news that 'the king of glory is swimming in his own blood'. With an array of chants and cries the host was brought to the church and the table of abuse was hung up there for all to see. Some Jews converted but those who did not, some 150 in number, were thrown into the flames, while the custodian and his wife were hanged.

The Wrocław case is here transformed into a universal tale of eucharistic proof. Instances of reported Jewish speech both lend it credence, and express openly doubts which might have been current among Christians, doubts which were then crushed by the power of the miracle. Orthodoxy is thus clearly vindicated, and a further distancing between audience and doubt is achieved by the relevant example of the Jews as carriers of such doubt. The Christian accomplices were represented as weak people tempted through Jewish wiles and riches, as was the peasant who had been the protagonist of the judicial versions of the tale. The *exemplum* also discarded the bloody events which followed the trial in other Silesian towns. Eucharistic truth is at the centre of this tale, and local variegations of punishment were less interesting than the pristine act of abuse and its miraculous consequences.[57] The author, an adherent of the *devotio moderna* and situated in north-west Europe, was telling here a recent tale, news of which must have travelled in religious orders and soon through the medium of print. The story of Wrocław thus travelled across Europe in a few years, and was deemed to be the stuff of useful contemplation and effective instruction.

Exempla are clearly tales stored for performance and action. Their importance is twofold when associated with the host desecration accusation: they not only provided patterns of action in suggesting the habitual tendencies of Jews and the proper Christian response to them, but report enactments of host desecrations in named communities, lending credence to the narrative, its relevance and performability, and the benefits attached to it. Such acts remain a possibility, a potential, their attractions suggested in telling *exempla*, but awaiting a clinching link to a community's current practices and expediencies.

IMAGES

Communities which had experienced the violence of host desecration accusations chose to remember it through images. Images after all habitually contained the holy, enshrined and continually mediated divine power, and provided the backdrop for clerical action. How is violence transformed from the passing and ephemeral to the inspirational, devotional, eternal, sanctioned, holy?

What is the particular power of images, their power to display individuals and groups, as carriers of memory, knowledge and thus of identity?[58] In the sacral images and commemorative rituals which flowed from dramatic and violent events, we encounter processes of repetition and encapsulation by which communities – local, regional, national – celebrated history and memory through the aid of a variety of symbolic forms. Among such forms the visual, particularly in commissioned artefacts, was deemed to be of special effect and value.

Images not only retained memory but also bred the expectation of veracity by their very existence. Thus a case of which there is no other contemporary historical trace can be told boldly by an image. In the textile town of Lauingen on the Danube we encounter a panel of *c.*1490, painted by Hannes Schühlein of Ulm (figure 15). It represents the finding of miraculous hosts in the hollow of a tree, in the presence of priests, monks and the arrested Jewish culprit (to the left). The caption which accompanies a slightly later copy, by Peter Reyser the town surgeon, now in Lauingen Museum, reports: 'in the year MCCCIII [*sic*] the Sacrament was stolen in Lauingen and then discovered and worshipped.'[59] The image reveals what the caption does not, that it was thought in the late fifteenth century, when the painting was made, that the local eucharistic miracle had been prompted by Jewish abuse. The Jews of Lauingen had known killing at the hands of the Rintfleisch forces; they were made to leave during the great expulsion of Jews from the Duchy of Bavaria-Landshut in 1450–1.[60] Yet there is no historical vestige of a host desecration accusation in the intervening years. Might this memory not be linked, however, to quite a different historical case? In her visionary writings, the mystic Margaretha Ebner (*c.*1291–1351) recounted a case of 1346 when a Christian woman stole some hosts

15. The finding of the host in 1404, St Martin's church, Lauingen on the Danube. By Hannes Schühlein of Ulm, *c.*1490.

16. The Case of Paris (*from left to right*) (a) the exchange of the host for a garment; (b) host desecration and discovery; (c) a solemn procession with the miraculous host; (d) Christian woman executed; (e) Jew, wife and children executed by fire; (f) devils and angels dispute over the Christian woman's soul. Paolo Uccello, *predella* to the Altarpiece of the Communion of the Apostles, Palazzo Ducale, Urbino.

from an abbey church and attempted to sell them to a Jew in Lauingen, only to be rebuffed, discovered and executed.[61] Was this the event which led to the birth of a local tradition about *Jewish* abuse of the host? What we can be sure of is that the image captured a story, stabilised it and rendered it worthy of worship and remembrance.

The destruction of Jewish space and the use of the void for the erection of Christian commemorative tokens was a single and pervasive act of replacement. The space which had previously been inhabited by Jews was almost always razed and reallocated for the erection of chapels after the killing or banishment of Jews.[62] Images were often contained in them, marking high altars or decorating newly dedicated side chapels.

The visual strategies employed in the turning of a host desecration tale into images were of three main types: telling the tale, sacramental use, and universal extension.

Telling the Tale

Images related to host desecration accusations were often made to commemorate the event by narrative disclosure of its crucial parts. Such telling assumed that the story was known through some other means, and would be crystallised and kept alive with the help of the image, altarpiece or panels.

Without doubt the most famous image of the host desecration (of Paris) is that painted by Paolo Uccello between 1465 and 1468. Originally commissioned to execute the altarpiece and *predella* for the patrician confraternity of Corpo di Cristo of Urbino, Uccello never got beyond the execution of the *predella*, which accomodated six scenes (figure 16), while the northerner, Joos Van Ghent, executed the Communion of the Apostles above.[63] The tale unfolds from left to right and includes (a) the scene of exchange of the host for some garments between a Jewish moneylender and a woman;[64] (b) a domestic scene in which the host is seen bleeding within a pan placed over a fire in the presence of a distressed wife, son and daughter, and with a group of Christians breaking down the door as the blood flows out of the wall;[65] (c) the bringing of the miraculous host in a procession for safe-keeping on the altar in an apse, a strange nocturnal scene; (d) the execution of the Christian woman by hanging; (e) the execution of the Jewish family, bound together in a fire; (f) the quarrel over the Christian soul between demons and angels. Scenes (c) to (f) are set against a continuous nocturnal background of a hilly countryside, while the scenes of purchase and abuse occur within the built-up spaces of the Jew's house and business. The *predella* – Uccello's last work – is colourful, dramatic, full of characters, and unfolds like a good play. The scenes were based closely on the influential version of Giovanni Villani's *Cronica*, which also provided the bare facts around which the *sacra rappresentazione* of the host desecration was composed.[66]

The commemoration of the act of eucharistic abuse and vindication is cast forcefully into contrast by the austere paleness of the scene above it, the main altarpiece of Joos Van Ghent. If the altarpiece bespoke eucharistic certainty as grounded in scripture, the *predella* exposed and demolished whatever doubt these claims might have nonetheless raised. The altarpiece ensemble thus borrowed from the variety of didactic resources which underpinned eucharistic instruction and which coexisted in the religious culture. When one reflects upon the identity of the patrons, the members of the Corpo di Cristo fraternity, the aptness of a eucharistic scene becomes clear. It is particularly significant when it is noted that this fraternity underwrote and promoted the creation of a *monte di pietà* in Urbino in 1468, which was meant to rid the town of the need for Jewish loans, and of the Jews themselves. The process of *monte* foundation was one facilitated and enabled by the efforts of the Observant Franciscans, whose rhetoric of reform often bound up internal Christian improvement with the excision of Jews through expulsion or conversion.[67] The powerful anti-usury thrust of their preaching to Christians converged neatly with their anti-Jewish arguments. These provided a poignant and animating context for the commissioning, making and viewing of the altarpiece in their chapel of the Corpo di Cristo.

Less elaborate in its parts, but no less direct and poignant, was the pair of altar paintings which were made for the chapel of the Holy Blood in Pulkau around 1518–22, and which similarly recounted a version of the narrative of accusation as experienced in Pulkau (figures 17a–c). Nicholas Breu, an exponent of the 'Danube School', produced six altarwing Passion scenes, four in front and two on the obverse of the (closed) wings, and the lower register which contained, as a sort of *predella*, two scenes of the host desecration tale. Breu's style is most distinctive, and is characterised by very wild and stark landscapes which contain figures in sweeping movement sporting wild clothes and hair.[68] The two scenes are contained within framing arches and are not now on view. The right-hand painting (a) portrays three Jews, bearded and in long cloaks, around a wooden table placed out of doors, just after the act of piercing a host, an act which has produced the dramatic result of the host's transformation into a Christ Child, now hovering over the table. The left-hand scene (b) depicts the same men's efforts at destroying the evidence: they are trying to get rid of the host by throwing it into a stream of water. According to some versions, the Jews threw the host into a well, and this produced mysterious lights which called forth Christians to discover it. Others claimed that the chapel of the Holy Blood was built on that very site.[69]

Similar local colour and detail is reflected in the single remaining part of what must have been a more elaborate altarpiece, which commemorates the host desecration at Regensburg of *c.*1476. A highly complex case, in which the host desecration also brought forth accusations of ritual murder, it is captured visually in a panel now stored in the

17. The altar of the Holy Blood Chapel by Nicholas Breu *c*.1520, Pulkau (a) (*left*) the desecration of the host; (b) (*right*) the attempt to hide the host (these two panels showing the host desecration tale are no longer on view); (c) (*opposite*) full view of the altar.

18. The finding of the host in Regensburg (*c.*1476).

German Museum in Nuremberg. The panel bears the captions 'The thief throws the hosts into a cellar' ('Der Dieb wirft die Hostien in einen Keller'), and 'The discovery of the hosts in the cellar' ('Die Auffindung der Hostien im Keller') (figure 18).[70] The panel falls into two sections divided vertically: on the right a brightly coloured town scene, with men and women around the city's fountain; on the left the darker scene of a man holding what appears to be a metal container from which two hosts had fallen or been placed through a grill and into a cellar. At the same time, over this dark scene of crime hover two angels, whom we have already encountered as heralds and markers of miraculous hosts. This panel probably formed part of an ensemble which would have clarified the larger narrative; but its painter clearly pursued the 'telling the tale' option, with the details of a given local accusation of abuse in a recognisable setting.

A more detailed treatment was offered in the church of St Eloi at Rouen, in a series of three sixteenth-century double windows which offer six scenes, each accompanied by an explanatory quatrain and all recreating the story of the miracle of Paris.[71] The narrative begins with a 'bourgeoise' who pawned her dress (window 1), and who was seduced by a cursed Jew into delivering the host to him (window 2). Fearlessly she handed the host to the Jew, who in turn gave her the dress without payment (window 3). He then put the host on a table, struck the host until it bled, and then thrice repeated the action (window 4). The woman then entered the Jew's house while he slept and took away the host (window 5) and brought it, still bleeding, to the Provost of Paris, seated on his throne (window 6).[72] The setting is highly classicised, with ornate arches as frames for the exchanges. Indeed, each scene sees an exchange between two main figures, except for the one depicting the Jew's abuse. Here the sumptuously dressed Jew stands alone at a dark table/altar, raising his knife with great deliberation over the pristine host.[73]

Visual representations were thus sometimes made to tell the story embellished with local colour, and were situated in the local church to be nourished by local knowledge. In them the Jews are vividly portrayed in the act of abuse, which was also the act of their unmaking, the discovery. This choice laid the emphasis on the abuse and the local identity of the actors. Even in Uccello's *predella*, about events which had occurred in Paris many years earlier, the story is greatly localised and drew immediacy from the very specific context of its use, the private chapel of a fraternity engaged in eucharistic piety. The host desecration accusation could thus be 'localised' even if it happened elsewhere; the effect was achieved through details of representation of gesture and space, and the familiarisation which these achieved. To a Nuremberger or a Pulkauite, recognition might have been prompted by this encounter with the tale in mundane and familiar spaces, within spheres of local knowledge which could make memories live.

Miraculous Emphasis and Sacramental Use

A different choice was made by some producers of images of host desecration, one we may call the sacramental or cultic approach. In it images were chosen not to retell a historical event, but to contain the resulting relic, the miraculous host, or its related relic, the bloody cloth which had contained it, and to celebrate the continuous emanation of the miraculous powers it had brought forth. The historical was set aside as the immanent and sacramental were emphasised in images which themselves became sacred objects. The best example of this type is the beautiful portable altarpiece and reliquary now (since 1821) at the Augustinian monastery of Klosterneuburg, made in Lower Austria around 1470, and commemorating the miracle of Korneuburg, 1305.[74] It is a small wooden gilt altarpiece (overall size, 26 × 42 cm; middle section, 26 × 21 cm), containing a central section in which was once displayed a piece of the bloodied and miracle-working cloth within a rectangular space; this is flanked by panels, each subdivided horizontally into two (see figure 10a above, p. 60). The Jew occupies a single square at the top right, as guarantor of the relic's origins. He is dressed in sumptuous Jewish garb, marked with a Jewish sign, and carries a bleeding host inscribed with the mark of the Crucifixion and held in a white cloth. The scene is explained with the caption 'Here the Jew shows the sacrament'. The remaining three scenes display the very types of miracles which the witnesses reported so willingly to Ambrose of Heiligenkreuz during his investigation: first, at the top left, the caption 'The first sign was that of the candles lighting up of themselves', and then similar captions announced the images depicting the cure of the crippled ('Zwen krump send geslecht worden'), showing a lame man, at the bottom left section; the cure of two blind people, at the bottom right ('Zwen plint send gesehend worden'). The blind and the lame are accompanied by a well-dressed man, the putative recorder of the events. When closed, the portable altar displays an image of a gothic monstrance within which a glowing white host is contained. Two small hooks secure its wings when closed.[75] Here the relic was contained, and only sketchy reference to its source, the host desecration, is provided. The visual is the context for the display of the host's miraculous powers (through its blood).

One Among Many: The Universal Tale

Any local eucharistic tale could be made to fit into a wider set of continuous eucharistic emanations. Just as reports of host desecrations and miracles were inserted into the late medieval collections of *exempla*, so they could be represented visually within a broader eucharistic series.

The choice to represent the tale as part of a larger set of unfolding miracles was made in a number of media, in artefacts which were not always related to a specific local or regional *cause célèbre* of a host desecration accusation. In such cases, the desecration scene is inserted among other well-known tales of eucharistic miracles.

In Orvieto Cathedral's chapel of the Corporal, constructed to commemorate the miracle of Bolsena, which may have helped influence Pope Urban IV to found the feast of Corpus Christi in 1264, the wall paintings of 1357–64 pursue such a strategy.[76] Their painter, Ugolino di Prate Ilario, decorated the whole chapel in the north transept with scenes of well-known eucharistic miracles, while upon the altar stood the chapel's magnificent enamelled tabernacle of the corporal stained in eucharistic blood, the emblem of the city's own experience, the miracle of neighbouring Bolsena. The tabernacle interacted with the stock of eucharistic tales already encountered such as the Jewish Boy (with three scenes: communion, throwing into oven and saving by the Virgin) or the woman who tested the eucharist in a burning pan only to see it bleed (figures 19a–b).[77]

There is a striking cluster in Aragon in the later fourteenth century: a pair of altar-frontals has survived from the parish of Las Monjas (Lérida diocese). The host desecration accusation is removed from any identifying context and is elevated to the universal field of eucharistic truths with several other miracles (figures 20a–b). It is further enhanced, as it is inserted into the larger Christian story, by being placed within frontals which celebrate the Incarnation, Crucifixion and Trinity. One altar-frontal has at its centre the Virgin and Child, the other the Trinity around the figure of the crucified Christ.[78]

These Catalan altar-frontals contain scenes in which a Jew boils the host in a cauldron or two Jews pierce it on a table. These were the commonest forms of abuse imputed to Jews, and they usually followed each other: as the piercing brought forth blood and failed to destroy the host, Jews were said to move on to further attempts at destruction by boiling water, which in turn become blood-red. As we have seen, the boiling cauldron is also strikingly similar to the way in which Jews were seen, and represented themselves as preparing their crockery and cutlery for the Passover: vats of boiling water were prepared, often for communal use, as is seen in a Castilian Haggadah of the first quarter of the fourteenth century (see figure 11, p. 73, above).[79]

The large context, both historical (Last Supper) and contemporary (host miracles), which host desecrations are here made to fit is reinforced by the overarching figures of Christ as Child and Christ in the Trinity, which turn the abusers into offenders against every Christian and all Christians, as far removed as possible from any immediate context.

The altarpiece of Jaime Serra of *c.*1400 in the monastery of Sijena

QVO QVIDA PVER IVDEVCV ALIIS PVERIS XPNS
RECEPIT CORPV XI CLA PATRE·⟵⟶

QVO PATER INDIGNATVS ARRIPVIT PVE-
RVM IN FVRNVM VITRARIVM CONIECIT

QVO MATRE ADVOCANTE HOCCVRRETES VIC
ERIPIVIT PVERV INCOLVME PATRE SVPDOI

ISTA FEV MVLIA MVLOTES CORP X INMEDIA ARDENTE Q IDVETA SI
ET STVPEFACTA MISIT CINERE· S: SANGVIS MVLIE HABVNDABI

19. Frescoes by Ugolino di
Prate Ilario, Chapel of the
Corporal, Cathedral of the
Assumption of Mary, Orvieto,
c.1357–64 (a) (*above*) the
Jewish Boy; (b) (*opposite*) the
woman who cooked the host.

near Huesca also inserts a host desecration tale into a larger scene. Here it appears on the right flank of the *predella*, alongside the Last Supper scene at the *predella*'s centre. It is paralleled on the left by a scene of host desecration: the host being struck by a Jewish man on a wooden table, with the appearance of Christ as wounded child in a boiling pot, as his wife and son look on (figure 21). Above, the altarpiece represents the Virgin and Child in the centre, and above them is situated a smaller scene of the Crucifixion. These central panels are surrounded by twelve smaller narrative panels showing the life of Christ.[80] The host desecration described here is of the Paris type: the abusing Jew has round him his wife and son, and the abused host on the table bleeds, while it has also been transformed into the Christ Child in the midst of the boiling cauldron. The architectural arrangements even provide a space on the left in which the exchange of garment for host is transacted. The Christian woman's cap is decorated with pseudo-Hebrew letters, a common attribute of Jewish identity in medieval art, and a sign of her complicity in the Jewish crime.[81] The Jew's attire and the placing of the bloodied host resemble the scene devoted to such abuse in the Las Monjas altar-frontal just examined. Indeed, Serra's altarpiece collapses the central themes of the altar-frontals, as in its centre are located both Christ on the Cross and as Child. It is tempting to relate the production of this *predella*, devoted as it is to the themes of host desecration, to the memory of such an accusation made against the Jews of Huesca in 1377, but this cannot be proven. Whereas the altarpiece is anything but local in its gestures, its meanings could have been enhanced by the memory of such recent accusations, even those that had been proven false.

In a similar way to the two Catalan altar-frontals, Serra's altarpiece embeds the host desecration accusation within a broad history of eucharistic tale and miraculous proof. All three surround the accusation with other famous miracles, mostly collected from the pages of *exempla* books, the famous and ubiquitous *Dialogue of Miracles* by Caesarius of Heisterbach, or the *Alphabet of Tales*. This universalising effect is also evident in a later case: the Paris miracle of 1290 was represented as one of many scenes in a sixteenth-century series of tapestries. Its subject-matter was similarly drawn from the world of *exempla* into which more recent host desecration tales were inserted in support of the traditional edifice built upon edifying tales. In 1573–8 these twelve tapestries were made for the Ronceray monastery in Angers, following a testamentary bequest by Bishop Jacques Fourré of Chalon-sur-Saône. The whole cycle deals with manifestations of the eucharist through miracles in the world and was meant to be hung in the abbey choir during the Corpus Christi festivities. Each tapestry contained at least two scenes (some more) and the miracles included are the Mass of St Gregory (on priestly doubt), the death of an undeserving communicant, the cure of a demoniac by

20. Las Monjas altar-frontals, late fourteenth century (a) (*above*) desecration of
the host by two Jewish men with a knife; (b) (*opposite*) a Jewish man throws the
host into a cauldron of boiling water.

the host, a horse kneeling to the eucharist, and bees adoring the host.
Among these is inserted a set of scenes depicting the host desecration
accusation at Paris, 1290. Each scene was accompanied by captions, in
a manner reminiscent of broadsheets, which we will encounter later.
Those around the host desecration scene recalled:

> There was a Jew, a resident of Paris, who bought
> the host and cut it with a knife until it bled
> and then put it to boil and it bled over
> as a crucifix became present within it.[82]

The stages of the abuse are juxtaposed in this single tapestry, as part of
the larger ensemble of the set as a whole: a series of manifestations of
eucharistic truth and power.

Processional Afterlife: Holy Knife and Sacred Host in Fifteenth-Century Paris

If ritual actions inform by the enactment of foundation myths, and make palpable the relation between the natural and the supernatural realms, in an attempt to bring them into harmony, then the processional rituals around the miraculous host of Paris may be seen as another visual encapsulation of the memory of the case. As we have seen, the house of the Jew of Paris and some adjacent houses were turned, with royal aid and the munificence of a rich merchant, into a *capella miraculorum* which contained the holy knife of abuse and existed alongside the parish church of Saint-Jean-en-Grève, where the miraculous host was reserved. It was between this chapel, in the street which came to be known within a few years as the 'street where God was boiled', on the precise site of the abuse, and the parish church, to which the bleeding host had been brought for safe keeping following its abuse, that the benefit and duties of commemoration of the Paris case were divided. These were integrated into processional trajectories which bound them and other notable points on the ecclesiastical map of Paris, on either side of the river, into a liturgical whole. Whereas material for the

21. The host desecration (according to the Case of Paris). Detail of Jaime Serra's altarpiece for the monastery of Sijena, Catalonia (*c.*1400).

fourteenth century is lacking, from the fifteenth century we possess a number of revealing records about the visual and ritual nature of these events.

On 15 May 1444 a procession for the promotion of peace between the King of England and the King of France was mounted in the presence of the bishops of Paris and Beauvais, and the abbots of Saint-Maur, Saint Magloire and Saint-Germain-des-Prés. It began in the parish church, where the miraculous host was collected, then proceeded to the miracle chapel, where the holy knife was added, together with other relics and crosses, perhaps like the one depicted in a nineteenth-century engraving of the fifteenth-century processional staff which belonged to the *praelector* of the chapel of Billettes.[83] They processed to the church of St Katherine Val-des-Escoliers, with 500 torches and some 9,000–10,000 people. Behind this multitude followed a wagon on which the mystery of the Jew was enacted – his abuse, his execution and the fate of his wife and children; the roads through which it passed were decorated as on Saint Saviour's day.[84]

Another such occasion was 3 June 1456 when the meeting of the court royal was cancelled and its members joined the general procession of the clergy. The crowd, consisting of barefoot clergy and a multitude of townspeople, paraded to the parish of St-Jean-en-Grève where the miracle of Billettes took place, whence the host was carried to Notre Dame, and to the Gate of the Royal Palace, and then to Notre Dame and to St Geneviève. Among the multitudes there may have been some poor folk, perhaps the recipients of charitable tokens such as the one found in the bend of the River Seine just under the Hôtel-Dieu, depicting Christ rising from a boiling cauldron, on one side, and a knife piercing Christ's monogram INRI, on the other.[85]

Procession, host in monstrance, relics, processional cross, mystery enacted, all in the space of the streets of Paris with some of the greatest people of the realm involved. The single eucharistic miracle of Paris was thus transformed into a focus for supplication of a national nature, which saw a culmination of visual and ritual effort.[86] While the Paris case was absorbed locally into the life of a new chapel, a parish, and of a royal capital, news of the event travelled widely and prompted efforts of commemoration in countries which had never lived through the host desecration and its violence.

WORD AND IMAGE: IMAGE AND PRAYER

The Carew-Poyntz Book of Hours

This English Book of Hours was made *c.*1350–60, probably for the wife of John Carew, Lord Deputy of Ireland, who died in 1363.[87] It contains a calendar, prayers for the Passion and for the mass, the Salutations of the Virgin, Hours of the Virgin, penitential psalms, gradual psalms, a litany to the Virgin and prayers for the Virgin and Christ. It is on the pages of prayers to the Virgin and Christ that a series of images of miracles of the Virgin appears, among which is the tale of the Jewish Boy.[88] These images are four lines high, at the *bas-de-page*, and the text above them fills fourteen lines. On the preceeding folios, however, occurs a series of images related to the host desecration story in the Paris version, as well as another tale which associates illicit keeping of the eucharist with its transformation into gold coins, another familiar tale (figures 22a–d). The host desecration sequence shows a woman hand-ing over a garment in exchange for a bag of coins taken out of the Jew's chest, in which coins lie glittering (fol. 183ᵛ) (a); the next scene has the woman at communion, receiving the host over a housling cloth, but also removing it from her mouth (fol. 184ʳ) (b). We next see the woman again involved in an exchange: this time she offers a cross-inscribed host as she receives back her pawned garment from the Jew (fol. 184ᵛ) (c). Abuse of the host by two Jews follows on fol. 185ʳ (d): one Jew is dressed in a typical fashion, but his accomplice is lightly dressed and has a rather distorted thick-lipped face. They perpetrate the attack on the eucharist upon a table with sharp lances, held by each. Behind each figure stands another: to the left a figure reminiscent of a man of law,[89] and to the right, a sergeant or baillif; these may represent the officers who were to arrest the Jews after the discovery of their act. Next follow two scenes involving the Virgin, and on fol. 185ᵛ the torments inflicted on the Jews on the way to execution are shown, as both men are dragged half-naked by a pair of horses with riders (and the attached prayer is 'Domine Ihesu Christi fili dei vivi').

Within the Latin pages of a Book of Hours, intended for personal intercession to the Virgin and the contemplation of her qualities, we witness the associative rendering of tales old and new. Whereas the prevailing theme of *bas-de-page* decoration here is that of Marian tales, an exemplary eucharistic story – which like so many Marian tales involves Jews – is interpolated here, offering an ending quite different from that of the traditional Marian tale, the story of the Jewish Boy.

In England and Ireland there was little resonance within the world of chronicle, experience or memory to interact with a host desecration tale. It was thus turned from recent event to 'classic' narrative within an environment of unqualified Marian piety, purity and justice.

The Holy Host of Dijon

Miraculous hosts, and particularly those which had responded to Jewish attacks, were seen as magnificent manifestations of the sacred, and sources of inspiration, health and grace. They were frequently venerated within the space of the community which had originally witnessed the events, and which needed to turn violence into memory, where the host had been saved, guarded and elevated to worship. An interesting and unusual case of sharing in the miraculous host occurred in the rarefied and privileged circle of the Burgundian court in the fifteenth century. Following their close collaboration during the years of the Council of Basel, in 1433, Pope Eugenius IV granted Duke Philip the Good of Burgundy a miraculous host, which was alleged to be the product of a Jewish attack. The papal bull describes the gift:

> We concede and donate to your pious devotion a host of the sacrament with the image of the Saviour seated on a throne, the wondrous Sacrament of the Lord's Body, perforated in many places by some madman with the ferocity of a sword's blows, and stained with blood in the said places, [a host] which is deposited in our sacristy.[90]

A perforated, blood-encrusted host was thus translated from the papal sacristy to the court at Dijon, and there placed in the Sainte Chapelle within the Burgundian family mortuary in the Charterhouse of Champmol.[91] It soon became an object of veneration within the small group of privileged users of the chapel. One such was René of Anjou, King of Sicily (1434–80), who was the Duke of Burgundy's prisoner in Dijon in 1435–7. The new relic kindled a devotion later expressed in its appearance in a full page illumination in a lavish Book of Hours commissioned by him. The image of a host hoisted on a cross held and adored by angels was placed between the pages of suffrages of the saints and prayers to the Virgin.[92]

The image of this family relic became a subject of special devotion among Duke Philip's closest circle. The relic received a magnificent pure gold monstrance in 1454, a gift from the Duke's third wife, Isabella of Portugal.[93] A further elaboration occurred in 1501 when King Louis XII granted 400 livres tournois for repair to the chapel, followed in 1505 by the gift made after his recovery from a grave illness, of the coronation crown, which henceforth was to be hung above the pinnacle of the sumptuous monstrance.[94] The Hours of Mary of Burgundy received an addition of a bi-folio *c.*1505, which incorporated the relic in its new setting. A full-page Host of Dijon in a meadow was accompanied by the prayer 'O salutaris hostia' on the facing page (figures 23a–b). This side also describes the cult's origins. The four stanzas begin with Jewish abuse, located neither in place nor in time:

> A Jew has mutilated the
> Host of the holy sacrament
> By striking ten blows and more,
> And making it bleed abundantly.
>
> Eugene, treasure of the church,
> Took it as his witness
> And had it transmitted
> To Philip Duke of Burgundy.

> Having arrived in Lille
> On business the Duke
> Received it devoutly
> In the year 1430.
>
> But in order to keep the
> Holy relic sacredly
> He had it decently placed
> In the chapel in Dijon.[95]

It describes the granting of the gift, its reception in Burgundy, and its placing 'honestement' in the chapel in Dijon.

22. The Case of Paris (*from left to right*) (a) the Christian woman pawns her garment; (b) receives communion; (c) hands over the host; (d) the Jew desecrates the host. Carew-Poyntz Book of Hours (*c.*1350–60), fols 183ᵛ, 184ʳ, 184ᵛ, 185ʳ.

Other members of the court participated in the exultation of the Host of Dijon. Not many years after its arrival, an officer of Philip the Good, Hughlein de Bregilles (who appears in the fiscal accounts of 1446) composed a celebratory poem about the host of Dijon and its cult. This survives in a sixteenth-century manuscript, the large part of which contains the text of a morality play on the Passion. Separated from the play text by a blank folio, the poem follows in a different hand, but is clearly linked by association.[96] The poem tells of a host desecration by a Jew, but names no place or time:

When the cursed and miserable Jew
With criminal heart and hateful courage
Had wounded the venerable sacrament
An event befell, both piteous and miraculous,
As real miraculous blood spurted from the wounds.[97]

23. Additions of *c.*1500 to the Hours of Mary of Burgundy (1465) (a) (*above*) The host of Dijon, fol. 1*ᵛ; (b) (*right*) the prayer 'O salutaris hostia', fol. 2*ʳ.

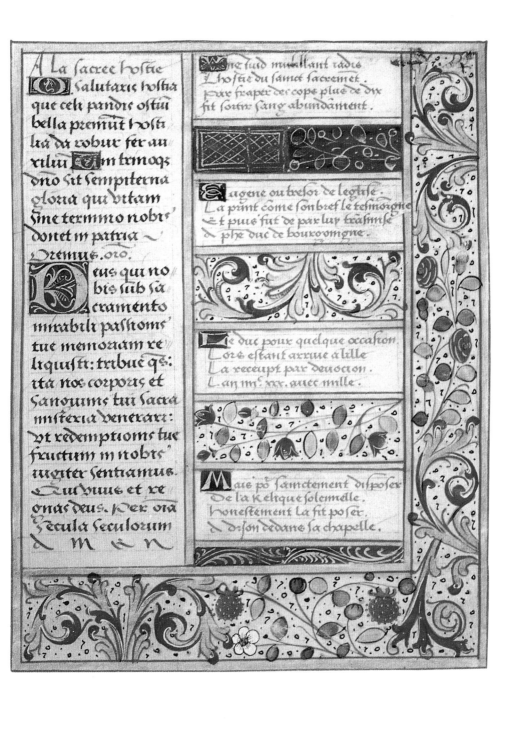

A La sacree hostie
Salutaris hostia
que celi pandis ostiu
bella premut hosti
lia da robur fer au
xiliu In trinoqs
dno sit sempiterna
gloria qui uitam
sine termino nobis
donet in patria
Oremus. oro.
Deus qui no
bis sub sa
cramento
mirabili passionis
tue memoriam re
liquisti: tribue qs:
ita nos corporis et
sanguinis tui sacra
misteria uenerari:
ut redemptionis tue
fructum in nobis
iugiter sentiamus.
Qui uiuis et re
gnas deus. per oia
secula seculorum
AMEN

ne suid muuillant radis
Lhostie du sainct sacremet
par frapper des cops plus de dix
fit sortir sang abundament.

Sagene ou tresor de leglise
La print come son bref le tesmoigne
Et puis fut de par luy trasmise
A phe duc de bourcoigne.

Le duc pour quelque occasion
Lors estant arriue a lille
La receupt par deuocion
Lan iiiC xx. auec mille.

Mais po sainctement disposer
De la Relique solemnelle
honestement la fit poser
A dison dedans sa chapelle.

24. The host of Dijon, Ogier Benigne's Book of Hours, fol. 17.

As in fifteenth-century Paris, a miraculous host is made the focus of hopes for national, indeed Christian, salvation. The poem ends with an invocation for the host's help and protection against the Turks:

Be our shield, defence and vanguard
against the Turks of the infernal force.
Without your grace we are too feeble.[98]

Clearly, in the Burgundian court, the local cult of the host was detached from any local resonances of host desecration accusations, in the absence of Jews, but was nourished by eucharistic piety, in association with the eucharistic prayer 'O salutaris hostia'. The miraculous host's local and current cult, its endorsement by the papacy, and the sumptuousness of its setting, were the foci for devotion. Thus the family of Ogier Benigne, the Comptroller of Dijon waterways, had a bi-folio added to a Book of Hours of *c*.1500, showing a full-page image of the host, resplendent in the monstrance crowned by Louis XII's crown, accompanying the prayer 'O salutaris hostia' (figure 24).[99]

Just as in the visualisations on altarpieces, the re-enactment of a host desecration could gain a grounding – of the sort offered by local reference in other cases – from gestures to the rich world of eucharistic association. Eternal cult, ubiquitous power – in these celebrations of the miracle, the Jews recede somewhat into the background.

Drama

Dramatic commemoration of the acts of host desecration imputed to Jews survive within three linguistic spheres: the English Croxton *Play of the Sacrament* of *c*.1461, the French *Mistere de la saincte hostie*, and the Italian rendering of the Paris case in a sixteenth-century drama named *Un miracolo del Corpo di Cristo*. Strangely, no version has survived in a German dialect, from any of the regions which so often repeated host desecration accusations and violence.[100] Such dramas as survive from other regions are embedded in distinctive cultural traditions and differ greatly in tone and emphasis. The Croxton play is a gentle and comic tale about Jewish doubt which is turned into faith, in a mode which by the late thirteenth century might be considered old-fashioned;[101] the French text is a close dramatisation of the local Parisian traditions as captured in the chronicle of St Denis and its satellites;[102] and the Italian version is a much expanded drama based on the Paris case, and linking it to the Miracle of Bolsena, to papal promotion of the Corpus Christi feast and to the liturgical offerings of Thomas Aquinas and St Bonaventure for the feast.[103]

It is immediately striking that the dramas of host desecration were composed and perhaps enacted in cultural spheres which did not give rise to regular host desecration accusations. England and Italian regions had never made such accusations, and after Paris in 1290 nor were these known on French soil. The tens of German towns which had accused, tried and executed, or accused and murdered, Jews for having abused the host have left no trace of dramatic rendering. The dramas about host desecration were far from the landscape of immediate memory, and thus had to mediate or make immediate the message of the narrative in other ways.[104] The English play achieved this through narrative resolution and a happy ending, with an interlude and comic scenes to boot; the French by assimilation into the Passion play style with detailed description of Christ's suffering together with an extrapolation which told of the later years of the 'mauvaise femme', the Christian accomplice; and the Italian version by presenting the narrative as a complex pan-Christian tale grounded in papal associations and grafted on to another well-known eucharistic miracle.

In contrast to the painful and gruesome *Crucifixio* play of the York Corpus Christi pageant, which explores the physical details and rhythms of torture which Christ's body suffered,[105] the Croxton *Play of the Sacrament* is an inversion of such a style. It is situated in Heraclea in Spain and in it the Jew Jonathan persuades a Christian merchant, Aristorius, to procure the host for him. Christ in the host is nailed to a 'piller', plucked off the wall again with pincers and then covered by a cloth before being jettisoned into a pot of boiling water, and later into an oven. Christ's body undergoes all the injuries which the growing traditions of the host desecration narrative inflicted upon it, and which likened its latter-day abuse to the original Crucifixion.[106] In depicting these torments, the *Crucifixio* and the Croxton play mirror each other, and equally demand of the spectator a great deal of imaginative work, drawing on the outrageous claim which drama and sacrament alike make of viewer and believer.[107] Both plays are steeped in Passion imagery, but in the Croxton play the author has used the kernel of the host desecration narrative to create a Passion play with a happy ending.[108] The eucharistic moment triumphs over the Passion: Christ moves with ease in and out of the bread, strengthening faith and finally even converting a Jew. He emerges from an oven as unscathed as the Jewish Boy repeatedly did in that old-fashioned tale. While it may have fulfilled a didactic function, as has often been claimed,[109] the Croxton play is much more useful as a platform for the discussion of sacramentality, and particularly of the issues of faith, the reality of faith. It thus holds up the Jew as a didactic prop, as he conveniently converts to Christianity in the face of eucharistic miraculous manifestation.

Much more didactic if much less dramatic is the French *Mistere de la saincte hostie*.[110] The Jewish moneylender Jacob Mousse induces a Christian woman to bring him the host in return for the freeing of her 'surcot', which had been pawned as surety for a loan. The woman shows some torment at the dilemma, complaining 'tu me requiers chose trop dure', but ultimately relents, in the desire to appear well dressed at Easter.[111] Here the Jewish personages are again the carriers of Christian faith and its proof, as members of the abusing Jewish family are made to reiterate tokens of eucharistic amazement. As the host is brought into the Jewish home the daughter says to her mother:

> Ha mere qu'il est blanc et tendre
> Laissez le moy ung peu tenir
> [Oh mother, how white and tender he is
> Let me hold him a little.]

Her brother adds, as siblings do:

> Et moy laissez le moy tenir
> et par Mahe il mest moult bel.
> Il est aussi blanc quang aignel
> Ha hay montrez le moi ma mere.[112]
> [No, let me hold him.
> By Mahomet! how lovely he is!
> He is white like a sheep.
> Ah! mother, show me it!]

As the children witness a series of attacks on the eucharist – with a knife, in a fire, with a lance, with a kitchen knife – the daughter expresses their horror:

> Helas doulx pere ie vous prye
> Que vous ne le despecez pas
> Helas il seigne helas hela
> Mon pere pour dieu cessez vous.[113]
> [Alas! sweet father I beg you
> do not hurt him so.
> Alas! he bleeds, Alas! Alas!
> My father, for God's sake, stop it!]

The mother similarly recognises the enormity of her spouse's actions as a crucifix arises from the abused host:

> Doulxdieu doulxdieu merci te crie
> Vraye hostie sacrifie.[114]
> [Sweet god, sweet god thank you cries out to you
>   the true host sacrifice]

The play follows closely the narrative line offered by the vernacular versions of the case of Paris studied above.[115] The Jewish boy leads to the

25. The *sacra reppresentazione* of the host desecration accusation. Biblioteca dell 'Academia e dei Lincei e Corsiniana, Rome, frontispiece.

discovery of his father's crime and inaugurates a whole process of recovery and celebration of the miraculous host enacted in parallel to the trial and execution of the father. Special emphasis is laid upon the treatment of the new relic, the holy knife, which, as we have seen, formed part of the emblematic relics of Paris in the fifteenth century.[116] A description of the performance in Metz in 1513 attests to the elaborate use of devices in attempts to render fantastical yet persuasive the workings of the miracles in the host.[117]

The fifteenth-century Italian play interpolates far more extensively and provides a familial and social context of great vivacity and precision. It opens with the announcement of an angel, whose prologue summarises the play's contents (figure 25). Based largely on the Paris case, it nonetheless invokes the Bolsena miracle (alleged to have occurred *c.*1264) and papal endorsement of the feast of the eucharist. The action begins with Guglielmo, who loses at dice and pawns his wife's greatcoat, the *cioppa*, with Manuel, the Jewish moneylender. The aggrieved wife wishes to have her garment for Easter and so she approaches Manuel with an offer of 'some exchange or money' in return for three days' use of the garment. Manuel agrees to return the pawn and pay her in exchange for 'bringing to him the body of her living God' ('corpo del suo dio vivo qui recharlo'). He claims that the host is needed for his sick son and that having it might persuade him to convert. The woman agrees and the exchange is completed.[118]

With the host in hand the Jew begins to act: he throws it into a pan and fries it, then stabs it and sees it bleed. When two men enter to take out a loan, they see the offence and report it to the king. Manuel is arrested and taken to the *podestà*, to whom he reveals the identity of his accomplice. The woman is soon arrested but she claims piteously that she had been tempted by the devil. The bishop is then summoned and attempts to remove the host from the Jew's house. When it is found it is carried away ceremoniously as the Corpus Christi hymn composed by Thomas Aquinas, the *Pange Lingua*, is chanted. Judgement is passed and the Jew is executed, but the woman is freed and a chapel built on the site of the Jew's house.

Here is an embellished version of the Paris case and the text from which Uccello may have drawn his inspiration for the narrative of the *predella* scenes. As opposed to the French version it involves more people and is less interested in the Jew's family than in the Christian one. At the end of the play Jews were brought on stage and beaten up, thus demonstrating the sort of violence which almost always followed a local accusation.[119]

Broadsheets and Poems: Passau 1477–8, Sternberg 1492 and Deggendorf 1337

The new technology of print allowed images and words, extolling host desecration tales and ensuing miracles, to publicise recent events and attract people from far afield to the new shrine. In this fashion what had been an experience encountered by locals, and by pilgrims, and spread in the *exempla* of preaching and in casual tales, was now captured in little pamphlets and broadsheets, which were relatively cheap and which could form the core of collective reading.[120] Moreover, recent events could be combined in new writing and printing projects such as the Nuremberg Chronicle produced by Hartmann Schedel (1440–1514) in 1493, 'the world chronicle' which juxtaposed in a single paragraph Wrocław (1453), Passau (1477–8) and Regensburg (1478). A single woodcut of the burning heads of Jews spoke for these widely disparate events, which Hartmann Schedel combined into a single theme, used to illustrate the report on Rintfleisch (1298) and Deggendorf (1337).[121]

The broadsheets and pamphlets examined here were produced in

Bavaria, an area we have seen to be dense with memories of host desecrations and their aftermath. The infectious nature of the accusations was paralleled by the regional spread of printed responses. When the Passau host desecration accusation took place in 1477–8, printing was truly in its infancy, and we have no surviving attempts at broadsheet dissemination before c.1481. As Passau had no print workshops before 1481, the first version was probably printed nearby in Nuremberg, and was later incorporated into the surviving broadsheet with a new text, printed by Caspar Hochfeder, entitled attractively 'A gruesome story which has taken place in Passau, about the Jews, as follows below' ('Ein grawsamlich geschicht Geschehen zu passaw Von den Juden als hernach volgt').[122] The upper half of the broadsheet contains a set of captioned images and its lower half contains a description of the event in Bavarian dialect, a version closely reliant upon confessions and trial records. In twelve images in three rows of four, older than the text and cut in a fairly crude but vivid manner, the story is told in great detail and definite emphasis.[123] It begins in a church (St Mary in the Freiung), with the theft of the hosts, and ends in one, with the scene of veneration of the miraculous hosts in the new chapel ('hye hebe man an zw pawen, unserm herren zu lob eyn gotshaus. Auss der juden synagog'). Five of the twelve scenes describe in detail the punishments meted out to the offenders: the arrest of the Jews, the beheading of the converted Jews, the torture with glowing tongs, the burning of their feet, the execution of Christoph the thief. Such images and their explanatory texts were made available in the region, which was already dense with eucharistic pilgrimage destinations and with awareness of miracles.[124]

By 1490 a poem was written about the Passau case ('Von der Juden zu Passau'), one which closely follows the evidence of the trial hearings, and which draws from an earlier poem in Latin, probably based on the trial protocols.[125] The poem, by Fritz Fellhainer, is of twenty-three six-line stanzas, and offers a colourful rendition of the events. It sounds almost like a script for a street drama; one can sense the immediacy of market-place or town square. The poem is lively and appealing, to the Christian men and women who had vindicated their God, and to the poet's lord, bishop Ulrich III Nussendorf (1451–79), who had responded aptly to the events. It opens and closes with invocations of God and the Virgin and displays throughout the rhetorical marks of public recitation in appeals to the audience: 'Now mark my words good pious Christians!' ('Nu merkt ir frumen kristen gut') opens six of the poem's stanzas.[126]

The poem is confident in its allocation of blame. Christoph Eisengeissamer – a Christian who had forgotten his identity and behaved like Judas – approached the Jews of Passau with the offer 'Would you buy the sacrament if I were to bring it to you?'[127] Two Jews, Mandel and Ungar, who like all Jews in this poem are named, assured Christoph of their willingness to trade and promised to pay him well for the sacrament.[128] He then broke into the church of St Mary in Freiung, stole eight host and waited three days (!) before he took them to the Jews, and was compensated by them with a Rhenish gulden, a scene nicely captured in the broadsheet (see, again, figure 12, p. 82). Christoph committed further mischief when he broke into another church, this time stealing $8\frac{1}{2}$ pfennig from the poor-box, following which he was arrested. He confessed to the judges the sale to the Jews and this led to their arrest. The accused Jews confessed to having taken the hosts to their synagogue, where they placed them on a marble table and one of their number, Veygel, pierced the hosts with a knife, bringing forth an issue of blood. They then took the hosts to Veygel's house for the night, and returned on the morrow to the synagogue to decide their fate. Fellhainer names all the Jews involved and meticulously details the distribution of the eight hosts in Jewish hands:

> They sent two particles to the Jews of Prague
> two to (Wiener) Neustadt,
> two to Salzburg,
> and they kept two particles
> which were pierced by Veygel (Veidl) the Jew.[129]

These were taken by Kalman to the bakery for destruction, but when they were placed in the fire, he witnessed two white doves flying out. Another Jew, Walg, saw a child in the fire and two angels. A great wind then arose from the fire and dizzied the attending Jews. Where the oven had stood a 'Got'shaus' now stands, attracting masses and devotees.

The medium of cheap broadsheets belonged to the world of public recitation and comment and interacted with other forms of commemoration such as procession and drama. Fellhainer's attention was drawn to the case some twelve years after the event, displaying the vitality of a cult the news of which had already spread through a broadsheet combining words and images.

The accusation of host desecration brought against the Jews of Sternberg in Mecklenburg in 1492, which occasioned the expulsion of the Duchy's Jews, was taken up by a second generation of printers, who showed imagination and enterprise. As we have seen, according to a dominant version, a clerk of Mecklenburg, Peter Dane, had recently broken off a relationship with a concubine, following admonition by his bishop.[130] The poor priest, in need of a loan, approached the Jew Eleasar and pawned a utensil – an iron pot. But the abandoned partner tracked him down, demanding the return of her pot in drunken shouts. Peter approached the Jew for the return of his pot and the Jew made him an offer: Peter would receive four shillings and the pot in return for some hosts. This was agreed, and at mass on 10 July Peter consecrated three hosts, two of which he hid in his gown. He then covered them in a piece of silk cut out of an altarcloth and brought the parcel to Eleasar on the morrow. A week or so later, Eleasar's prosperous household was celebrating his daughter's wedding. The real climax of this feast was to be the desecration of the host. He chose Simon the bridegroom and three male guests who had come to the wedding from neighbouring communities: Michael son of Aaron of Brandenburg, Schunemann of Friedland and Salomon of Teterow. At eight o'clock on the morning of 20 July, Eleasar placed the hosts upon a table. Those assembled were now to discover what the 'baked God' really was. He wielded a knife and needles to pierce the hosts, and where he led the others followed. Blood issued from the hosts on to the tablecloth and spilt over the edge of the table. He repeated the attack and with the same result. The horrified Jews ran away, all but Eleasar who calmly wrapped the hosts in a cloth and hid them in a wooden candle-holder.[131]

The wedding guests were now ready to return to their homes and Eleasar escaped with them, leaving to his wife the task of destroying the hosts. She tried to do so by throwing them into a fire, but to no avail, then into a stream, but found that she could not move away from the stone on which she was standing on the river bank unless she retrieved the hosts. She decided to approach Peter Dane for help, and on 21 August, a whole month after the original attack, she handed the hosts over to him during a walk in the ruins of the ducal castle. Peter tried to return the hosts to the church whence he had stolen them but found that he was rooted to the spot, so he buried them among the ducal ruins and put an apple branch to mark the burial place.

Peter's next action brought him in touch with the bishop and chapter of Schwerin, his superiors. He recounted a vision which directed him to unearth two hosts buried in the ducal grounds. Bishop Conrad Loste told this to Duke Balthasar and to his chapter and proceeded to investigate. The party set off to the grounds and Peter was ordered to dig at the appointed place indicated in the vision. The recovered hosts were then carefully taken to the high altar of St Michael's church, bearing marks of knife and needle wounds. Peter was arrested and confirmed what had already been suspected by all: namely, that the Jews were involved. Eleazar's wife and Jacob were arrested and on 22 October confessed that Eleazar had planned an abuse for some time. Years ago he had offered a Franciscan, who served as a chaplain in Prenzlin, a gulden for a host, and this was handed over to him between Easter and Pentecost. Additionally, the guests were induced to travel to the wedding with the promise of the eucharistic game: they came from Franconia, Leipzig, Hamburg, and the towns of Mecklenburg (Friedland, Teterow, Röbel).

Hearing of this large-scale plot, the dukes Magnus and Balthasar had all the Jews of Mecklenburg arrested. On 24 October, twenty-five men and two women were burnt on a hill outside Sternberg. To the ducal question, 'Why do you not follow the holy faith?' a Jew answered, 'I believe in the God of Abraham and Isaac, who made me a Jew.' A boy, Aaron, was pulled out of the fire, and in his fear he claimed to be able to show where two more hosts were buried in Neubrandenburg. Those who were not guilty, 265 in all, were expelled from the region without their property, punished for their brethren's offence. Eleasar's house was destroyed and turned into a chapel, which received indulgences in 1494, and was completed in 1496.[132] The chapel of the Holy Blood displayed the pot on one wall and the table used in the abuse on another. On an outer wall beside the portal, the stone on which Eleasar's wife was stuck can be seen, and the Rathaus sports a tablet engraved with the Jews' confession.

The is the tale conveyed to thousands of readers who were reached by the pamphlet of 1492, printed by Simon Koch of Magdeburg within weeks of the Sternberg trial. It is heavily anti-clerical (the sellers of the host were a secular priest and a Franciscan friar), redolent of misogyny, full of miracles, visions and supernatural turns of narrative, with an insistence upon the conspiratorial and cunning nature of Jewish abuse. Jewish rituals are seen as occasions for the planning and perpetration of abuses against Christianity, as Jewish networks facilitate the escape and disappearance of culprits.

The accusation in Sternberg followed a few months after the synod of Schwerin (3 April 1492), which reiterated the programme of clerical reform and liturgical probity. The very Bishop Conrad Loste who was to be the saviour of the eucharist and accuser of the Jews had decreed in detail the rules which were to pertain to the main actors of the tale: eucharist and priest. Canon 20 of the synod insisted upon the need to treat the eucharist properly, to keep it in locked vessels and safe places, and to allow no one but a priest (not even the *custos*) to handle it.[133] When carried to the sick the host had to be properly handled by a vested priest and heralded by bells. The next canon further addressed the issue of frequency of exposure which the reforming legate Nicholas of Cusa had treated so energetically, if not always effectively, in the 1450s: it should not be carried frequently nor exposed daily, but only on a few and suitable festivals.[134] A few clauses later the issue of clerical marriage is addressed in canon 26, entitled 'That clerics should not have concubines' ('Ne clerici habeant concubinas').[135] Here the cohabitation of clerics and women is strongly condemned, be the woman a concubine or a servant. A month was allotted for these cohabiting clerics to sever their ties with their partners and to enter celibate living, or face a fine of ten florins.

The response to the Mecklenburg accusation of host desecration in the medium of print was very quick and wide-ranging.[136] As Sternberg had no print workshops in 1492, Simon Koch of Magdeburg produced the first record of the case soon after 24 October in an unadorned broadsheet.[137] The broadsheet contains a text of 77 lines printed on a page of 35.2 × 22.3 cm, which begins 'After the birth of Christ MCCCCXxcii'.[138] Later printing initiatives employed an illustrated opening page with a caption, and then four to six pages of text telling the elaborate tale. Two woodcuts came to accompany these short pamphlets: a cruder and a finer composition, the former being a reworking of the latter. The cruder woodcut has four perpetrators around a table, three of them striking at the host, and, at the other end, a woman carrying away a pot. In a printing by a workshop in Cologne this image is captioned 'All Christian people be so informed that in the land of Mecklenburg, in the town of Sternberg, a great miracle has occurred, of the blinded Jews upon the most holy and precious sacrament, which they pierced with a knife so that blood flowed and the figure still shows';[139] it was occasionally decorated with black ink. A more refined piece of wood engraving, related to the former, but displaying greater emphasis upon shading and perspective, adorned Simon Koch's second effort, a six-page quarto pamphlet captioned 'Of the abuse of the holy sacrament by the evil Jews in Sternberg' ('Van der mysehandelinge des hilligen Sacramentes der boesen ioeden to den Sterneberge'). This woodcut was used in 1495 in Basel by Johannes Bergmann von Olpe in a Low German version of Koch's six-page pamphlet under the caption 'The story of the Jews in Sternberg in the land of Mecklenburg' ('Die geschicht der Juden zym Sternberg ym landt zu Mecklenburg').

Yet another very complex image was cut for a promoter of Sternberg and printed in Lübeck. Here the opening page shows a scene of a feast. A table occupies the centre of the scene, divided into two sections: on the right a wedding feast is laid on a cloth-covered part of the table with platters and wine jugs and five guests seated or standing around it; while on the left the table cloth has been removed from the table as a group of six (five men and a woman) stand around it piercing two hosts of differing sizes. Above the image-frame appears the word 'Sterneberche', and below the frame the couplet:

A story follows about the evil Jews,
one which is a noteworthy poem.[140]

In 1493 the story of Sternberg was told in the encyclopedic *Weltchronik* of Hartmann Schedel, the Nuremberg Chronicle, entering yet another, albeit limited, circle of dissemination. It may be that the Chronicle's brutal portrayal of Jews burnt in a fire influenced the cutter of the opening page which accompanied the text of Nikolaus Marschalk, the *Mons Stellarum* of 1512, printed in Rostock.[141] The opening page is decorated with a woodcut in four scenes, the four parts of a rectangle: top left, the monstrance containing the host; top right, the exchange of the pot; bottom left the abuse at a round table by seven Jews; and bottom right, the burning of the Jews while the grandees (the dukes) and officials look on.

The response to these late medieval accusations, experienced after the making of print, was swift and wide-ranging. Rather than seeing here a new departure, it is instructive to think of the broadsheet and pamphlets which spread the fame of Passau and Sternberg as a reworking of traditions of preaching, vernacular poetry and *novelle* before the 1460s, medieval material which has left little trace and which was available in smaller quantities.[142]

Thus new technology and older rhetoric, words and images, were combined to evoke and spread the awe of knowledge of the host desecration accusation, to vindicate the past and to offer guidelines for the future. Yet the transmission of memory is fragile; only seven years after the event, the royal document which endowed the church and monastery of Corpus Christi in Poznań, on the site of the Jews' property, recalled the place 'known to be where that Body of Christ was once miraculously found', without a mention of Jewish involvement.[143] It was not only the passage of time, but also the fragmentation of access to its commemorative traces that could lead to oblivion. Occasionally such loss was countered by a later revival, at places and times when solace or assurance was sought in the lost traces of righteous violence.

Such revival could benefit from the new technology and a sustained enthusiasm for the spread of news of miracles. Around 1500 the memory of the Deggendorf host desecration accusation (1337) was retold in a vernacular poem printed in a four-page pamphlet and heralded by a verse caption on the title page:

Von Tegkendorff das geschicht
wie die Juden das hailig sacrament haben zuͤgricht
Werdt ir in disem buͤchlein verston
was den schalckhafftigen Juden ist worden zuͦ lon.[144]

Under the caption a woodcut appears depicting the veneration of a host in a monstrance held up by two angels.[145] The poem's narrative tells of a Jew who approached a Christian woman in his service with the offer of money in return for the sacrament she was to receive at Easter. Having procured the host, several Jews congregated to discuss their actions on it. One Jew pierced it and witnessed blood coming forth and then the appearance of a child. Another attacked it with an axe, wishing to crack the host, but the child appeared again. A third Jew placed the host in a fire, but it remained unburnt. The fifth abuse occurred when a Jew put the host in his mouth, but a white child appeared in it. At the sixth Jew's approach, Mary appeared crying 'You false, blind Jews, how you have tortured my beloved son!' ('si sprach: "ir falschen Juden plind, wie martert ir mein liebes chind!"').[146] And the angel accompanying her also brought great illumination and thus the discovery of the Jews' offences by the watchmen, who alerted the town council. The Jews' seventh offence is then described, an attempt to poison the wells, bringing disaster to the town and its surroundings. Next a group of men gathered, fifty strong, and swore on a cross in the church of Schaching, on the outskirts of Deggendorf, to take revenge, in a gesture akin to departure on crusade. Early one morning Hartman of Degenberg led them to the town and there approached the burgers, and the town council allowed them to enter, kill the Jews, men and women, and burn down their houses. Unscathed by fire, the miraculous host continued to display its power: it escaped and appeared to a pious old smith in whose lap it settled. It also visited a recently ordained monk of Niederaltaich during the celebration of a trental, which led him to transfer it to safety. The miraculous host was recovered by a procession of clergy and layfolk. Many other miracles followed: the healing of the blind, the lame, the paralysed. News of the events spread near and far; this had happened in 1337 in Bavaria, in Deggendorf, in the church of the Holy Sepulchre.[147]

This lively account, punctuated by the ten miraculous signs displayed by the host, is opened by the poet's claim to veracity. Some time after the events he establishes a tradition of transmission of the true narrative: it had been told him by a pious burger who led him to the Holy Sepulchre church and recounted the tale as he had seen it happen.[148] If it was linked to the cycle of paintings which decorated the presbytery *c*.1450, then the poet's intervention came a good century after the events. Yet it is not known to us in manuscript form, so it is probably close in date of composition to the making of the pamphlets, and the introductory device a link back to an eye-witness. We see here an interaction between various forms of commemoration. The chapel, which contained an altar and an inscription about the events, provided a stage for the transmission of the tradition by a putative 'pious burger'. A chain of transmission was thus anchored in the fabric, linking up in closure with the invocation of the chapel in the poem's final stanza, in the call for commemoration of the Bavarian shrine of Deggendorf, a call for pilgrims to share in its miracles.[149] Deggendorf and Holy Saviour of Bettbrunn were Bavaria's two great pilgrimage shrines, of more than regional prominence.[150]

Poems on host desecration cases could also circulate outside a localised tradition; as translations they could travel far. Such was the case of the fifteenth-century poem in southern Netherlandish, most likely translated from a north German dialect. It tells of a host desecration accusation similar in many details to the Wrocław case, with several other elements from other tales. It possesses a homiletic opening, which praises the eucharist and reminds listeners of the guilt of Jews and their unwillingness to believe:

The Jews altogether
refuse to believe
that in the pure host
one consecrates God's body
as it happens in the priest's hands;
thereby hangs all of Christian belief.[151]

The poem then follows with a narrative of abuse which occurred in the month of September, when Jews tempted a custodian and his wife to sell the host. Having bought the host, the Jews placed it on a table to see how it would behave when pierced. Blood flowed from the host, leading to discovery by the town watchmen; the Jews were punished and the host was carried in procession to church. The story is told in lively detail in fifteen stanzas, and ends with a gesture to its audience calling them towards belief in transubstantiation, which cites almost directly some of its opening words:

You men and you women too
who believe firmly in this,
that in the pure host
we indeed receive with confidence God's body
from the priest's hand –
upon this stands all Christian faith –
May God punish all the Jews
in the whole wide world.[152]

As we have seen above in the case of *exempla*, the inherent confirmatory quality of the tale was appreciated and exploited by those intent not only on amusement, but also on instruction. A whole spectrum of generic uses arises around the news of a host desecration accusation: forcefully and often repeatedly in the locality soon after the event, but also more faintly and in more fanciful a manner following a number of mediations and translations, and with the passage of time.

The late fifteenth-century interest in the shoring up of lapsed or forgotten cults of miraculous hosts was supported by more recent manifestations of miracles, proof of the host's ever-present power. Some of the means by which memory was revived and supported throughout that century are particularly evident in the history of the cult of the miraculous hosts of Brussels.

THE FRAGILITY OF MEMORY: BRUSSELS 1370, AND LATER

The host desecration accusation at Brussels in 1369–70 was the single event of its kind in Brabant, an area which had seen the settlement of many Jews, particularly migrants from the Rhineland, since the thir-teenth century.[153] During the period of alliance between Jeanne, heiress to the Duchy of Burgundy, and Wenzel of Luxembourg, the host des-ecration accusation was brought against the most prominent Jew of Brabant, Jonathan of Enghien, a substantial financier and community leader, whose stature was reflected in his residence, a fortified stone house, a *steen*.[154] The tale begins with an approach made by Jonathan to a Jewish convert with a request for a number of consecrated hosts which were to be procured by theft from an outlying chapel, St Katherine at Molenbeek. John of Louvain, the convert, duly broke into the chapel and handed over to Jonathan the contents of the *ciborium*: sixteen hosts. These were then taken by Jonathan and his Jewish friends to the syna-gogue where they were thrown on a table and pierced with knives and other instruments. A fortnight later Jonathan was killed by four men while walking with his son in the garden, after which his wife decided to get rid of the hosts. She summoned another convert, this time Katherine, and asked her to carry the hosts far away to Cologne. Katherine agreed, but then thought better of her action and approached her priest, the curate of Notre Dame de la Chapelle, with the details of the events. This priest, Peter van de Heede, accepted the hosts from her and then together with the auxiliary-priests of St Gudule and the porter of the church of St Nicholas, brought them to the church of Notre Dame. Two of the hosts remained in this church and nine others were passed on to the mother church of Brussels, St Gudule.

When news of the events reached the Duke and Duchess of Brabant, they summoned Katherine; after interrogating her they ordered the detention of all the Jews of Brussels and Louvain in the Steenport prison. John of Louvain gave testimony against the Jews, but was ultimately implicated as the thief who had stolen the hosts. The ducal treasury also became involved as the prospect of mass confiscations of Jewish property loomed, attested by two entries in the account books for consecutive days, 16 and 17 May 1370.[155] The Jews were led through the streets of Brussels, through the Grande Place, and were executed in front of St Katherine's chapel, at Flanders Gate, whence the hosts had been stolen, on Ascension Day, 21 May 1370.[156] Jewish property then passed into the hands of the Receiver-General of Brabant, Geoffrey de la Tour, who reported tersely the circumstances which led to the windfall.[157]

The story of abuse was never doubted, but the fate of the precious hosts gave rise to discord between the churches involved. St Gudule sent two messengers to the Bishop of Cambrai to ask for support against the claims of the chapel of St Katherine. Bishop Robert of Geneva's response was in the form of a decree to the parishioners to return some of the hosts to St Gudule. It is important to remember that Brussels only possessed a single church, the collegiate church of St Gudule, to which all other churches serving parishioners were related as daughter chapels. So the hosts were translated to the church of St Gudule in the presence of the Duchess and Duke Wenzel, their vassals and officials, while the Abbot of Grimberge carried the *ciborium*. A cult soon developed around the miraculous hosts at St Gudule, the church chosen as the most appropriate location for the newly miraculous hosts. A record of the accounts for 1383 notes large expenses on a procession about the theft of the sacrament.[158]

But the veracity of the events which led to the production of the miraculous remains was cast into doubt a generation after the cult's inception. When visiting Brussels in 1401, the Bishop of Cambrai, the famous scholar Pierre d'Ailly, was asked to approve the cult. He was only willing to authenticate the cloth (corporal) which had touched the holy species, and granted indulgences to those venerating that, but set up an inquiry into the status of the hosts themselves. This was headed by the Dean of Brussels, John de Saint Géry.[159] John summoned six witnesses, among them two men who had been active in 1370: Peter van Heede (Ede), once curate of Notre Dame de la Chapelle, now curate of Erembodegem, and John Esche, *scholasticus* of St Gudule and now Archdeacon of Brabant.[160]

The two ancients, Peter and John, told a similar and complementary tale: that in 1370 a female convert, Katherine, had approached the rector of Notre Dame de la Chapelle and confessed to having been approached by some Jews on a night around the feast of St Bavo (1 October), with the request to hide away for them sixteen stolen hosts. They had kept the hosts and abused them, and blood drops had issued from them. They begged her to take the hosts 'to some secret place, the price considered carefully, entreating her not to bring the affair to the knowledge of the Christians'. She initially took the hosts and the payment offered, but then repented and confessed, handing the hosts over to her parish priest at Notre Dame de la Chapelle. He summoned a number of witnesses from local churches and after consultation received the hosts from her. He also called in the *scholasticus* of St Gudule, the very same John Esche, who examined Katherine too. After consulting his chapter, a decision was reached, that the hosts should be shared between the churches. Peter describes the growing fervour of the crowd of parishioners waiting to approach the hosts, and his apprehension: 'at a multitude of parishioners and folk flowing to the place, and lest they resolve to take counsel . . . fearing them he placed on the high altar the keys and the pyx in which the said hosts were kept'.[161]

The next witness, John Esche (Ysche), reported similar details, stressing that it was considered better to transfer the hosts to St Gudule. John adds details about the interrogation of Katherine by the Duke and Duchess of Brabant and the decision about Jewish guilt taken in audience. He also recounted that Katherine was asked to repeat her story in the presence of the Jews and held fast to her testimony:

The Jews having been captured and examined about the above-mentioned issues and questioned thoroughly, they confessed completely to all the above as Katherine had presented and claimed them to be and then were sent to the fire and to final punishment.[162]

Katherine herself was freed.

The next witness in 1402 was the royal chaplain, who had witnessed the same interrogation and added the interesting detail that John of Louvain, the convert-thief, flippantly opined: 'Why do these putrid dogs not admit the truth without such a cruel punishment, since they know that they committed and perpetrated the above-mentioned things?'[163] He thus gives a chilling insight into the torture which accompanied examination. John of Louvain's quip cost him his life, as his involvement in the affair was revealed, and he was led with the other Jews, chained hand and foot, to the fire. The inquiry ends with the testimonies of two chaplains of St Gudule and of a townsman, a master of the fabric of St Gudule, on the translation of the host to their church.

Here is a complex tale of intrigue, around a rich Jew, and a female convert, a male convert and a theft from a church. The competition over control of the budding cult erupts immediately and forcefully, while the inquiry of 1402 attests to the fragility of memories about cults and the possibility of continuous contestation over the very question of its authentic basis.

Attempts to bolster the cult continued throughout the fifteenth century, with the procuring in 1436 of an indulgence from the papal delegate, Nicholas Albergali, for the benefit of visitors to the miraculous host at St Gudule.[164] This year also saw the reconsecration of the chapel of St Gregory in the apse of St Peter's in St Gudule as the altar of the Holy Sacrament, pre-empting the construction of other votive altars in Brussels. So the host had two sites: a humble one in the chapel whence the hosts were stolen (St Katherine's) and a sumptuous one in the collegiate church of St Gudule, the only church of parochial status within the city walls.[165] It was also commemorated more widely. Charity tokens, which may have been distributed to the poor on commemorative occasions, bear a face of Christ inscribed as upon a host and pierced by a knife, with the Lamb of God on the obverse.[166]

How did knowledge of this tale spread? Brussels, the prime city of Brabant, displayed the tale in its mother church, where by the sixteenth century a set of stained glass windows depicted the whole narrative.[167] Yet knowledge of the popular media of *exempla* and vernacular poems is fragmentary. There is a trace of a short chronicle entry in Latin from the fourteenth century, preserved in the compendium of Jacob de Meyere *c.*1561: a short report on an abuse with daggers and swords, which brought forth an issue of blood and led to the burning alive of the city's Jews.[168] The fifteenth-century Netherlandish *Kronyk van Vlaenderen* provides a longer and more detailed account, according to which in June 1369 Jews stole the host from its container in the church of St Katherine, abused it in their synagogue with knives and swords, producing big holes which bled like fresh wounds ('in groete gaten, dewelke bloedden ghelijc varssche wonden'). When all was discovered, all the Jews of Brussels were arrested and burnt, and their quarter was destroyed (the only mention of the fate of the Jewish street, 'ende de joderye te nieute ghedaen'). The instigator is here named, Abraham, a Jew under ducal protection. The *Kronyk* also claims that the hosts were still on show in St Gudule at the time of its composition, at some point in the fifteenth century.[169]

A much more elaborate version of the events emanates from an anonymous manuscript now in the Royal Library in Brussels, dating from *c.*1450.[170] The text opens with the tale of the Holy Sacrament in St Gudule, based on the investigation conducted by John of St Géry, a story which should be a sign to all god-loving Christians ('welcke geschiedenisse es en deeteelc aen sien voer alle God minnende herten').[171] This is a popular version *par excellence*, with all the colour and detail of a story much retold and enjoyed, like the poem of Fritz Fellhainer about Passau. It is homiletic in style, a sermon which draws clear lines of responsibility and fills the action with colour and psychological insight. Indeed, it opens in sermon style with an invocation to 'All the good Christian people, who wish to know how the worthy holy sacrament of miracles, which rests in St Gudule in Brussels . . .' ('Alle ghi goede kerstene menschen, die begheren te wetene hoe dat werdeghe heyleghe Sacrament van Miraculen, dat te Sinte Goedelen te Bruesele rustende es . . .'). Here the instigator is clearly 'yonathas die goede yode' who ought in truth to be called 'Jonathas, die quade jode', whose wealth and standing are described with relish. He had a convert, John of Louvain, steal eighteen hosts for sixty *moutons d'or*. These he kept until the next Good Friday (1370), when he took them out and abused them. But Christ did not leave him unpunished and soon he was killed on his way to the court. His wife and son Abraham brought the hosts to the Jews of Brussels, who in turn shared them with the Jews of Louvain and Burgundy. Later on, on the great feast day of *Zebahot* (this must mean *Shavuot*, the festival of reception of the Torah, which would have been later, in May), reflecting on the processions held on Good Friday with the eucharist, they decided to use the hosts in their possession to show how stupid the Christians are ('Besiet nu end merct hoe die kerstene nu rasen, ende hoe dul si lopen achter straten, naect, wullen ende bervoet, van kerken te kerken, ter eeren van dien nuwelen ende broedekine dat wi onder ons heben'). On Saturday in Holy Week they congregated and had another discussion, this time blaming the host for much of the suffering which had afflicted their forefathers. They took the host, put it on a table, emitted blasphemies at it and spat on it as if on a carcass!

Some cut it with knives, and saw it bleed, others started to taunt the host: 'Now, you host, you little bread, let us see a miracle and avenge yourself on us, if you are indeed the real God, as Christians say.'[172]

Seeing the host bleed frightened the Jews, who took counsel as to the best next action, as they feared revenge and expulsion from Brabant. They approached the woman Katherine, a convert who still had contact with Jews. They invited her to eat and drink and begged her to take the hosts to safety in Cologne for a reward. She agreed but then worried and repented and went to the auxiliary priest of St Gudule and to Jan van Woeluwe, who was then rector of the chapel of St Nicholas. The host was taken to St Nicholas, and the rector then informed John of Esche, brother or brother-in-law of the Duke and the Duchess (the priest who gave testimony in 1402). This tale is obviously the story as it came to be known and confirmed in 1402, and which favoured St Gudule as the repository of the hosts. Here in the form of a sermon, it is a lively, confident version, which is little short of the text for a religious play.

The case of Brussels is at once enigmatic and revealing. It accounts for and recounts the circumstances which led to the expulsion of the Jews from Brabant in 1370. It also attempts to resolve the competition among the city's churches around the right to house the miraculous hosts, and thus to become the centre of a new cult. Here the collegiate church of St Gudule won, and the authentic place of recuperation (St Nicholas's, Notre Dame de la Chapelle) or the site of the theft (St Katherine's) remain secondary and ultimately obscure. In a sequence reminiscent of the Korneuburg and Pulkau cases, it also demonstrates the way in which unease and discomfort, lack of total faith in the claim for authenticity made by those who care for the miraculous hosts, can persist and elicit official treatment in the form of commissions of inquiry. It was a purely clerical affair in 1402, with more interest in the appropriate site of final veneration than in the possibilities of authentication for the Jews' actions. The inquiry spoke to those who still had most at stake, the keepers of the holy hosts, old men and their memories.

So by the mid-fifteenth century, the results of the events of Brussels of half a century earlier had produced a fairly coherent Latin narrative. When the canon of the Rouge-Cloître, near Brussels, John Gielemans (1427–87), undertook the making of a compendium of the saints of Brabant since 1300, the *Novale sanctorum*, he also included a version of the Brussels case.[173] The preface to the tale conveys John Gielemans's general aim neatly: to show that the Lord still manifests himself to his people, still feeds them the food of miracles, even in recent times.[174] It is a fanciful and stylised version which John presents: the notable Jonathan is made the thief who stole the host, by breaking into the church (and cracking a pane of glass). It is also he who brings the hosts to the synagogue where they are furiously attacked by Jews knowingly re-enacting the Passion. As they do so they shout: 'If you are God, let us see! Show yourself then, if you can.'[175] Blood then began to issue from the hosts and the terrified Jews sought an escape. They approached the convert Katherine but she went to the church of St Nicholas for advice, and the rector of St Nicholas took the hosts to the chapel of Notre Dame outside the city wall. The rector of St Nicholas and the chaplain of Notre Dame then approached the curate of St Gudule and all three decided upon the Jews' guilt: 'they postulated a fitting judgement upon the Jews, one which the Jews merited.'[176] The Jews were offered the choice between conversion and death, and some of their children were led off to baptism. As to the hosts, these were removed from Notre Dame to St Gudule and 'ecclesiastical men' determined that for the sake of the promotion of devotion they should be carried annually in procession, on which day the Duchess appeared splendidly and adored them.

John Gielemans thus reduces the story in time and complexity and emphasises the cultic lineage of the hosts. He then produces even more recent events in the hosts' history. Once during a procession, the hosts became wet and thus turned pale, no longer showing the marks of blood. It was then decided to remove them from show and reserve them in a cupboard within the church. It seems that without this processional prop the eucharistic cult of St Gudule diminished. In an attempt to revive it note was taken of a vision which appeared to a young man, John, who spent much time in St Gudule, contemplating the host. When he began to hear voices he tried to ignore them some five or six times, but ultimately, on one such occasion, refulgent lights appeared with the voices, and these could no longer be ignored. The host claimed: ' "It is fitting that I be adored by all living human creatures, and yet I am hidden and neglected, abolished and banished from the eyes and hearts of men in this place." '[177] He was thus forced to bring his tale to a canon of St Gudule. His visions were followed by a miraculous cure of his son, and by visions appearing to his wife. All this prompted renewed attempts at energising the cult. A bull of 1436 issued by Eugenius IV encouraged participation in the cult by offering a variety of spiritual rewards to those taking part in the eucharistic cult at St Gudule. An indulgence was granted to those who attended the Thursday mass sung before the relic; another was offered to those visiting St Gudule on Sunday in the octave of Corpus Christi or on the Sunday following 13 July, or to those who contributed donations to the maintenance of the chapel of the Holy Sacrament.[178] The bull was carefully kept in the chancery of St Gudule, despite the fact that it had been cancelled in the papal chancery. There was a multitude of corrections, since the bull had originally mentioned the hosts as being kept in a chapel, when in fact this chapel had not yet been completed. Corrections to the bull had spoiled its appearance, and so the copy was destined for the waste-basket; except that some-how, the friends of St Gudule managed to extract it. The evidence of endorsements on the document shows that it had a place in St Gudule's archives and that it was used there.

Memories require spurs, advocates; artefacts alone will not speak, move, they can become trivial, boring, forgotten; they need to be used and loved, inserted into narratives of life, in order to earn value. They need even more attention and care if their effect is to be directed and control-led: towards piety, uniformity or violent action against enemies. Shrines thus need continuous nurturing, the quickening which a zealous preacher can furnish, as he draws the link between its erstwhile founda-tion myth and the realities of life in communities which might use it in the present. Even the visual potential to tell a tale is as nothing without interpretative gestures, seals of approval, without acts which draw the symbol into a world of meaning. Memory enshrined in altarpieces, chapels, rituals is thus both vulnerable and potent, it is a resource waiting for renewal, for the drawing out of its implications. Memory is 'susceptible to the most elaborate elaboration'.[179]

That cults might lose their power has to do not only with forgetfulness or apathy, but with the very contested nature of cults and their relation to the transcendent within late medieval culture. It was after all the most important host-miracle pilgrimage site of the later Middle Ages, that at Wilsnack, which became the subject of repeated investigation and offi-cial disapproval by a commission of inquiry which included Jan Hus in the 1410s, and later of course the subject of some of Martin Luther's barbed comments. The sites of host desecration accusations often raised doubts as to the circumstances of their foundation: what was at issue was not the justice of the accusation against the Jews who were its victims, but rather the nature of the host before its abuse, and the authority upon which reports of miracles relied. This was the case in Pulkau and in Korneuburg, to name only two of the sites we have already encountered.

Thus, in the face of oblivion, the rupture of traditions, and official doubt, memories of sacred violence must be nurtured, or using David Freedberg's mantra: be enshrined, embellished, multiplied and dissemi-nated.[180] They cannot stand alone. The conservation of memory thus emerges as a highly active option, one which reveals its potency only through engaged application in the present. The person who erected a collective headstone for the victims of Rintfleisch in Rothenburg lamented the oblivion into which earlier massacres had sunk. He thus chose to carve in stone his lacrimose memories: 'In bitterness of soul and in bitter lament, for we have forgotten the tribulations of old, I have carved on this tablet of stone [the names of the] holy ones of Rothenburg, who were killed and burned for the sanctification of God's name in 1298.'[181] For Christians the memory of the violent and the sacred was thus transformed into emblematic tokens, redolent of authenticity, which provided occasions for experiencing power and pleasure, and which, as they did so, could lead to further violence, further pleasure.

7

Conclusion

Some two hundred years old, the host desecration tale had achieved monstrous shape, metamorphosing into an aged and poisonous creature. In the winter of 1510 it structured a case in which the Pomeranian thief and murderer Paul Fromm confessed to having broken into the village church of Knoblauch in Brandenburg, and stolen a monstrance containing two consecrated wafers, one small and one large. He also recounted that on the following morning he inspected his booty, and, when he abused one of the hosts, was immediately thrown into darkness. He next travelled to Spandau and attempted to rid himself of the hosts by selling them to the Jew Salomon who, after some haggling, agreed to pay six silver *groschen* for them. When Paul returned home some six months later, he repented and attempted to dispose of the monstrance by throwing it out of the window. The monstrance was found, however, and Paul was caught; he confessed under torture to having eaten a host, and given the other to Salomon, the Jew of Spandau. The Jew, for his part, battered and pierced the host repeatedly, and in his frustration at the host's indestructibility, taunted it to reveal itself as God. This it did, breaking up into three blood-encrusted pieces, taking the form of the host broken by the priest during the mass.

A year later Salomon sent a third of a host each to Jacob of Brandenburg and Marcus of Stendal, carefully packed and in the trusty hands of his son. With the remaining third he repeated the abuse, again with no success at annihilating it. So he decided to knead the host into the *matza* dough and thus have it baked for Passover. When he did so a luminescence shone from the dark oven, and floating above the bread was the thumb-size figure of a child. Salomon was terrified, but he could not run away from Spandau. Marcus, one of the recipients of the wafer morsels, abused his piece in turn, but failed to destroy it, and sent it to Braunschweig (or maybe to Frankfurt).

Jacob of Brandenburg, for his part, brought forth blood by beating and piercing his morsel. He brought it to the rich Jew Mayer of Osterburg, who bequeathed it to his son for use on his wedding night, but not before the wedding guests had abused it, offering Isaac the bridegroom the honour of the first blow. Ultimately the host was sent to Braunschweig, together with the table on which Jacob had abused it. In Braunschweig prison[1] the Jews ('blind dogs') confessed to having bought seven children, whom they tortured and killed, and whose blood they served as a delicacy, with pomegranates. For all of this the accused were sentenced to death by Landgrave Joachim of Brandenburg (1484–1535): first Paul Fromm was shredded with tongs and burnt, and then thirty-eight Jews were chained by the neck and burnt. At the stake they sang, stuffed their mouths with straw and died unflinchingly. Three of the Jews converted; two were beheaded, and a third was allowed to enter the Franciscan monastery in Berlin.[2] The remaining Jews were expelled and on the site of the abuse a chapel was built.

The strands of this accusation are familiar to you by now; we have encountered them before, especially in the large, elaborate trials of the fifteenth century: Wrocław, Sternberg, Passau. But the density of this sixteenth-century narrative is quite astounding: Jewish conspiracy, Christian theft, numerous hosts subdivided and bleeding, travels in the countryside by host-carrying Jews, Jewish weddings and a hint of Jewish sexual appetite, the combination in the Jews of evil intent and a testing attitude towards the host, and the gruesome deaths. The accusation ultimately led to the initiative which saw the expulsion of the Jews from Mark Brandenburg later that year.

In the face of so unremitting a narrative, the density of its details, the conviction of its storyline, it is easy to forget that the symbolic world within which it made sense was under assault, or at least experiencing significant pressure, in these very years. Only a few years later, in 1524, Martin Luther was to mock the cult of the holy host of Sternberg, just as earlier in the fifteenth century a commission of which Jan Hus was a member rejected the claims of that most popular eucharistic shrine at Wilsnack in Saxony, the scene of pilgrimage from far afield and of famous miracles.[3] In his letter to the prior of Sternberg, Luther wrote of the town's cult:

> I rejoice in the fact that you have cut short the superstitions that have prevailed among you and have put an end to Godless profit. May God grant that the knowledge of God grow into perfection among you and the Word of Grace rule among you in ample display of the Holy Spirit.[4]

As in the case of the ritual murder accusation, studied and interpreted by Ronnie Hsia, the host desecration accusation lost much of its potency in decades which saw the 'disenchantment of the world', or at least the refiguring of claims made in sacramental language around the traditional symbols of medieval Christianity.[5] It was no longer to be made west of the Elbe, and although the Austrian Counter-Reformation gloried in sumptuous wall-paintings which depicted host desecrations and miracles of yore, these were never re-enacted, even in those regions – Bavaria, Franconia, Austria – where the telling of the tale had been most virulent. This unmaking was not only the product of the sixteenth-century onslaught on the sacramental-sacerdotal world order,[6] it was also linked to the critique offered by voices of Christian reform since the late fourteenth century: a loathing for excessive external displays of piety such as those which surrounded the eucharist, a call for internal conversion and purification of individual and collective Christian lives, always coupled with resounding cries against usury, that easily turned to anti-Jewish rhetoric and campaigns. Repeated attempts were made by fifteenth-century reformers to restrict the laity's eucharistic access and power to name miracles and shrines, even though such initiatives often came up against resistance, indeed, dismantling, by archbishops.[7] The calls for improvement and purification of the Christian body sometimes took a malign turn, seduced by the easier, more antagonistic populism which advocated self-improvement through the creation and expulsion of bearers of pollution, such as Jews. Arch-preachers such as John of Capistrano spread this enthusiasm and encouraged not the introspective movement towards conversion to a better Christian life, but the easier self-fashioning which preys upon others, and which, once having excised them, deems the work done, the cleansing and purification achieved.[8]

The fifteenth century had also seen a widespread series of expulsions of Jews from cities and regions, sometimes occasioned by host desecration accusations, as in Brussels, Wrocław, the Kingdom of Austria, Silesia, Mecklenburg, Brandenburg. The density of Jewish settlement declined as Jews moved to smaller towns and villages, or moved eastward altogether.[9] What is so striking is the triumph of an urban pietism in dominating large areas of political discourse. What Hervé Martin has called the 'fonction tribunicienne' of religious spokesmen is evident throughout, as these increasingly dominated the media, reinforced at the end of our period by the immense possibilities offered by communication through cheap print.[10]

We have examined the use of a tale in the unfolding of violence against Jews. Where possible we have attempted to distinguish the motivating figures who launched or authorised the host desecration as the appropriate narrative frame within which a set of circumstances might be interpreted and according to which action might be structured. In early tellings of the tale we have noted the role of knights and regional lords, particularly in Franconia, as leaders of vengeful crowds, in areas where there was deep indebtedness on the part of small landlords, and a close proximity between the actions of men from towns and those from their hinterlands in a highly urbanised region. A strong administration could ensure that a trial rather than a massacre followed; but then a trial – secular or inquisitorial – could lead to brutal torture, punishment and banishment. The host desecration narrative possessed the power to offer modes of communal purification, the vindication of virtue and merit even in a varied and complex polity such as a late medieval *Reichstadt*.[11] The familiarity of the tale's setting acted as a foil for highly specific and local struggles and aspirations. But it is striking that towards the end of our period rulers availed themselves of the rhetoric of the tale more readily than their predecessors in the fourteenth century had done: the rhetoric of urban virtue and probity had triumphed over rulers' privileges, among them, clearly, that of preferring and protecting their Jews.[12] The position of Jews provided an emblematic flash-point for the eruption of tensions between towns and lords, towns and emperor.[13] The cries for expurgation and expulsion of Jews in the fifteenth century are like so many heated cries of self-justification from speakers who were as deeply engaged in the money business, who were likely to be attracted by anti-clerical sentiment and in some doubt about the sacraments, and from groups seeking dispensation from burdens related to self-governance.

That this process is most prominent in the Empire and that our story deals most frequently with German-speaking regions is understandable within this political framework. The expulsions from England and France left the Empire as the home of most European Jews outside the Iberian Peninsula in the late Middle Ages. But should we call the host desecration accusation a 'German' tale? Better not. As we have seen, the tale was located at the heart of late medieval religious culture, in its attitudes to Jews, its knowledge about the eucharist, and in the desires for self-definition to which it gave form. That it could turn into a social drama of horrific dimensions and outcome was the result of the embedded Jewish presence, its perceived privilege, the complexity of the political structure and the insidious location of Jews between jurisdictions and between people and ruler. Where circumstances of this kind arose elsewhere – as in mid and late fourteenth-century Catalonia/Aragon – similar accusations could develop, even if their outcome was again inflected quite differently within the specificity of that political system.

The process by which tales are expressed and representations evolve into action is exactly the historical *explanandum* that cannot be captured in its wholeness and variety by statements about national character or even claims about the predisposition of a culture's distinctive traits.[14] We have encountered and analysed here the fragility and limits of representation, as well as its potency. Medieval men and women became willing executioners on occasions not because this came naturally to them, but when and only when the act of violence became the most compelling way of making sense of the world and asserting identity and interest. They did so knowingly, they did so out of complex choices, they did so under influence, and always in a set of unique circumstances blended into local histories and resonating with memory. In the Middle Ages, just as in this century, it was possible for some persons to resist, to have examined the alternatives to and consequences of widely endorsed courses of action; above all, participation was an act of choice and knowledge, not the following of an irresistible urge. As I have shown, each atrocity depended on the working of particular agents who captured the imagination in the construction of narratives which led to a single and obvious course of action: we have seen preachers, councils, inquisitors; and some fifty years ago these were teachers, *Burgermeister*, doctors, lawyers.[15]

The host desecration narrative existed, thick with associations, embedded in local memory and universal Christian lore. It could move crowds to action but could also raise doubt and bring forth resistance. It was a *resource* of late medieval culture, which could be used, applied. It represented a possibility for violent action, for the expression of rage and fear. In a similar way to the pervasive anti-clerical discourse, its use could be opportunistic, credulous, manipulative; it was deployed as a rallying call which rulers and ecclesiastics did well to recognise and heed; its subject/victims, the Jewish communities, were the living proof of its veracity and poignancy.[16] Inasmuch as communities harboured a variety of authoritative traditional narratives which could animate action, the host desecration became one of these in several late medieval regions. Such action in turn fed into the traditions, and contributed to them something new, renewing and revalidating them.

If generalisations about the capacities of past generations to exclude are to be replaced by understandings which also raise a mirror to ourselves, such understandings must be at once very broad and very specific. All societies contain the capability to develop persecuting processes and possess the cultural resources for exclusion. But some are more given to such collective action than others at specific moments, as movements of violence and structures of intolerance become more acceptable within them. These are not unassailable resources and structures, nor durable ones. The attraction of excluding has differed between societies and within societies over time: be it the late medieval heretic or the early modern beggar, the medieval leper or the early modern witch. Even when narratives and cultural stereotypes exist as a resource within the culture, and they always do, these must be mobilised from thought to action. Once violent intolerant language is about, increasingly heard, spoken with impunity, then violent action is almost sure to follow.[17] Words are thus never 'only words'.[18] It is in facilitating the movement from word into action that we must locate responsibility. And this is not only related to what is so frequently called 'medieval' violence or 'popular' outrage alone; it concerns those most likely to read this book – educated, thoughtful, influential wielders of words and thoughts. The only historical lesson to be learnt is one of vigilance, of respect for language, of scrutiny of ritual, of alertness at the *inception* of narratives of exclusion, not only at their end. The licence for violence is not necessarily encoded in secret or sectarian codes, it is penned at the heart of cultures, with an ink coloured by their most familiar symbols, tinted by their most cherished desires.

Appendix: Rabbi Avigdor Kara: All the Afflictions (Et kol ha-tela'a)

All the afflictions which have befallen us, no one can tell,
  nor all that has been visited upon us.
  All this has happened and yet we have not forgotten God's name,
  the God of the Hebrews has been etched upon us.

Burning shame and indignity we have suffered, for so many trials and
    tribulations,
  trouble and loss which cannot be counted.
  Each affliction seems to suffice in its time, with nowhere to turn,
  as it replaces the memory of earlier ones.

Chastisement hit flourishing Prague
  in the year five thousand one hundred and forty-nine after creation.
  As the just fell before evil, the line spoilt.
  How the staff of fortitude, the rod of magnificence, has been broken.

Blood touched blood in that spring month
  on the last day of Passover, the feast of sweet salvation.
  And now a roasting fire has burnt me, has baked the Matzos,
  since I have heard the libel of many and danger around me.

Evil men's counsel was heard on this woeful day,
  rushing, running nameless sons of villainy,
  Each of them with weapon in hand, bows and arrows,
  with axes they came, like wood-cutters.

From every gate, from every opening they entered,
  gathering in groups, hovering in troops,
  their chants tremulous and joyful,
  as they spilt pure blood for swift robbery, to do and to have done
    with.

Going quickly to exhort each other,
  if anyone approached their camp they struck him down.
  Be ready in your posts to sanctify the exalted name
  and deem it a Passover sacrifice.

Having waited till nightfall they plotted their attack
   as they saw a Jew they seized him with a glance.
   First they try to persuade him,
   and then the killer strikes him dead.

Innocent children aplenty, pure children of Israel,
   offered themselves to suffer scandals and stings.
   If they are asked to consent,
   they say: 'do as you wish, here your servants are fallen.'

Just like the father of many, the father of few
   turns his intention to heaven and his soul towards the act.
   Father spares not his baby, his infant –
   all his fruits shall become sacred offerings.

Killing is the task of the most timid,
   and mothers spare not their sons, nor save them.
   An offering by each who is thus moved,
   male and female will be sacrificed.

Left without comfort as the head of the holy congregation, its guardian,
    falls;
   the rabbi, his pious brother and his only son.
   Is there such a sage, his book in hand?
   He will be lamented, woe to the master, woe to his flowering.

Master of old, respected among his people,
   hastens, lest they degrade him,
   and massacres his sons and kin with him;
   my heart is terrified, it leaps out of my chest.

Now my soul is eaten up for these great men, experts in book and in
    discourse,
   for leaders and cantors and community benefactors,
   for scholars and men of manners [ethics].
   Take them from me, they are my congregation.

Old synagogue was the meeting-place of their families
   their house of a prayer.
   There the sword of fire will devour them.
   They were sacrificed whole to their God.

Proud boys and girls were subjected to
   yet another abomination, father of all defilement.
   Until when, O God, will your sons and daughters be given
   to another people, and your eyes remain closed?

Rushing they entered the new and old synagogues.
  I cried in a faint voice
  as they mocked, burnt and shredded holy books,
  The Torah given by Moses as our inheritance.

Shout, hasten, rush, rob, loot,
  grab their silver, steal gold and all that you can find.
  They are free for the taking and their property and belongings too.
  All those who find them may devour and be deemed guiltless.

Tear away the clothes of the fallen haughtily,
  our boys and old men, struck by the sword of war.
  Naked they are thrown for shame and calumny,
  the human corpse fallen into the soil of the earth.

Unto us the fallen are too numerous to name,
  the infant with the elder, youths and maids.
  Why, they are in your number, Lord of all souls.
  God will know, since he is the knower of all secrets.

Verily, God, call a halt to the many killed and fallen,
  we have been nothing but robbed and beaten for so long.
  We have become an example and testimony to the nations,
  the Zuzims in Ham and the Emims.[1]

Why, they have committed atrocities and acted in malice,
  devised schemes to cover up the killing –
  burning Israel's bodies with gentiles –
  and mix Israel's seed with gentiles.

Your free house they have destroyed, the place where my fathers are
      buried,
  unearthing bones and breaking their headstones.
  My conscience has sunk and my feelings are low
  and my soul was terrified. How long will you allow this to go on?

All around me moan and groan
  pressed by the trouble of their brothers and the oppression of their
      enemies.
  Captured and tortured, beaten and afflicted,
  here is the cry of my people from afar.

Call, O God, a day of consolation, and put an end to sin and evil.
  Gather the exiled and draw routes in the desert.
  To those who deserve the consolation of Isaiah uplift quickly.
  Because my salvation is soon to come, my justice to appear.

Notes

Abbreviations

AGRB	Archives Générales du Royaume, Brussels
BL	British Library
BN	Bibliothèque Nationale
CUL	Cambridge University Library
HM	*Historiae memorabiles. Zur Dominikanerliteratur und Kulturgeschichte des 13 Jahrhunderts*, ed. E. Kleinschnidt, Cologne, 1974.
MGH	*Monumenta germaniae historica*
MGH.SS	*Monumenta germaniae historica. Scriptores*
ÖNB	Österreichische Nationalbibliothek
PL	*Patrologiae cursus completus. Series latina*, ed. J.-P. Migne, 217 plus 4 index vols, Paris, 1841–64.
REJ	*Revue des Études Juives*
RHGF	*Recueil des historiens des Gaules et de la France*, ed. M. Bouquet with L. Delisle, 25 vols, Paris, 1840–1904, repr. Farnborough, 1967–8

1   *Introduction*

1. On attitudes to Jews see J. Cohen, *The Friars and the Jews: the Evolution of Medieval Anti-Judaism*, Ithaca, N.Y., 1982, *passim* and comments on p. 256; on this book see D. Lasker's review in *Speculum* 58 (1983), pp. 743–5; see also A. Patchovsky, 'Der Talmudjude', in *Juden in der christlichen Umwelt während des späten Mittelalters*, ed. A. Haverkamp and F.-J. Ziwes, Berlin, 1992, pp. 13–27, esp. pp. 15–20. On the eucharist, M. Rubin, *Corpus Christi: the Eucharist in Late Medieval Culture*, Cambridge, 1991, chs 1 and 2.

2. Such a view is potently expressed in the works of G.I. Langmuir, *History, Religion and Antisemitism*, London, 1990 and *Towards a Definition of Antisemitism*, Berkeley

Calif., 1990. It has also been noted that such an approach 'seek[s] to establish a continuity between the hatreds of long ago and those of the here and now', D. Nirenberg, *Communities of Violence: Persecution of Minorities in the Middle Ages*, Princeton, N.J., 1996, pp. 4–5.

3. I have greatly benefited from discussion with E. Valentine Daniel, see his *Charred Lullabies: chapters in an anthropology of violence*, Princeton, N.J., 1996.

4. As discussed in P. Ricoeur, *Temps et récit*, I, Paris, 1983, esp. p. 87.

5. On the limitations of the use of textuality as a critical entry to the study of images see M. Bal and N. Bryson, 'Semiotics and art history', *Art Bulletin* 73 (1991), pp. 174–208, esp. pp. 202–6.

6. H. White, *The Content of the Form: Narrative, Discourse and Historical Representation*, Baltimore, Md., 1987; C. Segre, *Structures and Time: Narration, Poetry, Models*, Chicago, 1979.

7. See Michel de Certeau's comments in his discussion of proverbs: 'they signify the *operations* whose object they have been . . . more generally, they thus indicate a social *historicity* in which systems of representations or processes of fabrication no longer appear only as normative frameworks but also as *tools manipulated by users*', M. de Certeau, *The Practice of Everyday Life*, ed. S. Rendall, Berkeley, Calif., 1984, p. 21.

8. On textuality see N.Z. Davis, 'Du conte et de l'histoire', *Le Débat* 54 (1989), pp. 138–43. Readers of David Nirenberg's *Communities of Violence* will appreciate the parallel routes we have travelled in reflecting upon the nature of our work in this area; those who have not read it yet may be inspired by the introduction, pp. 3–17. Hayden White has found the attempt to apply textual insights to Holocaust narratives and revisionist counternarratives to be painful and intellectually unwieldy, H. White, 'Historical employment and the problem of truth', in *Probing the Limits of Representation: Nazism and the 'Final Solution'*, ed. S. Friedlander, Cambridge, Mass., 1992, pp. 37–53. For the core of Hayden White's position see White, *The Content of the Form*; Carlo Ginzburg has answered claims that treatment of textuality necessarily diminishes the possibility of discerning truth and making ethical judgements on the basis of texts, C. Ginzburg, 'Just one witness', in *Probing the Limits of Representation*, ed. Friedlander, pp. 82–96.

9. D. LaCapra, *Rethinking Intellectual History: Texts, Contexts, Language*, Ithaca, N.Y., 1983, p. 312.

10. P. Brooks, 'Changes in the margins: construction, transference, and narrative', in *Psychoanalysis and Storytelling*, The Bucknell Lectures in Literary Theory 10, Oxford, 1994, pp. 46–75, at p. 51.

11. On the exchange between storyteller and listener as a contract see ibid., pp. 51, 72.

12. On storytelling and transference see ibid., p. 51.

13. This is a point made, of course, in contexts of postcolonial criticism such as H.K. Bhabha, 'Introduction: narrating the nation', in *Nations and Narration*, ed. H.K. Bhabha, London, 1990, pp. 1–7, at p. 4: 'The "other" is never outside or beyond us; it emerges forcefully within cultural discourse, when we think we speak most intimately and indigenously "between ourselves".' From a different angle, see Gerd Mentgen's argument, which does away with the view of Jews as a marginal group in medieval Germany, 'Die Juden waren stets eine Randgruppe: über eine fragwürdige prämisse der actuellen Judenforschung', in *Liber amicorum necnon amicarum für Alfred Heit*, ed. F. Burgard, C. Cluse and A. Haverkamp, Trier, 1996, pp. 393–411. For a similar view expressed poetically see J.-F. Lyotard, 'La force des faibles', *L'Arc* 64 (1976), pp. 4–12, at p. 6.

14. T. Morrison, *Playing in the Dark: Whiteness and the Literary Imagination*, New York, 1992, p. 17.

2   *From Jewish Boy to Bleeding Host*

1. J. Cohen, *The Friars and the Jews: the Evolution of Medieval Anti-Judaism*, Ithaca, N.Y., 1982, ch. 1, pp. 19–32; A.S. Abulafia, *Christians and Jews in the Twelfth-Century Renaissance*, London, 1995, pp. 65–6, 137–8.

2. On miracles of the Virgin see H.L.D. Ward, *Catalogue of Romances*, II, London, 1893, pp. 586–94; C.N.L. Brooke, *From Alfred to Henry III, 871–1272*, London, 1974, p. 29.

3. B. Blumenkranz, 'Juden und Judisches in christlichen Wundererzählungen', *Theologische Zeitschrift* 10 (1954), pp. 417–46, at pp. 430–46.

4. Rutbeuf, *Le Miracle de Théophile. Miracle du XIIIe siècle*, ed. G. Frank, Paris, 1925; on Theophilus see D.A. Carpenter, 'Social perception and literary portrayal: Jews and Muslims in medieval Spanish literature', in *Convivencia: Jews, Muslims, and Christians in Medieval Spain*, ed. V.B. Mann, T.F. Glick and J.D. Dodds, New York, 1992, pp. 61–81, at p. 65. On the play version, G. Frank, *The Medieval French Drama*, Oxford, 1954, pp. 106–13.

5. H. Schreckenberg, *The Jews in Christian Art: an Illustrated History*, London, 1996, pp. 253–4. Rutbeuf's version of *c*.1261, the *Miracle de Théophile* (1260 × 70), is unusual in having a magician who was not Jewish, but Muslim! Rutbeuf, *Le Miracle de Théophile*, first appearance on p. 2 lines 44–7. See also G. Dahan, 'Salatin du *Miracle de Théophile* de Rutbeuf', *Le Moyen-Age*, 4th ser., 32 (1977), pp. 445–68, at pp. 445–9, 468.

6. H. Kraus, *The Living Theatre of Medieval Art*, London, 1967, p. 155, North Wall, fig. 108, p. 156; L. Réau, *Iconographie de l'art chrétien*, III (3), Paris, 1959, p. 1257 and II (2), Paris, 1957, pp. 628–30. For some English manuscript examples see the thirteenth-century De Braille Hours (*c*.1240) (BL Add. 49999), fol. 44, in C. Donovan, *The De Braille Hours: Shaping the Book of Hours in Thirteenth-Century Oxford*, Oxford, 1991, plate 9, and the Carew-Poyntz Hours, see below

pp. 18–19.

7. Under the title 'De quodam Iudeo', lib. 1, c. 10, *PL* LXXI, col. 714; for English translation, see *The Glory of Martyrs*, ed. R. Van Dam, Translated Texts for Historians, Latin Series 3, Liverpool, 1988, no. 9, pp. 29–32. On Gregory's use of miracle tales see K. Winstead, 'The transformation of the miracle story in the *Libri historiarum* of Gregory of Tours', *Medium Aevum* 59 (1990), pp. 1–15.

8. There is an early version of the tale in the pseudo-Bedan text *Ascelta*, *PL* XCIV, col. 557. Here the miracle concerned a Jewish boy who received the host from the hands of St Boniface. His father punished him by throwing him into the fire, and in this version the mother who turned to the Virgin for help was punished by the Jewish father and thrown into the fire with her son. Boniface extracted both from the fire. The *moralitas* exhorted towards worthy reception of the eucharist. I have benefited from discussions with Dr Julia Crick, who brought this text to my attention, and to whom I am most grateful.

9. Less openly it also expresses anxieties about the access of Jews to Christian holy spaces, on which see interesting evidence from tenth-century annotations to Amalarius of Metz's *De officiis ecclesiasticis*, BN nouv. acq. lat. 329, fol. 84, A. Wilmart, 'Un lecteur ennemi d'Amalaire', *Revue Benedictine* (1924), pp. 317–29, at pp. 317–20 and B. Blumenkranz, *Juifs et chrétiens dans le monde occidental, 430–1096*, Paris, 1960, pp. 85–8.

10. For other examples see the tale recorded in the annals of Ravenna, about a Jew who saw a lamb on the altar during mass, and was led to baptism, 'Agnelli abbatis S. Mariae ad blachernas liber ponitifcalis', *PL* CVI, cols 697–8.

11. 'Quo dum propinquaret, diuina, ut estimo, prouidentia in sibi reuelante, uidit super altare mulierem quandam honestae admodum formae in cathedra sedentem, paruulumque puerum super genibus suis tenentem qui propria manu sacram communionem sacerdoti porrigebat, ut et ipse plebi fideliter accedenti distribueret', Paschasius Radbert, *De corpore et sanguine domini*, ed. B. Apulus, CCCM 16, Turnholt, 1969, pp. 60–1 [*PL* CXX, cols 1299]; the tale appears in small print in Paulus's edition, indicating that it is a later addition by Paschasius (p. lviii). On the Paschasian polemic and its aftermath see M. Gibson, *Lanfranc of Bec*, Oxford, 1978, pp. 63–97. Gezo of Tortona was much influenced by Paschasius, see his *c.*950 'De corpore et sanguine Christi', *PL* CXXXVII, cols 370–406, at col. 390.

12. E. Wolter, *Der Judenknabe*, Bibliotheca Normannica 2, Halle, 1879, no. 9, pp. 44–5.

13. 'Ut in aecclesia sanctae matris Christi Jesu corpus et sanguinem Christi perceperit, propter hoc a patre suo proiectus in fornacem ardentem, illesus inde a christianis extractus est, asserente quod mulier, quae in illa aecclesia puerum tenens depicta erat, pallio suo flammas ignis in se eventillaset', 'Sigeberti Gembacensis Chronica', *MGH.SS* VI, pp. 300–74, at p. 317.

14. 'Crudam carnem a sacerdote accepit', Honorius Augustudonensis, 'Speculum ecclesiae', *PL* CLXXII, cols 807–1108, at col. 852.

15. On the Marian genre in England see M. Clayton, *The Cult of the Virgin Mary in Anglo-Saxon England*, Cambridge Studies in Anglo-Saxon England 2, Cambridge, 1990, p. 47.

16. CUL Ii.2.18, fols 218v–219r; *The Life, Letters and Sermons of Bishop Herbert de Losinga*, ed. E.M. Goulburn and H. Symmonds, 2 vols, Oxford, 1878, II, pp. 30–3.

17. 'quod de christiana ara sacram accepisset porcionem matri revelavit', ibid., p. 30.

18. On the connection between Mary and the eucharist see also M. Rubin, *Corpus Christi: the Eucharist in Late Medieval Culture*, Cambridge, 1991, pp. 39, 142–7; see also J.A. Holladay, 'The iconography of the high altar, Cologne Cathedral', *Zeitschrift für Kunstgeschichte* 52 (1989), pp. 472–98.

19. P.N. Carter, 'The historical context of William of Malmesbury's miracles of the Virgin Mary', in *The Writing of History in the Middle Ages: Essays Presented to Richard William Southern*, ed. R.H.C. Davis and J.M. Wallace-Hadrill, Oxford, 1981, pp. 124–65; R. Thomson, *William of Malmesbury*, Woodbridge, 1987, pp. 24–5, 198; H. Farmer, 'William of Malmesbury's life and works', *Journal of Ecclesiastical History* 13 (1962), pp. 39–54, at pp. 39–42, 51; *El libro De laudibus et miraculis sanctae Mariae de Guillermo de Malmesbury OSB (d. 1143)*, ed. J.M. Canal, Rome, 1968, p. 18.

20. My emphasis. '"Illa", inquit, "pulchra femina quam uidi in cathedra sedentem, et cuius filius populo diuideuatur, affuit mihi, in camino aestianti', *El libro De laudibus*, no. 33, pp. 137–8, at p. 138. William's version is close to that of Honorius of Autun, and as he could not have known the *Speculum ecclesiae*, they probably shared a source which transmitted Paschasius' version.

21. This interest is also explored in his *Gesta regum* of 1127 where he discusses Berengar's views on the eucharist and cites three of Paschasius' miracles in contradiction to these views, including that of the Jewish Boy, who saw a child torn to pieces member by mem-

ber and distributed individually to the people at the altar: William of Malmesbury, *Gesta regum*, II, ed. W. Stubbs, London, 1889, cc. 284–6, pp. 338–42 (c. 286 includes the tale).

22. 'presbiter angelico pane cibauit eum', 'Cuius heri populo puer est partitus in escam', Nigel of Canterbury, *Miracles of the Virgin Mary, in verse (Miracula sanctae dei genitricis Virginis Mariae, versifice)*, Toronto, 1986, pp. 62–4, at line 1485, p. 62 and at line 1527, p. 63.

23. Ibid., lines 1537–8.

24. John of Garland, *The Stella Maris of John of Garland*, ed. E.F. Wilson, Publications of the Mediaeval Academy of America 45, Cambridge, Mass., 1946, pp. 95–6, 157–9.

25. R.W. Southern, 'The English origins of the Miracles of the Virgin', *Medieval and Renaissance Studies* 4 (1958), pp. 176–216, at pp. 190–1, 199, 202–3, 211–12; Thomson, *William of Malmesbury*, p. 202; Adgars edition M.D. Legge, *Anglo-Norman Literature and its Background*, Oxford, 1963, pp. 187–91; J.A. Herbert, 'A new ms. of Adgar's Mary-legends', *Romania* 32 (1903), pp. 394–421, esp. pp. 414–15. Another translation into Anglo-Norman French followed in the thirteenth century, C. Meale, 'The miracles of Our Lady: context and interpretation', in *Studies in the Vernon Manuscript*, ed. D. Pearsall, Woodbridge, 1990, pp. 115–36, at p. 125.

26. James of Voragine, *Legenda aurea*, ed. T. Graesse, Leipzig, 1850, c. 119, pp. 515–16.

27. 'Qui continuo combustus et penitus consumatus est', ibid., p. 516.

28. The manuscript is of *c.*1300 and edited in *The South English Legendary*, ed. C. d'Evelyn and A.J. Mill, EETS OS 235, London, 1956; St Theophilus' story is on pp. 221–38 and within it the story of the Jewish Boy is on pp. 227–9. See A. Samson, 'The South English Legendary: continuity and context', in *Thirteenth-Century England*, I, ed. P.R. Coss and S.D. Lloyd, Woodbridge, 1986, pp. 185–94; M. Görlach, *The Textual Tradition of the South English Legendary*, Leeds, 1974.

29. *South English Legendary*, lines 230–4, pp. 228–9.

30. Hugo of Trimberg, 'Das Solsequium', in *Hugo von Trimbergs lateinische Werke*, ed. E. Seeman, Münchner Texte 9, Munich, 1914, no. 39, p. 70. On Hugo von Trimberg see ibid., pp. 8–14 and L. Behrendt, *The Ethical Teaching of Hugo of Trimberg*, Catholic University of America Studies in German 1, Washington DC, 1970.

31. *La Scala Coeli de Jean Gobi*, ed. M.A. Polo de Beaulieu, Paris, 1991, no. 368, p. 667; tale of transformed host, no. 367, p. 667.

32. For some interesting thoughts on *exempla* see L. Scanlon, *Narrative, Authority and Power: the Medieval Exemplum and the Chaucerian Tradition*, Cambridge, 1994, pp. 30–5.

33. Gautier de Coinci, *Les Miracles de Nostre Dame*, ed. V.F. Koenig, I, Geneva and Paris, 1955, pp. vii–l; II, Geneva and Paris, 1961, pp. 95–100; G. Dahan, 'Les Juifs dans les miracles de Gautier de Coinci (II)', *Archives Juives* 6 (1980), pp. 59–80. On the power of localisation and detail see B. Cazelles, *La Faiblesse chez Gautier de Coinci*, Stanford French and Italian Studies 14, Saratoga, 1978, pp. 85, 86–8. Gautier translated and composed his collection during his period as prior of Vic-sur-Aisne. On the quality of Marian worship and related anti-Judaism in northern France in this period, see W.C. Jordan, 'Marian devotion and the Talmud trial of 1240', in *Religionsgespräche in Mittelalter*, ed. B. Lewis and F. Niewöhner, Wolfenbütteler Mittelalter-

Studien 4, Wiesbaden, 1992, pp. 61–76, esp. pp. 68–73.

34. *Les Miracles de Nostre Dame*, ed. Koenig, II, lines 30–4, p. 96.

35. Ibid., lines 94–8, p. 98.

36. A.P. Ducrot-Granderye, *Études sur les Miracles Nostre Dame de Gautier de Coinci*, Annales Academiae Scientiarum Fennicae B, 25, 2, Helsinki, 1932, pp. 149–50. Gautier had great influence on Rutbeuf's work, see Gautier de Coinci, *Les Miracles de Nostre Dame*, ed. Koenig, I, p. vii.

37. Ibid., II, lines 140–2, p. 100. On this attitude see P.-M. Spangenberg, 'Judenfeindlichkeit in den altfranzösischen Marienmirakeln. Stereotypen oder Symptome des Veränderung der kollektiven Selbsterfahrung', in *Die Legende von Ritualmord. Zur Geschichte der Blutbeschuldigung gegen Juden*, ed. T. Erb, Dokumente, Texte, Materialen 6, Berlin, 1993, pp. 157–77, at pp. 168–9.

38. See BN nouv. acq. fr. 24541, fol. 35r; H. Focillon, *Le Peintre des miracles de Notre Dame*, Paris, 1950, p. 34 and plate 6.

39. The Tale of the Bishop of Toledo, in Gautier de Coinci, *Les Miracles de Nostre Dame*, II lines 209–12, p. 13; see also line 316, 'Jez bruïroie toz ensanble' ('I would burn them all together'). On the use of Jews as witnesses to Christian faith see ibid., IV, Geneva, 1970, the tale 'Dou giuis qui reçut l'ymage diet en wage', pp. 110–33, at lines 440–6, pp. 127–8, and lines 448–54, p. 128. See also Spangenberg, 'Judenfeindlichkeit in den altfranzösischen Marienmirakeln', pp. 166–7.

40. I am most grateful to Dr Peter Linehan for translating these lines of the *Cantiga* for me; Alfonso X, *Cantigas de Santa Maria*, ed. W. Mettmann, 4 vols, Coimbra, 1959–72, I, pp. 11–14, lines 3–6, p. 11. On influences upon the *Cantigas* see E. Levi, 'I miracoli della vergine nell'arte del medio

evo', *Bollettino dell'Arte* (1918), pp. 1–32, esp. pp. 1–3, and on antisemitism within them V. Hatton and A. Mackay, 'Antisemitism in the Cantigas de Santa Maria', *Bulletin of Hispanic Studies* 61 (1983), pp. 187–99 and A.I. Bagby Jr, 'The Jews in the *Cantigas* of Alfonso X, El Sabio', *Speculum* 46 (1971), pp. 670–88.

41. Alfonso X, *Cantigas de Santa Maria*, I, lines 97–105, p. 14. See also Carpenter, 'Social perception and literary portrayal', pp. 61–72.

42. The *Cantigas* were rendered into Castilian prose later in the century, in a version which also named the parents Rachel and Samuel, and which was more elaborate in detail, Alfonso X, *Cantigas de Santa Maria*, I, ed. W. Mettmann, 3 vols, Madrid, 1986, pp. 317–19.

43. *Alfonso X and the Jews: an Edition of and Commentary on Siete Partidas 7.24 'De Los Judíos'*, ed. D.E. Carpenter, Berkeley, Calif., 1986, pp. 64–5.

44. Gonzalo de Berceo, *Obras Completas. II: Los Milagros de Nuestra Señora*, ed. B. Dutton, London, 1971, pp. 125–30.

45. Ibid., quatrail 372, p. 127; for the praise of the Virgin see p. 128 n. 353b. On Berceo's treatment see R. Marsan, *Itinéraire espagnol du comte médiéval (XIIIe–XVe siècles)*, Témoins de l'Espagne 4, Série Historique, Paris, 1974, pp. 546–7.

46. M. Vloberg, *L'Eucharistie dans l'art*, Art et Paysages 11, Grenoble, 1946, pp. 213–14.

47. M.P. Lillich, 'Gothic glaziers: monks, Jews, tax payers, Bretons, women', *Journal of Glass Studies* 27 (1985), pp. 72–92, fig. 1, p. 73; for all three scenes see Kraus, *The Living Theatre*, figs 112–14, pp. 160–1; E.E.F. Hucher, *Vitraux peints de la cathedrale du Mans*, Paris and Le Mans, 1865.

48. N. Morgan, *The Medieval Painted*

Glass of Lincoln Cathedral, Corpus vitrearum medii aevi, London, 1983, p. 30; description of the window on p. 11 (images in 1c); see description by J. Lafond, 'The stained glass decoration of Lincoln cathedral in the thirteenth century', *Archaeological Journal* 103 (1946), pp. 119–56, at pp. 129–31 (life), pp. 132–4 (miracles) and images nos 34–5.

49. M. Anderson, *A Saint at Stake*, London, 1964, plate 7; M.R. James, *The Sculpted Bosses in the Cloisters of Norwich Cathedral*, Norwich, 1911, p. 25.

50. *An Alphabet of Tales: Fifteenth-Century Translation of the Alphabetum Narrationum*, ed. M.M. Banks, EETS OS 127, London, 1905, no. 308, pp. 210–11.

51. Rubin, *Corpus Christi*, p. 176; see above, figure 19a, p. 156.

52. An unexpected context for which this scene was chosen is an early fourteenth-century manuscript of the decretals of Gregory IX, made in Italy for Parisian use and illustrated in England, BL Royal 10 E IV; tale on fols 210v–213v.

53. *The Frescoes of the Chapel of Eton College*, ed. M.R. James with R.H. Essex, Eton, 1907, pp. 3, 12, and on Winchester, pp. 2, 5. The inscription at Eton associates the tale with *Legenda sanctorum*, which may be the *The Golden Legend*, see above, p. 11.

54. See for example the Miracles of the Blessed Virgin Mary (*c.*1310–20), BL Royal 2 B VII, fols 207v–208r; Ward, *Catalogue of Romances*, II, p. 601.

55. Cambridge, Fitzwilliam Museum MS 48; *A Descriptive Catalogue of the Manuscripts in the Fitzwilliam Museum*, ed. M.R. James, Cambridge, 1895, pp. 100–20, at p. 109. L.F. Sandler, *Gothic Manuscripts 1285–1385*, II, A Survey of Manuscripts Illuminated in the British Isles, Oxford, 1986, no. 130, pp. 143–5, at p. 144; for an image of the female owner see fol. 86r. On Mary and Jews in this manuscript see D.L. Despres, 'Immaculate flesh and the social body: Mary and the Jews in Cambridge Fitzwilliam MS 48, the Carew-Poyntz Hours', *Jewish History* 12 (1998), pp. 47–69, at pp. 50–6.

56. The Lovel Lectionary, BL Harley 7026, fol. 13r.

57. Oxford Bodleian Auct. D.4.4, fol. 203v; M.R. James (with an introduction by E.G. Millar), *The Bohun Manuscripts*, Oxford, 1934, p. 29, plate 32b; see reproduction in B. Blumenkrantz, *Juden und Judentum in der mittelalterlichen Kunst*, Stuttgart, 1965, p. 21, fig. 11.

58. James, *The Bohun Manuscripts*, pp. 42–3. See also reproduction in Blumenkrantz, *Juden und Judentum*, p. 20, figs 9 and 10.

59. E. Rickert, *Painting in Britain: the Middle Ages*, London, 1954, pp. 167, 148; Meale, 'The miracles of Our Lady', pp. 115–36.

60. *The Vernon Manuscript: a Facsimile of Bodleian Library, Oxford, ms. Eng. Poet. a.1*, ed. A.I. Doyle, Cambridge, 1989; Meale, 'The miracles of Our Lady', pp. 126–7, 129.

61. See figure 1, p. 14, above. See also Brussels, Bibliothèque Royale 3354 (II), fol. 12.

62. It is the second volume of the pair (vol. 1 contains the *Legenda aurea*) Brussels, Bibliothèque Royale 9229–30, MS 9230, fol. 34v, C. Gaspar and F. Lyna, *Les Principaux Manuscrits à peintures de la Bibliothèque royale de Belgique*, Brussels, 1984, I (2), notice 109, pp. 51–3, at p. 52 (see also I (1), notice 109, pp. 259–66).

63. BN Paris fr. 9198, fol. 68.

64. Wolter, *Der Judenknabe*, lines 41–6, p. 116.

65. Ibid., lines 97–100, p. 117.

66. Ibid., line 211, p. 120.

67. Ibid., lines 248–51, p. 121

68. 'Puer masculus . . . in ostia sacerdotis elevata puerum pulcherrimum vidit eum sibi dari per

totam diem a se nutrientibus postulavit', *Les Annales et la chronique des Dominicains de Colmar*, ed. C. Gérard and J. Liblin, Colmar, 1854, pp. 144–5. See also the interesting chastisement of a sinful priest offered when the host turned into a child during the mass, *Das Magnum Speculum Exemplorum als Ausgangspunkt populärer Erzählungstraditionen. Studien zur seiner Wirkungsgeschichte in Polen und Russland*, ed. R. Alsheimer, Frankfurt, 1971, no. 79, p. 138.

69. In for example the *Alphabetum narrationum*, see *An Alphabet of Tales*, c. 308, pp. 210–11.

70. For a comprehensive consideration of the convergence of eucharistic and Marian imagery see B. Williamson, 'The Virgin *lactans* and the Madonna of Humility: image and devotion in Italy, Metz and Avignon in the thirteenth and fourteenth centuries', Ph.D. dissertation submitted to the Courtauld Institute, University of London, 1996, ch. 10, pp. 207–28.

71. *Acta sanctorum aprilis*, ed. G. Henschenius and D. Papebroch, III, Antwerp, 1675, cols 694–5.

72. G. Kaftal, *Iconography of the Saints in the Painting of North East Italy*, Florence, 1978, fig. 1114, cols 847–8 (a painting by Antonio Vivarini, panel of a polyptych).

73. See A. Timmermann, 'Representing the eucharist: the Presentation in the Temple in German fourteenth and fifteenth century painting', unpublished paper delivered at the Third Medieval Postgraduate Research Seminar in Cambridge 1996.

74. 'Utrum, quando in hoc sacramento miraculose apparet vel caro vel puer, sit ibi vere corpus Christi', Thomas Aquinas, *Summa theologiae*, III, q. 76, a. 8; trans. W. Barden, London and New York, 1965, vol. 58, pp. 118–

23, at p. 118.

75. Ibid., answers *ad* 1, 2 and 3, p. 122.

76. As suggested by Mary Minty in '*Kiddush ha-shem* in German Christian Eyes in the Middle Ages', *Zion* 59 (1994), pp. 209–66 (in Hebrew).

77. *The Old French Evangile de l'Enfance: an Edition with Introduction and Notes*, ed. M.B.M. Boulton, PIMS Studies and Texts 70, Toronto, 1984, pp. 16–17.

78. Ibid., pp. 4–6.

79. Ibid., line 1472, p. 68. For another version see *Les Enfaunces de Jesu Crist*, ed. M. Boulton, London, 1985, lines 1132–6, p. 65:

E ki sunt ci enfermé?
Les Gius firent serement
Ke pors furent verrément.
Jesu dist dunc a cele gent:
'E pors serrunt certainement.'

The whole tale appears on lines 1111–56, pp. 64–5; on the illustrations, see ibid., p. 5.

80. *The Old French Evangile de l'Enfaunce*, pp. 67–8. Holkham Bible fol. 16r. For illustrations see *Les Enfaunces de Jesu Crist*, p. 5. On other tales which link Jews and pigs see O. Dähnhardt, *Natursagen*, II, Leipzig and Berlin, 1909, pp. 102–7; M. Albert-Llorca, *L'Ordre des choses*, Paris, 1991, p. *24; C. Fabre-Vassas, *The Singular Beast: Jews, Christians and the Pig*, trans. C. Volk, New York, 1997, pp. 93–4; M. Pastroureau, *Couleurs, images, symboles: études d'histoire et d'anthropologie*, Paris, 1989, pp. 252–4.

81. See, for instance, a mundane scene of baking, in which the oven resembles in all details the one often depicted in scenes of the Jewish Boy, in the month of December in a calendar from Utrecht diocese, *Manuscrits à peintures du IXe au début du XVe siècle. Catalogue d'éxposition*, Brussels, 1985, facing caption 'Cat. 12'

and p. 17 (Brussels, Bibliothèque Royale 2910-20, fol. 41v).

82. M.-C. Pouchelle, *The Body and Surgery in the Middle Ages*, trans. R. Morris, Cambridge, 1990, pp. 134-6, 139.

83. C. Ferguson O'Meara, '"In the hearth of the virginal womb": the iconography of the holocaust in late medieval art', *Art Bulletin* 63 (1981), pp. 75-88; for an example of testing of the eucharist within an oven see Ward, *Catalogue of Romances*, III, p. 699 (from a fourteenth-century manuscript BL Harley 2316, fol. 13r).

84. It is hard to evaluate the currency of the tale, but the linkage between mother as womb, and oven as annihilation, also appears in the tale of Miriam of Beit Azov, originally told by Josephus Flavius in his *History of the War of the Jews*. This is a tale of a Jewish woman of Jerusalem who is driven to roast and eat her own little son during the siege of Jerusalem by Titus in the year 70. This story came into vernacular circulation in the twelfth century and was incorporated into drama in the fourteenth and fifteenth centuries. Interpretations of the act vary in attributing to the mother hunger, madness, unnatural cruelty, or mercy for her son (devouring him lest he die himself of hunger or by the sword). See Guy N. Deutsch, 'Déicide et vengeance', *Archives Juives* 6 (1980), pp. 69-3; H. Schreckenberg, *Rezeptionsgeschichtliche und Textkritische Untersuchungen zu Flavius Josephus*, Arbeiten zur Literatur und Geschichte des Hellenistischen Judentums 10, Leiden, 1977, pp. 26-48.

85. 'Wie mac aber daz gesîn daz sich der grôze verbirget in einer kleinen oblaten? . . . Nû, war; umbe læt er sich niht sehen, læt er ist? . . . Wer möhte ein rôez fleisch geniezen oder rôez bluot getrinken? Wer möhte einem kindelîn sîn houbetlîn sîniu hendelîn oder sîniu füezelîn abe gebîzen!', Berthold of Regensburg, *Vollständige Ausgabe seiner Predigten mit Anmerkungen und Wörterbuch*, ed. F. Pfeiffer and J. Strobb, 2 vols, Vienna, 1862-80, II, pp. 266, 270.

86. This is a standard characterisation of the wolf in medieval bestiaries, see for example CUL Ii. 4.2, fol. 16r-v; or *A Medieval Book of Beasts: Pierre de Beauvais' Bestiary*, trans. G.R. Mermier, Lewiston, N.Y., 1992, c. 37, pp. 209-11.

87. '*Dyabolus*: Nota dyabolus comparatur volpi propter assimilacionem in actione; non enim habet vulpes nisi malignas operaciones, ut dicit philosophus . . .'; on a wolf pretending to be dead and eating birds (*aves*), 'Item dyabolus facit sicut Iudei qui loco Christi crucifigunt ymaginem ceream et quandoque pueros', *La Tabula exemplorum secundum ordinem alphabeti*, ed. J.T. Welter, Paris and Toulouse, 1926, no. 57, p. 19.

88. J. Delumeau, *La Peur en Occident (XIVe-XVIIIe siècles). Une Cité assiégée*, Paris, 1978, pp. 63-5. A peculiar domestication of a Jewish goblin, *das Jüdel*, in German folktale has him dwelling in ovens. He preys on children, and is, therefore, given various distractions to play with, and leave the children alone. When a child laughs in its sleep, it is said that the *Jüdel* is playing with him, J. Grimm, *Deutsche mythologie*, ed. E.H. Mayer, Berlin, 1878, nos 62, 389, 454, 473, pp. 436, 447, 449, 473.

89. Vienna, ONB 2554, fol. 30r; see the facsimile *Bible moralisée*, ed. R. Haussherr, Codices selecti phototypice impressi, Vienna, 1973, I, p. 58; II, pp. 50-1. I am most grateful to Dr Sarah Lipton who shared with me her insights and erudition and introduced me to this image.

90. 'Domine, tu non comedis carnes mortuas et coctas sed vivas, quid

iniuste depredaris nos. Devora ergo nunc duos filios meos et comede eos', John Gobius, *Scala coeli*, ed. M.-A. Polo de Beaulieu, Paris, 1991, under the rubric *Abstinentia*, no. 20, p. 172. For a later version in the *Magnum speculum exemplorum*, See *Das Magnum speculum exemplorum*, p. 133. On abuse of the poor as a form of devouring, or cannibalism, see P. Buc, *L'Ambiguité du livre. Prince, pouvoir et peuple dans les commentaires de la bible au moyen âge*, Théologie Historique 95, Paris, 1994, pp. 227–8.

91. These narrative elements, as well as its eucharistic potential, made the story of the Jewish Boy into the most frequently illustrated Marian tale in English manuscripts, Meale, 'The miracles of Our Lady', p. 127. On Mary and the Jews see also D.L. Despres, 'Mary of the eucharist: cultic anti-Judaism in some fourteenth-century English devotional manuscripts', in *From Witness to Witchcraft: Jew and Judaism in Medieval Christian Thought*, ed. J. Cohen, Wolfenbütteler Mittelalter-Studien 11, Wiesbaden, 1996, pp. 375–401.

92. On the 'family romance' see S. Kay, *The Chansons de Geste in the Age of Romance*, Oxford, 1995, pp. 83–90, 103–15.

93. H.-F. Rosenfeld, 'Das Jüdel', *Die deutsche Literatur des Mittelalters. Verfasserlexikon*, IV, Berlin and New York, 1983, pp. 891–3; of Bavarian or East Swabian origin, see R. Spenger, 'Die Legende vom Judenknaben', *Germania* 27 (1882), pp. 129–44, text on pp. 130–5; for an analysis of the text see Minty, '*Kiddush ha-shem*', pp. 241–5, and on the later history of the tale in German versions see pp. 239–41. See an interesting reading of a Marian tale involving the killing of a Christian boy in L.O. Fradenburg, 'Criticism, anti-semitism, and the Prioress's

Tale', *Exemplaria* 1 (1989), pp. 69–115.

94. The section on Giordano da Rivalto (da Pisa) is edited in *Racconti esemplari di predicatori del due e trecento*, II, ed. G. Varanini and G. Baldassari, Rome, 1993, pp. 1–491, quote from no. 167, p. 322, whole sequence is nos 167–8, pp. 322–8.

95. Trier, Stadtarchiv MS 1139, fols 66r and 89v: 'et credit eum pro sacramento xristi ymmo ipsum in xristo ut historia cavit occisum'; 'verumque dum habere non poterant suam seviciam converterunt in copus xristi misticum scilicet puerum sanctum et ipsum suspenderunt'. A. Vauchez, *La Sainteté en Occident aux derniers siècles du moyen âge*, Bibliothèque des Écoles Françaises d'Athènes et de Rome 241, Rome, 1981, pp. 107–8.

96. See below, pp. 129–30. See also Robert C. Stacey, 'From ritual crucifixion to host desecration: Jews and the Body of Christ', *Jewish History* 12 (1998), pp. 11–28.

97. On the use of Marian imagery for the expression of historical identity in contemporary Alicante see M.A. Albert-Llorca and J.-P. Albert, 'Mahomet, la Vièrge et la frontière', *Annales* 50 (1995), pp. 855–86, at pp. 881–6.

98. On this making of difference, with particular interest in images of rustics, see P. Freedman, 'Sainteté et sauvagerie: deux images du paysan au moyen-âge', *Annales* 47 (1992), pp. 539–60, esp. pp. 541–2.

99. The Jew is also made into the enemy of conversion in tales which plotted violent opposition to the desire of a young person to receive baptism, see the 1241 tale from Frankfurt in a chronicle of Erfurt, 'Cronica S. Petri Erfordensis moderna', *MGH.SS* XXX, Hanover, 1896, pp. 354–455, at pp. 394–5.

100. Rubin, *Corpus Christi*, pp. 35–49.

101. On processions see ibid., pp. 243–71.

102. *Decrees of the Ecumenical Councils,* ed. N.P. Tanner, Washington DC, 1990, c. 1 'De fide catholica', pp. 230–1.

103. See ibid., cc. 68–9, p. 266; on usury see c. 67, pp. 265–6.

104. Ibid., c. 20, p. 244.

105. For Wrocław see *Concilia,* XXIII, ed. J.D. Mansi, and others, Venice, 1779, cols 1174–6, clauses 15–19. These clauses were absent from the statutes promulgated by the Legate in dioceses further to the west.

106. *Concilia Germaniae,* III, ed. J. Hartzheim, Cologne, 1760, pp. 632–6, at p. 636; or *Concilia,* XXIII, cols 1169–76; for the canons, see also 'Continuatio Vindobonensis', *MGH.SS* IX, pp. 698–722, on synod pp. 699–702. On the synod see W. Trusen, *Spätmittelalterliche Jurisprudenz und Wirtschaftsethic dargestellt an Wiener Gutachten des 14. Jahrhunderts,* Vierteiljahrschrift für Social- und Wirtschaftsgeschichte Beiheft 43, Wiesbaden, 1961, pp. 93–7; for renewal in the Salzburg provincial synod of 1418, see C.-J. Hefele and H. Leclercq, *Histoire des conciles,* VII (1), Paris, 1916, c. 33, p. 599. Statutes protecting the host were renewed periodically, often with special mention of heretics, as in 1389 in Prague, *Concilia pragensia, 1353–1413,* ed. K.A.C. Höfler, Prague, 1862, pp. 37–9.

107. H. Ollendiek, *Die päpstliche Legaten im deutschen Reichsgebiet von 1261 bis zum Ende des Interregnums,* Historische Schriften der Universität Freiburg Schweiz 3, Freiburg, 1976, pp. 144–6; on these synods in general see pp. 103–4 (Wrocław) and pp. 106–8 (Vienna). See also P. Johanek, 'Das Wiener Konzil von 1267, der Kardinallegat Guido und die Politik Ottokars II', *Jahrbuch für Landesgeschichte von* *Niederösterreich* 44/45 (1978/79), pp. 312–40.

108. *Der Passauer Anonymus. Ein Sammelwerk über Ketzer, Juden, Antichrist aus der Mitte des 13. Jahrhunderts,* ed. A. Patschovsky, Schriften der MGH 22, Stuttgart, 1967, pp. 50, 51, 180.

109. See for example the twelfth-century font of Sainte Larme at Sélincourt, Kraus, *The Living Theatre,* fig. 101, p. 152, and the thirteenth-century glass of Troyes cathedral, ibid., fig. 99, p. 151. See also Schreckenberg, *The Jews in Christian Art,* pp. 16–18.

110. R. Branner, *Manuscript Painting in Paris during the Reign of Saint Louis: a Study in Style,* Berkeley, Calif., 1977, fig. 391 (Padua Bibliotheca Capitolaria D34, fol. 113ra).

111. M. Camille, *The Gothic Idol: Ideology and Image Making in the Middle Ages,* Cambridge, 1989, p. 178.

112. 'Item, statuimus, ad honorem Dei et reverentiam, quod, dum corpus Christi portabitur ad infirmos, nullus Judeus vel Judea major novem annis remaneat in Carreria in ejus presentia, sed se removeant et abscondant, et si quis contrafecerit, pro qualibet vice in v sol. puniatur', M.A. de Maulde, *Coutumes et règlements de la République d'Avignon au treizième siècle,* Paris, 1879, no. 125, p. 595; for restrictions during Holy Week see ibid., pp. 594–5. These restrictions and others appear under the heading 'Quo tempore Judei non exeant juzatariam'.

113. Vatican Apostolic Library Lat. 14779, fol. 12r; this case is also recorded in 1365, Lat. 14775, fol. 57r.

114. Vatican Apostolic Library Lat. 14778, fol. 29v. For a similar case of Guinevra, wife of Vinerie the Jew, see Vatican Library, Lat. MS 14776, fol. 47v. A fine was imposed for presence in the streets on Maundy Thursday in Vatican Library Lat. MS 14779, fol. 10r.

115. Vienna, ÖNB 2680, fol. 86ra–b: 'Es sal en uzlich Iude wen man mit gotis lichnam get hinder sich treten in ein hus do her(r)ynne wonende ist. Und wo her an der gasse get do sal her ouch wichen in ein hus adir in ein andir gasse en sal ouch nymant leid czu czihen.'

116. *Episcopal Registers, Diocese of Worcester: Register of Bishop Godfrey Giffard*, ed. J.W. Willis Bund, 2 vols, Worcester Historical Society, 1898–1902, II, p. 71. I am grateful to Dr Joan Greatrex for her help with this entry which we consulted at the Hereford and Worcester Record Office, b716.093.

117. On the issue of the excommunication of Jews see W.C. Jordan, 'Christian excommunication of the Jews in the Middle Ages: a restatement of the issues', *Jewish History* 1 (1986), pp. 31–8; on England esp. pp. 33–4; see also J. Shatzmiller, 'Jews "separated from the communion of the faithful in Christ" in the Middle Ages', in *Studies in Medieval Jewish History and Literature*, ed. I. Twersky, Cambridge, Mass., 1979, pp. 307–14.

118. See examples from the 1360s and 1370s in Vatican Apostolic Library, Vat. lat. 14777, fol. 4v; Vat. lat. 14776, fol. 47; J. Chiffoleau, *Les Justices du pape: délinquance et criminalité dans la région d'Avignon au quatorzième siècle*, Publications de la Sorbonne, Série Histoire Ancienne et Médiévale 14, Paris, 1984, p. 204.

119. 'Qui fertur sacerdotem cum corpore dominico euntem luto nescio vel lapide vulnerasse', Henry of Heimburg, 'Annales', *MGH.SS* XXVII, p. 717.

120. *The Apostolic See and the Jews, I: Documents*, ed. S. Simonsohn, PIMS Studies and Texts 94, Toronto, 1988, no. 357, pp. 376–7.

121. For Latin text see ibid., no. 93, pp. 98–9 or *PL* CCXVI, no. 84, cols 885–6; the English translation is from S. Grayzel, *The Church and the Jews in the Thirteenth Century*, rev. edn, New York, 1966, no. 29, pp. 136–8; on the case S. Simonsohn, *The Apostolic See and the Jews, VII: History*, PIMS Studies and Texts 109, Toronto, 1991, pp. 59–60, 247–8.

122. I am grateful to Professor Carlo Ginzburg for his inspiring comments on my reading of this tale, see C. Ginzburg, 'Representations of German Jewry: images, prejudice, ideas: a comment', in *In and Out of the Ghetto*, ed. R.P. Hsia and H. Lehmann, New York, 1995, pp. 209–12; see also on coins and the eucharist, M. Shell, *Art and Money*, Chicago, 1995, pp. 39–42. The thirteenth century saw a particular preoccupation with the significance of the Jewish occupation of moneylending, and this was sometimes seen as a form of idolatry, the worship of money, S. Lipton, 'The root of all evil: Jews, money and metaphor in the *Bible Moralisée*', *Medieval Encounters* 1 (1995), pp. 301–22. When money was miraculously transformed in chastisement of the Jews, this could also take the form of a more polluting and sinister turning into toads, see the case of Metz in 1385, J. Weill, 'Un juif brulé à Metz vers 1385 pour profanation de l'hostie', *REJ* 53 (1907), pp. 270–2, at p. 272. On the toad in *exempla* see J. Berlioz, 'L'homme au crapaud. Genèse d'un *exemplum* médiéval', in *Tradition et histoire dans la culture populaire. Rencontres autour de l'oeuvre de Jean-Michel Guilcher*, Grenoble, 1990, pp. 169–203.

123. On parallel representations of Jews and heretics in the thirteenth century see S. Lipton, 'Jews, heretics and the eye of the cat', *Word and image* 8 (1992), pp. 362–77. For a case of what might have been mockery of the mass by a group of youths of Orvieto in Holy Week 1295 see C. Lansing, *Purity and Power: Cathar Heresy in*

124. Gerald of Wales, *Gemma ecclesiastica*, in *Opera*, II, ed. J.S. Brewer, RS, London, 1862, D. 1, c. 11, Rolls series, pp. 38–43. The sacraments were clearly the issue over which error was most frequent and most dangerous, as articulated in an early fourteenth-century handbook for the Bohemian inquisition: 'Plerumque heretici tam stulta dogmata, tam execranda sacramanta proferunt, ut eciam Iudeorum et paganorum ebetent, et qui racione divine carent agnicionis', *Die Anfänge einer ständigen Inquisition in Böhmen. Ein Prager Inquisitoren-Handbuch aus der ersten Hälfte des 14. Jahrhunderts*, ed. A. Patschovsky, Berlin, 1975, no. 149, p. 229.

125. Under the rubric 'de eukaristia et ejus virtutibus' and dated 1298(!), *Le Speculum laicorum. Édition d'une collection d'exempla composée en Angleterre à la fin du XIIIe siècle*, ed. J.T. Welter, Paris, 1914, no. 269a, pp. 54–5.

126. On the devil's tricks and temptations in medieval literature see M. Schumacher, 'Der Teufel als "Tausendkünstler". Ein wortgeschichtlicher Beitrag', *Mittellateinisches Jahrbuch* 27 (1992), pp. 65–76.

127. Grayzel, *The Church and the Jews*, pp. 23, 25–6; and no. 18, pp. 114, 117; no. 69, pp. 198–201; no. 71, pp. 204–7; and conciliar initiatives in 1195 no. III, pp. 298–9; no. XVIII, pp. 316–19.

128. *The Apostolic See and the Jews, I: Documents*, no. 82, pp. 86–7.

129. 'Nam sunt qui, quod nephandum est dicere, nutrices christianas habentes non permittunt lactare filios, cum corpore Christi sumpserunt, nisi primo per triduum lac effuderint in latrinam; quasi intelligere quod corpus Christi incorporetur et ad secessum descendat. Sed falsum est', Henry of Segusio (Cardinal Hostiensis), *Summa aurea*, Basle, 1573, c. 1204. Dahan, 'Les Juifs dans les miracles', p. 28. For this persistent anxiety see also the Polish synod of Breslau in 1446, *Concilia poloniae: études critiques et sources*, Wrocław, Warsaw and Krakow, 1963, c. 51, pp. 453–4.

130. On discussion of digestion of the eucharist see Rubin, *Corpus Christi*, p. 37; for a later example of preoccupation with the problem of Christian women breastfeeding Jewish children see the urban statutes of Perugia of 1439 against the practice: 'Item che niuno Giudeio nè Giudeia possa nè deggha dare a bayla, nè far dare latte, nè nutrire, ne appoppare a veruna cristiana niuna loro reda o matura, sotto la dicta pena de libre conquanta', *A Documentary History of the Jews in Italy*, II, ed. A. Toaff, Leiden, 1994, doc. 952, pp. 492–5, c. 10 on p. 494.

131. E. Kanarfogel, 'Attitudes towards children and childhood in medieval Jewish society', *Approaches to Judaism in Medieval Times*, II, ed. D.R. Blumenthal, Brown Judaic Studies 57, Chico, Calif., 1985, pp. 1–34; esp. p. 18.

132. I am here enormously grateful to my colleague and friend Professor Gary Macy who discovered and transcribed this question from Paris Bibliothèque Mazarine MS 795, fol. 90v2 and shared it with me: 'Panis autem fastidiosus est febricantibus sic et panis ille qui de celo descendit fastidiosus est et nauseam facit rebellis hereticis et pessimis Iudeis quid dixerit in figuram hereticorum . . . Putant enim isti pessimi heretici et Iudei et alii infideles quod non sit ibi nisi bucella panis parva.'

133. 'Jurati presentant quod Abraham de Warwike Petithake Jsaake Cappelanus Judeorum de Norwico cum pluribus aliis tam Christianis quam Judeis ignotis Burgaverunt Ecclesias de

Newentonia et Sweynestorp calices vestimenta Libros et alia ornamenta Ecclesiarum illarum noctanter furati fuerunt et pixidem in qua corpus Christi posituum [*sic*] fuit viliter fregerunt et corpus domini sub pedibus calcaverunt', PRO Justices Itinerant Roll 1/575, m. 4 (Hundred of Hunnherd), transcribed in Z.E. Rokeach, 'The Jewish churchrobbers and host desecrators of Norwich (ca. 1285)', *REJ* 141 (1982), pp. 331–62, at p. 348. Another case is brought to light by Rokeach, in which Christians and Jews are said to have broken into the church of Lodnes, and were charged with a payment of bail for their release, ibid., p. 349.

134. 'Et respondetur in sententia diffinitiva, quod in hoc casu voluntas venditionis gravior est iudicanda quam actus furti. Unde dicti malefici potius tamquam heretici in favorem fidei igni sunt tradendi, quam sicut fures poena patiboli tormentandi', under the rubric 'De poena subtrahantis sacramentum eucharistiae', in *Právní Kniha mesta Brna z poloviny 14. stoleti*, I, Brno, 1990, no. 526, p. 332.

135. 'er ein ostye schelkkelichen in eins juden hus truog', *Oberrheinische Stadtrechte. III. Elsäßische rechte. I. Schlettstadter Stadtrechte*, ed. J. Gény, Heidelberg, 1902, p. 125.

136. *Viaticum narrationum* in *Beiträge zur lateinische Erzählungsliteratur der Mittelalters. III. Das Viaticum narrationum des Henmannus Bononiensis*, ed. A. Hilka, Berlin, 1935, no. 72, pp. 100–2. An adjacent tale in the collection also describes removal of the host into the palm of a recipient for fear of undeserving reception, ibid., no. 70, pp. 97–100. On the representation of Jews in some thirteenth-century *exempla* see I.G. Marcus, 'Images of Jews in the *exempla* of Caesarius of Heisterbach', in *From Witness to Witchcraft: Jews and Judaism in*

Medieval Christian Thought, ed. J. Cohen, Wolfenbütteler Mittelalter-Studien 11, Wiesbaden, 1997, pp. 247–56.

137. F. Pfeiffer, 'Niederdeutsche Erzählungen aus dem XV. Jahrhundert', *Germania* 9 (1864), pp. 257–89, no. 11 'Der jude mit der Hostie' at pp. 284–7. The story is said to have taken place in Strassburg in 1417. See also BL Add. 15833, fol. 141, for a fourteenth-century version from Upper Austria.

138. *La Tabula exemplorum secundum ordinem alphabeti*, ed. J.-T. Welter, Thesaurus Exemplorum 3, Paris and Toulouse, 1926, note 57, pp. 101–2, at p. 102.

139. 'Schoepffer und loeser rihter und behalter, bist du got und mensche so erbarme dich uiber mich armen suindigen moenschen', *Johannes von Sterngassen und sein Sentenzenkommentar*, ed. W. Senner, Berlin, 1995, lines 25–8, p. 369. See text also in F. Pfeiffer, 'Sprüche deutscher Mystiker', *Germania* 3 (1858), pp. 225–43, no. 11 at p. 237. I am most grateful to Dr W. Senner OP, for bringing his edition of John's work to my attention.

140. 'wan du bist got und moensche so erbarme dich uiber mich armen suindigen moenschen', *Johannes von Sterngassen*, lines 5–8, p. 369.

141. John Bromyard, *Summa praedicantium*, Antwerp, 1614, p. 254b. This *exemplum* is followed by another about a French Jew who pretended to be a Christian (p. 255a) and by another about a Jew who returned a pawn to a woman in exchange for a consecrated host (ibid.).

142. On gender and the making of the tale, see below, chapter 4, pp. 74–7.

143. The manuscript has been discovered, identified and discussed by Nicole Bériou to whom I am most grateful for providing me with a typescript of her article 'Le premier récit du "miracle de

l'hostie" – 1273 (ms. Paris BN lat. 16482', forthcoming.

144. On the figure of the *vetula* see J. Agrimi and C. Crisciani, 'Savoir médical et anthroplogie religieuse: les répresentations et les fonctions de la *vetula* (XIIIe–XVe siècle)', *Annales* 48 (1993), pp. 1281–308.

145. M. Lillich, *Rainbow like an Emerald: Stained Glass in Lorraine in the Thirteenth and Early Fourteenth Centuries*, University Park, Pa., 1991, plates IV 14–16 and pp. 78–84; for the text by J. Ruyr of 1634, see pp. 112–13.

146. For a similar role attributed to a priest see the miracle from Cologne (1150), in Jean d'Outre-meuse (des Preis) (d. 1400), *Ly myreur des histors*, IV, ed. S. Bormans, Brussels, 1877, pp. 403–4.

147. For general discussions of the host desecration accusation see G. Langmuir, 'The tormentors of the body of Christ', in *Christianity and its Discontents: Exclusion, Persecution and Rebellion, 1000–1500*, ed. S.L. Waugh, Cambridge, 1996, pp. 287–309; M. Despina, 'Les accusations de profanation d'hosties portées contre les juifs', *Rencontre. Chrétiens et juifs* 22 (1971), pp. 150–73 and 23 (1971), pp. 179–96; P. Browe, 'Die Hostienschändung der Juden im Mittelalter', *Römische Quartalschrift* 34 (1926), pp. 167–97; J. Trachtenberg, *The Devil and the Jews*, New Haven, Conn., 1943, pp. 109–18.

148. C. Ginzburg, 'Représentation: le mot, l'idée, la chose', *Annales* 46 (1991), pp. 1219–34, at p. 1230.

3   Patterns of Accusation

1. A host desecration by Jews is sometimes claimed to have occurred in Beelitz (Mecklenburg) in 1247. This is based on a sixteenth-century tradition which has no support from the thirteenth-

century indulgences granted to a local shrine, and which do not mention Jews at all, *Germania Judaica*, II (1), ed. Z. Avneri, Tübingen, 1968, pp. 61–3. See, for example, the mention in W. Treue, 'Schlechte und gute Christen. Zur Rolle von Christen in antijüdischen Ritualmord- und Hostienschändungslegenden', *Aschkenas* 2 (1992), pp. 95–116, at p. 99.

2. On whom see D.L. d'Avray, *The Preaching of the Friars: Sermons Diffused from Paris before 1300*, Oxford, 1985.

3. 'De miraculo hostiae a Judaeo Parisiis anno Domini MCCXC', *RHGF* XXII, p. 32; 'Chronicon ecclesiae sancti Dyonisii', *RHGF* XXIII, p. 145; *Les grandes chroniques de France*, VIII, ed. J. Viard, Paris, 1934, pp. 144–5; on the *Grandes chroniques* see G. Spiegel, *The Chronicle Tradition of Saint-Denis*, Medieval Classics: Texts and Studies 10, Brookline, Mass., 1978, pp. 72–6, 94 and L. Delisle, 'Notes sur quelques manuscrits du Musée Britannique', *Mémoires de la Société de l'histoire de Paris et de l'Ile-de-France* 4 (1877), pp. 183–238; 'Iohannis de Thilrode Chronicon', *MGH.SS* XXV, ed. J. Heller, Hanover, 1880, p. 578. On the making of the accounts of the case see J. Dehullu, ' "L'Affaire des Billettes" en de beschuldiging van hostieprofanatie in Parijs, 1290', Licensiat dissertation, Catholic University of Louvain, 1992.

4. Paris Archives Nationales L663 (readings for the Office of the Holy Sacrament); Paris Archives Nationales L1492B, Cartulary (sixteenth century); Paris BN lat. 10981 (readings for the feast).

5. 'Sciam, inquit, an vera sint quae de re hujusmodi insani garriunt Christiani', 'De miraculo hostiae', p. 32.

6. Ibid.

7. On the parish see R. Cazelles, *Nouvelle histoire de Paris de la fin du*

règne de Philippe Auguste à la mort de Charles V, 1223–1380, Paris, 1972, pp. 48, 116 and J.-A. Dulaure, *Histoire physique, civile et morale de Paris*, II, Paris, 1854, p. 142.

8. For a legal opinion as to the appropriate judicial context for a trial of a Jew who threw mud at a crucifix see the view of Petrus de Ancharano (1330–1416) in J. Muldoon, *Popes, Lawyers and Infidels*, Philadelphia, Pa., 1979, p. 170 n. 88.

9. For a similar claim of indestructibility of heretical books when burnt see Jordan of Saxony, *Opera ad res ordinis spectantia*, ed. J.-J. Berthier, Fribourg, 1891, c. 17, pp. 9–10.

10. F. Autrand, M. Foisil, J. Longère and L. Pietri, *Histoire du diocèse de Paris*, I, Histoire des diocèses de France 20, Paris, 1987, p. 159.

11. 'Iohannis de Thilrode Chronicon', p. 578.

12. 'In illo loco civitatis Parisiensis, in quo quidam Iudei ...', *The Apostolic See and the Jews. Documents*, I, ed. S. Simonsohn, PIMS Texts and Studies 94, Toronto, 1988, no. 275, pp. 283–4.

13. S. Moreau-Rendu, *A Paris, rue des Jardins ...*, Paris, 1954, p. 41.

14. This was one of many new orders created in the thirteenth century, founded in 1286 at Boucheromont in the diocese of Châlons-sur-Marne by Lord Gui de Joinville, A. Boinet, *Les Églises parisiennes*, I, Paris, 1958, p. 339. Like so many other orders it was dissolved after the decrees of the Council of Vienne, and in 1317 became amalgamated with the Augustinian Order. A description of the churches of Paris made in 1325 describes the chapel with a short poem:

Puis, siet apres une chapele
Dediées par miracle bele
D'un Juif qui en son ostel
Bouilli le sacrement d'autel
Dont trouvez fu vermaus entiers.

BN ms supp. fr. 1133, fol. 118–19; H.L. Bordier, *Eglises et monastères de Paris*, Paris, 1856, p. 38, lines 223–7. For the cartulary of this chapel see BN lat. 10981. For a drawing of the seal of the Billettes see P. Perdrizet, *Le Calendrier parisien à la fin du moyen-âge d'après le breviaire et les livres d'heures*, Paris, 1913, p. 159, fig. 15; it depicts a Jew fanning the fire under a cauldron.

15. F. de Mallevoüe, 'Saint-Jean-en-Grève au temps d'Henri IV', *La Cité* 13 (1914), pp. 414–30; also printed in the parish breviary *Offices propres à l'église paroissiale de St-Jean-en-Grève*, Paris, 1742, from Paris Archives Nationales L663, no. 1, also in BN lat. 10981.

16. de Mallevoüe, 'Saint-Jean-en-Grève', p. 422.

17. Ibid., pp. 425, 419 (for use on Corpus Christi and its octave).

18. See the list of cases in Map 1, p. xiv.

19. G. Villani, *Nuova cronica*, I, ed. G. Porta, 3 vols, Parma, 1990–91, c. 143, pp. 616–17.

20. G. Acquilecchia, 'Dante and the Florentine chroniclers', *Bulletin of the John Rylands Library* 48 (1965), pp. 30–55, at p. 36 n. 2 and p. 44. I am grateful to Professor Daniel Bornstein for some helpful and authoritative comments about Villani's principles of selection of tales.

21. See below, pp. 141–2; Giovanni could not of course, have attended the sermon of November 1304 discussed here, as he was away from Florence at the time.

22. 'MCCCVI omnes judei in Francia commorantes, precepto regis, uno die scilicet in festo sancte Marie Magdalene, capiuntur pro quodam crimine nephando quod egerant ex sacramento altaris, prout accusati fuerant apud regem', *La Chronique liegoise de 1402*, ed. E. Bacha, Brussels, 1900, p. 252; on dating see p. xxxiii. This claim is taken literally by R. Chazan, *Medieval Jewry in*

Northern France: a Political and Social History, Baltimore, Md., 1973, pp. 181–2. See discussion in W.C. Jordan, *The French Monarchy and the Jews*, Philadelphia, Pa., 1989, pp. 192–4; S. Menache, 'The king, the church and the Jews: some considerations on the expulsions from England and France', *Journal of Medieval History* 13 (1987), pp. 223–36.

23. 'Intelleximus quod Iudei... et quam plures aliciunt muneribus et promiensis, in tantum quod a plerisque receperunt et suis nephandis manibus presumpserunt nequiter pertractare sanctissimum corpus Christi et alia sacramenta nostre fidei blasphemare, simplices plurimos seducendo et circuncidendo seductos', G. Saige, *Les Juifs de Languedoc antérieurement au XIVe siècle*, Paris, 1881, pp. 235–6; M. Kriegel, 'La Jurisdiction inquisitoriale sur les juifs à l'époque de Philip le Hardi et Philip le Bel', in *Les Juifs dans l'histoire de France. Premier colloque international de Haïfa*, ed. M. Yardeni, Leiden, 1980, pp. 70–7, at pp. 74–5.

24. N. Valois, 'Jacques de Thérines, cistercien', in *Histoire littéraire de la France*, XXXIV, Paris, 1914, pp. 179–219, at pp. 188–9.

25. 'hec fecit urgens causa eiectionis gentis iudaice a christianissimo regno Francie', *Fortalitium fidei contra Judeos saracenos aliosque fidei inimicos*, Lyons, 1511, book 3 (on Jews, consideration 9, expulsion 2, fol. 216rb, on Paris, fols 216vb–217vb). On the sources and making of the *Fortalitium*, see B. Netanyahu, 'Alfonso de Espina, was he a new Christian?', *Proceedings of the American Association for Jewish Research* 43 (1976), pp. 107–65. On the expulsion see Jordan, *The French Monarchy and the Jews*, pp. 179–238.

26. M. Esposito, 'Notes sur le "Fortalitium fidei" d'Alphonse de Spina', *Revue d'Histoire*

Ecclésiastique 43 (1948), pp. 514–36; on expulsion see pp. 515–16. The *Fortalitium fidei* itself was an extremely successful compilation, one which was soon translated into French by Pierre Richart (dit Loiselet) as *La Fortresse de la foy*, and which survives in numerous northern European manuscripts of the fifteenth century, J. Bruyn, *Van Eyck Problemen*, Orbis Artium 1, Utrecht, 1957, n. 2, p. 48. For dissemination see for example *Catalogue des manuscrits de la Bibliothèque royale de Belgique*, III, ed. J. van den Gheyn, Brussels, 1903, nos 1711–14, pp. 103–4. It was widely published in Germany in the later fifteenth century, no. 209, p. 93. On this see also S. Simonsohn, *The Apostolic See and the Jews, VII: History*, PIMS Studies and Texts 109, Toronto, 1991, pp. 36–7.

27. Jean Gerson, *Opera omnia*, VIII, ed. P. Glorieux, Paris, p. 389: 'Sic refert Lyra de Judaeis, quod idololatras nos exinde pessimos execrantur. Facit ad hoc historia Judaei bullientis et transverberantis hostiam consecratam Parisius; sed miraculum confutavit illum aliosque convertit.'

28. As, for example, according to the chronicler of the Cumbrian priory of Lanercost, *Chronicon de Lanercost, MCCI–MCCCXVVI*, ed. J. Stevenson, Edinburgh, 1839, pp. 134–6, at p. 135.

29. On the *predella* see below, figure 16f, p. 147.

30. Jordan, *The French Monarchy and the Jews*, pp. 239–51.

31. M. Wenninger, *Man bedarf keiner Juden mehr. Ursachen und Hintergründe ihrer Vertreibung aus den deutschen Reichstädten im 15. Jahrhundert*, Beihefte zum Archive für Kulturgeschichte 14, Vienna, 1981.

32. *Westfalia judaica. Urkunden und Regesten zur Geschichte der Juden in Westfalen I: 1005–1350*, ed. B.

Brilling and H. Richtering, *Studia Delitzschiana* 11, Stuttgart, 1967, no. 31, p. 56. A. Cohausz, 'Vier ehemalige Sakramentswallfahrten: Gottsbüren, Hillentrup, Blomberg und Büren', *Westfälische Zeitschrift* 112 (1962), pp. 283–6.

33. 'maxime propter varias negligencias quae in diocesi nostra contingerunt, heu per Iudaeos quam per alios, hoc sanctissimum viaticum indigne tractaverunt', P. Fürstenberg, 'Zur Geschichte der Fronleichnamsfeier in der alten Diözese Paderborn', *Theologie und Glaube* 9 (1917), pp. 314–25, at p. 316.

34. 'Annales Zwettlenses', *MGH.SS* IX, p. 658.

35. On Jewish settlement and location within towns like Rothenburg see *Arbeiten zum historischen Atlas von Südwestdeutschland*, V, ed. H. Veitshans, Stuttgart, 1970, pp. 16–20 and maps.

36. For the most thorough survey of chronicle accounts see F. Lotter, 'Die Judenverfolgung des "König Rintfleisch" in Franken um 1298. Ein endgültige Wende in den christlich-jüdischen Beziehungen in deutschen Reich des Mittelalters', *Zeitschrift für Historische Forschung* 15 (1988), pp. 385–422 and *idem*, 'Hostienfrevelvorwurf und Blutwunderfälschung bei den Judenverfolgungen von 1298 ("Rintfleisch") und 1336–1338 ("Armleder")', in *Fälschungen im Mittelalter. Internationaler Kongress des MGH München, 16–19 September 1986* 5, MGH Schriften 33 (5), Hanover, 1988, pp. 533–60.

37. 'Eodem eciam anno exorta est fama quedam de Iudeis, quod corpus dominicum in mortario contuderint, et sanguis in multa quantitate emanaverit, qui postea a Iudeis non poterat occultari. Et ob hoc omnes Iudei in Herbipoli, Nuernberch, Rothenburch et eciam per totam Franconiam per insultum populi et quosdam,

qui se in magna multitudine collegerant et quendam qui Rintflaisch dicebatur, quem pro principe elegerant, volencium vindicare tam recentem iniuriam salvatoris, incendio sunt cremati', 'Continuatio Ratisbonensis', *MGH.SS* XVII, p. 419.

38. 'Quod permissa fuit a deo persecutio eorundem', in 'Gesta Rudolfi et Alberti regum romanorum 1273–1299', in *Hermannus Altahensis und ordere Geschichtsquellen Deutschlands im dreizehnten Jahrhundert*, Fontes rerum germanicarum, II, ed. J.F. Boehmer, Stuttgart, 1845, pp. 111–47, at p. 144.

39. 'Continuatio Florianensis', *MGH.SS* IX, ed. W. Wattenbach, Hanover, 1851, p. 751; Lotter, 'Die Judenverfolgung', p. 390.

40. 'Puerum cuiusdam nobilis et potentis viri in contemptum Christiani nominis impie iugulasse', c. 28 'De occisione Iudeorum', *MGH.SS* XXIV, pp. 480–81; 'Iudeos ferociter invaserunt, nulli parcentes', p. 480.

41. 'Gesta Boemundi Archiepiscopi Treverensis', *MGH.SS* XXIV, pp. 480–81.

42. The Annals of Colmar described the name's etymology: 'Veniens in Franckoniam carnifex Rintfleisch, id est caro bovis, nomine, qui Iudeos cepit et interfecit et eorum res disripuit violenter . . . nec erat impedire', *Les Annales et la chronique des Dominicains de Colmar*, ed. C. Gérard and J. Liblin, Colmar, 1854, pp. 178–9; Lotter, 'Hostienfrevelvorwurf', pp. 415–16.

43. The Heilbronn annalist described the movement as one from smaller towns to greater ones, 'Annales Halesbrunnenses maiores', *MGH.SS* XXIV, p. 46.

44. See map in *Germania judaica*, II (2), at end.

45. *Das Martyrologium des Nürenberger Memorbuches*, ed. S. Salfeld, Quellen zur Geschichte der Juden

in Deutschland 3, Berlin, 1898, pp. 270–1.

46. A.M. Habermann, *Gzerot Ashkenaz ve-Tsarfat*, Jerusalem, 1971, lines 6–15, p. 230 (my translation from Hebrew).

47. See introduction on pp. 3–35; and F. Lotter, 'Das Judenbild im volkstümlichen Erzählgut um 1300: Die "Historiae memorabiles" des Rudolf von Schlettstadt', in *Herrschaft, Kirche, Kultur: Beiträge zur Geschichte des Mittelalters*, ed. G. Jenal and S. Haarländer, Stuttgart, 1993, pp. 431–45; and M. Rubin, 'Rudolph of Schlettstadt OP: reporter of violence, writer on Jews', in *The Dominicans in the Medieval World*, ed. K. Emery Jr, Notre Dame, Ind., 1997, pp. 283–92.

48. P. Herder, 'Problemen der christlich-jüdischen Beziehungen in Mainfranken im Mittelalter', *Würzburger diözesan-geschichtsblätter* 40 (1978), pp. 79–94; Kraft had to sell property as he was so badly in debt, see Lotter, 'Hostienfrevelvorwurf', pp. 401–3; on his lordship and finance see H. Schwillus, 'Hostienfrevellegende und Judenverfolgung in Iphofen. Ein Beitrag zur Entstenhungsgeschichte des Kirche zum hl. Blut im Gräbenviertel', *Würzburger Diözesan-Geschichtsblätter* 58 (1996), pp. 87–107, esp. pp. 98–9.

49. *HM*, c. 1, pp. 41–3.
50. Ibid., p. 43.
51. F. Graus, 'Die Juden in ihrer mittelalterlichen Umwelt', in *Die Juden in ihrer mittelalterlichen Umwelt*, ed. A. Ebenbauer and K. Zatloukel, Vienna, 1991, pp. 53–65, at p. 65.
52. Schwillus, 'Hostienfrevellegende und Judenverfolgung', pp. 100–1.
53. The chapter is entitled 'De plaga quam iudaei plurimi sustinerunt in Alemannia annus domini 1296', *Die königsaaler Geschichtsquellen mit den Zusätzen und der*

Forsetzung des Domherrn Franz von Prag, ed. J. Loserth, Fontes Rerum Austriacarum I (8), Vienna, 1875, c. 55, pp. 137–8; alternatively, *Chronicon aulae regis*, ed. J. Emler, Prague, 1884, c. 55, pp. 66–7.

54. 'opiniantur tamen alii, quod factum fuerit pro amore pecuniam rapiendi', *Die königsaaler Geschichtsquellen*, p. 138.

55. Rintfleisch rex iste tibi gens iudaica triste
Excidium fecit, the namque repente reiecit,
Et quasi delevit, te namque deus modo sprevit,
Ipseque tortorem dat, quod te sic ad amorem
Ipsius alliciat, tibi quod sua gratia fiat.
O iudaee dole! quia tu cum duplice mole
Semper pressus eris, hic ac illic crucieris.

Die königsaaler Geschichtsquellen, c. 55, p. 138.

56. Lotter, 'Hostienfrevelvorwurf', pp. 411–12.
57. 'Prope Mechlin Mulin opidum rivus fluebat et quasi insula faciebat, in qua non nisi pauperes et meretrices habitabant', *HM*, no. 2, pp. 43–4, at p. 43.
58. K. Geissler, *Die Juden in Deutschland und Bayern bis zur Mitte des vierzehnten Jahrhunderts*, Zeitschrift für Bayerische Landesgeschichte Beiheft 7(b), Munich, 1976, pp. 222–3.
59. 'Christiani namque, ut dicitur, post interfectionem ipsorum ipsa secreciora eorundem purgantes invenerunt corpus Christi plurimis locis confossum', *Monumenta Erphesfurtensia*, ed. O. Holder-Egger, MGH. Scriptores Rerum Germanicarum in Usum Scholarum 42, Hanover and Leipzig, 1899, p. 39.
60. N.Z. Davis, *Fiction in the Archives: Pardon Tales and their Tellers in Sixteenth-Century France*, Stanford, Calif., 1987, p. 114.

61. According to the Jewish martyrology this happened on 25 July 1298, *Das Martyrologium des Nürnberger Memorbuches*, p. 53, translation on pp. 206–7.
62. *HM*, c. 6, pp. 49–51.
63. 'De eucharistia vendita. Anno 1299 perfidissimi Iudei sacrum corpus Christi in nocte sancta pasche emptum a custode ecclesie in civitate Franconie que Rotingin dicitur per diversas civitates et castella aliis Iudeis distribuerunt. Quedam autem religiose mulieres, que sacras vigilias ad tumulum Crucifixi observabant, sicuti moris est in Theotonia, cum, hora matutinarum de ecclesia prodeuntes, irent ad excitandum presbyterum ecclesie, ut Crucifixum de monumento ante matutinas secundum consuetudinem sublevaret, viderunt super domum Iudei qui dictum sacramentum emerat, duo luminaria rutilare. Cumque attonite starent et secum quererent, superveniens presbyter interrogat, quid conferant; vidensque cum ipsis luminaria, compertoque, quod Iudeus cum custode in ecclesia fuisset et iuxta altare, caute vocat iudicem civitatis et quosdam de civibus. Qui irruentes in domum Iudei, ipsum et custodem ecclesie ceperunt. Qui statim coacti confessi sunt facinus perpetratum. Iam vero ut dictum est, idem corpus Christi per diversas Iudeorum dispersum fuerat mansiones. Qui sepe dictum corpus Christi sacratissimum acubus et subulis pungentes et in mortariolis tundentes et per illas puncturas et tunsiones sanguinem elici conspicientes, tandem in diversis locis in terra suffoderunt. Sed Deus omnipotens sacramentum salutis multis miraculis prodientibus suis fidelibus propalavit. Quapropter Christiani insurgentes contra Iudeos, eos per diversas civitates et loca turmatim occiderunt', *MGH.SS* XXV, pp.

714–15.
64. Ibid., p. 715. The chronicler of Regensburg similarly describes the efforts of older Jews to stop boys and girls from receiving baptism in order to escape the fire, 'Continuatio Ratisbonensis', p. 419.
65. E.G. Gudde, *Social Conflict in Medieval German Poetry*, University of California Publications in Modern Philology 18, Berkeley, 1934, p. 107.
66. Lotter, 'Die Judenverfolgung', pp. 408–9.
67. 'jussu magistratus et dominorum superiorum multi capti et persecuti [sunt]. Demum omnes, quorum magna erat multitudo, igne consumpti, occisi et aboliti sunt', *HM*, c. 5, p. 47. Such towns came to be known as blood-cities in the Hebrew sources, as a memorial tablet discovered in 1980 shows, I. Güssow, 'Die Gemeinde der Juden', in *Reichstädte in Franken. Katalog zur Ausstellung*, ed. R.A. Müller, B. Buberl and C. Grimm with E. Brockhoff, Veröffentlichungen zur Bayerischen Geschichte und Kunde 14, Augsburg, 1987, p. 84.
68. It turned into an even costlier set of massacres than those of Rintfleisch, Lotter, 'Hostienfrevelvorwurf', pp. 562–4, with a contemporary estimate of some 6,000 victims.
69. K. Arnold, 'Die Armlederbewegung in Franken 1336', *Mainfränkisches Jahrbuch für Geschichte und Kunst* 26 (1974), pp. 35–62; Lotter, 'Hostienfrevelvorwurf', pp. 560–71.
70. 'Quidam enim vir nobilis tunc temporis in partibus Franconie a Iudeis fraudulenter, maliciose ac turpiter interfectus est. Quod audiens frater eius de ordine Hospitalariorum, vir robustus et animosus, nimium dolens de occisione fratris surrexit et multorum virorum animos sibi concilians in ulcionem fratris

Iudeos gravissime persecutus est in illa terra', John of Winterthur, *Chronicon*, ed. C. Brun and F. Baethgen, *MGH.SS* Rerum Germanicarum New Series 3, Berlin, 1924, pp. 138–9.

71. 'sub pretextu passionis Christi illate ab eis vindicande ab eo, zelo fidei accensus tanquam esset, magnam multitudinem extreminium et necem Iudeorum provocavit', John of Viktring (Iohannis abbatis Victorensis), *Liber certarum historiarum*, II (book 6), ed. F. Schneider, Scriptores Rerum Germanicarum in Usum Scholarium, Hanover and Leipzig, 1910, p. 139.

72. This extraordinary tale has been interestingly discussed by C. Cluse, ' "Blut ist im Schuh". Ein Exempel zur Judenverfolgung des "Rex Armleder" ', in *Liber amicorum necnon et amicarum für Alfred Heit*, ed. F. Burgard, C. Cluse and A. Haverkamp, Trier, 1996, pp. 371–92.

73. For a view of the movement as a peasant uprising see S. Hoyer, 'Die Armlederbewegung – ein Baueraufstand 1336/1339', *Zeitschrift für Geschichtswissenschaft* 13 (1965), pp. 74–89.

74. *Nova Alemanniae*, ed. E.E. Stengel, Berlin, 1921, I, letter 411, pp. 236–9. The letter claims that some 1,500 Jews were killed and that the Archbishop was very worried lest the violence spread down the Rhine valley, p. 238.

75. 'uf den eyde nimmer daruz czu chomen, biz die, die daz getan hatten, nach minne und nach rehte daz gentzlich und gar haben geriht', Arnold, 'Die Armlederbewegung in Franken 1336', pp. 48–62, esp. pp. 60–2, quote on p. 61.

76. 'nescio pro certo quo motivo instigatus, insurgens contra Iudeos populari turma copiose constipatus mangna (sic) plaga eos percussit . . . allegans se divina inspiracione et celesti oraculo in mandatis accepisse', John of Winterthur, *Chronicon*, p. 139.

77. Hoyer, 'Die Armlederbewegung – ein Baueraufstand 1336/1339', p. 82.

78. Arnold, 'Die Armlederbewegung in Franken 1336', p. 41; L. Schwinden, 'Die Judenverfolgungen des "Armleder" 1336/1339 in Herrschafts- und Socialgefüge deutscher Landschaften', Prüfungsarbeit, University of Trier, 1976, p. 39. I am most grateful to Mr Schwinden for allowing me to consult this unpublished and most useful work. There is little mention of the events in local chronicles.

79. K. Hausberger, *Geschichte des Bistums Regensburg*, 2 vols, Regensburg, 1989, I, pp. 259–60.

80. *MGH.SS* XVII, p. 565; Schwinden, 'Die Judenverfolgungen des "Armleder" ', pp. 41–2.

81. Hausberger, *Geschichte des Bistums Regensburg*, I, p. 259.

82. In a bond of 19 May 1338, the Jews paid for protection, John of Winterthur, *Chronicon*, p. 142. See the map of the regional repercussions of the Deggendorf violence in *Germania Judaica*, II (1), p. 58.

83. M. Wiener, *Regesten zur Geschichte der Juden in Deutschland wahrend des Mittelalters*, Hanover, 1862, nos 109, 123, pp. 40, 42.

84. John of Winterthur, *Chronicon*, p. 140.

85. 'in sinagogis suis katholicam eukaristiam irriserint et inter alia ludibria spinis acutis usque ad effusionem sangwinis transfixerint. Quocirca circa festum sancti Michaelis in omnibus civitatibus preter Ratisponam et Wiennam per totam Babariam et Austriam a populo pauperum miserabiliter et crudeliter sunt occisi', 'Chronica de ducibus bavariae', in *Bayerischen Chroniken des XIV. Jahrhunderts*, ed. G. Leidinger, Scriptores Rerum Germanicarum in Usum Scholarium 19, Hanover and Leipzig,

1918, p. 167.

86. Ibid.

87. 'Et quamvis in nece domini nostri plura hiis promeruerint, tamen causam istius persecutionis aliam nisi suprascriptuam non inveni nec audivi, nisi quod in Austria corpus Christi male tractaverant Iudei, prout a quodam qui inde venit percepi', *Heinricus de Diessenhofen und andere Geschichts-quellen Deutschlands im späteren Mittelalter*, ed. J.F. Boehmer (and J. Huber), Stuttgart, 1868, pp. 28–9.

88. 'Tumulus eius pro fidei merito pluribus miraculis dicitur corus-casse', *Liber certarum historiarum*, p. 196.

89. John of Winterthur, *Chronicon*, p. 142.

90. 'Modo queritur utrum pro tali causa in tali casu . . . ut occidantur pro hac causa', Klosterneuburg Library MS 825, fols 11v–12r; the discussion then follows first *pro* and then *contra* until fol. 14v. In posing such a question he was not alone: after the 1290 case of Paris, the foremost theologian of Paris, Henry of Ghent, dealt with a quodlibetal question on whether a Jew who, having desecrated the host and witnessed its miracles, was moved to conversion should be punished for his crime, Henry of Ghent, *Quodlibeta*, Paris, 1518, quodlibet XV, q. 15, fols 470v–472v: 'Utrum Iudaeus pungens hostiam consecratam qui videns sanguine emergente . . . conver-titur et bapizatur, debeat delicto puniri a iustitia publica.' See also G. Dahan, *Les Intellectuels chrétiens et les juifs au moyen-âge*, Paris, 1990, p. 547.

91. Vienna Haus-, Hof- und Staatsarchiv, protocols for 16 Dec. 1305, transcribed (with many errors) in A. Legler, *Das Notariats-Instrument über den Korneuburger Blutwunder-Prozess*, private edn, n.d., pp. 3–28. For some transcrip-tions of the testimonies and of

Ambrose of Heiligenkreuz's tract of 1312, see *Urkundenbuch des Stiftes Klosterneuburg bis zum Ende des vierzehnten Jahrhunderts*, II, ed. H. Zeibig, Fontes Rerum Austria-carum: Abtheilung Diplomataria et Acta 28, Vienna, 1868, pp. 172–4.

92. 'Exorto quoque contra me odio Civium prefatorum, quasi ego apponerem iudeis et processum negocii impedirem', *Urkunden-buch*, p. 173; W.S. Koller, 'Die Korneuburger Bluthostie – Historische Quellen und Wirkungen', Master of Theology dissertation, Catholic Theology Faculty, University of Vienna, 1991, p. 10; K. Lohrmann, *Judenrecht und Judenpolitik im mittelalterlichen Österreich*, Hand-buch zur Geschichte der Juden in Österreich B(1), Vienna and Co-logne, 1990, p. 105.

93. On this altarpiece see Koller, 'Die Korneuburger Bluthostie', pp. 32–3 and below, p. 154.

94. On the procedures for the investi-gation of miracles in the four-teenth century see M. Goodich, *Violence and Miracle in the Fourteenth Century: Private Grief and Public Salvation*, Chicago, 1995, ch. 1, esp. pp. 1–15.

95. Cluse, 'Blut ist im Schuh', *passim*.

96. On the Jewish house, the *Judenhof*, a complex of dwellings which becomes increasingly common in the fourteenth century, see A. Haverkamp, 'The Jewish quar-ters in German towns during the late Middle Ages', in *In and Out of the Ghetto: Jewish–Gentile Relations in Late Medieval and Early Modern Germany*, ed. R.P. Hsia and H. Lehmann, New York, 1995, pp. 13–28.

97. Koller, 'Die Korneuburger Bluthostie', p. 28.

98. F. Ilwof, 'Zur Geschichte der Judenverfolgung in Steiermark im Jahre 1310', *Mitteilungen des historischen Vereins für die Steyermark* 12 (1863), pp. 210–16; Koller,

'Die Korneuburger Bluthostie', pp. 14–16.

99. 'Anonymus Leobiensis', in *Scriptores rerum austriacarum veteres ac genuini*, I, ed. H. Pez, Vienna and Regensburg, 1743, p. 907.

100. Ambrose of Heiligenkreuz studied the Cistercian miraculous lore contained in his monastery's library as he continued to ponder and write on the subject of miraculous authentication, Klosterneuburg MS 825, fol. 120v. The tract which resulted from these researches, the 'De hostia mirifica', also formed the basis for future consideration of the subject, see for example the extract made from Ambrose's tract in answer to a question: 'Queritur: si iveniatur oblata in domo Judei val alibi, quis habebat congnoscere', ÖNB 4827, fols 3ra–4va. This may have been used in the investigation conducted by Frederic of Bamberg after the Pulkau events, see below, pp. 67–8.

101. 'Annales Zwettlenses', *MGH.SS* IX, p. 683; Lohrmann, *Judenrecht und Judenpolitik*, p. 155.

102. G. Gugitz, *Österreichs Gnadstätten in Kult und Bild*, Vienna, 1955, pp. 149–50.

103. 'Eodem quoque anno dicitur pasca christianorum et pasca Iudeorum uno eodemque die fuisse, quapropter maximum exterminium factum est Iudeorum nam in Pul(t)ka circa festum sancti Georgii reperta est sacra hostia in domo cuiusdam Iudei ex toto cruentata et miraculis plurimis ut dicebatur approbata et cum maxima veneracione ad ecclesiam sancti Michaelis prope . . . deportata', 'Calendarium Zwettlense', *MGH.SS* IX, p. 691.

104. 'Continuatio Zwettlensis', *MGH.SS* IX, p. 683.

105. 'Calendarium Zwettlense', *MGH.SS* IX, p. 691.

106. 'exceptis his qui in civitatibus, sicut Winna et in Nova civitate sitis in Austria, a ducibus et baronibus sunt protecti', *MGH.SS* IX, p. 671.

107. John Neplacho, 'Kronika Neplachova', in *Fontes rerum Bohemicarum*, III, Prague, 1882, p. 481; *1000 Jahre österreichisches Judentum. Ausstellungskatalog*, ed. K. Lohrmann, Eisenstadt, 1982, p. 307.

108. 'Thesauris, bonis, litteris eorum spoliat, submersi, exusti, precipitati, eviscerati misere perierunt', *Liber certarum historiarum*, p. 209; 'In pluribus locis terrarum principes eos quantum poterant defenderunt. Christus enim suam causam vindicavit', ibid, pp. 209–10.

109. 'ante domum cuiusdam Iudei extra tamen limites eius, in strata sub paleis a quodam laico fuit inventa', *The Apostolic See and the Jews, I: Documents*, ed. S. Simonsohn, no. 354, p. 372. The papal letter to the Bishop of Passau reports extensively from the Duke's initial letter, about local doubts and of the precedent in (Kor)neuburg (Neumburch) and in 'Fyntz' (Linz?) and 'Werchartstorp' (Wernhartsdorf?); for the whole letter, pp. 371–4.

110. The ducal suspicions of fraud were clearly put, and reproduced in the papal mandate ordering an inquiry into the Pulkau affair: 'quod olim in ducatu Austrie, in opido Neumburch, prefate tue diocesis, quedam hostia non consecrata madefacta cruore, per quemdam clericum in ecclesia dicti opidi posita fuit, qui postmodum in presentia bone memorie Wernhardi, episcopi Pataviensis predecessoris tui presentibus fide dignis personis adhuc . . . entibus . . . confessus fuit se dicto cruore prefatam hostiam madidasse, ad presumptionem inducendam, quod a Iudeis contumeliose dehonestata taliter extitisset', ibid., p. 372.

111. 'Timens ne populus idolatriae committeret crimen', *Die*

königsaaler Geschichtsquellen, p. 559.

112. John of Winterthur, *Chronicon*, pp. 142–3; on the chronicle see A. Lhotsky, *Quellenkunde zur mittelalterlichen Geschichte Österreichs*, Mitteilungen des Institut für Österreichische Geschichtsforschung- Ergänzungband 19, pp. 277–8. F. Baethgen, 'Franziskanische Studien', *Historische Zeitschrift* 131 (1925), pp. 421–71, esp. pp. 453–71.

113. 'Propter quendam sacerdotem nimia inopia oppressum, qui hostiam sangwine aspersit et a se proiectam iuxta Iudeos ipsos suspectos reddidit et graviter infamavit', John of Winterthur, *Chronicon*, pp. 142–3. For an accusation of 1434, against a priest who sprinkled blood on a host in order to attract people to his church, see 'Gesta archiepiscoporum Magdeburgensium', *MGH.SS* XIV, ed. W. Schum, Hanover, 1883, p. 464: 'unus presbiter, qui cruorem in hostia consecrata in Wardenberg prope Wittenberg ad concursum faciendum subdole fecerat, ibidem incarceratus ab archiepiscopo Gunthero, exclamavit, ut eriperent eum, et sic per foramen extractus.'

114. *Die königsaaler Geschichtsquellen*, pp. 558–9; reports of the miracles of St Wenzel and of flocks of locusts which were repelled by birds then followed, p. 560.

115. Vienna, ÖNB 350, 1ra–17vb; it is followed by another canonlaw discussion of the authentication of eucharistic miracles by Ullmann, an Austrian Franciscan friar (fols 17vb–32rb) and by a tract on the mass (fols 32rb–103r); the manuscript was in Salzburg Cathedral Library in 1433. M. Anselgruber has edited and discussed this text in his *Institutsarbeit* submitted to the Institute for Austrian Historical Research in Vienna. Unfortu-

nately I have not been able to consult his edition fully, but have consulted the manuscript on microfilm. See also *idem*, 'Das "Hostienwunder" von Pulkau aus der zeitgenossischen Quelle des Fridericus von Bamberg', in *Dies trug sich zu anno 1338. Pulkau zur Zeit des Glaubenswirren*, ed. M. Anselgruber and H. Puschnik, Pulkau, n.d., pp. 53–68.

116. Vienna ÖNB 350, fol. 14rb.

117. '*Discipulus*: Questio octava. Quanta sit culpa et que pena debetur iudei tenere attractantibus istud venerabile sacramentum? . . . *Doctor*: Quia corpus christi a iudeis attractatum sub striquilinio fuit inventum in pulcha et fimo contenctum et perfidi iudei ibi proieceran et fimum superiecerant et ut sic obtegerent et occultarent sanguinem defluentem . . . Quanto maior gloria tanto maior offensa.'

118. See on this theme below, pp. 137–8.

119. I have not seen the original manuscript but have used the Handwritten Catalogue 'Manuscripten-catalog der Stifts-Bibliothek Göttweig. Band I', pp. 639–40 (the description is on p. 640 of the catalogue and refers to the entry at the *bas-de-page* margin on fol. 249), and have seen the reproduction in *Dies trug sich zu anno 1338*, p. 68.

120. On the endowment see *Urkunden der Benediktiner-Abtei unserer lieben Frau zu den Schotten in Wien*, ed. E. Hauswirth, Vienna, 1859, no. 371, pp. 448–50, no. 372, pp. 350–3.

121. For a description of these *predella* images see K. Lohrmann, 'Die Juden in mittelalterliche Niederösterreich', in *Die Kuenringer: das Werden des Landes Niederösterreich. Ausstellung – Stift Zwettl 16. Mai-26. Oktober 1981*, ed. H. Wolfram, K. Brunner and G. Stangler, Vienna, 1981, pp. 119–23, no. 116, pp. 121–2; *1000 Jahre österreichisches Judentum*, ed. Lohrmann, no. 35,

p. 30. The two panels (120 × 55 cm) are not on public display, and I am grateful to Frau Dr H. Puschnik for having explained the circumstances surrounding the treatment of these images in Pulkau. I am most grateful to Professor Gerhard Yaritz of the Institut für Realienkunde des Mittelalters und der Frühen Neuzeit in Krems for help in procuring reproductions of the images, figures 17a–b, p. 151, below.

122. On Bavaria's late medieval shrines see S.D. Sargent, 'Miracle books and pilgrimage shrines in late medieval Bavaria', *Historical Reflections* 13 (1986), pp. 455–71.

4   Persons and Places

1. R. Morse, *Truth and Convention in the Middle Ages: Rhetoric, Representation and Reality*, Cambridge, 1991, p. 95.

2. J. Alexander, *The Films of David Lynch*, London, 1993, p. 12.

3. On Jewish bodily difference W. Johnson, 'The myth of male menses', *Journal of Medieval History* 24 (1998), pp. 273–95. For the converse view, of Christian men as virile, see M. Saperstein, *Decoding the Rabbis: a Thirteenth-Century Commentary on the Aggadah*, Cambridge, Mass., 1980, pp. 99–100 (from a Provençal Jewish writer).

4. 'Money can transform itself into the body of Christ only because it can buy everything, including the body of Christ', C. Ginzburg, 'Representations of German Jewry: images, prejudices, ideas – a comment', in *In and Out of the Ghetto: Jewish–Gentile Relations in Late Medieval and Early Modern Germany*, ed. R. P. Hsia and H. Lehmann, Cambridge, 1995, pp. 209–12, at p. 211.

5. 'Hoc anno pasca christianorum convenit cum pasca Iudeorum, propter quid maximum exterminium factum est Iudeorum', 'Annales Zwettlenses', *MGH.SS* IX, ed. G.H. Pertz, Hanover, 1851, p. 683. In Remaghen it was said to have been Christmas; William the Procurator, 'Chronicon comitum et nobilium Hollandiae', in A. Matthaeus, *Veteris aevi analecta*, IV, The Hague, 2nd edn, 1738, pp. 496–718, at p. 611. On Eastertide anti-Jewish harassment see G. Mentgen, 'Der Würfelzoll und andere antijüdische Schickanen in Mittelalter und Früher Neuzeit', *Zeitschrift für Historische Forschung* 22 (1975), pp. 1–48, esp. pp. 15–23.

6. 'Annales Glogauenses', in *Scriptores rerum silesiacarum*, ed. H. Margraf, Wrocław, 1877, p. 18.

7. Yomtov Lippmann of Mühlhausen, *Sefer ha-nizzahon*, ed. F. Talmage, Kuntresim Texts and Studies 59–60, Jerusalem, 1983, no. 354, p. 194.

8. See P. Biller, 'Views of Jews from Paris around 1300', *Studies in Church History* 29 (1992), pp. 187–207; S. Kruger, 'The bodies of Jews in the late Middle Ages', in *The Idea of Medieval Literature: Essays in Honor of Donald R. Howard*, ed. J.M. Dean and C.K. Zacher, London and Toronto, 1992, pp. 301–23; J. Trachtenberg, *The Devil and the Jews: the Medieval Conception of the Jew and its Relation to Modern Anti-Semitism*, Philadelphia, Pa., 1943, p. 149.

9. W. Treue has recently begun to consider the role of Christians in the tales of Jewish abuse, including the host desecration accusation, see 'Schlechte und gute Christen. Zur Rolle von Christen in antijüdischen Ritualmord und Hostienschändungslegenden', *Aschkenas* 2 (1992), pp. 95–116; on women, pp. 97–100.

10. See figure 16a, p. 146, below.

11. Joannis Długosz Senioris Canonici Cracoviensis, 'Historiae poloniae libri XII', in *Opera omnia,*

XII, ed. A. Przezdiecki, Krakow, 1876, p. 538. For the *exemplum* see Poznań Raczynski Library 161, fol. 133v. See H. Kowalewicz, 'redniowieczne exempla polsko-łacińskie', in *Kultura elitarna a kultura masowa w Polsce późnego Średniowiecza*, ed. B. Geremek, Wrocław, 1978, pp. 283–90. I am most grateful to Dr Stephen Rowell for bringing this unpublished *exemplum* to my attention, and to the Librarian of Raczyński Library, Mr Janusz Dembski, who responded promptly to my request for a copy of this folio.

12. See the story of Rudolph of Schlettstadt, *HM*, no. 10, pp. 55–7.

13. 'cultum non visitavit, confessa non fuit nec ipso tempore sacrosanctum sacramentum non sumpsit anima ipsius pessime obcecata', *Urkundenbuch der Stadt Osnabrück 1301–1400*, ed. H.-R. Jarck, Osnabrücker Urkundenbuch 6, Osnabrück, 1989, doc. 1264, pp. 1088–9. See also a later case in the Polish town of Sochaczew where in 1556 a Christian maid was said to have stolen the host and sold it to Jews; the woman and the Jews were executed, 'Spominki swietokrzyski', in *Monumenta poloniae historica*, III, Lwow, 1878, pp. 117–18.

14. 'quidam solo nomine christicola'; 'Corpus Christi horribiliter a Iudeis torquetur!', John of Winterthur, *Chronicon*, ed. C. Brun and F. Baethgen, *MGH.SS* Rerum Germanicarum New Series 3, Berlin, 1924, p. 107.

15. 'dass ihnen eine gewisse Notzin das heilige Sakrament zum Kauf gegeben haben sollte', *Quellen zur Geschichte der Juden im Hessischen Staatsarchiv Darmstadt 1080–1650*, ed. F. Battenberg, Quellen zur Geschichte der Juden in Hessischen Archiven 2, Wiesbaden, 1995, no. 1070, p. 284.

16. 'filia diaboli, suis utique fratribus, dicti etiam filiis, Judaeis videlicet',

William the Procurator, 'Chronicon comitum et nobilium Hollandiae', pp. 611–12. In a version of the Paris tale contained in the chronicle of the Cumbrian priory of Lanercost the woman was described as 'una mulier, Evae filia', *Chronicon de Lanercost MCCI–MCCCXLVI*, ed. J. Stevenson, Edinburgh, 1839, p. 135.

17. 'Et comme bleiz soy vendit mal elle s'en conseilla ung Juys qui ly dit selle ly voloit livrer le St corps Nostre Segneur et le sacrement il ly aideroit', transcribed from a manuscript in Turin into Paris Bibliothèque Nationale nouv. acq. fr. 4857, fol. Q262; J. Weill, 'Un juif brulé à Metz vers 1385 pour profanation d'hostie', *REJ* 53 (1907), pp. 270–2, at p. 271.

18. *Margaretha Ebner und Heinrich von Nördlingen. Ein Beitrag zur Geschichte der deutscher Mystik*, ed. P. Strauch, Freiburg in Breisgau, 1882, pp. 116–17.

19. 'prodita per alias mulieres christicolas, que viderant ante necem Iudeorum eam bursam, in qua reconditum erat Christi corpus, Iudeis afferre ac vendere eis voluisse, certissime, quasi per hoc ipsam criminis ream notantes ipsam ceperunt, et ad penam et ad supplicium mortis traxerunt', John of Winterthur, *Chronicon*, p. 108.

20. Ibid., 'Et sic Iudei, immunes et alieni a prefato reatu quamvis existaverunt, deleti sunt.'

21. Thomas Ebendorfer, *Chronica Austria*, ed. A. Lhotsky, MGH Scriptores Rerum Germanicarum New Series 13, Berlin and Zurich, 1967, pp. 370–1, at p. 370. For the decree of 16 April 1421, ordering the execution by fire of the custodian's wife, see *Das Judenbuch der Scheffstrasse zu Wien (1389–1420)*, Quellen und Forschungen zu der Geschichte der Juden in Deutsch-Österreich I, ed. A. Goldmann, Vienna and Leipzig, 1908, p. 133: 'das weib, die man

auf heut richten wirdet, vor zeiten mesnerinn dacz Enns gewesen ist, die hat das heilig Sacrament Gots leichnam meniger stukch aus der pharrkirchen daselbs ze Enns verstollen und das ainer Judinn und aim Juden umb gut verkaufft und ubergeantwurtt . . . da obgenant weib auf heutigen tag auch geschafft und empholhen ze richten mit dem prannt.'

22. 'brevissima consultatione cum uxore praehabita', 'De expulsione iudaeorum', *Monumenta poloniae historica*, III, p. 786.

23. See below, pp. 122–3.

24. *HM*, no. 11, p. 58.

25. H. Maschek, *Deutsche Chroniken*, Deutsche Literatur – Reihe Realistik des Spätmittelalters 5, Leipzig, 1936, pp. 135–8, at p. 135. For a rare case of a respectable young man's agency see the case in Coimbra before 1397, in which a youth associated with the cathedral treasurer procured a silver cup with three consecrated hosts and handed it over to the Jews, *The Apostolic See and the Jews, I: Documents*, ed. S. Simonsohn, PIMS Studies and Texts 94, Toronto, 1988, no. 484, pp. 514–16: 'quidam iuvenis, familiaris dilecti filii thesaurarii ecclesie Colimbriensis, seductus per quendam Iudeum', p. 515.

26. On children in tales of eucharistic miracle see M. Rubin, *Corpus Christi: the Eucharist in Late Medieval Culture*, Cambridge, 1991, pp. 117, 135, 137–8, 143, and an example in *Magna vita sancti Hugonis*, ed. D.I. Douie and H. Farmer, NMT, London, 1962, II, c. 3, pp. 85–92, esp. p. 86.

27. *Beiträge zur lateinische Erzählungsliteratur des Mittelalters III. Das Viaticum narrationum*, ed. A. Hilka, Berlin, 1935, p. 99, and above, p. 35.

28. *HM*, no. 9, pp. 53–5.

29. 'vox . . . quae etiam apertissime auribus Christianorum foris existentium implicatur', William

the Procurator, 'Chronicon', pp. 611–12.

30. J. Perles, 'Die Geschichte der Juden in Posen', *Monatsschrift für Geschichte und Wissenschaft des Judenthums* 13 (1864), pp. 281–95, 321–34, 361–73, 409–20, 449–61.

31. See below, figure 17a, p. 150.

32. Rudolph of Schlettstadt, *HM*, c. 8, pp. 51–3.

33. *HM*, no. 7, p. 51.

34. On the role of the clergy in one of the towns which suffered the violence of Rintfleisch see H. Schwillus, 'Hostienfrevellegende und Judenverfolgung in Iphofen. Ein Beitrag zur Entstehungsgeschichte des Kirche zum hl. Blut im Gräbenviertel', *Würzburger Diözesan-Geschichtsblätter* 58 (1996), pp. 87–107, at pp. 97–8.

35. See again Uccello's treatment in the third scene of his *predella*, an enigmatic nocturnal scene of outdoor recovery of the host, figure 16c, p. 146.

36. Eike von Repgow, *Sachsenspiegel*, ed. C. Schott, Zurich, 1984, book 3, c. 2, p. 161.

37. See the highly stylised evidence of Konrad of Megenburg's poem *Planctus ecclesiae in Germaniam*, on the violence of 1338:

Nitentur layci, credas, velut audi dici,
Quod male prespiteri simul et perdantur Hebrei;
Nam bona prespiteri sua devastent et Hebrei;
Hii nimis usura, primi perimant sua iura,
Prespiterique regant sua, sed layci male degant,
Ducant in claustra rerum plaustrissima plaustra.

Konrad of Megenburg, *Planctus ecclesiae in Germaniam*, ed. R. Scholz, MGH. Die Deutschen Geschichtsquellen des Mittelalters C2 II (1), Leipzig, 1941, p. 46, lines 602–7. See also on the insurgence of peasants in 1439, L.

Rothkrug, 'Religious practices and collective perceptions: hidden homologies in the Renaissance and the Reformation', *Historical Reflections* 7 (1980), p. 111.

38. See above, pp. 67–8. In Weickersheim it was a bell-ringer; *HM*, no. 1, pp. 41–3, at p. 41.

39. *Monumenta Aquensia*, I, ed. J.-B. Moriondus, Turin, 1789, cols 339–40, at col. 339.

40. Vienna, Haus-, Hof- und Staatsarchiv, protocols of the hearings of 16 Dec. 1305, fol. 2r.

41. 'cum ergo ille sacerdos hanc culpam in se retorserit et confessus fuerit, se auctorem sceleris huius certe ipsum solum pena deberet tenere nec iudei', Klosterneuburg MS 825, fol. 14v.

42. Even in those versions of the tale which omit the mention of Peter's concubinage, his transgression is explained by clerical indigence, see *Deutsche Chroniken*, pp. 134–8.

43. 'Ad correccionem Christianorum obstinatorum vel ad Iudeorum terrorem perversorum', *Monumenta poloniae historica*, IV, Lwow, 1884, pp. 1–5, at p. 2.

44. *Lexicon mediae et infimae latinitatis poloniae*, II, ed. M. Plezia, Krakow, 1959–67, col. 494.

45. The sorts of use to which stolen hosts might be put are discussed in Rubin, *Corpus Christi*, pp. 334–42.

46. Ibid., pp. 77–82.

47. 'Gesta abbatum Magdeburgienseium', *MGH.SS* XIV, p. 429. See a later version in Low German, *Die Magdeburger Schöppenchronik*, ed. C. Hegel, Die Chroniken der Deutschen Städte 7 – Die Chroniken der Niedersächsischen Städte 1, Leipzig, 1869, pp. 184–5.

48. 'Chronicon Salisburgense a. S. Rudberto usque ad annum Christi MCCCCXCV', *Scriptores rerum austriacarum*, II, ed. H. Pez, 3 vols in 2, Vienna and Regensburg,

1745, cols 427–46, at col. 429.

49. 'De persecutione iudaeorum vratislavensium a.1453', in *Monumenta poloniae historica*, IV, pp. 1–5, at p. 2.

50. See the instance from the casebook of Brno, in the failed attempt of two poor scholars to sell hosts to Jews, above, p. 34.

51. Z.E. Rokeah, 'The Jewish church-robbers and host desecrators of Norwich (ca.1285)', *REJ* 141 (1982), pp. 331–62; see above, p. 34.

52. 'De persecutione iudaeorum vratislavensium a.1453', pp. 1–5.

53. See below on this case, pp. 130–31; and R. Po-chia Hsia, *The Myth of Ritual Murder: Jews and Magic in Reformation Germany*, New Haven, Conn., 1988, pp. 50–6.

54. *Urkundenbuch der Stadt Leipzig*, III, ed. J. Förstemann, 3 vols, Codex Diplomaticus Saxoniae Regiae II 8–10, Leipzig, 1894, no. 69, p. 51.

55. J. Miret y Sans, 'El procés de les hostias contra is Jueus d'Osca', *Annuari de l'Institut d'Estudios catalans* 4 (1911–12), pp. 59–80, at p. 71.

56. J. Fischer, 'Ein neues Dokument zur Geschichte der Judenvertreibung aus Schlesien im Jahre 1453', *Monatschrift für Geschichte und Wissenschaft des Judentums* 66 (1922), pp. 299–305, at p. 301.

57. 'qui te regat, ducat et gubernet', J. Schneller, 'Der Hexenwesen im sechszehnten Jahrhundert', *Das Geschichtsfreund: Mitteilungen des historischen Vereins der fünf Orte Lucern, Uri, Schwijz, Unterwalden und Zug* 23 (1868), pp. 351–70, at p. 368.

58. 'cum devote expiravit', ibid., p. 370. For a case of theft from the *Sakramenthaus* of Lungern see J. Ming, 'Die Sacramentswald-Capelle ob Giswil', *Der Geschichtsfreund* 19 (1863), pp. 222–6.

59. See the Prague case of 1389 and the chronicler's account, below, pp. 135–7.

60. On fantasies associated with Jewish female converts see R. Po-chia Hsia, 'Witchcraft, magic and the Jews in late medieval and early modern Germany', in *From Witness to Witchcraft: Jews and Judaism in Medieval Christian Thought*, ed. J. Cohen, Wolfenbüttler Mittelalter-Studien 11, Wiesbaden, 1997, pp. 419–33, at p. 427.

61. See above, p. 42.

62. Here she protests her innocence, as only after the fact did it become clear to her that her father was cooking a consecrated host 'quod tamen michi tunc temporis ignotum fuit, ad ignem seu caldare se inclinans hostiam in manu habebat', Rudolph of Schlettstadt, *HM*, no. 9, pp. 53–5, at p. 55.

63. *HM*, no. 16, pp. 64–6. On flux and menstruation in Jewish men as discussed by thirteenth-century theologians, see Biller, 'Views of Jews from Paris', pp. 199–201, 204. On this view see also G. Mentgen, *Studien zur Geschichte der Juden in mittelalterlichen Elsaß*, Forschungen zur Geschichte der Juden A2, Hanover, 1995, pp. 422–3.

64. *HM*, no. 16, p. 65: 'Sanantur autem per sanguinem hominis Cristiani, qui nomine Cristi baptisatus est. Id intellexi ab una ancilla eorum, que erat Cristiana, quod eis a quodam sacerdote vel sacrista in quadam villa pro pecunia sacramentum dominicum ministratum [est].'

65. As told in the text of *c.*1450 in E. Bunte, *Juden und Judentum in der mittelniederländischen Literatur (1100–1600)*, Frankfurt, 1989, pp. 100–8, at p. 105; P. Lefèvre, 'Le thème du miracle des hosties poignardées par les juifs en 1370', *Le Moyen Age* 8 (1953), pp. 373–98, at pp. 385–6.

66. Fischer, 'Ein neues Dokument', pp. 303–4.

67. 'Respondit quod quidam capellanus vendidit [qui]dem sibi, quod quamdiu teneret, faceret de son greu sed quod plau diligebat argentum quam ostias et pro contemptu projicit eas per quandam mensam, ita quod ceciderunt in terram, dicendo quantum appreciebatur eas', J. Régné, 'Rapports entre l'inquisiton et les juifs d'après le mémorial de l'inquisiteur d'Aragon (fin du XIVe siècle)', *REJ* 52 (1906), pp. 224–33, at p. 231; H. Omont, 'Mémorial de l'inquisiteur d'Aragon à la fin du XIVe siècle', *Bibliothèque de l'École des Chartes* 66 (1905), pp. 261–8. For some interesting examples of tension and denunciations among Jewish converts or new Christians see I. Peri, *Restaurazione e pacifico stato in Sicilia, 1377–1501*, Bari, 1988, pp. 115–20.

68. See on this S. Grayzel, *The Church and the Jews in the Thirteenth Century*, rev. edn, New York, 1966, pp. 35–6.

69. On the use of converts by the inquisition see Y.H. Yerushalmi, 'The inquisition and the Jews of France in the time of Bernard Gui', *Harvard Theological Review* 63 (1970), pp. 317–76, at pp. 322, 355–6.

70. On forms of execution see H. Zaremska, 'Lieux d'exécution à Cracovie aux XIVe–XVIe siècles', in *Lieux du pouvoir au moyen-âge et à l'époque moderne*, Warsaw, 1995, pp. 185–96, at pp. 188, 191.

71. On banishment as punishment for the poor see H. Zaremska, 'Le banissement et les bannis en Europe Centrale: XIVe–XVe s.', in *Le migrazioni in Europe, secoli XIII–XVIII*, ed. S. Cavaciocchi, Istituto Internazionale di Storia Economica F. Datini. Atti delle Settimane di Studi e Altri Convegni Ser. II, 24, Florence, 1994, pp. 731–54, esp. p. 739.

72. 'se, mentis alienatione preoccupatum, fidem katholicam abnegasse, multis coram astantibus, ac in Judaica perfidia, se dixisse mori

velle', L. Ölsner, 'Schlesische Urkunden zur Geschichte der Juden in Mittelalter', Archiv für Kunde Österreichischer Geschichts, quellen 31 (1864), pp. 57–144.

73. For some thoughts about attitudes to conversion see J.M. Elukin, 'From Jew to Christian? Conversion and immutability in medieval Europe', in *Varieties of Religious Conversion in the Middle Ages*, ed. J. Muldoon, Gainesville, Fla., 1997, pp. 171–89.

74. See below, pp. 135–9.

75. 'fideles fidei zelo accensi, commoto in eos impetu aliquos trucidaverunt, vulgo mobili atque ut semper improvido aliquid de eorum substantiis rapiente', 'Annales Zwettlenses', *MGH.SS* IX, p. 663.

76. 'lacrimis et querulosis clamoribus civibus propalavit', John of Winterthur, *Chronicon*, p. 108.

77. 'Quod audientes cives Constancienses turmatim concurerunt et ulcisci Dei sui iniuriam et contumeliam illatam a Iudeis conantes, plures Iudeos in insania et furore magno deprehendentes in scelere necaverunt, ipsos tanquam boves securibus mactantes', John of Winterthur, *Chronicon*, p. 107.

78. 'Propter quod factum zelo divino promoti ... occiderunt et combusserunt et in pulverem redigerunt', 'Annales Zwettlenses', p. 683.

79. See below, pp. 136–7.

80. The artisan who cut the scenes depicted in woodcuts in the Nuremberg Chronicle used the same image when describing the punishment of Jews in the cases of the Franconian massacres of Rintfleisch and Deggendorf, see M. Eger, *Der 'Deggendorfer Gnad'*, Deggendorf, 1992, p. 252.

81. See above, pp. 62–3.

82. E. Peters, *The Magician, the Witch and the Law*, Philadelphia, Pa., 1978, appendix 1, pp. 183–95.

83. *Monumenta poloniae historica*, IV, p. 5.

84. On pain, torture and abjection see L.O. Fradenburg, 'Criticism, anti-semitism, and the Prioress's Tale', *Exemplaria* 1 (1989), pp. 69–115, esp. pp. 74–84.

85. For an initial and general exploration of the Marian themes prevalent in some transformations of vacated Jewish quarters in late medieval towns (following expulsions or massacres) see H. Röckelein, 'Marienverehrung und Judenfeindlichkeit in Mittelalter und Früher Neuzeit', in *Marie in der Welt. Marienverehrung im Kontext der Sozialgeschichte 10.–18. Jahrhundert*, ed. G. Signori and G.P. Marchal, Clio Lucernensis 2, Lucerne, 1993, pp. 279–307.

86. On this see F. Graus, 'Randgruppen der städtischen Gesellschaft im Spätmittelalter', *Zeitschrift für Historische Forschung* 8 (1981), pp. 385–437, at p. 398; see Rudolph of Schlettstadt's description of the Jewish neighbourhood in Mochmühl, *HM*, no. 2, pp. 43–4.

87. 'Verum impiissimum scelus prodidit candens lumen ... et demolitis Judaei aedibus, praesens excitata est capella', I. Gropp, *Collectio novissima scriptorum et rerum Wirceburgensium*, II, Frankfurt, 1744, p. 3a; for bull see ibid., pp. 3b–4a.

88. *Westfälische Urkundenbuch*, IV, ed. R. Wilmans and H. Finke, 1892, no. 485, p. 999. P. Fürstenberg, 'Zur Geschichte der Fronleichnamsfeier in der alten Diözese Paderborn', *Theologie und Glaube* 9 (1917), pp. 314–25, at p. 316; on this also J. Spanke, 'Nachrichten über die Sakramentskapelle in Büren und ihre Stiftungen', *Zeitschrift für Vaterländische Geschichte und Alterthumkunde* 48 (1890), pp. 192–210; and A. Cohausz, 'Vier ehemalige Sakramentswallfahrten: Göttsbüren, Hillentrup,

Blomberg und Büren', *Westfälische Zeitschrift* 112 (1962), pp. 275–304, at pp. 281–2.

89. *Inventare der nichtstaatlichen Archive des Kreises Büren*, ed. L. Schmitz-Kassenberg, Veröffentlichungen der Historischen Kommission der Provinz Westfalen 2, Münster, 1915, no. 29, p. 54; a commemorative chapel had already existed within the Busdorf monastery since 1299, *Die Urkunden des Stiftes Busdorf in Paderborn*, ed. J. Prinz, Westfälische Urkunden (Texte und Registen) 1, Paderborn, no. 65, pp. 72–4.

90. 'Annales zwettlenses', *MGH.SS* IX, p. 658.

91. 'Et qualiter ecclesia ibidem edificaretur, fideliter cogitabant', *HM*, no. 8, pp. 51–3. See below, on the reliquary of the bloodied cloth of Korneuburg, pp. 59–61. The dedication to the Holy Blood is extremely popular in Bavaria, see P. Soergel, *Wondrous in his Saints: Counter-Reformation Propaganda in Bavaria*, Berkeley, Calif., 1993, pp. 23–4.

92. 'Annales zwettlenses', *MGH.SS* IX, p. 683. See on the Corpus Christi chapel in Korneuburg W.S. Koller, 'Die Korneuburger Bluthostie: Historische Quellen und Wirkungen', Master of Theology Thesis, Catholic Theology Faculty, University of Vienna, 1991, p. 28.

93. *Die Kunstdenkmäler von Niederbayern. XVII. Stadt und Bezirk Deggendorf*, ed. K. Gröber, Munich, 1927, repr. Vienna, 1982, p. 42. An alter was dedicated in 1400, ibid., pp. 27–8. The north aisle pillars of this chapel bear the inscription: 'ANNO DOMINI M°CCC°XXXVII° DES NACHSDE TAG NACH SAND MICHELS TAG WURDEN DI JUDEN ERSLAGEN DI STAT SI ANZUNDEN DO BART GOTES LAICHENAM FUNDEN DAZ SAHED FRAUEN UND DO HUAB MAN DAZ GOTSHAUS ZE

BAUN AN', ibid., p. 27; for a reproduction see Eger, *Der 'Deggendorfer Gnad'*, p. 224.

94. 'propter miracula que ibidem fiunt, magna populi multitudo confluit', *Codex diplomaticus maioris Poloniae*, new ser., VII, Warsaw and Poznań, 1985, no. 414, pp. 22–3, at p. 22.

95. 'ecclesiam una cum monasterio ordinis predicti in laudem omnipotentis Dei et in honorem sacrosancti Corporis Domini nostri Ihesu Christi in suburbio civitatis nostre Poznanie, in loco ubi ipsum Corpus dominicum miraculose olim inventum esse dignoscitur', *Codex diplomaticus maioris Poloniae (1400–1444)*, ed. F. Piekosinski, Warsaw, 1877, no. 91, pp. 86–8, at p. 87.

96. See the confirmation by King John I of Portugal in 1397, *The Apostolic See and the Jews, I: Documents*, no. 484, pp. 514–16.

97. On the power of ruins to retain memory and beg questions about ancestry see A. Janovitz, *England's Ruins: Poetic Purpose and the National Landscape*, Oxford, 1990, p. 4.

98. U. Eco, *Travels in Hyper-reality*, London, 1986, pp. 199, 200.

99. Ibid., p. 209. For other such reflections on narrative, see R. Kearney, 'Postmodern culture: apocalypse now?', in *The Wake of Imagination: Ideas of Creativity in Western Culture*, London, 1988, pp. 299–347.

100. 'Celui qui perçoit l'événement doit opter pour l'une des deux solutions possibles: ou bien il s'agit d'une illusion des sens, d'un produit de l'imagination et les lois du monde restent alors ce qu'elles sont; ou bien l'événement a véritablement eu lieu, mais alors cette realité est régie par des lois inconnues de nous...', T. Todorov, *Introduction à la littérature fantastique*, Paris, 1970, p. 29.

Interjection

1. M. Rubin, *Corpus Christi: the Eucharist in Late Medieval Culture*, Cambridge, 1991, pp. 243–71.
2. A. Abulafia, *Christians and Jews in the Twelfth-Century Renaissance*, London, 1995. But there is clearly an awareness of eucharistic Christian practice, if not an interest in it, before the later Middle Ages, see some references to the host in I.G. Marcus, *Rituals of childhood: Jewish Acculturation in Medieval Europe*, New Haven, Conn. 1996, p. 155 n. 89; also *idem*, 'Images of the Jews in the *exempla* of Caesarius of Heisterbach', in *From Witness to Witchcraft: Jews and Judaism in Medieval Christian Thought*, Wolfenbütteler Mittelalter-Studien 11, Wiesbaden, 1997, pp. 247–56, at pp. 252–3.
3. For Jewish discussion of transubstantiation see D. Lasker, *Jewish Philosophical Polemics against Christianity in the Middle Ages*, New York, 1977, pp. 135–51. For a list of Jewish polemical treatises see G.M. Weiner, 'Jewish anti-Christianism from the Crusades to the Reformation', in *The Culture of Christendom: Essays in Medieval History in Commemoration of Dennis L. T. Bethell*, ed. M.A. Meyer, London and Rio Grande, 1993, pp. 281–93, at pp. 290–3.
4. R. Joseph b. R. Nathan Official, *The Book of Joseph the Zealot (Sepher Yosef ha-mekaneh)*, ed. J. Rosenthal, Jerusalem, 1970. On this text see Z. Kahn, 'Étude sur le Livre de Joseph le Zélateur. Recueil de controverses religieuses du moyen âge', *REJ* 1 (1880), pp. 222–46 and 3 (1881), pp. 1–38, and H. Trautner-Kromann, *Shield and Sword: Jewish Polemics against Christianity and the Christians in France and Spain from 1100–1500*, Tübingen, 1993, pp. 90–1.
5. *The Jewish-Christian Debate in the High Middle Ages*, ed. D. Berger,

Philadelphia, Pa., 1979; on the authorship of the text, see pp. 32–7. On the title see Weiner, 'Jewish anti-Christianism', p. 286. On these thirteenth-century books see also A. Shapira, 'Anti-Jewish polemic in the twelfth century [Pulmus anti-notzri bameah hayod bet]', *Zion* 56 (1991), pp. 79–85, at p. 80.
6. On the book's subjects see Kahn, 'Étude sur le livre de Joseph le Zélateur', pp. 18–23, and on the eucharist, p. 23.
7. Missing word here, *The Book of Joseph the Zealot*, n. 2, p. 85.
8. Ibid., c. 91, p. 85.
9. Ibid., n. 4.
10. Ibid., no. 13, p. 39.
11. *The Jewish-Christian Debate*, no. 175, pp. 184–5; Hebrew text on p. 122.
12. F.I. Baer, *Die Juden im christlichen Spanien: Urkunden und Regesten*, I, Veröffentlichungen der Akademie für die Wissenschaft des Judenthums – Historische Sektion 4, Berlin, 1929, no. 253, pp. 350–9, at p. 352.
13. On Rabbi Lippmann see E. Zimmer, *Jewish Synods in Germany during the Late Middle Ages (1286–1603)*, New York, 1978, pp. 27–8.
14. I.J. Yuval, 'Kabbalisten, Ketzer und Polemiker. Das kulturelle Umfeld des Sefer ha-Nizachon von Lipman Mühlhausen', in *Mysticism, Magic and Kabbalah in Ashkenazi Judaism*, ed. K.E. Grözinger and J. Dan, Studia Judaica 13, Berlin and New York, 1995, pp. 155–71, at pp. 161–2; S. Baron, *A Social and Religious History of the Jews*, XI, New York, 1965, p. 336 n. 9.
15. R. Yomtov Lippmann of Mühlhausen, *Sefer ha-nizzahon*, ed. F. Talmage, Jerusalem, 1983, Genesis no. 8, pp. 10–11, at p. 11; there is a cursory mention in Numbers no. 116, p. 7, against Christian claims 'that God exchanged the *matsot* of the Penta-

teuch with other such wafers as the Christian believes'. The modern introduction prefaces a reproduction of the seventeenth-century edition *Liber Nizachon Rabbi Lipmanni*, ed. T. Hackspan, Nuremberg, 1644.

16. Yomtov Lippmann of Mühlhausen, *Sefer ha-nizzahon*, no. 354, p. 194; Zimmer, *Jewish Synods in Germany*, p. 77.

17. For the latter see the image in a *Haggadah* (book of Passover rites and readings) from Barcelona, of the fourteenth century, where *matza* is held in a manner which resembles the handling of the host in contemporary illuminations, BL Add. 14761; B. Narkiss, *Hebrew Illuminated Manuscripts in the British Isles: a Catalogue Raisonné*, Oxford, 1982, plate 12, p. 64.

18. G. Sed Rajna, *Le Mahzor enluminé: les voies de formation d'un programme iconographique*, Leiden, 1983, no. 3, of *c*.1320–5 German cauldron; for perceived similarity between *matza* and host see the example of the attribution of hiding the desecrated host in the *matza* dough in the Berlin case of 1510, below, pp. 190–91.

19. Israel Yuval has argued that the *Book of Contention* was an attempt to harmonise Kabbalah, philosophy and mysticism into a system which was not so much apologetic, but protective of Jews' own views from error, Yuval, 'Kabbalisten, Ketzer und Polemiker', *passim* and esp. pp. 170–1.

20. On which see J. Edwards, *The Jews in Christian Europe 1400–1700*, London, 1988, pp. 28–9. On Duran's writings see F. Talmage, 'The Polemical Writings of Profiat Duran', *Immanuel* 12 (1981), pp. 69–85.

21. Peter Lombard's *Sentences*, IV, distinctions 10–13, in *The Polemical Writings of Profiat Duran*, ed. F. Talmage, Jerusalem, 1981 (in Hebrew), p. 35. On this book see also Y. Baer, *A History of the Jews in Christian Spain*, II, Philadelphia, Pa., 1966, pp. 151–2.

22. A. Hudson, 'The mouse in the pyx: popular heresy and the eucharist', *Trivium* 26 (1991), pp. 40–53; G. Macy, 'Of mice and manna: *quis mus sumit* as a pastoral question', *Recherches de Théologie Ancienne et Médiévale* 58 (1991), pp. 157–66.

23. *The Polemical Writings*, pp. 36–7.

24. Ibid., p. 39.

25. H. Crescas, *Bittul iqqarei ha-nozrim*, ed. D.J. Lasker, Ramat Gan, 1990, pp. 70–74 on 'their sacrifices'.

26. Ibid., pp. 70–71.

27. Ibid., pp. 71–3.

28. *The Polemical Writings*, p. 77; Trautner-Kromann, *Shield and Sword*, no. 46, p. 160.

29. The translation is from *Disputation and Dialogue: Readings in the Jewish-Christian Encounter*, ed. F.E. Talmage, New York, 1975, p. 121 – I would prefer the usage 'substance' rather than 'essence'; for the original see *The Polemical Writings*, p. 78; Y. Baer, *A History of the Jews in Christian Spain*, II, Philadelphia, Pa., 1966, pp. 150–8.

30. Written *c*.1385 and revised *c*.1400, see the introduction to *The Gospel of Matthew according to a Primitive Hebrew Text*, ed. G. Howard, Macon, Ga., 1987.

31. *Judaism on Trial: Jewish-Christian Disputations in the Middle Ages*, ed. and trans. H. Maccoby, London and Washington, 1993, pp. 193–4.

32. F. Talmage, 'From the Writings of R. Avigdor Kara and R. Menachem Shalem', in *Thought and Action. Essays in Memory of Simon Rawidowicz on the Twenty-fifth Anniversary of his Death* (in Hebrew), ed. A. Greenbaum and A. Ivri, Haïfa, 197, pp. 43–52, esp. pp. 43–5.

33. Yomtov Lipmann of Mülhausen, *Sefer ha-nizzahon*, p. 24.

34. Oxford Bodleian Opp. 585, fol. 81r–82r; see edition in F. Talmage, 'An anti-Christian disputation in eastern Europe in the style of the disputation in Spain – a unique manuscript (in Hebrew), *Kiryat-Sefer* 56 (1981), pp. 369–72.

35. Ibid., p. 371 (my translation).

36. Henry of Segusio, *Summa aurea*, Venice, 1570, Liber quintus, 'De Iudeis, sarracenis et eorum servis', cols 1202–11; 'Et in quibus tolerentur', col. 1203; 'Et in quibus graventur', col. 1204.

37. 'Nam sunt quidam, qui ... nutrices Christianas habentes non permittunt lactare filios, cum corpus Christi sumpserunt, nisi primo per triduum lac effunderint in latrinam: quasi intelligunt, quod corpus Christi incorporetur, et ad decessum descendat. Sed falsum est ... credere', ibid., col. 1204.

38. Rubin, *Corpus Christi*, p. 37.

39. J. Cohen, 'The Jews as killers of Christ in the Latin tradition', *Traditio* 39 (1983), pp. 1–27.

40. '*Non habebis deos alienos coram me – None facies sculptile – neque similitudinem eorum quae in caelis sunt* etc.', Bonaventure, 'De decem praeceptis collatio III', in *Opera omnia*, V, Quaracchi, 1891, no. 8, p. 516 and developed on pp. 516–17 *et seq.*

41. 'De tertio: *neque similitudinem* etc., in quo prohibet Deus adorare corporalem naturam, dicunt quod adoramus frustrum panis, et hoc maxime videtur eis absurdum', ibid., no. 13, p. 517. For a survey of Bonaventure's writings on Jews see G. Dahan, 'Saint Bonaventure et les juifs', *Archivum franciscanum historicum* 77 (1984), pp. 369–405, and on this text p. 393. There is also a short mention in L.I. Newman, *Jewish Influence on Christian Reform Movements*, Columbia University Oriental Series 23, New York, 1925, p. 118. For representation of Jews in de-

votional writings by Bonaventure see Anne Derbes, *Picturing the Passion in Late Medieval Italy: Narrative Painting, Franciscan Ideologies, and the Levant*, Cambridge, 1996, pp. 91–2.

42. J.M. Millás Vallicrosa, 'Un tractado anónimo de polémica contra los Judiós', *Sefarad* 13 (1953), pp. 3–34; G. Dahan, *Les Intellectuels et les juifs au moyen-âge*, Paris, 1990, pp. 502–3.

43. 'Quod autem arguitur ultra: quod Christiani comedunt corpus Christi, quod est horribile: Dicendum quod verum, esset si acciperetur in propria specie, sed ipsum accipere sub speciebus panis nos est horribile, sed magis suave et venerabile. Non enim ipse Christus vel eius corpus in ista comestione frangitur vel atteritur sentibus vel laceratur, sicut imaginantur Iudaei, sed solae species panis franguntur vel atteruntur', Nicholas of Lyra, *Tractatus contra Iudeum impugnatorem evangelium secundum Mattheum*, Lyons, 1545, 4th particle, argument 2, fol. 280vb, and on to fol. 281ra.

44. On the Cathars see Rubin, *Corpus Christi*, p. 321 and examples in *Le Registre d'inquisition de Jacques Fournier (1318–1325)*, ed. J. Duvernoy, Toulouse, 1965, I, pp. 214–15, II, pp. 245–6; and on Lollards, see *eadem*, '*The Stripping of the Altars*: traditional religion and the challenges of history', *Assays* (1997), pp. 1–7, at pp. 4–6.

45. 'postmodum in carcere fassus esset quod christianus non erat, sed judaeus Samoeque vocatus, quodque Christiani comedunt Dominum suum, cum instantiaque petiisset ut, si mori contigerat, de ipso fieret sicut de judaeo', 'Continuatio chronici Girardi de Fracheto', *RHGF* XXI, Paris, 1855, pp. 3–70, at pp. 29–30, esp. p. 30.

46. My translation from *Das Martyrologium des Nürenberger Memor-*

buches, ed. S. Salfeld, Berlin, 1898, p. 341; see also A.M. Habermann, *Gzerot Ashkenaz ve-Tsarfat* (in Hebrew), Jerusalem, 1971, pp. 230–3; see above pp. 50–51.

47. Habermann, *Gzerot*, pp. 213–19, at p. 215.

48. S. Bernfeld, *The Book of Tears (Sefer ha-demaot)* (Hebrew), Berlin, 1924, p. 266. The last line of this quatrain like all such lines invokes the pleas of the Jews in the Book of Esther (Esther 3:9, 5:4, 5:8, 7:3, 8:5, 9:13); indeed, the whole poem is cast in the metre of the Book of Esther.

49. Do sprach der Jud: 'noch eins mir prist:
    Seyt Jhesus nun ein mensch auch ist,
    Wie wirt sein leyb so weit geteylt
    In prots gestallt und unvermeylt,
    Als an vil enden teglich gschicht.
    Kein mensch so weyt sich teylet nicht',

    Hans Folz, *Die Reimpaarsprüche*, ed. H. Fischer, Münchner Texte und Untersuchungen zur Deutschen Literatur des Mittelalters 1, Munich, 1961, no. 27, 'Christ und Jude', pp. 226–42, at p. 241, lines 551–6. On this see H.H. Ben-Sasson, 'Jewish-Christian disputation in the setting of Humanism and Reformation in the German Empire', *Harvard Theological Review* 59 (1966), pp. 369–90, at p. 375.

50. On this argument see D. Lasker, 'Transubstantiation, Elijah's chair, Plato, and the Jewish-Christian debate', *REJ* 143 (1984), pp. 31–58.

51. Zurich Staatsarchiv Rats und Richterbucher B VI 205, fol. 135ʳ; see a Middle English *exemplum* based on a tale of an amicable disputation between a Christian and a Jew, *Middle English Sermons*, ed. W.O. Ross, EETS 209, London, 1940, pp. 127–31.

52. I.G. Marcus, *Rituals of Childhood: Jewish Acculturation in Medieval*

Europe, New Haven, Conn., 1996, pp. 74, 83–5; at p. 74: 'school-child, like the Christ Child for Christians, can be seen as a pure sacrifice who brings vicarious atonement for the community.'

5 Making the Narrative Work

1. M. de Certeau, *The Practice of Everyday Life*, trans. S. Rendall, Los Angeles, 1984, p. 23.

2. M. Méras, 'Une prétendue persécution de Juifs à Moissac sous l'abbatiat de Durand de Bredon', *Annales du Midi* 79 (1967), pp. 317–19, at p. 317, n. 1.

3. *Recueil des actes des comtes de Provence appartenant à la maison de Barcelone*, ed. F. Benoit, Paris, 1925, between p. xxxvi and p. xxxvii. I am grateful to Dr Dominic Selwood for directing me to this book.

4. E.G. Gudde, *Social Conflict in Medieval German Poetry*, University of California Publications in Modern Philology 18/1, Berkeley, Calif., 1934, p. 107.

5. H. Fisher, *Die verfassungsrechtliche Stellung der Juden in den deutschen Städten während des dreizehnten Jahrhunderts*, Breslau, 1931, pp. 57–62.

6. In the heat of the Rintfleisch events, there is at least the hint that, where trials took place, Jews may have sought defence against the accusation of host desecration in the testimony of Christians, see the case described by Rudolph of Schlettstadt in *HM*, no. 6, pp. 49–51, at p. 50: 'Tunc iudei falsos testes Cristianos per-dixerunt innocenciam eorum excusare volentes.'

7. *Exhibitor* of the document of the official of Paris, in 'Iohannis de Thilrode Chronicon', *MGH.SS* XXV, ed. J. Heller, Hanover, 1880, p. 578.

8. *Quellen zur Geschichte der Juden im Hessischen Staatsarchiv Darmstadt 1080–1650*, ed. F. Battenberg, Quellen zur Geschichte der Juden in Hesse 2, Wiesbaden, 1995, no. 1070, p. 284.

9. 'darum dar er ein ostye schelkklichen in eins juden hus truog', *Oberrheinische Stadtrechte. III. Alsässische Rechte. I. Schlettstadter Stadtrechte*, ed. J. Gény, Heidelberg, 1902, p. 129.

10. *Urkundenbuch der Stadt Osnabrück, 1301–1400*, ed. H.R. Jarck, Osnabrücker Urkundenbuch 6, Osnabrück, 1989, no. 1264, pp. 1088–9. The distance from Rothenburg to Osnabrück is 370 km as the crow flies; but people do not. This would have been the end of a lengthy wandering involving much river crossing and travel.

11. E. Lourie, 'A plot which failed? The case of the corpse found in the Jewish *call* of Barcelona (1301)', *Mediterranean History Review* 1 (1986), pp. 187–220.

12. M. Esposito, 'Un procès contre les Juifs de la Savoie en 1329', *Revue Historique* 34 (1938), pp. 785–801; it is suggested on p. 795 n. 2 that *aharace* is a corruption of the word *rakik*, a wafer or host. But it would seem more like *harosset*, a fruity Passover dish.

13. Ibid., pp. 799–801.

14. On the Infant and his emulation of French royal style see D. Nirenberg, *Communities of Violence: Persecution of Minorities in the Middle Ages*, Princeton, N.J. 1996, p. 248 n. 60.

15. Pere III of Catalonia (Pedro IV of Aragon), *Chronicle*, ed. J.N. Hillgarth, trans. M. Hillgarth, PIMS Texts in Translation 23–4, Toronto, 1980, I, pp. 2–6; J.N. Hillgarth, *The Spanish Kingdoms, 1250–1516*, 2 vols, Oxford, 1976–8, I, ch. 2, pp. 347–71; on Eleanor see I, p. 350. On this case see Y. Baer, *A History of the Jews in Chris-*

tian *Spain*, II, Philadelphia, Pa., 1966, pp. 88–9.

16. F.I. Baer, *Die Juden im christlichen Spanien: Urkunden und Regesten*, I, Veröffentlichungen der Akademie für die Wissenschaft des Judenthums – Historische Sektion 4, Berlin, 1929, no. 253, pp. 350–8, at p. 352; *The Apostolic See and the Jews, I: Documents*, ed. S. Simonsohn, PIMS Studies and Texts 94, Toronto, 1988, pp. 65–6.

17. The Infant reigned 1387–95 and brought much tribulation, including an uprising of the nobility in 1391. On his failures and weaknesses, see the the dream-voyage written by Barnat Metge, an erstwhile royal clerk, around 1395, *Lo somni*, ed. M. Jordà, Barcelona, 1980.

18. The Infant's letter to the King of 6 July 1367, Baer, *Die Juden im christlichen Spanien*, I, no. 284, pp. 399–404.

19. Baer, *A History of the Jews in Christian Spain*, II, pp. 39–40 and D. Lasker, *Jewish Philosophical Polemics against Christianity in the Middle Ages*, New York, 1977, pp. 139, 142–3, 144, 147, 149, 150; see above, pp. 96–7.

20. Baer, *Die Juden im christlichen Spanien*, I, p. 403.

21. See summary, ibid., pp. 404–5

22. 'per ço com no son estats trobats culpables', ibid., p. 406. Little evidence remains in the Jewish sources, except for a mention of a nasty accusation, ibid.

23. J. Miret y Sans, 'El procés de les hostias contra los jueus d'Osca a 1377', *Anuari d'Estudis Catalanas* 4 (1911–12), pp. 59–80, at p. 62; Baer, *A History of the Jews in Christian Spain*, II, pp. 89–90.

24. The family was involved: 'El dito Ahim con su muller e sus fillos et companyas sea fuydo de la dita ciudat de Huesca', Miret y Sans, 'El procés de les hostias', pp. 63–4 n. 1. They were accused of 'buying badly' five hosts: 'haya comprado

malament cinco hostias consa-
gradas, la qual cosa es fuert
abominable et de mal exemplo',
ibid.
25. 'qual precio priso de los dictos
judios tres aniellos dargent de los
quales die dos a una fembra seglar
qui es amiga e concubina...',
ibid., p. 64.
26. Ibid.
27. Ibid., n. 1.
28. He addressed his father 'Suplich
a la vostra gran segnoria', ibid.,
pp. 64–5 n. 2.
29. Ibid., p. 67 n. 1.
30. 12 Dec. 1377, ibid.
31. 'que per odi et malvolença son
estades posades moltes coses',
ibid., p. 69 n. 2.
32. 'los juheus dixeren que per força
de turments hauien dit ço que dit
hauien contra veritat', 18 Jan.
1378, ibid., p. 69 n. 3.
33. On Lope see Hillgarth, *The
Spanish Kingdoms*, I, p. 32.
34. 'nos qui en tiempos de guerras
et de tribulaciones que hauemos
houidas en nuestros Regnos et
tierras los hauemos conseruados
bein los puede et los deue
conseruar el Duch en tiempo de
paç et de benenança', Miret y
Sans, 'El procés de les hostias', p.
70 n. 2.
35. 'lo original del proces de qual vos
nos tramesses trallat es escrit de
ma del confessor lo desencol-
pament quel christia feu fels
juheus qui daço eren encolpats',
ibid., p. 71 n. 1.
36. 'dixeren que no plagues a Deu
que ells hi sabossen res et nuill
tempo havien tengudes hosties
ni sabien ques era', ibid., p. 73;
'ells nulls temps ha gussen iustes
hosties ne sabien qu seren', ibid.,
p. 74.
37. Ibid., p. 76.
38. Ibid., p. 78.
39. 'falses tractaments e maneres, per
persones quils volen mal'; 'no si a
per falses acusacions condempnat
ne punit', Baer, *Die Juden im
christllichen Spanien*, I, no. 361, pp.

547–8 or Miret y Sans, 'El procés
de les hostias', p. 80 n. 1.
40. In the letter to his nephew the
King wrote 'que segons lur
presumpcio e creença lo dit
Sentou no es culpable en lo fet,
allegants diverses raons, per les
quals pretenen, que semblant acte
raonablament no pot ne deu
caure en cor de juheu', Baer, *Die
Juden im christlichen Spanien*, I, no.
361, pp. 547–8, at p. 547; Baer, *A
History of the Jews in Christian Spain*,
II, pp. 91–2.
41. On the concept of *chronotopos* see
M.M. Bakhtin, 'Forms of time and
of the chronotope in the novel',
in *The Dialogic Imagination: Four
Essays*, ed. M. Holquist, trans. C.
Emerson and M. Holquist, Austin,
Tex. 1981, pp. 74–258; the
chronotopos encompasses 'The
intrinsic connectedness of temporal and spatial relationships that
are... expressed in literature',
M.V. Montgomery, *Carnivals and
Commonplace: Bakhtin's Chronotope,
Cultural Studies, and Film*, American University Studies Series 4
173, New York, 1993, p. 84. For
further exploration of the *chronotopos* see M. Holquist, *Dialogism:
Bakhtin and his World*, London,
1990, pp. 109–15, 154–5.
42. M. Despina, 'Les accusation de
profanation d'hosties portées
contre les juifs', *Rencontre. Chrétiens et Juifs* 22 (1971), pp. 150–
73, at pp. 168–9.
43. The Jewish sources call her
komeret, 'priestess'. On *presbytera* as
a term for a Greek priest's wife see
A.J. Minnis, '*De impedimento sexus*:
women's bodies and medieval
impediments to female ordina-
tion', in *Medieval Theology and the
Natural Body*, ed. P. Biller and A.J.
Minnis, York Studies in Medieval
Theology 1, Woodbridge, 1997,
pp. 109–39, at p. 127.
44. The main source is the Hebrew
Chronicle of Eliahu Capsali,
Seder Yehuda Zuta, II, ed. A.
Shmuelevitch, S. Simonsohn and

M. Benayahu, Jerusalem, 1977, pp. 225–7; N. Porgès, 'Elie Capsali et sa Chronique de Venise', *REJ* 77 (1923), pp. 20–40; J. Starr, 'Jewish life in Crete under the rule of Venice', *Proceedings of the American Academy for Jewish Research* 12 (1942), pp. 59–114, at pp. 66–7.

45. Starr, 'Jewish life in Crete', pp. 66–7.

46. See in 'Die kleine Klosterneuburger Chronik (1322 bis 1428)', ed. H.J. Zeibig, *Archiv für Kunde Österreichischer Geschichts-Quellen* 7 (1851), pp. 227–52, at p. 245; U. Weiss, *Die frommen Bürger von Erfurt. Die Stadt und ihre Kirche im Spätmittelalter und in der Reformationszeit*, Weimar, 1988, p. 36. On Sigismund's politics and the crusade see S. Wefers, *Das politische System Kaiser Sigmunds*, Veröffentlichungen des Instituts für Europäische Geschichte Mainz – Abteilung Universalgeschichte 138, Stuttgart, 1989, pp. 77, 81–2, 87.

47. For the First Crusade see R. Chazan, *European Jewry and the First Crusade*, Berkeley, Calif., 1987; for Jewish reports see *The Jews and the Crusades: the Hebrew Chronicles of the First and Second Crusades*, ed. and trans. S. Eidelberg, Madison, Wis. 1977.

48. 'in eadem congragacione mencio facta fuit de confederacione Iudeorum et Hussitarum ac Waldensium, item de multitudine Iudeorum, de delicata vita ipsorum et de quibusdam libris execrabilibius, quos habent in contumeliam creatoris et blasphemiam Christi, omnium sanctorum et maximam iniuriam omnium Christianorum', *Die Akten der theologischen Fakultät der Universität Wien (1396–1508)*, ed. P. Uiblein, Vienna, 1978, I, p. 37; trans. in M.H. Shank, *'Unless You Believe, You Shall Not Understand': Logic, University and Society in Late Medieval Vienna*, Princeton, N.J.,

1988, p. 188.

49. I.J. Yuval, 'Jews, Hussites and Germans in the chronicle *Gilgul bnei Hushim*', *Zion* 54 (1989), pp. 275–319, at p. 281 (in Hebrew); idem, 'Kabbalisten, Ketzer und Polemiker. Das kulturelle Umfeld des Sefer ha-Nizachon von Lipman Mühlhausen', in *Mysticism, Magic and Kabbalah in Ashkenazi Judaism*, ed. K.E. Grözinger and J. Dan, Studia Judaica 13, Berlin and New York, 1995, pp. 155–71, esp. p. 167; J.E. Scherer, *Die Rechtsverhältnisse der Juden in den deutschen-österreichischen Ländern*, Leipzig, 1901, p. 125.

50. Shank, *'Unless You Believe'*, p. 188 (*Die Akten der theologischen Fakultät*, I, p. 36). The Duke had renewed the Jews' privileges in 1417 for four years, following a payment of 6,000 gulden made to him by the Jews in January of that year, to finance his debts, Shank, *'Unless You Believe'*, p. 191.

51. On Henry see ibid., *passim*.

52. W. Trusen, *Spätmittelalterliche Jurisprudenz und Wirtschaftsethic dargestellt an Wiener Gutachten des 14. Jahrhunderts*, Vierteiljahrschrift für Sozial- und Wirtschaftsgeschichte Beiheft 43, Wiesbaden, 1960, p. 101. On Langenstein's views and his suggestions for alternative credit arrangements see A. Hoffmann, 'Die wirtschaftlichen Verhältnisse zur Zeit Rudolfs IV', in Hoffmann, *Staat und Wirtschaft im Wandel der Zeit*, Munich, 1979, pp. 178–207, at pp. 199–201.

53. Shank, *'Unless You Believe'*, pp. 54, 191.

54. See some thoughts on the importance of the various accusations against Jews in causing the expulsion in I.J. Yuval, 'Vengeance and damnation, blood and defamation: from Jewish martyrdom to blood libel accusations [in Hebrew]', *Zion* 58 (1993), pp. 33–90, at p. 61 n. 103.

55. '*Item anno vicesimo* wurden die Juden gefangen in allen Lant ze Osterreich an den achten Tag zu der Auffart oder des Pfinztags vor Pfingsten, und Ir wurden vil getawft: Und dy sich nicht wolten bekheren, die hett man gefangen uncz in die Vasten. Und an Mitichn *Judica* ward Sand *Gregorii* Tag, da verprant man sew alle, Weib und Man', 'Anonymi Viennensis breve Chronicon Austriacum ab anno MCCCII ad MCCCCXLIIII', in *Scriptores rerum austriacarum*, II, ed. H. Pez, Vienna, 1743, col. 550.

56. A. Lhotsky, *Thomas Ebendorfer. Ein österreichischer Geschichtschreiber, Theologe und Diplomat des 15. Jahrhunderts*, Stuttgart, 1957, pp. 1–57 on his life; pp. 384–7 on the chronicle. See also J. Macek, *The Hussite Movement in Bohemia*, ed. E. Lauer, trans. V. Fried and I. Milner, London, 1965, pp. 41–3. On the *Geserah* and for the text see the appendix to *Das Judenbuch der Scheffstrasse zu Wien*, ed. A. Goldmann, Quellen und Forschungen zur Geschichte der Juden in Deutsch-Österreich I, Vienna and Leipzig, 1908, pp. 112–33.

57. 'multas sacramenti particulas comparasse et eas ad illudendum suis paribus destinasse, que sacrilegia et mulier prefata questionata confessa est', Thomas Ebendorfer, *Chronica Austriae*, ed. A. Lhotsky, *MGH.SS* Rerum Germanicarum New Ser. 13, Berlin and Zurich, 1967, p. 370.

58. For the record of the deaths of Jews in Vienna and Leitomitchl see the *Memorbuch* see *Jahrbuch der jüdische Literarischen Gesellschaft* 19 (1928), pp. 99–111. Similar claims were made in Prague, J. Jireček, 'Zprváa o židovském pobití v Praze r. 1389 z rukopisu Krakovského', *Sitzungsberichte der königliche böhmische Gesellschaft der Wissenschaften in Prag* (1880), pp. 227–9, at p. 228.

59. Shank, '*Unless You Believe*', pp. 198–9.

60. R. Gladstein, 'Eschatological trends in Bohemian Jewry during the Hussite period', in *Prophecy and Millenarianism: Essays in Honour of Marjorie Reeves*, ed. A. Williams, Harlow, 1980, pp. 241–56, at p. 250. Against this view, S. Eidelberg, 'Were there contacts between Czech Jews and the Hussite rebels? [in Hebrew]', in *Proceedings of the American Academy for Research: Hebrew Section* 44 (1977), pp. 1–14; H. Ben-Sasson, 'The Jews in the face of the Reformation', *Proceedings of the Israel Academy of Sciences and Humanities* 4 (1971), pp. 62–116, at p. 68; H. Kaminsky, *A History of the Hussite Revolution*, Berkeley, Calif., 1967, p. 256.

61. S. Eidelberg, *Jewish Life in Austria in the Fifteenth Century as Reflected in the Legal writings of I. Isserlein and his Contemporaries*, Philadelphia, Pa., 1962, pp. 12–13.

62. L.I. Newman, *Jewish Influence on Christian Reform Movements*, Columbia University Oriental Series 23, New York, 1925, pp. 435–53.

63. Kaminsky, *A History of the Hussite Revolution*, p. 256.

64. Macek, *The Hussite Movement in Bohemia*, pp. 41–3; R. Kieckhefer, *Repression of Heresy in Medieval Germany*, Liverpool, 1979, ch. 6, esp. pp. 85–6.

65. Ebendorfer recounts the variety of Jewish reactions to the calamity: suicide, conversion, false conversion: 'alii pertinaci furore succensi et coniugibus et propinquiis velatis faciebus sevum per facinus arteriis amputatis vitam miserius ademerent, quorum corpora asinorum tradita sunt sepulture. Ceteri autem sacro baptismate iniciati in fide perstiterunt, alii vero diversis sub coloribus ad vomitum reversi prosilierunt', Ebendorfer, *Chronica Austriae*, p. 371.

66. Shank, *'Unless You Believe'*, pp. 197–8
67. P.W. Knoll, *The Rise of the Polish Monarchy in Piast Poland in East Central Europe, 1320–1370*, Chicago, 1972, pp. 70, 73–4.
68. On John (Giovanni) see J. Hofer, *Johannes Kapistran: ein Leben im Kampf um die Reform der Kirche*, 2 vols, Bibliotheca franciscana 1–2, new edn, Heidelberg, 1964–5; on the mission see D. Sullivan, 'Nicholas of Cusa as reformer: the papal legation to the Germanies, 1451–1452', *Mediaeval Studies* 36 (1974), pp. 382–428; on the Observant Franciscan Order see P.L. Nyhus, 'The Franciscan Observant reform in Germany', in *Reformbemühungen und Observanzbestrebungen im spätmittelalterlichen Ordenswesen*, ed. K. Elm, Berliner Historische Studien 14, Berlin, 1989, pp. 207–17; see D.B. Nimmo, 'The Franciscan Regular Observance: the culmination of medieval Franciscan reform', in ibid., pp. 189–205 and R. Manselli, 'L'osservanza francescana: dinamica della sua formazione e fenomenologia', in ibid., pp. 173–87.
69. 'Venit devotus pater Johannes de Capistrano frater ordinis sancti Francisci de observancia, vite sanctimonia clarus, ab apostolica sede facultate magna contra hereticos Bohemos missus', *Acta sanctorum octobris*, ed. J. van Hecke and others X, Brussels, 1861, pp. 269–552, at pp. 393–4.
70. On John's treatment of Rokycana see Hofer, *Johannes Kapistran*, II, pp. 91–3.
71. M. Wenninger, *Man bedarf keiner Juden mehr. Ursachen und Hintergründe ihrer Vertreibung aus den Reichsstädte im 15. Jahrhundert*, Beihefte zum Archiv für Kulturgeschichte 14, Vienna, 1981, p. 222.
72. L. Olsner, 'Schlesische Urkunden zur Geschichte der Juden im Mittelalter', *Archiv für Kunde österreichischer Geschichts-Quellen* 31 (1864), pp. 91–2 and no. 39, p. 143. John lent an apocalyptic quality to his preaching and collected prophecies, see O. Bonmann, 'Zum Prophetismus des Johannes Kapistran (1386–1456)', *Archiv für Kulturgeschichte* 44 (1962), pp. 193–8.
73. 'De expulsione iudaeorum', in *Monumenta poloniae historica*, III, Lwow, 1878, pp. 786–9; Olsner, 'Schlesische Urkunden'; J. Fischer, 'Ein neues Dokument zur Geschichte der Judenvertreibung aus Schlesien im Jahre 1453', *Zeitschrift für Geschichte und Wissenschaft des Judenthums* 6 (1922), pp. 299–305; 'De persecutione iudaeorum vratislavensium a.1453', in *Monumenta poloniae historica*, IV, Lwow, 1884, pp. 1–5. On the sources see Hofer, *Johannes Kapistran*, II, Heidelberg, 1965, pp. 209–10.
74. On the sources see *Germania judaica*, III (1), ed. A. Maimon with J. Guggenheim, Tübingen, 1987, pp. 161–2; H. Wegrzynek, 'Accusations of host profanation against Jews in Poland', *European Review of History* pilot issue (1993), pp. 45–56, at pp. 49–50.
75. See above, pp. 80–83, 110–13.
76. Fischer, 'Ein neues Dokument', pp. 303–4.
77. 'darnach dy juden aber gesamt und haben das kindel genummen und das hälsel gedrukcht, das es nicht schreyn mocht, und also lembtig in das vässel verslagen und vermacht, das dye negel dem kindallen seinen leichnam verbundt und also getött haben. Darnach haben sy das vässel geöffnet und das kind daraus genummen und des pluets in weisse tuecher gefangen und mit wein das pluet ab dem leichnam des kindleins gewaschen, auch das vässel mit wein ausgewaschen und also den wein mit dem pluet in gleser gossen und mit wakchs wol vermacht und behalten und das

kindel in dem selben cheller such pegraben', Fischer, 'Ein neues Dokument', p. 304.

78. This is an early case; R. Po-chia Hsia has noted that 'in the 1470s legends of ritual murders and host desecrations began to converge, resulting in a stylized type of ritual murder discourse in which prepubescent boys and Eucharistic devotion play the central role', R. Po-chia Hsia, *The Myth of Ritual Murder: Jews and Magic in Reformation Germany*, New Haven, Conn., 1988, p. 52. See also below, pp. 129–31. For an earlier association between ritual murder and host desecration accusations see Robert C. Stacey, 'From ritual crucifixion to host desecration: Jews and the Body of Christ', *Jewish History* 12 (1998), pp. 11–28.

79. Yomtov Lippmann of Mühlhausen, *Sefer ha-nizzahon*, ed. F. Talmage, Kuntresim Text and Studies 59–60, Jerusalem, 1983, no. 354, p. 194.

80. A broad penny, probably a *grossus pragensis* (Groat of Bohemia) very common in these regions. I am grateful to Peter Spufford for his expert help, and see P. Spufford, *Handbook of Medieval Exchange*, Royal Historical Society Guides and Handbooks 13, London, 1986, pp. xx–xxiii, li.

81. This is a translation of the German word *Schulklopfer* used to describe the synagogue's beadle, the *gabbai*, a figure of some administrative and executive importance in medieval communities, R. Straus, *Regensburg and Augsburg*, trans. F.N. Gerson, Philadelphia, Pa., 1939, p. 22.

82. 'Qui offert diis, damnabitur, excepto Deo solo', 'De expulsione iudaeorum', in *Monumenta poloniae historica*, III, Lwow, 1878, pp. 786–9, at p. 788.

83. Ibid., p. 789.

84. Ibid.

85. 'Annales Glogauenses', in *Scrip-*
tores rerum silesiacarum, ed. H. Margraf, Wrocław, 1877, pp. 18–19. An iron cross was placed on the site of the execution, Hofer, *Johannes Kapistran*, II, p. 213.

86. *Monumenta poloniae historica*, IV, Lwow, 1884, pp. 1–5.

87. 'partibus nostris a deo missus de speciali gracia dei omnipotentis', ibid., p. 4.

88. 'Quoniam Judeorum augmentum multam operatur blasphemiam domini nostri Ihesu Christi et sue virginis matris Marie atque fidei katholice derogacionem', ibid., p. 5.

89. On the structure see A. Timmermann, 'Staging the eucharist: late Gothic sacrament houses in Swabia and the Upper Rhine: architecture and iconography', Ph.D. dissertation, University of London (Courtauld Institute of Art), 1996, p. 83.

90. On these structures see *Kunstdenkmäler der Stadt Breslau*, ed. L. Burgermeister, Kunstdenkmäler Niederschlesien 1, Wrocław, 1930, p. 217 (St. Elisabeth), pp. 212–13, 227 (Sandkirche).

91. See B. Pullan, *Rich and Poor in Renaissance Venice*, Oxford, 1971, pp. 606–9.

92. John's disciple Bernardino da Feltre (1439–94) was to carry on his anti-Jewish and anti-usury preaching, R. Segre, 'Bernardino da Feltre, i monti di pietà e i banchi ebraici', *Revista Storica Italiana* 90 (1978), pp. 818–33. He preached in Trent in 1475 on the eve of the greatest ritual murder trial of all, the trial over the death of little Simon of Trent, in which ritual murder accusation and host desecration accusation combined, see R. Po-chia Hsia, *Trent 1475: Stories of a Ritual Murder Trial*, New Haven, Conn., 1992. On *monti di pietà* see also S. Simonsohn, *The Apostolic See and the Jews, VII: History*, PIMS Studies and Texts 109, Toronto, 1991, pp. 220–7. The aims of the

movement were only partially achieved in the sixteenth century, M.G. Muzzarelli, 'Luoghi e tendenze dell'attuale storiografia italiana sulla presenza ebraica fra XIV e XVI secolo', *Società e Storia* 23 (1984), pp. 369–94.

93. R. Po-chia Hsia, 'Witchcraft, magic and the Jews in late medieval and early modern Germany', in *From Witness to Witchcraft: Jews and Judaism in Medieval Christian Thought*, ed. J. Cohen, Wolfenbütteler Mittelalter-Studien 11, Wiesbaden, 1997, pp. 419–33, at p. 422.

94. The experience of meeting John while on a mission from the Archbishop of Krakow may have prompted the historian Jan Długosz to report and embellish the memory of a host desecration accusation which had taken place in his town of Poznań some fifty years earlier.

95. Zurich, Staatsarchiv, Rats- und Richterbücher B VI 205, fols 134–5. I am most grateful to Susannah Burghartz for sending me transcripts of these entries and to Professor Hajo Schiewer for having read them with me.

96. Ibid., fol. 134r.

97. It is not clear which minster and which Neumarkt he is referring to: there is such a town near Linz and another near Nuremberg.

98. His testimony appears ibid., fol. 134v.

99. Ibid., fol. 135r.

100. R. Ben-Shalom, 'The Tortosa disputation, Vicente Ferrer, and the problem of converts according to Yitzhak Natan' (in Hebrew) *Zion* 66 (1991), pp. 21–45; on Ferrer's role in the Tortosa Disputation see Baer, *A History of the Jews in Christian Spain*, II, pp. 95–6, 166–71; Despina, 'Les accusations de profanation d'hosties', pp. 168–9.

101. 'Los apostolos qui conqueriren lo mon no portaven lança ne coltell, e por ço done materia . . . que los christians no deuen matar los juheus ab coltell mas ab paraules', E. Chabás, 'Estudio sobre los sermones valencianos de San Vicente Ferre. V', *Revista de Archivos Bibliotecas y Museos* 8 (1903), pp. 111–26, at p. 125; M.M. Gorce, *St Vincent Ferrier (1350–1419)*, Paris, 1935, p. 126. For some of the ideas which underpinned preaching to Jews from the thirteenth century see S. Lewis, *Reading Images: Narrative Discourse and Reception in the Thirteenth-Century Apocalypse*, Cambridge, 1995, pp. 219–21.

102. 'Los senyors temporals deuen convertir los infels de sa terra . . . pero sens força injuriosa, be jurídica'; 'Es necessari al preycador de publicar les veritats a fels e infels . . . E veus, per ço vosaltres veniu a la preycació', Chabás, 'Estudio sobre los sermones', p. 125.

103. A. Müller, *Geschichte der Juden in Nürnberg, 1145–1945*, Nuremberg, 1968, p. 46. The extracts from the Jew Wolf's confession were prepared by the Count of Ottingen, Staatsarchiv Nürnberg Rat. Nbg. Ratskanzlei A Laden no. 71, 12.

104. Müller, *Geschichte der Juden*, p. 81.

105. Hsia, *The Myth of Ritual Murder*, pp. 67–9.

106. *Urkunden und Aktenstücke zur Geschichte der Juden in Regensburg, 1453–1738*, ed. R. Straus, Quellen und Erorterungen zur Bayerischen Geschichte New Ser. 18, Munich, 1960, no. 149, p. 40.

107. Straus, *Regensburg and Augsburg*, pp. 149–50.

108. Hsia, *The Myth of Ritual Murder*, pp. 50–3.

109. 'in des Veidl Iuden bachofen geworffen da hab er ein figur zwayer Enngl gestallt aus dem ofen fliegen sehen und ist geschehen an ainem freytag', Munich Staatsbibiliothek MS cgm 753, fols 145r-150r, at fol. 145r.

110. See *Urkunden and Aktenstucke*, nos 531–2, pp. 179–80. A. Mayer, 'Die

Gründung von St. Salvator in Passau – Geschichte und Legende', *Zeitschrift für Bayerische Landesgeschichte (Festgabe Max Spindler)* 18 (1955), pp. 256–78. On the response of the Jewish leadership to the accusations see E. Zimmer, *Jewish Synods in Germany during the Middle Ages (1286–1603)*, New York, 1978, pp. 43–7; the leadership was aware of the 'infectious' nature of such accusations, p. 45.

111. R. von Liliencron, *Die historischen Volkslieder der Deutschen von 13. bis 16. Jahrhundert*, 5 vols in 4, Leipzig, 1865–9, II, no. 153, pp. 142–6, stanza 21, p. 145.

112. On this case see Baer, *A History of the Jews in Christian Spain*, II, pp. 398–423; J. Edwards, *The Jews in Christian Europe 1400–1700*, London, 1988, pp. 33–4 (a short summary of the case).

113. On memory and liturgical commemoration of massacres in the liturgy of Ashkenasi Jews see the very important recent article I. Yuval, 'Vengeance and damnation'.

114. J. Laplanche and J.-B. Pontalis, *The Language of Psychoanalysis*, trans. D. Nicholson-Smith, London, 1986, pp. 292–3.

115. Other accusations against Jews, such as miscegenation, could also lead to the unfolding of a host desecration accusation, as shown by David Nirenberg in the case of Boniach Deuslosal, a Jew of Puigcerda, in 1377, through a denunciation by two converts, Nirenberg, *Communities of Violence*, pp. 144–5.

6 Violence and the Trails of Memory

1. Those who undergo trauma have been aptly seen as changed and burdened by events which cannot, some might say ought not, be understood: 'The traumatised, we might say, carry an impossible history within them, or they become themselves the symptom of a history they cannot entirely possess', in C. Caruth, 'Introduction', in *Trauma: Explorations in Memory*, ed. C. Caruth, Baltimore, Md., 1995, p. 5.

2. A.M. Habermann, *Gzerot Ashkenaz ve-Tsrafat*, Jerusalem, 1971, pp. 230–3, these lines 1–2, 5, 6, 10, on pp. 230, 231, 232. *Das Martyrologium des Nürnberger Memorbuches*, ed. S. Salfeld, Quellen zur Geschichte des Juden in Deutschland 3, Berlin, 1898, p. 341. For similar laments on 'blood cities' see R. Joshua ben R. Menachem's lament which recounts Rothenburg, Würzburg, Nuremberg and Bamberg, in Habermann, *Gzerot*, pp. 213–19. See an earlier example, Paris, so named by 1242–3, in A. David, 'Pogroms against French Jews during the Shepherds' crusade of 1251 [in Hebrew]', *Tarbiz* 46 (1977), pp. 251–7.

3. H. Yerushalmi, *Zachor: Jewish History and Jewish Memory*, Seattle, 1982, pp. 39–40. I. Elbogen, *Der jüdische Gottesdienst in seiner geschichtlichen Entwicklung*, Frankfurt-am-Main, 3rd edn, 1931, pp. 221–31, or I.M. Elbogen, *Prayer in Israel and its Historical Development* (in Hebrew), Tel Aviv, 1972, pp. 165–73, esp. pp. 172–3.

4. *Leket Joscher des Joseph B. Mose*, ed. J. Freimann, 2 vols, Berlin, 1902–3, I, p. 112.

5. E. Zimmer, *Jewish Synods in Germany during the Late Middle Ages (1286–1603)*, New York, 1978, p. 19; the Hebrew text appears in n. 9 on that page.

6. See the vexed question of the status of women whose husbands were thought to be dead, Israel (Ben Petahia) Isserlein, *Sefer terumat hadeshen im pesakim u-khetavim*, Fürth, 1778, no. 241, cols 71rb–72va.

7. On this genre see Yerushalmi, *Zachor*, pp. 45–6. Historical writing becomes more notable in the sixteenth century, ibid., pp. 33–4. See for example on the Vienna *Geserah* Joseph Ha-Cohen and the Anonymous Corrector, *The Vale of Tears (Emek Habacha)*, trans. H.S. May, The Hague, 1971, pp. 58–9. Further on commemoration of events by medieval Jews with special reference to massacres see R. Chazan, 'Representation of events in the Middle Ages', in *Essays in Jewish Historiography: In Memoriam Arnaldo Dante Momigliano 1908–1987*, ed. A. Rapoport-Albert, History and Theory *Beiheft* 27, Middletown, Conn., 1988, pp. 40–55.

8. On memory as related to sites of memory see some reflections in P. Nora, 'Between memory and history: *Les lieux de mémoire*', *Representations* 26, no. 2 (1989), pp. 7–25.

9. See E.L. Santner, *Stranded Objects: Mourning, Memory and Film in Postwar Germany*, Ithaca, N.Y., 1990, pp. 1–30.

10. On Vatican Council II and attempts to rethink representations of Jews see R. Neudecker, 'The Catholic church and the Jewish people', in *Vatican II: Assessment and Perspectives Twenty-Five Years After (1962–1987)*, III, ed. R. Latourelle, New York, 1989, pp. 282–323. I am most grateful to my colleague Dr Norman Tanner for responding to my query about this subject and advising on appropriate reading.

11. A letter sent to the Abbot of the Scottish Monastery in Vienna in connecton with traces of the Pulkau cult has not been answered. There is a sense of unease among some scholars concerning access to the shrine and its historical remains.

12. As late as 1984 the decoration of the Iphofen pilgrimage church retold the tale of Jewish host desecration, H. Schwillus, 'Hostienfrevellegende und Judenverfolgung in Iphofen. Ein Beitrag zur Entstehungsgeschichte', *Würzburger Diözesan-Geschichtsblätter* 58 (1996), pp. 87–107, at pp. 94–5.

13. In Munich Bayerische Staatsbibliothek cgm 753, fols 119r–124r; P.E. Weiden-Willer, *Untersuchungen zur deutschsprachigen katechetischen Literatur des späten Mittelalters*, Munich, 1965, p. 30. Another copy is found in the archives of Nuremberg, having been directed from Passau to the council there, Nuremberg Staatsarchiv Ratschlagbücher 13*, fols 43–5. On communication between town councils during the unfolding of judicial cases against Jews see the comments in R. Po-chia Hsia, *The Myth of Ritual Murder*, New Haven, Conn., 1988, p. 53.

14. P. Lehmann, *Parodistische Texte*, Munich, 1923, pp. 36–41. On this see F. Graus, *Struktur und Geschichte. Drei Volksaufstände im mittelalterlichen Prag*, Sigmaringen, 1971, pp. 50–60; according to another version of the satire in a manuscript from Krakow, the Jews mocked the eucharist as an idol, ibid., p. 55 n. 25.

15. M. Bayless, *Parody in the Middle Ages: the Latin Tradition*, Ann Arbor, Mich, 1996, pp. 8–9.

16. Ibid., p. 134.

17. This fits in with the description 'von eine Jud ein klein steinchen geworfen ut do monstrancien', according to the Limbourg chronicle by the clerk Tilmann Elhen von Wolfhagen (1317–1377) of Trier diocese, *Die Limburger Chronik des Tillemann Elhen von Wolfhagen*, ed. A. Wyss, Deutsche Chroniken IV (1), Hanover, 1883, p. 79.

18. 'V tunnas plenas argento', 'Chronicon Engelhusii', *Scriptores rerum brunsuicarum*, II, ed. G.W. Leibnitz, Hanover, 1711, p. 1134. He was away from Prague just then, still in Eger, R.E. Weltsch,

Archbishop John of Jenstein (1348–1400): Papalism, Humanism and Reform in Pre-Hussite Prague, Studies in European History 8, The Hague, 1968, p. 61.

19. *Die Limburger Chronik*, p. 41.

20. Bayless, *Parody in the Middle Ages*, p. 13.

21. See parallel notions of rustic simplicity/decency in S. Justice, *Writing and Rebellion: England in 1381*, Berkeley, Calif, 1994, pp. 91–2. I am grateful to Peter Johanek and Willis Johnson for illuminating comments on this point. For a contemporary usage, albeit not satirical, see the text on the Passion of John Hus, 'Passio etc. secundum Johannem Barbatum rusticum quadratum', *Fontes rerum bohemicarum*, VIII, Prague, 1932, pp. 14–24.

22. Weltsch, *Archbishop John of Jenstein*, ch. 2, pp. 40–78.

23. The Jewish tradition saw the events as occurring against the royal will, see the version in the sixteenth-century chronicle of David Gans, *Sefer Zemah David (Prague 1592)*, ed. M. Breuer, Jerusalem, 1983, pp. 361–2.

24. Krakow, Jagellonian Library MS 2583 (DD.XIX.4), fol. 92v; the text is printed in J. Jireček, 'Zpráva o židovském pobiti v Praze r. 1389 z rukopisu Krakovského', *Sitzungsberichte der königlichen böhmische Gesellschaft der Wissenschaften in Prag* (1880), pp. 227–9.

25. I am most grateful to Professor Alfred Thomas for his translation and identification of the hymn's Czech title.

26. Weltsch, *Archbishop John of Jenstein*, p. 61. See also M. Tischler, 'Böhmische Judengemeinde 1348–1519', in *Die Juden in den böhmischen Ländern. Vorträge der Tagung des Colloegium Carolinum in Bad Wiessee vom 27. bis 29. November 1981*, Munich and Vienna, 1983, pp. 37–56, at pp. 50–2; W. Brosche, 'Das Ghetto von Prag', in ibid., pp. 87–122; there were some 4,000 Jews in the city around 1388, p. 106.

27. 'quia tamen hujusmodi usurarii nephas horrendum et detestabile . . . hodie nedum per populares verum etiam per magni status homines multimodis et quaesitis et fucatis coloribus, quod dolemur referimus, frequentatur, propter quod ab ipsis Iudaeis et aliis infidelibus in improperium nobis objicitur et fidelium cordibus in Dei ecclesia scandala gravantur', 16 Oct. 1381, *Concilia pragensia, 1353–1413*, ed. C. Höfler, Prague, 1862, p. 30.

28. Cited from Vatican Lat. 1122, fol. 228c: 'Nam bene videtis clerum et Christofideles cottidie in suis iuribus et libertatibus supplantari et subici multasque iniurias perpeti et magis synagogam quam Christi proficere ecclesia et inter principes plus unum posse Judeum quam procerem vel prelatum', in Weltsch, *Archbishop John of Jenstein*, n. 89, p. 62.

29. 'Ymmo per usurias inauditas principes et magnates adeo depauperantur, ac si cum thesauris illis suum dominum Antichristum ditare et adiuvare queant', ibid.

30. 'Non fuit temporibus illis qui vice regia justiciam faceret pupillis et viduis, ymmo nec baronibus, nobilibus et vassalis, quorum pars non modica, querelas emisit, de illata sibi regali violencia. Exosus igitur erat clero et populo, nobilibus, civibus et rusticis, solis erat acceptus Iudeis', in 'Catalogus abbatum Saganensium', *Scriptores rerum silesiacarum*, I, ed. G.A. Stenzel, Wrocław, 1835, p. 214.

31. 'quia christiana gens dissimilare et ferre non potuit, in vindictam blasphemiam illius, quadam die . . . in sollempnitate paschali . . . zelo mota Judeos ipsos et domus eorum igne cremavit', ibid.

32. 'Plebs autem audiens opus tam nepharium vociferabat dicens: "Merito delenda est iudaica perversitas, per quam blasphemiae tanta excreuit immensitas"', Jireček, 'Zpráva o židovském', p. 226.

33. Playing on the verse Matthew 26: 34: 'Amen dico tibi: In hac nocte, antequam gallus cantet ter, me negabis.'

34. See entry by E.-S. Bauer and G. Baeder in *Die deutsche Literatur des Mittelalters. Verfasserlexikon*, Berlin and New York, 1985, cols 584–90; on the *Dialogus*, cols 585–6.

35. O reges, reges pudeat vos criminis huius!

    Usuras capitis, quas gens maledicta lucratur,

    in quo vos ipsos maledictos esse probatis usuratores.

    . . . .

    Non propter eos, non propter eorum

    virtutes, quibus expertes sunt, nec racione

    iusticie, que subdit eos, sed propter eorum

    argentum vile vel cetera dona vel aurum

    istud fecisti. Tu scis, quod facta nephanda

    sepius intulerant hii Christi fidelibus, et tu

    munera sumpsisti, sed legis preteristi iusticiam crebro.

    E.S. Bauer, *Frömmigkeit, Gelehrsamkeit und Zeitkritik an der Schwelle der grossen Konzilien. Johannes von Wetzlar und sein Dialogus super Magnificat*, Mainz, 1981, pp. 274–6, lines 2084–7, 2103–10.

36. Sed consilliarie nequam

    qui contra cives Pragenses exacuisti

    regem, peniteas nec ultra tam malefidam

    gentem promoveas, ne contra corpus amandum

    Christi tale quid accidat amplius, esurientes

quo saciat Dominus.

Ibid., p. 280, lines 2177–82.

37. For Hebrew text, see S. Bernfeld, *Sefer Hademaot*, II, Berlin, 1924, pp. 159–64, and my modest translation below, appendix, p. 196; on the lament, S.W. Baron, *A Social and Religious History of the Jews*, XI, New York, 1967, p. 274. On Kara see F. Talmage, 'Angels, anthems and anathemas: aspects of popular religion in fourteenth-century Bohemian Judaism', *Jewish History* 6 (1992), pp. 13–20, at pp. 15–19. On laments see Elbogen, *Der jüdische Gottesdienst*, pp. 221–31.

38. See appendix p. 196, line 14. This is also the date offered in the necrology, *Das Martyrologium*, ed. Salfeld, p. 210.

39. A poem about the Rintfleisch crowd may have preserved the themes of chants, see above, p. 52.

40. For a later report on the massacre in Prague, in an early seventeenth-century Hebrew chronicle, blaming 'our iniquities' for the disaster see *A Hebrew Chronicle from Prague c.1615*, ed. A. David, trans. L.J. Weinberger and D. Ordan, Tuscaloosa, Ala. and London, 1993, p. 21.

41. *Das Martyrologium*, ed. Salfeld, p. 94, see also pp. 22, 69, 79.

42. Y.H. Yerushalmi, *Zakhor: Jewish History and Jewish Memory*, Seattle Wash., 1982; on this view see A. Funkenstein, *Perceptions of Jewish History*, Berkeley, Calif., 1993, pp. 10–15.

43. Interestingly, cults of miraculous hosts do not seem to have produced collections of miracle-tales such as saint's shrines often did, not even in Bavaria which had several eucharistic pilgrimage sites; S.D. Sargent, 'Miracle books and pilgrimage shrines in late medieval Bavaria', *Historical Reflections* 13 (1986), pp. 455–71.

44. As historical tales they operate by turning forms of difference into

45. sources of similarity, and events which might otherwise appear distant into relevant and poignant happenings; H. White, *The Content of the Form: Narrative Discourse and Historical Representation*, Baltimore, Md., 1987, p. 16.

45. On this aspect see M. Rubin, 'Rudolph of Schlettstadt OP: reporter of violence, writer on Jews', in *The Dominicans in the Medieval World*, ed. K. Emery Jr, Notre Dame, Ind., 1997, pp. 283–92, and on the *Historiae memorabiles* in general see F. Lotter, 'Das Judenbild im volkstümlichen Erzählgut dominikanischer Exempelliteratur: Die "Historiae memorabiles" des Rudolf von Schlettstadt', in *Herrschaft, Kirche, Kultur. Beiträge zur Geschichte des Mittelalters: Festschrift für Friedrich Prinz zu seinem 65. Geburtstag*, ed. G. Jenal with S. Haarländer, Stuttgart, 1993, pp. 431–45.

46. On his life see C. Delcorno, *Giordano da Pisa e l'antica predicazione volgare*, Biblioteca di 'Lettere Italiane' 14, Florence, 1975, pp. 4–13.

47. D.R. Lesnick, *Preaching in Medieval Florence: the Social World of Franciscan and Dominican Spirituality*, Athens, Ga., 1989, pp. 119–33.

48. 'Rifanno ancora la passione di Cristo non solamente nel cuore loro ... ma rifannola ancora nell'anima sua ... L'altro modo onde rifanno ... nel sacramento del Corpo suo, faccendone crudeli cose ... L'altro modo onde rifanno la passione di Cristo, si è nella immagine Sua, e questo è in due modi; l'uno si è nella persona d'alcuno uomo ... quando possono ... L'altro modo ... è nel secondo modo della immagine, come sono le figure dipinte di Cristo', in the sermon of 9 November 1304, the feast of the Holy Saviour, which was delivered in the square of the church of Santa Luperata, in *Racconti esemplari di predicatori del due e*

trecento, II, ed. G. Varanini and G. Baldassari, I Novellieri Italiani IV (2), Rome, 1993, nos 167–8, pp. 321, 324, 327, 330, or Giordano da Rivalto, *Prediche*, II, ed. D. Moreni, 2 vols, Florence, 1831, pp. 225–32; Delcorno, *Giordano da Pisa*, p. 300.

49. 'Io era in quelle contrade quando fu che un giudeo mandò una sua fante alla chiesa de'cristiani; e fece e procurò si, o per pecunia o per altra malizia, che si fece venire il Corpo di Cristo. Quando l'ebbe, fu egli e certi de'giuderi nella casa, e ricominciaro a ffare la passione di Cristo sí pessimamente e con tanta rabbia, ch'era una maraviglia; e nel mortaio il pestavano niquitosamente. Intervenne che apparve uno fanciullo, ch'era Cristo medesimo', *Racconti esemplari*, II, pp. 324–5; see also in Giordano da Rivalto, *Prediche*, II, pp. 227–8; Delcorno, *Giordano da Pisa*, no. 65, p. 300. When could he have visited? He was in Viterbo from 1295, and then in Rome and then by 1303 in Florence, ibid., pp. 11–13.

50. 'Levossi uno uomo laico, ispiritual persona, per volontà di Dio, avendo zelo della fede: e ffu insieme con un altro artefice e prese il gonfalone; e fecersi capo di questa cosa gridando: – Sieno morti i giuderi –, e scorsero tutta la cittade e tutta la provincia, ed ebber seguito di più di ventimilia persone; et tutti i giuderi uccisono, quanti ne potero trovare in tutta la provincia, e beato che gli potea uccidere', *Racconti esemplari*, II, no. 168, p. 325; Giordano da Rivalto, *Prediche*, II, p. 228. On this passage see also J. Cohen, *The Friars and the Jews: the Evolution of Medieval Anti-Judaism*, Ithaca, N.Y., 1982, pp. 239–41.

51. On the sources for the making of *exempla* see A. Murray, 'Confession as a historical source in the thirteenth century', in *The Writing of History in the Middle Ages: Essays*

Presented to Richard William Southern, ed. R.H.C. Davis and J.M.
Wallace-Hadrill, Oxford, 1981,
pp. 275–322, at pp. 286–305.

52. Another Florentine version is that
of Archbishop Antoninus of Florence in *Divi Antonini archiepiscopi
Florentini . . . Chronicorum opus,* 3
vols, Lyons, 1586, III, p. 231b.

53. *Ci nous dit: recueil d'exemples
moraux,* ed. G. Blangez, Paris,
1979, no. 146, p. 148.

54. 'de quodam alio Iudaeo, qui
cuidam mulieri totum debitum
remisit ea conditione quod ei
corpus Christi portaret', John
Bromyard, *Summa praedicantium,*
Antwerp, 1614, p. 255a.

55. (Attributed to) Gilles Aurifaber,
*Speculum exemplorum, editio
princeps,* Deventer, 1481, fols
302vb–303vb; a more accessible
edition is Johannes Major,
Magnum speculum exemplorum,
Douai, 1605, fols 333a–334b. On
the work see R. Alsheimer, *Das
Magnum Speculum Exemplorum als
Ausgangspunkt populärer Erzähltra-
dition. Studien zur seiner Wirkungsgeschichte in Polen und Rußland,*
Europäische Hochschulschriften
Ser. 19 3, Frankfurt-am-Main,
1971, pp. 17–19.

56. 'Quomodo Judaei corpus christi
in partes sciderunt et miracul-
osus sanguis de eodem corpore
prorupit: ne tamen pignum
atque simplicium mentium fides
circa terrificum sacramentum corpus Jesu Christi vaccilet . . . usque
nunc tam stupenda mirandaque
circa sacramentum Eucharistiam
prodigia fulgent', Johannes
Major, *Magnum speculum exemplorum,* fol. 302vb.

57. See also the *exemplum* based on
the case of Poznań in 1399, as
transmitted in an Easter sermon
by Friar Michael of Janowiec of
Trzemszno monastery 'de una
muliere, que Corpus Cristi Judeis
vendidit et hoc factum est
Poznanie', based on the mid
fifteenth-century version of the

case by the historian Jan Długosz,
Poznań Raczyński Library 161,
p. 133v, see H. Kowalewicz,
'Sredniowieczne exempla polsko-
łacińskie', in *Kultura elitarna a
kultura masowa w Polsce późnego
Sredniowieczna,* ed. B. Geremek,
Wrocław, 1978, pp. 283–90; H.
Wergzynek, 'Accusations of host
profanation against Jews in
Poland', *Europa* pilot issue
(1993), pp. 45–56, at p. 49.

58. P. Connerton, *How Societies
Remember,* Cambridge, 1989; D.
Freedberg, *The Power of Images,*
Chicago, 1989.

59. 'Anno MCCCCIII ist das
Sakrament zu Lauingen gestohlen
alda erfunden und erhebt
worten', W. Meyer, *Die Kunstdenkmäler des Landeskreises Dilingen
an der Donau,* Munch, 1972, p.
524, fig. 491; G. Rückert, 'Die
Auffindung des Hochwürdiges
Gutes', *Alt Lauingen* 3 (1908), pp.
45–6. I am most grateful to Mr
Bernhard Ehrhart, Honorary
Director of the Town Museum in
the Lauingen Heimathaus for his
kindness in writing to me about
this image and a related one,
and for sending me reproductions
of the images. Mr Ehrhart has
made the attribution to Hannes
Schühlein.

60. *Germania Judaica,* II (1), ed. Z.
Avneri, Tübingen, 1968, p. 473;
III (1), ed. A. Maimon, Tübingen,
1987, p. 722.

61. *Margaretha Ebner und Heinrich
von Nördlingen. Ein Beitrag zur
Geschichte der deutsche Mystik,* ed. P.
Strauch, Freiburg-in-Breisgau and
Tübingen, 1882, pp. 116–17.

62. See above pp. 89–92.

63. For good reproductions of the
predella see P. d'Ancona, *Paolo
Uccello,* trans. E. Andrews,
London, 1960, plates lxii–lxxiii.
On the altarpiece, which depicted
the Communion to the Apostles
and which was painted by Joos
Van Ghent (*fl.* 1460–75) in 1472,
see E. Panofsky, *Early Netherlandish*

Painting, I, Harvard University Charles Eliot Norton Lectures 1947–8, 2 vols, Cambridge, Mass., 1953, pp. 340–2; J. Levallaye, *Juste de Gand, peinte de Frédéric de Montefeltre*, Université de Louvain – Recueil de Travaux Publiés par les Membres des Conférences d'Histoire et de Philologie 2, 37, Louvain, 1936, pp. 49–74. On the image of the Jew observing the scene of Communion, see J. Hoffmann, 'Piero della Francesca's "flagellation": a reading from Jewish history', *Zeitschrift für Kunstgeschichte* 44 (1981), pp. 340–57, at pp. 345–9.

64. The ample *bodega* boasts a large fireplace, which may bear a eucharistic connotation, see C. Ferguson O'Meara, ' "In the hearth of the virginal womb": the iconography of the holocaust in late medieval art', *Art Bulletin* 63 (1981), pp. 75–88, at p. 87.

65. For a new interpretation of the blood gushing out of the wall see S. Greenblatt and C. Gallaghar, 'The wound in the wall', a paper which has been most kindly shared with me.

66. On which see the seminal article by M.A. Lavin, 'The altarpiece of Corpus Domini in Urbino: Paolo Uccello, Joos Van Ghent, Piero della Francesca', *Art Bulletin* 49 (1967), pp. 1–24, at pp. 5–8; M.A. Goukovskj, 'A representation of the *Profanation of the Host*: a puzzling painting in the Hermitage and its possible author', *Art Bulletin* 51 (1996), pp. 170–3.

67. J.R.H. Moorman, *A History of the Franciscan Order from its Origins to the Year 1517*, Oxford, 1968, p. 436. On the Jews in Urbino see C. Roth, *A History of the Jews in Italy*, Philadelphia, Pa., 1946, pp. 119–20; On Jewish moneylending see G. Luzzatto, *I banchieri ebrei in Urbino nell'età ducale*, Padua, 1902; A. Milano, 'Considerazioni sulla lotta dei Monti di Pietà contro il prestito ebraico', in *Scritti in memoria di Sally Meyer (1875–1953)*, Jerusalem, 1956, pp. 205–8.

68. *Gotik in Österreich*, ed. R. von Baldass, W Buchowiecki, R. Feuchtmüller and W. Mrzaek, Vienna, Hanover and Bern, 1961, pp. 73–7 or in A. Stange, *Malerei der Donauschule*, Munich, 1971, p. 149 and figs 235–6. I am most grateful to Mrs Puschnik of Horn for her helpful comments on the Pulkau affair.

69. See above, pp. 67, 91.

70. Nuremberg, Germanisches Nationalmuseum GM 1806/7. I am grateful to Dr Malcolm Vale for mentioning this image to me.

71. I am most grateful to Laurence Flavigny of the Musée Départemental des Antiquités (Seine-Maritime) in Rouen for his generous help in sending me material and images related to these windows.

72. A. Tougard, 'Les verriers du Miracle des Billettes au Musée des Antiquités', *Bulletin de la Commission Départementale des Antiquités de la Seine Inférieure* 16 (1912–14), pp. 415–18; images and captions reproduced between p. 417 and p. 418.

73. See below on the stained glass windows on the miracle of Brussels inserted in what had been Ste Gudule's church in Brussels, p. 184.

74. *Die Zeit der frühen Habsburger. Dome und Klöster 1279–1379. Wiener Neustadt 12. Mai bis 28. Oktober 1979*, Wiener Neustadt, 1979, no. 199, p. 364.

75. My warmest thanks are here offered to Mr Wolfgang Huber of the Klosterneuburg Museum, who very kindly helped me during my visit, showed me the altarpiece and then provided the reproductions essential for this study.

76. The corporal is a cloth for containment of the eucharistic host. On the Bolsena miracle see M. Rubin, *Corpus Christi: the Euchar-*

ist in Late Medieval Culture,
Cambridge, 1991, p. 176 and for
a suggestive discussion see C.
Lansing, *Power and Purity: Cathar
Heresy in Medieval Italy*, Oxford,
1997, pp. 161–6.

77. On the Jewish Boy see above, pp.
7–39; on women who tested the
eucharist by cooking or baking R.
Marsan, *Itinéraire espagnol du conte
médiéval, VIIIe–XVe siècles*, Paris,
1974, pp. 307–14. See also the
echo in the Croxton *Play of the Sacrament*, where the Jews are made
to cook the host while Jonathas's
hand is still attached to it, see
below, pp. 169–70.

78. To the left of the Trinity scene, at
the lower register, the scene of
the Last Supper is depicted, the
moment of inception of the
eucharist.

79. M. Metzger and T. Metzger, *Jewish
Life in the Middle Ages: Illustrated
Hebrew Manuscripts of the Thirteenth
to the Sixteenth Centuries*, New York,
1982, no. 114, p. 81 (London, BL
Oriental 2737, fol. 87r).

80. C.R. Post, *A History of Spanish
Painting*, II, Cambridge, Mass.,
1932, pp. 234–6; J. Gudiol,
Pintura medieval en Aragon, Saragossa, 1971, pp. 189, 192 (figs
101, 104).

81. On such lettering in the northern
art of the later Middle Ages see
R. Mellinkoff, *Outcasts: Signs of
Otherness in Northern European Art*,
I, California Studies in the History
of Art 32, 2 vols, Berkeley, Calif.,
1993, pp. 97–119.

82. Ung Juif ayant a Paris pans
achet(és)
l'hostie au sang la ferrit dung
coute(au)
Puys la mettant bouillir saillant
hor(s)
ung crucifix sest dedans presenté.

G. de Tervarent, 'Les Tapisseries
du Ronceray et leurs sources
d'inspiration', *Gazette des Beaux-
Arts* 10 (1933), pp. 79–99, fig. 8,
p. 97; M. Jarry, 'La collection

de tapisseries du château de
Langeais', *Bulletin de la Société de
l'Histoire de l'Art Français* (1972),
pp. 39–62, at p. 42. For contemporary examples of French
tapestries featuring eucharistic
miracles see *Tapestries of Europe
and Colonial Peru in the Museum of
Fine Arts, Boston*, I, ed. A.S. Cavallo,
Boston, 1967, I, pp. 69–74; II,
plate 16.

83. See a reproduction of a nineteenth-century copy of the staff
now in the Musée de Cluny, M.
Vloberg, *L'Eucharistie dans l'art*,
II, Grenoble and Paris, 1946, p.
214.

84. *Journal d'un bourgeois de Paris*, ed.
A. Tuetey, Paris, 1881, pp. 372–3.

85. E. Hucher, 'Méreaux de plomb',
Revue Numismatique 3 (1858), pp.
338–50; plate 17, 2.

86. In the twelfth-century church of
St Alpin in Châlons-sur-Marne,
around 1515, a pair of windows,
shaped as tri-lobed lancets,
depicts the miracle of Paris (Bay
1) culminating in a procession.

87. *A Descriptive Catalogue of the Manuscripts in the Fitzwilliam Museum*, ed.
M.R. James, Cambridge, 1895, pp.
100–20; *Gothic Manuscripts 1285–
1385*, II, ed. L.F. Sandler, A
Survey of Manuscripts Illuminated
in the British Isles, Oxford, 1988,
no. 130, pp. 143–5.

88. Cambridge, Fitzwilliam Museum
48, fols 188v–189r; above, pp. 18–
19.

89. See on the insertion of figures
of authority into illustrations J.-C.
Schmitt, 'Le miroir du canoniste.
Les images et le texte dans un
manuscrit médiéval', *Annales* 48
(1993), pp. 1471–95.

90. 'Tibi hostiam quamdam sub imagine Salvatoris in throno sedentis
mirabile sacramentum Dominici
Corporis, multis in locis a vaesana
cujusdam feritate gladii ictibus
perforatam, et ex ea sanguine
respersam in locis praefatis,
quae in sacrario nostro recondita,
tuae piae devotioni concedimus

et donamus', 27 Sept. 1433, Raynaldus, *Annales ecclesiastici*, XXVIII, Bari, 1874, cols 153b–154a. Eugenius was clearly fascinated by the cult of miraculous hosts abused by Jews, as he also supported the flagging cult in Brussels, see below, p. 187.

91. See discussion in association with the Ogier Benigne Book of Hours in V. Reinburg, 'Accessory texts', in *Time Sanctified: the Book of Hours in Medieval Art and Life*, ed. R.S. Wieck, Baltimore, Md., 1988, pp. 103–10, at pp. 107–8; *Medieval and Renaissance Manuscripts in the Walters Art Gallery, I: France 875–1420*, ed. L.M.C. Randall with J. Oliver et al., Baltimore, Md., see description in entry no. 180 on MS W291, pp. 393–400, esp. pp. 394, 396, 398–9.

92. BL Egerton 1070, fol. 110r; and see also a copy in BN lat. 1156A, fol. 22; O. Pächt, 'René d'Anjou – Studien I', *Jahrbuch der kunsthistorischen Sammlungen in Wien* 69 (1973), pp. 65–126, at pp. 90–2 (fig. 87 on p. 92).

93. The monstrance was destroyed during the French Revolution, but its shape can be garnered from a stucco altar-frontal which depicted it, now in the museum at Dijon; for an image see A.S. Cocks, 'The myth of "Burgundian" goldsmithing', *The Connoisseur* 194,781 (Mar. 1977), pp. 180–6, fig. 2, p. 183.

94. The king made a vow to 'la saincte hostie de Disjon' for which he entertained a special devotion, 'La cronique de France de l'an mille cincq cens et cincq', in *Chroniques de Louis XII par Jean d'Autun*, ed. R. de Maulde, Paris, 1895, p. 3.

95. Une Juid mutillant iadis
Lhostie du sainct sacrement
Par fraper des cops plus de dix
Fit sortir sang abundamment

Eugene ou tresor de leglise
La print comme son bref le

tesmoigne
Et pris fut de par luy transmise
A philipe duc de bourgouigne.

Le duc pour quelque occasion
Lors estant arrive a lille
La receupt par devocion
Lan iiijc xxx avec mille

Mais por sainctement disposer
De la relique solennelle
Honestement la fit poser
A dijon dedans sa chapelle.

Gebetsbuch Karls des Kühnen vel potius Stundenbuch der Maria von Burgund, ed. F. Unterkircher and A. de Schryver, 2 vols, Graz, 1969, II, pp. 12–13; see the facsimile at the end of the Book of Hours, reproduced in vol. I, fols 1*v–2*r, poem on fol. 2*r.

96. BN fr. 25466, play on fols 10r–28v; fol. 29 is blank; poem on fols 30r–31v.

97. Quant le juif mauldit et malheureux
Par ceur felon et couraige haynneux
Eust deplaye le digne sacrement
Ung cas advint piteux et merveilleux
des playes jaillit vray sang miraculeux.

BN fr. 24566, fol. 30v.

98. Soyes nous escu et targe et avantgarde
Contre les Turcs de linfernale garde.
Sans ta grace nous sommes trop debiles.

Ibid., fol. 31v.

99. Baltimore Walters Art Gallery 291, fols 17v*–18v*; Reinburg, 'Accessory texts', pp. 107–8, fig. 80.

100. It is often claimed that popular drama sponsored 'sensationalism, voyeurism, sadism and anti-semitism' (J.S. Gatton, ' "There must be blood": mutilation and martyrdom on the medieval stage', in *Violence in Drama*, ed. J.

Redmond, Cambridge, 1991, pp. 79–91, at p. 79). The absence of German host desecration plays poses a riddle concerning the relationship between dramatic representation and the desire or willingness of members of the audience to act (as) violently (as the play characters do). A Netherlandish drama on a eucharistic miracle survives, though it is unrelated to an accusation against Jews. It is dated after 1436 and was perfomed in Breda, a performance of 1500 being known, *Het spel vanden heiligen sacramente vander Nyeuwerveart*, ed. W.J.M.A. Asselberg and A.P. Huysmans, Zwolle, 1955.

101. See above, pp. 7–39.

102. A play is mentioned as part of the celebrations in the procession of 1444 discussed above, p. 161. This may have been a set of tableaux vivants.

103. The latter's contribution is not clear. On Corpus Christi liturgy see Rubin, *Corpus Christi*, pp. 185–96. For an Orvietan play for Corpus Christi, based on the Miracle of Bolsena, see V. de Bartholomaeis, *Laude drammatiche e rappresentazioni sacre*, 3 vols, Florence, 1943, repr. Florence, 1967, I, pp. 368–81. On a representation of the profanation of the host in a fifteenth-century painting (*c.*1500), now at the Hermitage Museum, probably based on a woodcut frontispiece to the text of the *sacra rappresentazione*, see Goukovskj, 'A representation of the *Profanation of the Host*', pp. 170–3. This may have been the play which was performed in May 1473 for Eleanor of Aragon, who visited the town on her way to her wedding in Ferrara. As reported: 'Fu fatta la rappresentazione di quel Giudeo che arrosto il Corpo di Cristo', A. d'Ancona, *Sacre rappresentazioni dei secoli XIV, XV e XVI*, I, Florence, 1872, pp. 287–8;

P. Francastel, 'Un mystère illustré par Uccello: le miracle de l'hostie d'Urbino', *Revue Archéologique* 39 (1952), pp. 180–91. This report resembles the opening of the prologue to the play, 'Detta una donna el corpo del signore a un giudeo / che frisse & scherni multo', Rome, Bibliotheca dell'Accademia dei Lincei e Corsiniana 92.F.22 (printed in Rome in 1498), fol. 52r.

104. Some plays about ritual murder were produced in the fifteenth century, K.J. Baum, 'Das Endinger Judenspiel als Ausdruck Mittelalterlicher Judenfeindschaft', in *Judentum in Mittelalter. Beiträge zur christlich-jüdischen Gespräch*, ed. P. Wilpert, Berlin, 1966, pp. 337–49, at pp. 340–9.

105. R.L. Homan, 'Mixed feelings about violence in the Corpus Christi plays', in *Violence in Drama*, ed. Redmond, pp. 93–100.

106. On the *Play* see G.M. Gibson, *The Theater of Devotion: East Anglian Drama and Society in the Late Middle Ages*, Chicago, 1989, pp. 34–6, 38–40.

107. I have been inspired in thinking about these issues by discussions with Sarah Beckwith and by reading her article 'Real presences: the York *Crucifixio* as sacramental theatre', in S. Beckwith, *Signifying God: Social Act and Symbolic Relation in York's Play of Corpus Christi*, forthcoming, Berkeley, Calif., 2000. See also V.I. Scherb, 'Violence and the social body in the Croxton *Play of the Sacrament*', in *Violence in Drama*, ed. Redmond, pp. 69–78.

108. On torture imagery see R.L. Homan, 'Devotional themes in the violence and humor of the Play of the Sacrament', *Comparative Drama* 20 (1986–7), pp. 327–40, at p. 335. See for example the reverse crucifixion described in the Play as Jonathan directs some Jews to remove the nails from his

hands, *The Non-Cycle Mystery Plays and Fragments*, ed. O. Waterhouse, EETS ES 104, London, 1909, pp. 55–89, lines 657–712 on p. 78. On the work of resolution in the Croxton play see C. Sponsler, *Drama and Resistance: Bodies, Goods, and Theatricality in Late Medieval England*, Medieval Cultures 10, Minneapolis, Minn., 1997, p. 159.

109. C. Cutts, 'The Croxton play: an anti-Lollard piece', *Modern Languages Quarterly* 5 (1944), pp. 45–60; on this see Gibson, *The Theater of Devotion*, p. 35.

110. *Mistere de la saincte hostie*, Aix, 1817. For a summary of the play see *Dictionnaire des mystères*, ed. Comte de Douhet, Paris, 1854, cols 885–901.

111. Ibid., Bi^v.

112. Ibid., Biii^v.

113. Ibid., Ci^r.

114. Ibid., Ciiii^r.

115. See above, pp. 40–47.

116. A burgess insists on the treatment of the *canivet* (*Dictionnaire des mystères*, cols 885–901, Eiv^v):

Sil plaist a dieu et a sainct-gille
Je emporteray ce canivet
Car le precieux sang y est
Qui de lhostie yssit hors ains.

117. J. Enders, 'Dramatic memory and tortured spaces in the *Jeu de la saincte hostie*', in *The Medieval Practices of Space*, Minneapolis, Minn., 1999.

118. Lavin, 'The altar piece of Corpus Domini', pp. 5–7.

119. Rome, Biblioteca dell'Accademia e dei Lincei e Corsiniana, frontispiece, 92.F.22, fol. 55r.

120. New shrines received the print treatment, and older ones were reassessed by newly produced broadsheets, see P. Soergel, *Wondrous in His Saints: Counter-Reformation Propaganda in Bavaria*, Berkeley, Calif., 1993, ch. 1, esp. pp. 25–43. See for example the broadsheet made for the pilgrimage to Wilsnack, *De hystorie unde erfind-*

inghe des hillighen Sacraments tho der Wilsnagk, fifteen scenes (5 × 3) with captions, see reproduction in *Das Wunderblut zu Wilsnack. Niederdeutscher Einblattdruck mit 15 Holzschnitten aus der Zeit von 1515–1520*, ed. P. Heitz, introd. W.L. Schreiber, Strassburg, 1904. For a later example of the reworking of medieval shrine legends see M.-E. Ducreux, 'L'Ordre symbolique d'un pélerinage tchèque dans l'espace habsbourgeois au 17e siècle: Stará Boleslav', in *Les Identités pélerines en Europe, XVIe–XIXe siècles*, ed. D. Julia, P. Boutry and P.A. Fabre, Paris, 1998. I am most grateful to Professor Robert Evans for informing me of this article.

121. On these cases see above, pp. 40–69. The Nuremberg Chronicle's full title is *Liber chronicarum cum figuris et ymaginibus ab inicio mundi* (1493), fols CCLVIIv, CCXXv, CCXXXv; the German translation appeared five months later, in December, with 350 woodcuts. On Hartmann Schedel see B. Hernad and F.J. Worstbrock, *Die deutsche Literatur des Mittelalters. Verfasserlexikon*, VIII, New York, 1992, cols 609–21. The Nuremberg Chronicle strongly influenced other, regional chronicles. See the report of Sternberg in Petermann Etterlin, *Kronica von der loblichen Eydtgnoschaft, jr harkommen und sust seltzam strittenn und geschichten*, ed. E. Gruber, Quellenwerk zur Entstehung der Schweizerischen Eidengenossenschaft III, 3, Aarau, 1965, no. 235, pp. 277–8.

122. Indeed the awkward cut-off at the bottom of the third row of images may indicate this secondary use of the images together with the later text, in a Passau printing 'hye zu passaw', W. Schmidt, *Die Inkunabeln des Kupferstichs in Königlichen Kabinet zu München*, 1886, p. 16, no. 33; W.L. Schreiber, *Handbuch der Holz- und Metallschnitt des XV.*

Jahrhunderts, Berlin, 1893–1900,
repr. Stuttgart, 1969, p. 108, no.
1965 (see no. 1966 too).

123. A similar structure was used by the
painter of a seventeenth-century
panel commemorating the Paris
host desecration for the church of
Saint Martin des Champs in Paris.
Nine scenes in three rows tell the
tale, Vloberg, *L'Eucharistie dans
l'art*, II, p. 212.

124. Soergel, *Wondrous in His Saints*,
pp. 37–8.

125. For the poem see R. von
Liliencron, *Die historischen Volks-
lieder der Deutschen von 13. bis 16.
Jahrhundert*, 5 vols in 4, Leipzig,
1865–9, II, no. 153, pp. 142–6;
*Die kleineren Liederdichter des 14.
und 15. Jahrhunderts*, I, ed. T.
Cramer, Munich, 1977, pp. 199–
204. On Fellhainer see U. Müller,
*Die deutsche Literatur des Mittelalters.
Verfasserlexikon*, Berlin and New
York, 1980, cols 721–2.

126. Liliencron, *Die historischen Volkslieder*, II, stanzas 2, 6, 20–3, pp.
19–22. On the use of invocations
in the texts of broadsheets and the
wider context of preaching and
broadsheets see G. Ecker,
*Einblattdrucke von der Anfänge
bis 1555. Untersuchungen zu ein
Publikationsform literarischer Texts*,
2 vols, Göppinger Arbeiten zur
Germanistik 314, Göppingen,
1981, I, pp. 96–109, esp. p. 97.

127. Liliencron, *Die historischen
Volkslieder*, II, stanza 2, lines 3–4,
p. 143.

128. ' "pring uns das sacrament, wir
wellen dirs bezahlen schon" ',
ibid., stanza 4, line 2, p. 14.

129. zwai partikeln schickten si den
        Juden gein Prag,
    die zwai in die Neustat,
    die zwai gein Salzpurg hin,
    die zwai behielten si under in,
    die der Veigel Jud gestochen hat.

    Ibid., stanza 13, lines 2–6, p. 144.

130. On clerical misbehaviour in
the tales see above, p. 79.

131. See the version in K. Schmidt, *Das
heilige Blut von Sternberg*, Verein
für Reformationsgeschichte –
Schriften für das Deutsche Volk
18, Halle, 1892, pp. 7–11.

132. V. Honemann, 'Die Sternberger
Hostienschändung und ihre
Quellen', in *Kirche und Gesellschaft
im Heiligen Römischen Reich des
15. und 16. Jahrhunderts*, ed.
H. Bockmann, Göttingen, 1994,
pp. 75–102, at pp. 78–9.

133. *Concilia Germaniae*, V, ed. J.
Hartzheim, Cologne, 1763: 'De
reverende portando sacramentum Eucharistie, ut infra', c. 20,
p. 646a.

134. Ibid., c. 21, p. 646b.

135. Ibid., c. 26, cols 647–8: 'vel eam si
habeat, infra mensem a se separet
. . . sub pena decem florenorum.'

136. For a summary see C. Borchling
and B. Claussen, *Niederdeutsche
Bibliographie: Gesamtverzeichnis der
niederdeutschen Drucke bis zum Jahre
1800*, I, Neumünster, 1931, cols
93–4.

137. Honemann, 'Die Sternberger
Hostienschändung und ihre
Quellen', p. 88; *Einblattdrucke des
15. Jahrhunderts. Ein bibliographis-
ches Verzeichnis*, Sammlung Biblio-
tekwissenschaftlichen Arbeiten
35–6, Halle, 1914, p. 378.

138. A copy survives in the collection of
Hildesheim Cathedral. The text is
published in *Deutsche Chroniken*,
ed. H. Maschek, Deutsche Literatur. Realistik des Spätmittelalters
5, Leipzig, 1936, pp. 134–8; see
reproduction in Honemann, 'Die
Sternberger Hostienschändung
und ihre Quellen', pp. 97–8.
For summary of texts see V.
Honemann, 'Sternberger Hostienschändung', in *Die deutsche
Literatur des Mittelalters. Verfasserlexikon*, IX, Berlin and New York,
1993, cols 306–8.

139. It begins 'Allen christen myn-
schen sy so wissen dat in den Land
van Mecklenberch in der stat
Sternenberch eyn groys myrakel

geseyet is van den verblynden Juden an dem allerhillychsten hoechwerdychsten Sacrament dat sy myt messer doerstochen haen dat bloet der vyß gevlossen is als dese Figuyr vyß wyset', Ludwig von Rencken, 1492.

140. 'Wan den bosen ioden volget hyr eyn gheschicht / Dar to van den suluen eyn merklik gedycht', see Borchling and Claussen, *Niederdeutsche Bibliographie*, no. 209, col. 93.

141. And reprinted in 1522 in the same city, Honemann, 'Die Sternberger Hostienschändung und ihre Quellen', pp. 90–1; F. Backhaus, 'Die Hostienschändungsprozesse von Sternberg (1492) und Berlin (1510) und die Ausweisung der Juden aus Mecklenburg und der Mark Brandenburg', *Jahrbuch für brandenburgische Landesgeschichte* 39 (1988), pp. 7–26, 12–13.

142. The medieval character of broadsheets is emphasised by H.A. Oberman in the summary of his article, 'Zwischen Agitation und Reformation: die Flugschriften als "Judespiegel"', in *Flugschriften als Massenmedium der Reformationszeit*, ed. H.-J. Köhler, Spätmittelalter und Frühe Neuzeit – Tübinger Beiträge zur Geschichtsforschung 13, Stuttgart, 1981, pp. 269–89, at pp. 287–8.

143. *Codex diplomaticus maioris Poloniae 1400–1444*, ed. F. Piekosinski, Warsaw, 1877, no. 91, pp. 86–8, at p. 87.

144. BL 11515.b.60, four pages with a title woodcut by Silvan Otmar of Augsburg c.1520; for the text of this pamphlet see Liliencron, *Die historischen Volkslieder*, I, no. 12, pp. 45–8. On the poem see B. Wachinger, 'Der Judenmord von Deggendorf', in *Die deutsche Literatur des Mittelalters. Verfasserlexikon*, IV, Berlin and New York, 1983, cols 893–6.

145. This is a typical image for host veneration, see figure 24, p. 168, above, and Rubin, *Corpus Christi*, pp. 293–4 and fig. 17 on p. 295.

146. Liliencron, *Die historischen Volkslieder*, I, no. 12, lines 60–1, p. 47. No fourth 'abuse' is told; the poem moves from 'Das dritte zaichen' (l. 47) to 'Zům funften mal' (l. 53).

147. The chapel was built on the site of the Jewish houses. M. Eder, *Die 'Deggendorfer Gnad'*, Deggendorf, 1992.

148. Zů Teckendorf in der stat
ain frumer purger mich da pat,
dass ich mit im gieng hinab
in die chichen zu° dem hailigen grab
und schawet an das große mord
das von den falschen Juden dort
am sacramante ward getan.

Liliencron, *Die historischen Volkslieder*, I, no. 12, lines 9–15, p. 46.

149. Soergel, *Wondrous in His Saints*, pp. 36–7, 172–81.

150. K. Hausberger, *Geschichte des Bistums Regensburg*, I, Regensburg, 1989, pp. 248–9.

151. Die joden al ghemeine,
si en wouleb gheloven niet,
dat men in die hostie reine
godes lichaem consakeriert
al tu schen des priesteres handen,
daer dat kersten ghelove aen stent.

W. Bunte, *Juden und Judentum in der mittelniederländischen Literatur (1100–1600)*, Judentum und Umwelt 24, Frankfurt, 1989, stanza 3, p. 384.

152. Ibid., stanza 15, p. 385.

153. J. Stengers, *Les Juifs dans les Pays-Bas au moyen-âge*, Académie Royale de Belgique – Classe des Lettres 45/2, pp. 13–15; Bunte, *Juden und Judentum*, pp. 111–21.

154. J. Bruyn, *Van Eyck Problemen*, Orbis Artium 1, Utrecht, 1957, pp. 123–6, 129–55; Stengers, *Les Juifs dans les Pays-Bas*, pp. 25–6; Bunte, *Juden und Judentum*, pp. 111–21.

155. 'Item Bevervoet misso versus Lucsenborg XVIa in meye occasione judeorum captorum Bruxellis IIII mottonen', P. Lefèvre, 'Le thème du miracle des hosties poignardées par les juifs à Bruxelles en 1370', *Le Moyen-Âge* 8 (1953), pp. 373–98, at p. 381 n. 12 (AGRB, Reg. 2356, fol. 16v); 'Item datum domino Johanni de Horten, misso ad dominum episcopum Cameracensem, causa Sacramenti, pro equo et expensis XXXVI libros', ibid., pp. 382–3 (AGRB, Archives ecclésiastiques, Caisse 517, no. 14).

156. AGRB, Reg. 2356, fols 13v, 14r: 'Iudei combusti ascencione domini.'

157. 'Item recepta de bonis dictorum judeorum, postquam combusti fuerant circa Ascencionem Domini lxx°, qui diffamati fuerant de sacramento punito [puncto?] et furtive accepto ex capella beate Katherine apud Bruxellam, in quantum dicta bona pervenerunt ad manus receptoris', Lefèvre, 'Le thème du miracle', pp. 377–80. On the sources see *Inventaris van het out archief van de kapitelkerk van sint Michil en Sint Goedele te Brussal*, ed. P. de Ridder, 2 vols, Brussels, 1987.

158. Lefèvre, 'Le thème du miracle', p. 395. The eucharistic procession continued throughout the years of Duchess Jeanne's widowhood, J. Rouyer, 'Méreaux du XIVe siècle et autres concernant la dévotion au Saint-Sacrement de miracle de Brussels', *Revue Belge de Numismatique* 4 (1888), pp. 246–75, at p. 260.

159. *Inventaris*, ed. de Ridder, II, nos 8460–2.

160. On the inquiry, and for a report, see P. Lefèvre, 'La valeur historique d'une enquête épiscopale sur le miracle eucharistique de Bruxelles en 1370', *Revue d'Histoire Ecclésiastique* 28 (1932), pp. 329–46, at pp. 342–6.

161. See above for pressures on those dealing with the status of material acclaimed as miraculous by the local community, see pp. 59–61.

162. 'ut huiusmodi hostias sacratas perfixas ad certum locum secrete asportaret, attentius precio appreciato, supplicantes ne res gesta ad cognitionem christianorum deveniret'; 'Qui pre multitudine parochianorum et populorum, ibidem confluentium, et ne deliberarentur insistentium, timens eosdem, claves suas et custodie, ubi dicte hostie reposite extiterant, posuit in altari majori'; 'Quibus judeis captis, et super premissis examinatis et enormiter questionatis, premissa omnia, prout dicta Katherina eadem referebat et proponebat, penitus sunt confessi, et demum igni et ultimo traditi sunt supplicio', Lefèvre, 'La valeur historique', pp. 343, 344, 345.

163. ' "quare hi canes putridi non fatentur veritatem, absque tanta et tam crudeli pena, cum utique premissa se sciant fecisse et perpetrasse?" ', ibid., p. 345.

164. *The Apostolic See and the Jews, II: Documents*, ed. S. Simonsohn, PIMS Studies and Texts 95, Toronto, 1989, no. 708, pp. 828–30.

165. The church of Notre Dame de la Chapelle to which Katherine belonged was outside the walls, *Inventaris*, ed. de Ridder, I, pp. 49–50. A bell was founded in Mechlin (Mâlines), called the Salvator, in 1481 for the votive Chapel of the Holy Sacrament in St Gudule, P. Lefèvre, 'Le miracle eucharistique à Bruxelles', *Analecta bollandiana* 51 (1933), pp. 325–36, at p. 335.

166. These tokens may be related to the Hospital of St John the Baptist in Brussels, see Rouyer, 'Méreaux du XIVe siècle', pp. 260–1, and plate 6.

167. Stengers, *Les Juifs dans les Pays-Bas*, pp. 57–9.

168. 'MCCCLXIX Mense Iunio Iudaei Bruccellae venerabile corpus Christi pugionibus et gladiis transfixerunt, unde cruor copiose effluxit; quod ob scelus eodem in oppido vivi fuere concremati', Jacobus de Meyere, in Bunte, *Juden und Judentum*, p. 100.
169. Ibid., pp. 99–100, at p. 100.
170. Brussels, Royal Library 3245, fols 284r–286v; transcribed in Bunte, *Juden and Judentum*, pp. 100–8.
171. Ibid., p. 100.
172. Ibid., p. 103.
173. 'Historia quomodo venerabile sacramentum nuper revelatum' in the *Novale sanctorum* published in parts in *De codicibus hagiographicis Iohannis Gielemans canonici regularis in Rubea Valle prope Bruxellas*, Brussels, 1895, pp. 419–28. On this see Lefèvre, 'Le thème du miracle', pp. 391–2. I am grateful to Ms. Stephane Boule'h for our conversation about Gielemans.
174. This is the general aim of the *Novale sanctorum*, pp. 416–17.
175. 'Si tu es Deus, videbimus. Manifesta ergo tu [sic] quoque, si potes', ibid., p. 420.
176. 'censuram condignam super Iudaeos non immerito postulaverunt', ibid., p. 421.
177. 'Ecce, fili mi, hic convenit me invocari et adorari ab omni creatura humana vivente; et en sum in hoc loco absconditus et neglectus atque ab oculis et a cordibus hominum abolitus et alienatus,' ibid., p. 422.
178. *The Apostolic See and the Jews*, II, no. 708, pp. 828–30. See above for Eugenius IV's other initiative, only three years earlier, in encouraging another cult around a host allegedly abused by a Jew, pp. 162–3. For further grants to the chapel in the 1430s and 1440s see Lefèvre, 'Le thème du miracle', p. 396 n. 37.
179. Nora, 'Between memory and history', p. 12.

180. Freedberg, *The Power of Images*. chs 5–6, pp. 82–135.
181. T. Kwasman, 'Die mittelalterlichen jüdischen Grabsteine in Rothenburg o. d. Tauber', in *Zur Geschichte der mittelalterlichen Jüdischen Gemeinde in Rothenburg ob der Tauber*, ed. H. Merz, Schriftenreihe des Reichsstadtmuseums Rothenburg o. d. Tauber – Museumheft 3, Rothenburg o. d. Tauber, 1993, p. 54 reproduction, p. 55 transcription, p. 56 translation into German.

7 Conclusion

1. The council arrested the Jews of Braunschweig on suspicion at the order of Landgraf Joachim. As no case was proven against them the Jews were released and expelled, see F. Backhaus, 'Judenfeindschaft und Judenvertreibungen im Mittelalter. Zur Ausweisung der Juden aus dem Mittelelbraum im 15. Jahrhundert', *Jahrbuch für Geschichte Mittel- und Ostdeutschlands* 36 (1987), pp. 275–332, at p. 330 n. 185.
2. This version is a paraphrase of the excellent translation offered in H.A. Oberman, *The Roots of Anti-Semitism in the Age of Renaissance and Reformation*, trans J.I. Porter, Philadelphia, Pa., 1984, pp. 97–9; the original text, from a woodcut printed in Nuremberg by Hieronymus Höltzel, appears on pp. 147–9. On Höltzel see ibid., p. 97 and *Buchdruckerlexikon des 16. Jahrhunderts (deutsches Sprachgebiet)*, ed. J. Benzing, Frankfurt, 1952, p. 331. For detailed analysis of the case see W. Heise, *Die Juden in Mark Brandenburg bis zum Jahre 1571*, Historische Studien 220, Berlin, 1932, ch. 15, pp. 210–27. A case in Saxony in 1514, which resulted in the killing of the Jew after torture with red-hot pincers, was occasioned by the similar accumulation of overlapping

accusations reported by a chronicler as 'umb etlicher schendlicher begangener stuk willen mit dem werdigen hilligen sacrament und andern sachen', in 'Chronik des Dietrich Westholf von 750–1550', in *Chroniken der deutsche Städte*, XX, Leipzig, 1887, p. 401.

3. On the complex debates around this shrine see C. Zika, 'Hosts, processions and pilgrimages in fifteenth-century Germany', *Past and Present* 118 (1988), pp. 25–64.

4. 'Ich freue mich dass Ihr dem bei Euch herrschenden Aberglauben das Maul gestopft und Euren gottlosen Erwerb abgethan habt. Der Herr gebe, dass die Erkentnis Christi bei Euch zur Volkommenheit wachse und das Wort von der Gnade bei Euch herrsche in reichlischer Erweisung des Geistes', K. Schmidt, *Das heilige Blut von Sternberg*, Verein für Reformationsgeschichte – Schriften über das Deutsche Volk 18, Halle, 1892, pp. 41–2. Article 20 of the *Twenty-seven Articles* dealt with the proliferation of 'chapels and field-churches ... and new pilgrimages'; here too Wilsnack and Sternberg are mentioned, ibid., p. 3.

5. R. Po-chia Hsia, *The Myth of Ritual Murder: Jews and Magic in Reformation Germany*, New Haven, Conn., 1988. The host desecration accusation declines in virulence and power just as the sacramental underpinnings of the tale are deconstructed and re-examined, see parallels in S. Clark, 'Le sabbat comme système symbolique: significations stables et instables', in *Le Sabbat des sorciers*, ed. N. Jacques-Chaguin and M. Préaud, Grenoble, 1993, pp. 63–74, esp. pp. 63–6, 73–4.

6. On the contemporary polemic about miracles see Hsia, *The Myth of Ritual Murder*, p. 147.

7. See, for example, the reforming activities of Nicholas of Cusa, E.

Meuthen, *Nikolaus von Kues, 1401–1464. Skizze einer Biographie*, Münster, 1964, pp. 91–9; C.J. Hefele and H. Leclercq, *Historie des conciles*, VII (2), Paris, 1916, pp. 1215–17, 1227.

8. See for example the language of the Council of Erfurt which expelled its Jews in 1458 (a few years after Capistrano's visit): 'Nu das die selbin yoden der stad burger, rich und arm, mit yrem wucher so sere vorterbeten, so greif sich der rad an trefflichen umbe eines gemeines nutzes willen und gap dem bischcove ein mergliche summe geldis, das da lieff na uf VII tusent gulden', *Die Chronik Hartung Cammermeisters*, ed. R. Reiche, Halle, 1896, no. 101, pp. 166–7.

9. For a contemporary list of expulsions see S. Baron, *A Social and Religious History of the Jews*, XI, Philadelphia, Pa., 1967, p. 275.

10. H. Martin in *Identità politica e identità religiosa*, ed. G. Gensini, San Miniato, 1999.

11. On the appropriation of a religious language into the urban discourse of self-legitimation see A. Vauchez, 'Introduction', in *La religion civique à l'époque médiévale et moderne (Chrétienté et Islam)*, ed. A. Vauchez, Collection de l'École Française de Rome 213, Rome, 1995, pp. 1–5, at p. 1.

12. On the use of rumours and regional accusations as points of pressure on rulers see the case of the Chinese witch-scare of 1768 in P.A. Kuhn, *Soulstealers: the Chinese Sorcery Scare of 1768*, Cambridge, Mass., 1990.

13. See the analysis of Backhaus, 'Judenfeindschaft und Judenvertreibungen', p. 332. For reciprocal vigilance over the treatment of Jews in neighbouring towns see the example of c.1387 when Nördlingen is forced to justify a recent uprising against Jews to its fellow-members in the Union of Swabian Towns (Swäbische

Städtebund), *Urkunden zur städtischen Verfassungsgeschichte*, ed. F. Keutgen, Berlin, 1899, no. 426, pp. 517–20, esp. p. 518, article 2.

14. From the perspective of this book's concerns, the central insight into violent atrocity offered by Daniel Goldhagen in his attempt to explain participation by 'ordinary' Germans in the making of the Final Solution seems shallow and ahistorical, cf. D.J. Goldhagen, *Hitler's Willing Executioners: Germans and the Holocaust*, London, 1996, esp. ch. 2, pp. 49–79.

15. I agree with Paul Brass's insight: ' "communal riots" are, I believe, undertaken mostly by "specialists", who are ready to be called out on such occasions, who profit from it, and whose activities profit others', *Theft of an idol: text and context in the reproduction of collective violence*, Princeton, N.J., 1997, p. 9.

16. For an analysis of the components of anti-clerical discourse in Germany see R.W. Scribner, 'Anticlericalism and the cities', in *Anticlericalism in Late Medieval and Early Modern Europe*, ed. P.A. Dykema and H.A. Oberman, Leiden, 1993, pp. 147–66.

17. See on this the insights in B. Scribner, 'Preconditions of tolerance and intolerance in sixteenth-century Germany', in *Tolerance and Intolerance in the European Reformation*, ed. P.O. Grell and B. Scribner, Cambridge, 1996, pp. 32–47, at pp. 46–7.

18. See a related, highly polemical, argument in C. MacKinnon, *Only Words*, London, 1994.

Appendix: Rabbi Avigdor Kara: All the Afflictions

1. Genesis 14:5.

Index